Moral Skepticisms

MORAL SKEPTICISMS

Walter Sinnott-Armstrong

OXFORD
UNIVERSITY PRESS

OXFORD
UNIVERSITY PRESS

Oxford University Press, Inc., publishes works that further
Oxford University's objective of excellence
in research, scholarship, and education.

Oxford   New York
Auckland   Cape Town   Dar es Salaam   Hong Kong   Karachi
Kuala Lumpur   Madrid   Melbourne   Mexico City   Nairobi
New Delhi   Shanghai   Taipei   Toronto

With offices in
Argentina   Austria   Brazil   Chile   Czech Republic   France   Greece
Guatemala   Hungary   Italy   Japan   Poland   Portugal   Singapore
South Korea   Switzerland   Thailand   Turkey   Ukraine   Vietnam

Published by Oxford University Press, Inc.
198 Madison Avenue, New York, New York 10016

www.oup.com

First issued as an Oxford University Press paperback, 2007.

Oxford is a registered trademark of Oxford University Press

Library of Congress Cataloging-in-Publication Data
Sinnott-Armstrong, Walter, 1955–
Moral skepticisms / Walter Sinnott-Armstrong.
   p.   cm.
Includes bibliographical references (p.) and index.
ISBN 978-0-19-518772-4; 978-0-19-534206-2 (pbk.)
1. Ethics.   2. Skepticism.   I. Title.
BJ1031.S56 2005
171'.2—dc22   2005040674

9 8 7 6 5 4 3 2 1

Printed in the United States of America
on acid-free paper

To Geoff

Preface

I have always held strong moral beliefs. Growing up in Memphis, I discovered early on that other people held their moral beliefs just as strongly as I held mine, even when we disagreed. Some of these people were then and remain now my close friends. These conflicts made me wonder whether they or I (or both or neither) were justified in our respective moral beliefs. That wonder led to this book.

When I first came to philosophy, I hoped to rule out moral nihilism and to prove my own moral beliefs. I thought that I succeeded in my undergraduate thesis on Kant's ethics. That was long ago. In this book, I argue that moral nihilism cannot be ruled out by any method and that moral beliefs can be justified only in limited ways.

Some readers will find my conclusions disappointing or threatening. They still want to establish their moral beliefs thoroughly, conclusively, and objectively. At least they want to refute moral nihilism. In contrast with scientists who feel free to ignore or make fun of skeptical hypotheses like Descartes' deceiving demon, most moral believers and theorists feel driven to fight moral nihilism. They are not satisfied by merely setting aside moral nihilism as irrelevant. That ploy strikes them as too arbitrary.

I respect their endeavor. Sometimes I share the urge to refute moral nihilism and moral skepticism. However, when I work through the details of moral epistemology carefully and consider extreme positions charitably, I don't see how to rule out moral nihilism. This inability leads to another: Many people cannot obtain the kind of justified moral belief that they long for. This is an important limit on the epistemic status of our moral beliefs. We ought to face that limit honestly.

Facing our epistemic limits need not lead us to accept moral nihilism. I am not a moral nihilist. I believe that some acts are morally wrong. I even feel confident in specifying some of the acts that are morally wrong. None of this changes when I admit that I cannot disprove moral nihilism or when I adopt my moderate moral skepticism.

Other people will still feel disappointed and threatened by my conclusions. However, this opposition should diminish when I show how our moral beliefs can be justified in modest ways. It should also help to distinguish moral epistemology from substantive ethics, because second-order beliefs about the epistemic status of moral beliefs cannot force us to give up the moral beliefs that we need to live well.

So, I hope that my readers will engage in this enterprise with an open mind. I will discuss and endorse some extreme positions, but these positions should not be rejected too quickly just because they seem weird or dangerous. They and the arguments for them need to be assessed carefully and fairly so that we can all end up with an accurate view of when, how, and how much our moral beliefs can be justified.

Acknowledgments

This book benefited from the generous and insightful comments of so many people that I am bound to forget to thank many of them. I apologize in advance.

The penultimate version of the manuscript was read by Russ Shafer-Landau and another reviewer for Oxford University Press, both of whom provided extremely helpful guidance. The previous version was discussed by a reading group at Dartmouth College, organized by Roy Sorensen and also attended by Julia Driver, Bob Fogelin, Bernie Gert, Joshua Gert, Jim Moor, Matthew Nudds, and Kathleen Wallace. Their profound challenges to my ideas are appreciated. The version before was read by Robert Audi, who straightened me out on a number of important points.

Parts of this book derive from earlier articles that received careful scrutiny from various readers. Published comments by Simon Blackburn and Mark Nelson were especially useful. So were conversations with (in addition to those already listed) Alexander Bird, Paul Bloomfield, Michael Bratman, David Brink, David Copp, Jonathan Dancy, Jon Ellis, Terry Horgan, Sam Levey, Don Loeb, Ram Neta, Diana Raffman, Mike Ridge, Bruce Russell, Geoff Sayre-McCord, Jonathan Schaffer, John Skorupski, David Sosa, Christie Thomas, Mark Timmons, Bill Tolhurst and Tim Williamson. In early stages of this project, I learned a great deal from participants in a Humanities Institute and two conferences at Dartmouth College, including (in addition to many of those already listed) especially Mitch Haney, Richard Hare, Stephen Jacobson, John Konkle, Chris Kulp, Paul Mac-Namara, Peter Railton, Stefan Sencerz, Ernie Sosa, Bill Throop, John Tresan, Margaret Walker, Doug Weber, Michael Williams, Susan Wolf, and Nick Zangwill. In later stages, I was helped by audiences at Dartmouth College; the American Philosophical Association; the Australasian Association of Philosophers; the Research School of Social Science at the Australian National University; Monash, Ohio State, Princeton, and Wayne State Universities; and the Universities of Auckland, Bristol, Cambridge, Connecticut, Edinburgh, Glasgow, North Carolina at Greensboro, Nebraska at Lincoln, Oxford, Reading, St. Andrews, and Stirling.

At the end, fellowships at the Center for Applied Philosophy and Public Ethics in Canberra and at the Princeton Center for Human Values enabled me to polish the final version.

I am also grateful for permission to use earlier publications in this book. Parts of chapters 1 and 4–6 derive from Sinnott-Armstrong 1996a. Section 2.2 descends from Sinnott-Armstrong 2000a. Section 3.3 is based on Sinnott-Armstrong 1995a. Chapter 5 owes a lot to Sinnott-Armstrong 2004a. Chapter 7 revises Sinnott-Armstrong 2000b. Section 8.1 is based on Sinnott-Armstrong 1999e. Chapter 9 builds on Sinnott-Armstrong 2001b and 2002c.

Although it will become obvious as I present my views, I would be remiss if I did not acknowledge my debts to the writings of some great philosophers. My Pyrrhonism is inspired by Bob Fogelin. My coherentism is due to David Brink and Geoff Sayre-McCord.

I am also grateful for the encouragement of wonderful editors at Oxford University Press, including Robert Miller, Peter Momtchiloff, and Peter Ohlin.

My heartfelt thanks to you all.

Contents

PART I

ISSUES

In 2003, two adults flew from their home in the United States to Canada in order to get married. Like most married couples, they had sex on their wedding night. This couple was unusual only insofar as both were male. Because of that, many observers think that their marriage and their sexual act were morally wrong. Others believe just as strongly that these particular acts were not morally wrong. Some view their acts as beautiful expressions of a moral ideal of love. A few people who knew about their acts formed no moral opinion at all about what these individuals did.

At a higher level of generality, many people believe that terrorism is always immoral. Others believe that this general kind of act is not immoral in a few special circumstances, such as when terrorism really is the only way to secure the basic human rights of a large population. Some others suspend belief about such unusual situations, so they also suspend belief about whether all terrorism is morally wrong.

At an even higher level of generality, utilitarians and Kantians disagree about the fundamental principles of morality and about whether consequences or intentions count at all in determining what is morally right. Many students study these debates carefully but still cannot make up their minds about which theory, if either, to accept.

Moral controversies like these raise higher-order questions about the formation and status of moral beliefs: If I have not yet reached any opinion about the morality of affirmative action, for example, how should I decide what to think? If I do come to believe that affirmative action is immoral (or morally permitted or morally required), is my belief justified? Can other people be justified in believing the contrary? Can anyone know whether affirmative action is immoral? How?

These questions arise even without disagreement. Almost everyone agrees that experimental surgery on conscious humans without anesthesia or consent is immoral. We also get a lot of agreement on generalizations such as that it is immoral to break promises without adequate reasons. But how can such moral beliefs be justified? Do we know that they are true? If some people disagree, what would or could or should we say to or about these deviants? Could we show them that their unusual moral beliefs are false or unjustified? How?

Such questions lie at the heart of moral epistemology. Whereas substantive ethics is about what is morally right or wrong or good or bad, moral epistemology asks whether and how anyone can know or be justified in holding substantive moral beliefs. The questions of moral epistemology arise at a higher level, for they concern the epistemic status of our substantive moral beliefs in general. These questions lead into fundamental issues about the nature of morality, language, metaphysics, and justification and knowledge in general.

When applied to ethics, these abstract issues are not just theoretical. They also have practical importance. Debates about when, if ever, an employee health plan should pay for abortions often turn on disputes about whether someone can know that abortion is morally wrong (or not). If nobody can obtain knowledge or justified belief about such controversial moral issues, then this might make it seem unfair to treat people differently on the basis of such beliefs, as employers do when they insist that health plans not pay for abortions. (Cf. Lockhart 2000.)

Similarly, hospital ethics committees often decide when terminal patients may (and may not) be taken off life support. Contrary moral beliefs are sometimes held strongly by relatives of the patients, so why should such decisions be handed over to ethics committees? One natural answer is that those ethics committees are more likely to be more justified in their conclusions about such moral issues, maybe because they are more impartial or less emotional or better informed. That answer obviously depends on some view about when moral beliefs are justified. Theories about justified moral belief might, then, affect how we organize ethics committees in order to make their moral conclusions as justified as possible.

Political theorists face similar issues when judges use their moral beliefs in overturning laws that were passed by elected legislatures and supported by public opinion. Why should judges have the power to impose their moral beliefs on so many people who disagree? One natural response is that the special position of judges makes them more justified in trusting their moral beliefs (maybe because they are better informed or less subject to unfair political pressures and self-interest). That response, again, depends on assumptions about what makes moral beliefs justified.

Moral epistemology also affects education. Most people agree that public schools should teach respect for other groups, cultures, and ways of life, but many parents balk at teaching respect for gay couples (with or without children). Before schools can feel comfortable teaching values that conflict with the values of parents, policy makers might need to decide which values can be justified well enough to be taught in the public schools of a free society. In these and many other ways, our public debates and institutions are deeply affected by our views on whether, when, and how moral beliefs can be justified.

Even in our personal lives, we often need to decide which moral claims to believe and how much confidence to place in them. Should you commit civil disobedience in support of a cause that seems just? Should you tell the spouse of a friend who is having a secret affair or report someone who is illegally downloading software or child pornography? Your decisions might sometimes hinge on whether you think that your moral belief is justified well enough. If you think that there can be reasonable disagreement on the moral issues, you will probably be less inclined to make a big deal out of it.

Most generally, when a moral problem is serious, many people want to have some belief about it. They do not want their moral belief to be arbitrary. They want it to be justified. The questions are whether and, if so, how and to what extent they can get what they want. Those are the basic questions for moral epistemology and for this book.

What Is Moral Epistemology?

The field of moral epistemology lies in the intersection between the larger territories of moral theory and general epistemology. Accordingly, this chapter will lead into moral epistemology by surveying moral theory in general and then moral skepticisms in particular.

1.1. Moral Theory

Any division of moral theory is bound to be controversial, but a framework can help in comparing various views. For this purpose, moral theory is often divided, first, into substantive ethics and meta-ethics.

Substantive ethics[1] includes claims and beliefs about what is morally right or wrong, what is morally good or bad, what morally ought or ought not to be done, and so on. These claims and beliefs might be about acts, states of character, persons, policies, institutions, or laws. They might be about particular cases or about general kinds. They might or might not be combined into moral systems, such as utilitarianism and Kantianism. Anyone who makes or implies any such claim is to that extent doing substantive ethics.

Some claims that seem substantive turn out to be true by definition. For example, if a speaker claims that murder is wrong and then defines murder as wrongful killing, the speaker's claim says only that wrongful killing is wrong. That does not tell us anything about which particular acts are wrong, since any act of killing that the speaker does not consider to be wrong will not be classified as murder. A theory in substantive ethics might include some claims like this and

---

1. This field is often called "normative ethics." I prefer "substantive ethics" because moral epistemology is also normative in a different way, as we will see.

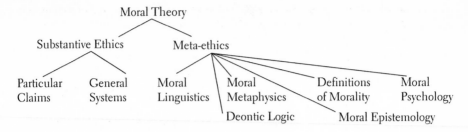

FIGURE 1.1.

some definitions, but it must also include some non-definitional claims about morality to count as a substantive moral theory.[2]

Meta-ethics then asks about the nature or status of substantive moral claims, beliefs, and theories. One prominent area of meta-ethics has been the study of moral language. When a speaker says, "Abortion is immoral," one might ask what this sentence means, what effect this utterance causes (or usually causes or is intended to cause), or what speech act is performed. Such questions are often said to fall under *moral semantics*, but semantics concerns meaning, so it does not strictly include theories about speech acts and effects, which fall under *pragmatics*. That makes it more precise to describe this area of meta-ethics as *moral linguistics*.

There is much more to meta-ethics than moral linguistics. Meta-ethics also includes *moral metaphysics*, which asks whether any moral properties and facts exist and, if so, what metaphysical status they have. These metaphysical issues are separate from moral linguistics, since moral language might refer to moral facts and properties even if no such facts or properties exist (just as a child can describe Santa Claus despite his non-existence).

There are also debates about *the definition of morality* as opposed to religion, law, custom, and so on. *Moral psychology* then asks about the nature and sources of moral beliefs and moral emotions, such as guilt and shame, as well as about our motivation to be moral. *Deontic logic* studies forms of argument or inference or reasoning that depend on the normative and evaluative terms in substantive moral claims. *Moral epistemology* is yet another area of meta-ethics, which concerns roughly whether, when, and how substantive moral claims and beliefs can be justified or known. These sub-fields are diagrammed in figure 1.1. Moral philosophers also discuss other issues, including moral authority or reasons to be moral, but this incomplete picture should be enough to impart some sense of the variety of issues within moral theory.

2. Some opponents might claim that all true moral judgments are true by definition, but this claim could not be plausible unless the proffered definitions were theoretical definitions like "Water is H$_2$O." I am referring, instead, to dictionary definitions. On these kinds of definitions, see Fogelin and Sinnott-Armstrong 2005, 368–72.

Of course, these divisions of moral theory are questionable. Some philosophers reject any distinction between substantive ethics and meta-ethics. It must be admitted that this line is often blurred. One reason is that many claims in moral theory are unclear and combine parts from different areas. Unclear conjunctions are often hard to classify. Moreover, some claims that are supposed to be neutral among all substantive moral theories are really neutral among only some but not other substantive moral theories. The distinction between substantive ethics and meta-ethics might, then, be seen as a matter of degree depending on the range of positions among which a certain claim is neutral.

The different sub-fields within meta-ethics are also often hard to distinguish. Ontological conclusions are often drawn from semantic premises. Semantic analyses of moral language can be tested by their ability to explain the validity of inferences or to fit within some formal semantics of deontic logic. Definitions of morality determine the range of emotions to be studied in moral psychology.

Such connections, conflations, and confusions should not cause concern here. Nothing I say will depend on any hard and fast line between substantive ethics and meta-ethics or between moral epistemology and other sub-fields of meta-ethics. Indeed, if someone insists on avoiding the word "meta-ethics" altogether, that would not affect my arguments. All I need from these distinctions is an initial, rough map of the terrain that surrounds the field to be explored in this book.

1.2. Epistemology Applied to Morality

The central topic here is moral epistemology, which is just epistemology applied to substantive moral beliefs. Epistemology is the study of knowledge and justified belief in general. It asks whether, when, and how people can know or be justified in believing anything. Moral epistemology asks these questions about moral beliefs in particular. Answers to such questions make second-order claims about the epistemic status of first-order moral beliefs.

Of course, we cannot determine whether any claim is justified or known if we have no idea what that claim means, so moral epistemology depends in some ways on moral semantics. Moreover, some philosophers (including Hare 1965, 1981; and Habermas 1990) try to justify moral beliefs by appealing primarily to a theory of moral language, so moral epistemology might be based on moral semantics. The same might be said for moral ontology, the definition of morality, deontic logic, and moral psychology. Nonetheless, moral epistemology differs from other areas of meta-ethics in that it focuses directly on knowledge and justified belief in morality and brings in other issues only when relevant to these central concerns.

Moral epistemology is also distinct from substantive ethics. Both fields ask whether something is justified, but they ask this question about different kinds of things. Moral epistemology asks whether *beliefs* are justified, whereas substantive ethics asks whether *actions* (or policies, institutions, etc.) are justified. For example, the question of whether I am justified in breaking the speed limit to get to class on time is a question of substantive ethics, but the question of whether I am justified in believing that I am justified in breaking the speed limit to get to class on time is a question of moral epistemology. People can be epistemically unjustified in believing that an act is morally justified, such as when they believe that capital punishment is morally justified, and they believe this only because they read it in a book that they are not epistemically justified in trusting. (This can happen whether or not capital punishment really is morally justified.) People can also be epistemically justified in believing that an act is morally unjustified, such as when they have a trustworthy basis for believing that capital punishment is unjustified. (Again, this can happen whether or not capital punishment is morally justified.) All of this shows that being epistemically justified is separate from being morally justified.

Similarly, people can have epistemic reasons for moral beliefs without moral reasons for action, and vice versa. Some philosophers do seem to assume that nobody can have a reason to do an act without having any reason to believe that he has a reason to do that act. Others assume that, if an agent has a reason to believe that there is a reason for that agent to do a certain action, then that agent does have a reason to do that action. I find both assumptions dubious. Moreover, even if reasons for action did follow from reasons for belief and vice versa, a reason for an action would still be distinguishable from a reason to believe in that reason for action, since the reasons have different objects. One is about actions. The other is about beliefs. That is enough to separate the fields of substantive ethics and moral epistemology.

These distinctions, admittedly, get confusing. Suppose a critic claims that it is morally wrong for colleges to use racial quotas in admissions. A defender of affirmative action quotas asks, "Why?" This question asks for some kind of reason or justification, but it is not clear whether it asks for a reason against the racial quotas themselves or, instead, for a reason for the belief that the racial quotas are morally wrong. In response to the former question, the critic might point to features of the racial quotas that make them morally wrong in his opinion, such as that some applicants will be affected adversely although they personally did nothing wrong. Then he is offering a reason not to use the racial quotas, which is a reason for action. In contrast, if the question "Why?" is interpreted differently, a critic of the racial quotas might say that he has studied racial quotas long and hard, consulting with many students and experts, and this long process has made it obvious to him that these racial quotas are immoral. This is not directly a reason for action. Instead, he is offering a reason for his belief, that is, a list of sources or factors that make him justified in believing that the racial quotas are immoral. These reasons for belief are facts about him (including his beliefs), whereas the reasons for action were facts about racial quotas. Other kinds of reasons for belief might seem closer to reasons for action. Sometimes a reason to believe that an action is morally right (or wrong) is a *belief* that the action has certain properties, and the *fact* that the action has those properties is a reason for (or against) doing the action. Since to state the fact is to express the belief, it is then hard to tell whether a speaker is referring to the reason for belief or, instead, to the reason for action. That explains why so many people conflate these distinct kinds of reasons. It is often not clear which kind of reason is being sought when someone asks "Why?" or which kind of reason is being given when someone answers that question. But here we need to avoid such confusions and unclarity. If we do, then moral epistemology can be distinguished from substantive ethics.

These fields are still related, insofar as an adequate moral epistemology must cohere with the best substantive ethics. Nonetheless, theories in moral epistemology are supposed to be neutral among competing substantive moral views, just as logic, semantics, and general epistemology need to be neutral among competing views in history or biology. When people disagree about the morality of abortion, they often want a method to resolve their dispute or a test of whether either view is justified. Moral epistemologists study and sometimes propose such methods and tests. To avoid begging the question, these methods and tests must be neutral among the views under dispute. Of course, some theories in moral epistemology are not really so neutral. Maybe no theory in moral epistemology can be completely neutral among all possible substantive moral views. Even so, some theories in moral epistemology can still be neutral among the competitors in a particular dispute. Then they might be useful in choosing among those particular alternatives. That would help a lot, but it remains to be seen whether even that much can be accomplished. If so, then moral epistemology is distinct from substantive ethics at least in such contexts.

Whether or not its questions can be answered independent of substantive ethics, moral epistemology at least asks distinctive questions. Indeed, several different questions that are not directly about substantive ethics are asked and answered within moral epistemology. A first question concerns *conditions* for justified belief and knowledge in morality. Some moral epistemologists attempt to spell out necessary or sufficient conditions for a person to be justified in believing a moral claim or to know that a certain moral claim is true. A second question concerns practical *procedures* or *methods*. Some moral epistemologists propose steps that a person can or must go through in order to gain justified moral belief or knowledge. A third question asks how we can *show* that moral claims or beliefs are true or justified or known. A fourth question asks about *degrees* to which moral beliefs can be justified—which are justified better or best—while admitting that different beliefs are justified also but not as well. Still other moral epistemologists ask parallel questions about justifications or arguments or epistemic virtues or reliability regarding moral beliefs, each of which is different from the question of when moral beliefs are justified.

All of these questions are important and lie within moral epistemology, but we cannot discuss all of them at once. In this book, I will focus on the questions of which conditions are necessary or sufficient for moral knowledge and for a person to be justified in believing a substantive moral claim.

1.3. Varieties of Moral Skepticism

The primary challenge in moral epistemology is posed by moral skepticism. However, many very different views have been described as moral skepticism. The best way to explain the particular kind of moral skepticism that will concern us here is to contrast it with the other views that sometimes go by the same name.

In general, what makes moral skepticism *moral* is that it concerns morality rather than other topics. Moral skeptics might go on to be skeptics about the external world or about other minds or about induction or about all beliefs, but these other skepticisms are not entailed by moral skepticism alone. What makes moral skeptics *skeptics* is that they raise doubts about common beliefs. Moral skeptics then differ in the *kinds* of doubts they raise and the *targets* of those doubts.

The most central versions of moral skepticism correspond to two varieties of general epistemological skepticism. These views are often conflated and confused, but the distinction between them is crucial to my project. One tradition descends from Plato's Academy, so it is called *Academic* skepticism.[3] This position is sometimes known as *Cartesian* skepticism, but that is misleading, because Descartes (1641) argued against it. Whatever you call it, this kind of skepticism is defined by the claim that nobody knows or is justified in believing anything.[4]

In contrast, this claim is neither asserted nor believed by skeptics in the other tradition. They also neither deny nor disbelieve it. They have so much doubt that they do not make any claim about whether or not anyone has any knowledge or justified belief. They suspend belief about Academic skepticism. This other variety of skepticism descends from the ancient philosopher Pyrrho, so it is often called *Pyrrhonian* skepticism.[5] Those who prefer descriptive names can think of Academic skepticism as dogmatic, doctrinaire, assertive, or committed skepticism, and Pyrrhonian skepticism as non-dogmatic, non-doctrinaire, non-assertive, and non-committed, since Pyrrhonians do not assert or commit themselves to any dogma, doctrine, or claim (positive or negative) about whether anyone knows or is justified in believing anything.

Moral skepticism comes in two corresponding varieties. *Pyrrhonian skeptics about moral knowledge* do not believe that anyone knows that any substantive moral belief is true. They doubt that anyone has moral knowledge. Still, they also do not believe the opposite, that nobody has moral knowledge. They doubt that too. Their doubts are so extreme that they do not adopt any position one way or the other about whether anyone has moral knowledge. In other words:

Pyrrhonian skeptics about moral knowledge suspend belief about whether or not anyone knows that any substantive moral belief is true.

Similarly:

Pyrrhonian skeptics about justified moral belief suspend belief about whether or not anyone is justified in holding any moral belief.

<hr/>

3. My stipulated usage should not be confused with the different meaning of "academical" skepticism in Hume ([1748] 1888).

4. Most skeptics in this tradition make the stronger modal claim that nobody *can* know or be justified in believing anything. I define Academic skepticism by the weaker non-modal claim about what people *do* know rather than what they *can* know, because I will criticize Academic skepticism, and I do not want to be accused of being unfair to this opponent by making its claim too strong. For various views on Academic skepticism, see DeRose and Warfield 1999.

5. For more on Pyrrho and recent Pyrrhonians, see Sinnott-Armstrong 2004b.

Pyrrhonian moral skeptics still might hold some substantive moral beliefs, but they do not endorse any higher-order epistemic claim about whether their own moral beliefs are justified or known.

In contrast, *Academic moral skeptics* make definite claims about the epistemic status of moral beliefs:

> *Academic skepticism about moral knowledge* is the claim that nobody ever knows that any substantive moral belief is true.

> *Academic skepticism about justified moral belief* is the claim that nobody is ever justified in holding any substantive moral belief.

The relation between these two versions of Academic moral skepticism depends on the nature of knowledge. If knowledge implies justified belief, as is traditionally supposed, then Academic skepticism about justified moral belief implies Academic skepticism about moral knowledge. However, even if knowledge does require justified belief, it does not require *only* justified belief, so Academic skepticism about moral knowledge does not imply Academic skepticism about justified moral belief. There might be no moral knowledge but plenty of justified moral beliefs.

In any case, both of these versions of epistemological skepticism need to be distinguished from yet another form of moral skepticism:

> *Skepticism about moral truth* is the claim that no substantive moral belief is true.

This claim implies Academic skepticism about moral knowledge, since knowledge implies truth. However, skepticism about moral truth cannot be based on skepticism about moral knowledge, since lack of knowledge does not imply lack of truth. For similar reasons, skepticism about moral truth also cannot be based on skepticism about justified moral belief. Instead, skepticism about moral truth is usually based on views of moral language or metaphysics.

Some philosophers of language argue that sentences like "Cheating is morally wrong" cannot be either true or false because of how they resemble pure expressions of emotion (such as "Boo, Knicks!") or imperatives (such as "Go, Celtics!"). These kinds of expressions and imperatives cannot be either true or false. Thus, if these analogies hold in this respect, then, because of their nature, substantive moral beliefs also cannot be either true or false. In other words, they are not apt for evaluation in terms of truth, so:

> *Skepticism about moral truth-aptness* is the claim that no substantive moral belief is truth-apt (that is, the right kind of thing to be either true or false).

This claim is often described as *non-cognitivism*. That label would be misleading here, however, since etymology suggests that cognitivism is about cognition, which is tied to knowledge both etymologically and in common use. Although skepticism about moral truth-aptness has implications for moral knowledge, it is directly about truth-aptness and not about moral knowledge.

Whatever you call it, skepticism about moral truth-aptness is often denied, for reasons to be discussed in chapter 2. Opponents of such views claim that moral assertions express *beliefs*. In particular, they express beliefs that certain acts, institutions, or people have certain moral properties (such as moral rightness or wrongness) or beliefs in moral facts (such as the fact that a certain act is morally right or wrong). This non-skeptical linguistic analysis presents moral beliefs as the right kind of thing to be true in the right conditions, but it still does not show that any moral claims are or even can be true, since assertions can express beliefs that are false or, at least, not true. Truth-*aptness* does not ensure *truth*. Thus, opponents of skepticism about truth-aptness still may endorse another version of moral skepticism, which claims that all moral beliefs must be erroneous:

> *Skepticism with moral error* (or a moral error theory) is the claim that some substantive moral beliefs are truth-apt, but none is true.[6]

This claim follows from the combination of the linguistic view that moral assertions express beliefs, a view of truth in which a belief cannot be true unless it corresponds to a fact, and a metaphysical thesis:

> *Skepticism about moral reality* is the claim that no moral facts or properties exist.[7]

This kind of skepticism will be discussed in chapter 3.

Moral error theorists and skeptics about moral truth-aptness disagree about the content of moral assertions, but they still agree that no moral claim or belief is true, so both are skeptics about moral truth. None of these skeptical theses is implied by either skepticism about moral knowledge or skepticism about justified moral belief. Some moral claims might be true, even if we cannot know or have justified beliefs about which ones are true. In contrast, a converse implication seems to hold: if knowledge implies truth, and if moral claims are never true, then there cannot be any knowledge of what is moral or immoral (assuming that skeptics deny the same kind of truth that knowledge requires). Nonetheless, since the implication holds in only one direction, skepticism about moral truth is still distinct from all kinds of epistemological moral skepticism.

Yet another non-epistemological form of moral skepticism answers the question "Why be moral?" This question is used to raise many different issues. Almost everyone admits that there is sometimes some kind of reason to do some moral acts. However, many philosophers deny various universal claims, including the claims that there is always *some* reason to be moral, that there is always a distinctively *moral* (as opposed to self-interested) reason to be moral, and/or that there is always an *adequate* reason that makes it irrational not to be moral or at least not irrational to be moral. These distinct denials can be seen as separate forms of *practical moral skepticism*.

---

6. Examples include Mackie (1946, 1977), who claims that positive moral beliefs are false; and Joyce (2001), who claims that positive moral beliefs are neither true nor false, despite being truth-apt. See also Robinson (1948), J. P. Burgess (1979), Hinckfuss (1987), Garner (1994), V. A. Burgess (1998), and Greene (forthcoming).

7. Compare Nietzsche [1888] 1954: "There are altogether no moral facts." The nature of moral facts will be discussed in sections 2.2.4 and 3.1.

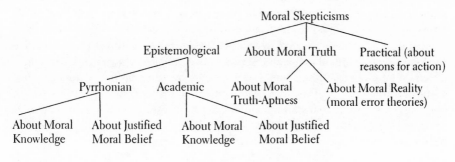

FIGURE 1.2.

Practical moral skepticism resembles epistemological moral skepticism insofar as both kinds of skepticism deny a role to reasons in morality. However, epistemological moral skepticism is about reasons for *belief*, whereas practical moral skepticism is about reasons for *action*. Moreover, practical moral skeptics usually deny that there is *always* enough reason for moral action, whereas epistemological moral skeptics deny or doubt that there is *ever* an adequate reason for moral belief. Consequently, practical moral skepticism does not imply epistemological moral skepticism. Some moral theorists do assume that a reason to believe that an act is immoral cannot be adequate unless it also provides a reason not to do that act. However, even if the two kinds of reasons are related in this way, they are still distinct, so practical moral skepticism must not be confused with epistemological moral skepticism.

Altogether, these forms of moral skepticism are diagrammed in figure 1.2. Epistemological moral skepticism will be the main topic in most of this book, so that group of views is what I will mean henceforth whenever I refer to moral skepticism without qualification. When the context does not already make it clear, I will specify whether I have in mind Pyrrhonian or Academic skepticism and whether this skepticism is about knowledge or justified belief.

1.4. Presumptions Against Moral Skepticism

All of these moral skepticisms come in for heavy criticism. Some opponents of moral skepticism are on a mission to save the world from horrible acts that are supposed to result when people become moral skeptics of any variety. However, skeptics about moral knowledge and justified moral belief can act well and be nice people. They need not be any less motivated to be moral, nor need they have or believe in any less reason to be moral than non-skeptics. Moral skeptics can hold substantive moral beliefs just as strongly as non-skeptics. Their substantive moral beliefs can be common and plausible ones. Moral skeptics can even believe that their moral beliefs are true by virtue of corresponding to an independent moral reality. All that moral skeptics deny is that their or anyone's moral beliefs are justified or known (and Pyrrhonian moral skeptics don't even deny that). This meta-ethical position about the epistemic status of moral beliefs need not trickle down and infect anyone's substantive moral beliefs or actions.[8]

Anti-skeptics might respond that moral skepticism does in fact often have detrimental effects on moral beliefs and actions. Nice moral skeptics might ascribe such effects to misunderstanding, but, if such misunderstandings are common, then moral skepticism might be dangerous. This fear is natural. Roy Sorensen, for example, reports that he loaned a book that defends moral skepticism to a student. As the student left, Roy wondered whether he would ever see his book again. He didn't. Still, this does not show that moral skepticism weakens moral beliefs. Maybe students with antecedently weak moral beliefs are drawn to moral skepticism.

Besides, overly strong moral beliefs can create other problems. Some busybodies might be less likely to interfere with other people's choices if they were moral skeptics. Moral skepticism might prevent bombastic moralists from being overbearing in ways that often thwart negotiation and sometimes ignite wars. When all such considerations are weighed, it is not at all clear that moral skepticism has bad consequences overall.

In any case, the main question here is whether moral skepticism is *true*. Even if adopting moral skepticism does have bad consequences, that cannot show that it is not true. Maybe belief in evolution or certain economic views also leads to bad consequences, but that would be no argument against evolution or the economic views. Similarly, even if opponents could show that it is dangerous to believe in moral skepticism, that could not show that moral skepticism is not true. So I will not spend any more time defending moral skepticism against such charges.

Critics still argue that moral skepticism conflicts with common sense. Most people think that they are justified in holding many moral beliefs, such as that it is morally wrong for parents to spank their children too hard. People also claim moral knowledge, such as when a neighbor says, "I know that it is wrong for him to spank his daughter so hard, but I don't know what I should do about it." Moral skepticism conflicts with these common ways of talking and thinking, so moral skeptics seem to owe us some argument for their claims.

Academic moral skepticism is, moreover, a universal and abstruse claim. It is the claim that all moral beliefs have a certain epistemic status. Normally one should not make such a strong claim without some reason. One should not, for example, claim that all astronomical beliefs are unjustified unless one has some reason for this claim. Analogously, it seems that one should not claim that all moral beliefs are unjustified unless one has some positive argument. Thus, its form, like its conflict with common sense, seems to create a presumption against moral skepticism.

Moral skeptics, in response, sometimes try to shift the burden of proof to their opponents. Anyone who makes the positive moral claim that homosexual sodomy (or abortion or adultery or arson) is morally wrong seems to need some reason for

---

8. Even if some moral skeptics did give up the belief that harming others is morally wrong, for example, they still might have enough non-moral reason not to harm other people if they care about other people. Thus, even the lack of moral belief need not lead to immoral action.

that claim, just as someone who claims that there is life on Mars seems to need evidence for that claim. If the presumption is always against those who make positive moral claims, then it is opponents of moral skepticism who must carry the burden of proof. Or, at least, moral skeptics can deny that the burden of proof is on moral skeptics. Then moral skeptics may criticize any moral belief or theory without needing to offer any positive argument for moral skepticism, and their opponents need to take moral skepticism seriously enough to argue against it (see Copp 1991).

This controversy about burden of proof can be resolved by distinguishing Academic moral skepticism from Pyrrhonian moral skepticism. Academic moral skeptics (about either moral knowledge or justified moral belief) make an abstruse universal claim that conflicts with common sense, so they seem to have the burden of arguing for their claim. In contrast, Pyrrhonian moral skeptics neither assert nor deny any claim about the epistemic status of any moral belief. They simply raise doubts about whether moral beliefs are ever known or justified. This difference suggests that Pyrrhonian moral skeptics do not take on as much burden of proof as do Academic moral skeptics.

Pyrrhonians also thereby avoid the infamous problem of the criterion (Chisholm 1982, Nelson 2003). Academic skeptics seem to assume that we can discover general criteria or conditions of knowledge before we decide which particular beliefs, if any, count as knowledge. Non-skeptics often respond that we need to determine which particular beliefs count as knowledge before we can figure out which general conditions need to be met in order for knowledge to occur. Pyrrhonians stand back from this whole debate and ask whether there is any adequate reason to begin either with general criteria or with particular cases. Since Pyrrhonians do not favor either starting point, they do not seem to need an argument for picking one starting point as opposed to the other.[9]

In any case, whether or not they need to do so, moral skeptics usually try to support their position with a variety of arguments. If knowledge requires justified true belief, as is often assumed, then arguments for Academic skepticism about moral knowledge can deny either that moral beliefs can be true or that moral beliefs can be justified. These two kinds of arguments will be discussed in the remainder of part I. Chapters 2–3 will focus on moral truth. Chapters 4–6 will discuss justified moral belief. In chapters 2–4, I will focus on Academic moral skepticism. I will return to Pyrrhonian moral skepticism in chapters 5–6.

I will end up rejecting both skepticism about moral truth and Academic moral skepticism, so my own views will not emerge until chapters 5–6. Nonetheless, it is worth considering these other moral skepticisms carefully, both because they set the stage for my account and also because they are more often discussed than the position that I will eventually adopt.

---

9. Pyrrhonian moral skepticism thereby avoids problems pointed out by Nelson (2003), who argued that my earlier Academic moral skepticism begs the question as much as its denial, which he endorses. I am very grateful to Nelson for his criticisms, which were part of what convinced me to become a Pyrrhonian moral skeptic instead of an Academic moral skeptic.

Are Moral Beliefs Truth-Apt?

One common argument for Academic moral knowledge skepticism runs like this: Knowledge requires true belief. No moral belief can be true. Therefore, no moral belief can be knowledge. This argument seems simple, but it raises deep issues in moral semantics and metaphysics, as well as in the analysis of knowledge. The last shall be first.

2.1. Does Knowledge Require True Belief?

The premise that knowledge requires true belief conjoins two separable parts: that knowledge requires belief and that knowledge requires truth. Each of these claims is traditional, common, and plausible, at least in the cases that will concern us here.

Knowledge clearly seems to require belief. I don't know where the Pope is right now if I do not have any belief about where he is. That lack of belief would be enough to make me say, "I don't know where he is," if someone asked me.

Common expressions like "I can't believe you did that" and the toast "To my friends, who know my failures but refuse to believe them" might seem to suggest knowledge without belief. However, these idioms merely flout rules of common usage for rhetorical effect.

Some philosophers (e.g., Radford 1966) deny that belief is necessary for knowledge because of examples where people answer questions correctly by guessing without believing that they are right. It is not clear what to make of such cases. However, even if knowledge does not require belief in situations like these, this kind of knowledge is not what is claimed by most theories in moral epistemology. Moral epistemologists who claim that certain moral beliefs count as knowledge do not feel as if they are guessing. So I will assume henceforth that the relevant kind of knowledge implies some notion of belief, even if only a thin one.

The second condition that is said to be necessary for knowledge is truth. I don't know where the Pope is right now if I believe that he is in Italy when actually he is in Africa (or anywhere other than Italy). The fact that I got it wrong seems to be enough to show that I didn't know as much as I thought I knew. Moreover, if I say to the Pope, "Go to Italy," or if I ask you, "Where is the Pope?" then what I say cannot be the object of knowledge, because imperatives and questions are not the kinds of things that could be either true or false.

Some psychologists seem to use the word "know" so that it does not imply truth and is compatible with falsehood. The word "know" then seems to describe little more than a level of confidence, regardless of truth. I suspect that this use by psychologists is a technical use that does not conform to common language. But that does not matter here. Even if the word "know" can legitimately be used in some contexts without implying truth, this use is absent from most theories in moral epistemology.

One noteworthy exception is Gilbert Ryle (1958), who argued that moral knowledge is a kind of know-how. In Ryle's view, we can know how to ride a bike without being able to say much, if anything, instructive about how to ride a bike and without having any definite beliefs about how bikes work. We might even hold many false beliefs about bikes. Analogously, Ryle claimed, we can know how to do morally right acts without having many, if any, beliefs about which acts are morally right or about what makes them morally right. We might even hold numerous false beliefs about morality. So this kind of knowledge does not seem to imply either belief or truth. This counterexample cannot be dismissed as trivial. For some practical purposes, know-how is more important than knowledge-that. Theoretically, it might be very useful for moral epistemologists to study moral know-how. Nonetheless, even if know-how is important, it is not the *only* kind of knowledge that is important. If someone knows how to act morally but does not have any beliefs about which acts are moral or why, then something valuable is missing. What is missing is that other kind of knowledge—knowledge that certain claims are true—which is usually studied in general epistemology and in moral epistemology. For such reasons, I will also focus here on knowledge-that, and I will assume that such knowledge implies truth as well as belief.

2.2. Expressivism

Even granting the first premise, the skeptical conclusion follows only if we add the second premise: that no moral belief can be true. In section 1.3, I labeled this premise skepticism about moral truth and mentioned two main ways to support it. One appeals to an expressivist analysis of moral language that is supposed to lead to skepticism about truth-aptness. The other cites metaphysical considerations to support a moral error theory. This chapter will discuss expressivist theories. Chapter 3 will consider error theories.

2.2.1. *What Is Expressivism?*

Expressivism is best understood in contrast with moral realism. Moral realists claim that some moral sentences are true by virtue of corresponding to the moral facts and properties that those moral sentences describe.[1]

In response, expressivists typically make three claims.[2] The first claim is that moral sentences do not have truth-values. The second claim is that moral assertions do not describe the world. The third claim is that moral assertions do express emotions or other non-cognitive states, such as attitudes or desires. The first two claims are negative, while the third claim is positive. The first claim is about semantics, whereas the next two claims are about pragmatics in a broad sense. Accordingly, I will refer to these claims as the negative semantic claim, the negative pragmatic claim, and the positive pragmatic claim, respectively.

These three claims, together with an account of the expressed non-cognitive state, are supposed to specify the meanings of moral sentences. It is partly because the negative claims rule out truth conditions and description that expressivists turn to an expressive function to explain the meanings of moral sentences. This expressive function is said to be all there is to those meanings because moral sentences are not used to describe or to state true propositions. So the three claims are related. That is why they are often conjoined into a single theory.

Nonetheless, these three claims are logically independent, so we need to ask which of them is crucial to moral skepticism. First, the positive pragmatic claim is that moral assertions express some non-cognitive state. Which state? Traditional emotivists hold that emotions or attitudes are expressed. Recent expressivists often instead refer to expression of desires or motivations or plans. These are all states of mind, but prescriptivists can also be seen as expressivists if prescriptions can also be expressed.[3] In all such variations, what is expressed is non-cognitive, because it is not a belief or any other kind of state that can be true or false. However, the positive claim that moral assertions express non-cognitive states does not entail the negative claim that moral assertions do not also express other states, such as beliefs, or that they do not perform other speech acts, such as describing and stating. A moral assertion might perform several speech acts at once, just as "That angry bull is charging right at us" can be used to state a fact, express fear, draw attention, and prescribe action. Thus, neither skepticism about moral truth nor

---

1. More precisely, the primary truth-bearer is the proposition expressed by a sentence, since the same sentence (such as "I am hot") can express different propositions with different truth-values in different contexts. For simplicity, I will follow the common practice of calling sentences true when they express true propositions and beliefs true when they are beliefs in a true proposition.

2. These claims are separated by Stoljar 1993, 81. Expressivists include Ayer (1946), Stevenson (1944), Hare (1952), Blackburn (1984, 1993, 1998), and Gibbard (1990, 2003). More recent expressivists often weaken the negative semantic claim in ways to be discussed. Although expressivism is usually about evaluative or normative judgments in general, I will focus on moral language in particular.

3. For convenience, I will sometimes write about expressing states of mind, which might not include prescriptions, but my main points about expressivism will also apply to prescriptivism.

epistemological moral skepticism follows from the positive pragmatic claim of expressivism.

The negative pragmatic claim also does not yield skepticism. It is coherent to grant that moral sentences "are not in the business of describing or representing anything," but they still do "make real assertions—evaluative assertions—that are genuinely truth-apt" (Timmons 1998, 20n17). Moreover, many (or even all) evaluative assertions do seem descriptive in a broad way. Evaluative assertions can describe, for example, a degree of disvalue (rape is worse than theft) or a kind of disvalue (disclosing the client's secret was unprofessional but not unpatriotic) or a moral status (refusing to help was far from ideal, but it was not wrong) (Sinnott-Armstrong 1999a). Thus, the negative pragmatic claim of expressivism is doubtful and, even if it could be defended, would not rule out moral truth or moral knowledge.

What matters for moral skepticism, then, is expressivism's negative semantic claim. That is why I will focus on that particular part of expressivism.

2.2.2. *Initial Problems of Embeddings*

Expressivism's negative semantic claim runs into trouble, because moral sentences fit smoothly into many contexts that seem to require truth-values. Most directly, proper English speakers don't blush when calling moral sentences true, false, known, and unknown:

> It's true that lying is usually wrong, but surprise parties are exceptions.
> The claim that terrorism can be justified is simply false.
> I was mistaken when I held that homosexuality is immoral.
> I know that my neighbor ought not to spank his children so hard, but I don't know what I should do about it.

Common speakers also ascribe propositional attitudes to moral claims:

> I believe that what I am doing is moral.
> I doubt that what I am doing is immoral.
> I fear that what I am doing is not moral.
> I hope that what I am doing is not immoral.

We talk about what is probably or really immoral:

> This law is probably fair, but there is a significant risk that it violates a fundamental right.
> A punishment should fit how bad the crime really and truly is, not how bad people think it is. (Cf. Brink 1989, 27.)

Tenses and counterfactuals seem to indicate what was or will be or would be true, and yet we say things like these:

> Yesterday plagiarism was wrong, and it will remain wrong tomorrow and long after we die.
> Cutting him open with a sharp knife would have been reprehensible if he had not consented to the operation.

The most widely discussed examples are logical operators:

> Negation: It is not the case that capital punishment is wrong. (Cf. Sinnott-Armstrong 1995a, 228–31.)
>
> Disjunction: Either contraception is morally wrong or abortion is not morally wrong. (Cf. Blackburn [1988] 1993, 191; and Gibbard 2003, 41–48.)
>
> Conditionals: If lying is wrong, then so is paying your little brother to lie for you. (Cf. Geach 1960, 1965; and Searle 1962, 1969.)

Contexts like these provide evidence that moral sentences can have truth-values, because it is hard to explain these uses of moral language without ascribing truth-values to moral sentences.

To see how serious this problem is, let's look in more detail at moral conditionals in arguments of the form *modus ponens*. Here's a standard example:

(1) Lying is wrong.

(2) If lying is wrong, then paying your little brother to lie for you is wrong.

∴ (3) Paying your little brother to lie for you is wrong.

It is obvious that argument (1)–(3) is valid. Because of the argument's form, it is not possible that both its premises, (1)–(2), are true and its conclusion, (3), is false.[4] The initial problem is that this obvious fact seems inconsistent with expressivism. The argument (1)–(3) would not be valid if the sentence "Lying is wrong" had different meanings in the two premises, since then the argument would commit a fallacy of equivocation. However, expressivism appears to imply that "Lying is wrong" does have different meanings in premise (1) and in the antecedent of premise (2). So expressivism seems to imply that argument (1)–(3) is not valid.

One source of this problem is that expressivists would analyze premise (1) as expressing something like disapproval of lying, but a speaker can believe and assert premise (2) without disapproving or expressing any disapproval of lying, since to assert the conditional (2) is not to assert its antecedent. More important here is that expressivists deny that (1) has a truth-value. However, the antecedent of the conditional premise (2) must have a truth-value, if the conditional connective in (2) is understood in the most common and natural way. Even if this conditional connective is not interpreted as a material conditional or as truth-functional, this conditional still seems to claim some relation between the truth-values of its antecedent and its consequent.

An expressivist might respond by analyzing conditionals in some way that does not require its components to be truth-apt. Such analyses are often supported by conditionals that embed questions (as in "If he's not home, where is he?") and

---

4. All expressivists whom I know admit that (1)–(3) is a valid argument. Moreover, common people use arguments like this and see them as valid arguments. If any expressivists denied either that (1)–(3) is valid or that (1)–(3) is an argument, then it would be hard to imagine how they would explain what common people mean by the components of (1)–(3). Such expressivists might escape this part of my argument, but they would not escape my main point.

imperatives (as in "If you can't stand the heat, get out of the kitchen"). Despite such examples, however, a conditional with indicative components can still claim some relation between the truth-values of the antecedent and of the consequent, just as a conjunction of indicatives claims a relation between its conjuncts' truth-values despite examples like "I'm not moving, and what are you going to do about it?" Indeed, some account that requires components of indicative conditionals to be truth-apt seems necessary to fit the common logical intuition that argument (1)–(3) is valid, since validity is most naturally explained in terms of truth-values. Moreover, the connective "If..., then..." seems to have the same meaning regardless of whether or not its antecedent or consequent is evaluative. When its components are not evaluative but are indicative and do have truth-values, then a conditional does seem to claim some relation between the truth-values of those components. This makes it seem that conditionals also operate on truth-values when their components are evaluative indicatives. For such reasons, the antecedent of premise (2) seems to have a truth-value. But the negative semantic claim of expressivism implies that premise (1) has no truth-value. This suggests, again, that (1) does not mean the same as the antecedent of (2), so (1)–(3) equivocates and is invalid, according to expressivism.

The problem is that argument (1)–(3) is not invalid. It's valid. If expressivism implies otherwise, then expressivism is inadequate to capture a crucial feature of moral language—namely, logical relations among moral sentences.

In response, expressivists need to show how they can explain the validity of (1)–(3) in particular and of moral instances of *modus ponens* in general. The most common and plausible attempt to explain such validity is to grant that moral sentences have a minimal kind of truth. Moral expressivists can still distinguish themselves from moral realists by denying that any moral sentences have the robust kind of truth that moral realists claim—correspondence to real moral facts. Not that much is required for truth, according to certain minimalist theories. Such minimal theories might be enough for expressivists to explain the logic of moral sentences.

To understand and assess this response, we need to explore minimal theories of truth. Such theories differ in various ways, but most derive from Alfred Tarski (1944). Tarski argued, roughly, that a theory of truth for a language would assign individuals to names and sets to predicates in such a way as to imply all instances of Schema T: "S" is true if and only if S. A minimal theory of truth then says, again roughly, that this is all there is to know about truth.

This theory puts constraints on which sentences can be true or express truths. A sentence will not fit into Schema T unless it is grammatical to substitute that sentence for "S" in the schema. That explains why questions and imperatives are neither true nor false. Some non-indicative phrases do get labeled "true." Suppose I ask, "When does the party start?" You respond simply, "7:00," and a listener remarks, "That's true, but almost nobody will be there before 7:30." The listener can call "7:00" true because "7:00" is here equivalent to "The party starts at 7:00," which is indicative. So, despite such elliptical examples, it seems that only indicatives or their equivalents (or what they express) can be true or false.

Still, not all indicatives have truth-values. Indicatives are neither true nor false, despite fitting into Schema T, when they are nonsense (such as "He is dlab") or indeterminate (such as "He is bald," when the subject pronoun has no specific referent, or "Hanover is north," if there is no definite answer to "North of what?"). Some philosophers add that "The present King of France is bald" is neither true nor false while there is no present King of France, and that "Walter is bald" is too vague to be either true or false while Walter is on the borderline between being bald and being hairy. Even if so, however, these latter examples are at least the kind of sentence that could be true or false if the world were different.

Moral sentences can also be meaningless or indeterminate in the same way as non-moral sentences. Just consider "He ought to abdicate" with no determinate subject referent or "Fear mongering is wrong" when it is not clear enough what counts as fear mongering. Moral assertions are often under-specified in ways that rule out any truth-value. Nonetheless, it is hard to see any reason why *all* moral assertions must *always* be underdetermined in ways that keep them from being true or false. Surely, many such moral assertions and beliefs seem determinate enough to meet these minimal conditions for truth-aptness.

Extreme expressivists might argue that moral sentences do not really have even minimal truth, because their logical form is different from their grammatical form. If a sentence like "You ought to return phone calls" has the grammatical form that it appears to have, but it has the logical form "Hooray to returning phone calls" or "Return phone calls," then its logical form does not fit into Schema T, so it cannot have minimal truth-aptness. Though tempting, this line of thought faces serious problems. On the traditional view of logical form, one sentence gives the logical form of another only if the first sentence means the same as the second, and one sentence means the same as another only if one is true whenever the other is. This test, however, creates problems for expressivists who claim that the logical form of an evaluative sentence is an exclamation or imperative. The whole point of this version of expressivism is that "You ought to return phone calls" is *not* true whenever "Hooray to returning people's phone calls" is, because the former is grammatically embeddable in contexts such as "It is true that . . ." while the latter is not. It follows that "Hooray to returning people's phone calls" is *not* the logical form of "You ought to return people's phone calls" on the traditional view of logical form. Extreme expressivists might respond by denying that one sentence means the same as another only if one is true whenever the other is. However, this restriction on logical form is accepted in all other cases. Philosophers reject an analysis of the logical form of a definite description (as by Russell 1905) or an action sentence (as by Davidson 1967) if there are any circumstances where the analyzed sentence is true but its analysis is not true. So it is hard to see why this test would not apply to extreme expressivism as well. If it does, then this distinction between grammatical form and logical form will not prevent moral sentences from having minimal truth.[5]

---

5. This is part of why Hare insisted from the start that his prescriptivism does not claim that the logical form of evaluations is given by imperatives: "It is no part of my project to 'reduce' moral language to imperatives" (1952, 2). Evaluations might have the same force as imperatives or exclamations, and might also be similar in other ways, without having the same logical form.

This is bad news for *extreme expressivists*.[6] However, it is good news for *minimal expressivists*, who admit that some moral sentences have minimal truth-values. This admission helps minimal expressivists explain why moral sentences are called "true" or "false" and how they fit into conditionals and other unassertive contexts.

In particular, expressivists can cite minimal truth to handle moral *modus ponens*. All sentences that are apt for minimal truth also fit into the antecedents of conditionals.[7] Whenever a sentence fits into the antecedent of a conditional, a *modus ponens* argument whose premises are this sentence and an appropriate conditional is valid.[8] The reason is that arguments with the form *modus ponens* are valid by virtue of the properties of the connective "if…, then…" not by virtue of any properties of the components that are connected by "if…, then…." Philosophers hold many views of the truth conditions of the connective "if…, then…." I do not need or want to commit myself to any controversial view of conditionals here. All that is essential here is that no analysis of the conditional connective in an instance of *modus ponens* can do justice to our logical intuitions unless it makes that argument formally valid. An argument is formally valid only if any argument with the same form is valid regardless of the content of its components. Thus, an instance of *modus ponens* is valid regardless of whether or not its components have evaluative content.

2.2.3. *Further Problems of Embeddings*

Minimal truth-aptness is, however, not enough by itself to save expressivism. One reason is that merely claiming minimal truth-aptness for a sentence does not tell us what that sentence means, even if we know its pragmatic force. This problem is pressed forcefully by Dreier.[9] Imagine a greetivist, who tells us that the expression "Hello, Bob" is used to greet Bob. It is not used to describe Bob, and it has no truth-value. In contrast, the indicative variation "Bob is hello" is also used to greet Bob, but it has minimal truth-aptness by virtue of its grammatical form and determinacy, so it can be used in valid arguments, such as "Bob is hello. If Bob is hello, then so is his little brother. Therefore, his little brother is hello." Dreier's

---

6. For more bad news, see Jackson and Pettit 1998; Smith 2001; and Dorr 2002. For more on minimal truth and expressivism, see Hooker 1996.

7. Some sentences without minimal truth-aptness fit into the *consequents* of conditionals (as in "If that is your attitude, go to hell!"). Dreier (1996) pointed out that imperatives might fit into the antecedents of *other* kinds of conditionals, such as "Stay in the kitchen only if you can stand the heat." It is not clear whether this antecedent is a true imperative or just elliptical for "You should stay in the kitchen." Anyway, imperatives never fill the space after "if" in a sentence with "if…, then…." That is the position at stake in evaluative instances of *modus ponens*.

8. I respond to some proposed counterexamples in Sinnott-Armstrong, Moor, and Fogelin 1986; and Sinnott-Armstrong 1999b. Even if these responses failed to validate *modus ponens* in general, the proposed counterexamples would not affect the point here as long as *modus ponens* works with evaluative sentences in the same way as it does with non-evaluative sentences.

9. See Dreier 1996, 42–44. Dreier imagines an accostivist, who says that "Hiyo, Bob" is used to accost Bob. I use greetivism because "Hello" is more familiar.

point is that none of this stipulation gives us any idea what "Bob is hello" means. It does not mean "Bob is greeted" or "The speaker greets Bob." Greetivists can say that to assert "Bob is hello" is to greet, but that does not help us understand a conditional with "Bob is hello" in its antecedent, since that conditional is not used to greet. This lack of understanding shows that merely saying that a sentence is used for a certain speech act and also has minimal truth-aptness and so fits into conditionals is not enough to explain what the sentence means. But that is all that expressivism tells us so far about moral sentences. Thus, the three central claims of expressivism plus minimal truth-aptness are not enough for expressivists to explain the meanings of moral sentences alone and in compounds.

In addition to minimal truth-aptness, expressivists also need some larger semantic theory to explain the positive content of moral sentences. Moreover, that theory must show that the meaning of a moral sentence does not change when that sentence is embedded in the antecedent of a conditional. Otherwise, that theory will not be able to explain why arguments like (1)–(3) do not equivocate and are valid.

One such semantic theory is proposed by Gibbard (1990, 94–102). Gibbard represents the content of an evaluative utterance as a set of factual-normative worlds or as ruling out the complement of that set. A factual-normative world is just a combination of a possible world with a set of general norms of the form "Do this" or "Don't do that." An evaluative sentence holds in a factual-normative world if and only if the facts in the possible world plus the norms that are also in the factual-normative world logically imply the evaluative sentence.[10] The content of a conditional is then the complement of the intersection of (a) the set of normative-factual worlds that gives the content of the antecedent with (b) the complement of the set of normative-factual worlds that gives the content of the consequent. In other words, a conditional rules out the intersection of (a) and (b).

This semantic apparatus is supposed to explain the validity of arguments like (1)–(3) as follows: Premise (1) rules out the set of all normative-factual worlds in which lying is not wrong. Premise (2) then rules out the intersection of the set of normative-factual worlds in which lying is wrong with the set of normative-factual worlds in which it is not wrong to get your little brother to lie. Together, premises (1)–(2) rule out the whole set of normative-factual worlds in which it is not wrong to get your little brother to lie. This includes every normative-factual world that the conclusion (3) rules out. Thus, this apparatus explains why argument (1)–(3) is valid. It also explains why the meaning of (1) does not change when it is placed in the antecedent of (2), since the sentence in both locations refers to the set of normative-factual worlds in which lying is wrong. This apparatus also explains the meaning of the whole conditional premise (2) in terms of another set of normative-factual worlds. So it might seem that expressivists could not ask or be asked for more.

---

10. The implication here is not completely clear, because the norms have the form of imperatives, and the evaluative sentences do not. But let that pass.

Gibbard's semantic apparatus does imply and to that extent explain the validity of (1)–(3) and other moral instances of *modus ponens*.[11] By providing a way to represent the content of (1)–(3), Gibbard can also specify how the meaning of (1) is shared by the antecedent of (2) and the meaning of (3) is shared by the consequent of (2).

It is doubtful, however, that even all of this is sufficient to specify what (1), (2), and (3) mean. If expressivists make the negative and positive pragmatic claims and the negative semantic claim, and then they add minimal truth and Gibbardian semantics, they still do not have enough to reveal the meanings of moral sentences. The point can be made by extending Dreier's argument. It is easy to construct Gibbardian semantics for "hello." We just introduce generalizations called "hellorms," such as "Hello, everyone here" or "Everyone here is hello" (analogous to Gibbard's norms). Next we construct a logic of "hello" in terms of "hellormative-factual worlds," which are combinations of possible worlds with hellorms (analogous to Gibbard's "normative-factual worlds"). The content of the sentence "Bob is hello" can then be represented as a set of hellormative-factual worlds or as ruling out all other hellormative-factual worlds. The content of the conditional "If Bob is hello, so is his little brother" rules out the intersection of the set of hellormative-factual worlds where Bob is hello and the complement of the set of hellormative-factual worlds where Bob's little brother is hello. The validity of the argument "Bob is hello. If Bob is hello, so is his little brother. So his little brother is hello" can then be explained by showing that every hellormative-factual world that is ruled out by the conclusion is already ruled out by the premises. Nonetheless, this semantic story does not help us to understand "Bob is hello" any better than we did before going through all of this rigmarole. This lack of understanding shows that such formal semantics is not enough to explain what "Bob is hello" means. Consequently, analogous moves by expressivists are also not enough. When expressivists add a formal semantics like Gibbard's on top of the three central claims of expressivism plus some story about minimal truth-aptness, they still do not succeed in analyzing the meanings of moral sentences. It might not be clear what more is needed, but my extension of Dreier's argument shows that something more is needed.

Expressivists might respond that all they need is to specify the non-cognitive state that is expressed. Gibbard does, after all, go to great lengths to explain acceptance of norms and the emotions that are expressed by assertions of evaluative sentences (Gibbard 1990, 55–82, 126–50). This is still not enough. "Hello, Bob" and "Bob is hello" are used to greet, which is to express a kind of respect or pleasure at contacting someone. But no analysis of respect or pleasure will make us understand "If Bob is hello, so is his little brother," even if that analysis is added to a logic of hellormative worlds. What we do not understand is the claim that Bob is hello, not just the non-cognitive state that is expressed when "Bob is hello" is asserted.

---

11. It is not clear why validity is good or inconsistency is bad in Gibbard's view, but that is a separate issue. See Sinnott-Armstrong 1993, 301–2, and Van Roojen 1996.

Analogously, then, no analysis of the non-cognitive state expressed by moral assertions can sufficiently fill out the expressivist theory. In neither case can meanings be adequately explained by a non-cognitive state, a logic, and central claims like those of expressivism.

Another likely response is that I demand too much. Although Gibbardian semantics is not enough to explain what "Bob is hello" means, that is because "hello" is odd in certain ways. Gibbard's semantics still might suffice to explain evaluative sentences, if we can assume a common understanding of evaluative sentences. But we can't. If the expressivist account depends on a prior understanding of evaluative terms, then it is not sufficient in itself to explain the meanings of those evaluative terms. The only reason expressivism seems to do a better job than greetivism is that we already have some sense of what evaluative sentences mean, and we take that prior sense for granted in interpreting theories like expressivism. This dependence on prior understanding, however, shows that expressivism by itself is not enough to specify those meanings.

Of course, expressivists might develop other semantic theories. Gibbard recently reformulated his theory in terms of plans, but he admits that his new version is his "own previous solution with a somewhat different gloss" (2003, 60), and none of the changes help solve the problems I raised. Blackburn has presented several similar accounts over the years: First, he explained unassertive contexts by propositional reflections ([1973] 1993, 125–29). Then, he employed meta-attitudes (1984; criticized in Sinnott-Armstrong 1987). Blackburn's next view ([1988] 1993, 193; criticized in Sinnott-Armstrong 2000) uses a variation on Hintikka's (1969) semantics for deontic logic. Most recently, Blackburn (1998, 73–74) seems to endorse Gibbard's approach, which runs into the problems that we just saw. None of these accounts solves the basic problem.

The general point is that formal logic cannot do the work of semantics at least for non-logical terms.[12] This is a serious problem for expressivists, because expressivists need to claim that their theory is complete in the sense that it includes everything necessary to understand the meanings of (at least some) evaluative sentences. My extensions of Dreier's argument show that it is not sufficient for expressivists to say just that evaluative sentences are minimally truth-apt and not descriptive but expressive, even if expressivists add formal semantics for these sentences. If this is all they say, the claims of expressivism do not amount to a complete theory of the meaning of evaluative sentences.

But then we cannot be sure that an expressivist theory could ever be completed without referring to maximal moral truths or something else that is incompatible with the core of expressivism. Indeed, it is hard to see how to explain the meanings of moral sentences in unassertive contexts without giving truth conditions along the lines proposed by moral realists. Moreover, it seems natural to fill the gap in expressivism by supplying realistic truth conditions for evaluative

---

12. And even for logical terms, according to Prior (1964, 191): "To believe that anything of this sort can take us beyond the symbols to their meaning is to believe in magic."

judgments. This will remain a reason to favor moral realism as a semantic theory over expressivism until expressivists complete their theories.

2.2.4. *Does Expressivism Matter?*

Even if expressivists can solve these problems, the only way to do so is to admit that moral sentences have minimal truth-values. This admission limits the relevance of expressivism for moral skepticism and moral epistemology. Once expressivists admit minimal moral truth, then it is not clear what they deny or what implications their theory has.

It might seem that expressivists can still deny moral facts, but that depends on what facts are (Blackburn 1998, 79; Gibbard 2003, 18). Minimal moral truth ensures minimal moral facts if facts are defined by truth like this: There is a *fact* that p if and only if "p" is true. Moreover, since "p" is true if and only if p, there is a fact that p if and only if p. If these equivalences tell us all there is to facts, then minimal expressivists must admit a moral fact whenever they admit a moral truth and even whenever they make a moral assertion. For example, if they assert, "Abortion is morally wrong," then they have to admit "It is true that abortion is morally wrong" and "It is a fact that abortion is morally wrong" at least in minimal senses.[13]

Moral sentences can also correspond to minimal facts in a minimal sense. A sentence "p" *corresponds* to the fact that p just in case the following biconditional holds: the sentence is true if and only if the fact holds (or "p" is true if and only if p). The relation of correspondence on this minimal view is no more than the logical relation of equivalence expressed by "if and only if." Thus, once minimal expressivists admit minimal moral truths and facts, they cannot avoid admitting this minimal kind of correspondence as well.

Minimal description comes next. A sentence "p" *describes* a fact that p if and only if: "p" is true if and only if p. Since they admit moral truth and facts, minimal expressivists have to admit that moral assertions describe moral facts in this minimal sense. This admission is also needed to explain why people often use moral assertions to describe how strong their moral obligations are, what kind of obligations they are, and so on. (See Sinnott-Armstrong 1999a.)

Minimal expressivists also have to admit moral beliefs. One essential feature of beliefs that distinguishes beliefs (among other cognitive mental states) from non-cognitive mental states is, supposedly, that beliefs aim at truth. If so, my mental state does not count as a belief unless I care about whether it is true and also unless enough evidence against its truth would bother me and induce me to adjust my belief to achieve truth. On this basis, extreme expressivists often deny that there are any moral beliefs, since there is no moral truth for them to aim at. Minimal expressivists cannot take this position, because they admit minimal moral truth. A mental state can then aim at such a minimal moral truth and thereby meet the conditions necessary to count as a belief.

---

13. Gibbard 1990, 112, denies moral facts on a more substantive notion of fact, but he grants my point here in Gibbard 2003, 18.

Moral assertions come next. An utterance of a sentence by an actor on a stage is sometimes said not to be an assertion because the actor does not believe or claim that it is true. However, speakers who assert moral sentences do believe (and express their beliefs that) those moral sentences are true in a minimal way, so their speech acts can be described as a minimal assertion.

What is believed or asserted? A proposition. But what is that? Philosophers of language sometimes say that different sentences express the same proposition when they mean the same thing, as when Ann says "I am angry" and Betty says "Ann is angry," or when an English speaker says "It is raining" and a French speaker says "Il pleut." Similar translations work for moral sentences. If Ann says "I did wrong" and Betty says "Ann did wrong," these sentences are related in the same way as the sentences when Ann says "I am angry" and Betty says "Ann is angry." Moral sentences can also be translated into other languages, and a correct translation will then express the same proposition as the original. Consequently, expressivists cannot plausibly deny that moral sentences express propositions of this linguistic kind.[14]

Philosophers of mind mean something else when they identify propositions with the objects or contents of propositional attitudes, like belief. However, we already saw why minimal expressivists must grant moral beliefs, and different people can believe the same thing, so minimal expressivists also must grant moral propositions of this doxastic kind.

Some metaphysicians build much more into propositions when they define propositions as sets of possible worlds. However, once expressivists grant moral truth, they can talk about moral sentences being true in the worlds of the set that defines the proposition.[15] So they must grant this metaphysical kind of proposition as well.

What, then, is left for minimal expressivists to deny? One tempting view is that minimal expressivists deny that moral truth-values are mind-independent. Moral realists typically claim that the truth-value of a moral sentence is conceptually independent of the mental states (especially beliefs and emotions) of the judger who believes or asserts the moral sentence. In contrast, subjectivists hold that "That was wrong" means "I disapprove of that," so its truth-value depends on the emotions of the speaker.

Do expressivists deny such mind-independence? This would make sense of their negative semantic claim, after they grant minimal truth-values. It also seems

14. Expressivists still might deny that the kind of proposition that is expressed by moral sentences has any truth-value. Ayer is usually interpreted as denying all moral propositions, but he actually writes, "If I . . . say, 'Stealing money is wrong,' I produce a sentence which has no factual meaning—that is, expresses no proposition which can be either true or false" (1946, 107). This quotation allows moral propositions of a kind that cannot be either true or false. Then moral sentences could express such propositions without being either true or false. So expressivists could grant that moral language expresses propositions without giving up their negative semantic claim that moral language is not used to state propositions that are true or false.

15. Alternatively, expressivists could define propositions in terms of the normative-factual worlds in the semantics of Gibbard 1990, 94–102, or fact-plan worlds as in Gibbard 2003, 57.

natural to think that, if moral assertions express non-cognitive mental states, then whether they are minimally true depends on whether the speaker has those non-cognitive mental states.

However, this denial of mind-independence would create trouble. People who believe that it is morally wrong to eat meat usually believe that it would still be morally wrong even if we (humans!) all approved of it and thought that it was morally right or permissible. We do not believe that such moral truths vary with our opinions or feelings. If minimal expressivists claim otherwise, then they fail to capture an important aspect of much moral thought. Most contemporary expressivists admit this.

In response, most contemporary expressivists claim to capture mind-independence. To see how, we need to define mind-independence in terms of counterfactuals: to say that the truth-value of "meat-eating is wrong" is mind-independent is to say that its truth-value would not change if the people who believe and assert it changed their moral beliefs and attitudes. Such counterexamples are endorsed, for example, by Blackburn when he writes:

> Suppose someone said "if we had different sentiments, it would be right to kick dogs," what could he be up to? Apparently he endorses a certain sensibility: one which lets information about what people feel dictate its attitude to kicking dogs. But nice people do not endorse such a sensibility. What makes it wrong to kick dogs is the cruelty or pain to the animal. *That* input should yield disapproval and indignation as the output.... So we should not say or think that were our sentiments to alter or disappear, moral facts would do so as well. This would be endorsing the defective counterfactuals, i.e. endorsing the wrong kinds of sensibility, and it will be part of good moralizing not to do that. (1984, 218–19n)

Thus, Blackburn accepts mind-independence.

It is not clear that Blackburn's expressivist gloss captures the counterfactuals that are implicit in common moral thought according to moral realists. One reason is that Blackburn takes these counterfactuals to be substantive truths of "good moralizing," whereas moral realists take these counterfactuals to be conceptual or metaphysical truths independent of any particular substantive moral view. (Cf. Zangwill 1994.) Moreover, Blackburn glosses the counterfactuals as claims about which patterns of sensibilities are or are not acceptable, but people take themselves to be talking about kicking dogs rather than about attitudes when they assert such claims or counterfactuals. If some people fail to disapprove of kicking dogs but still do not perform acts of kicking dogs, then I might think less of them, but at least they do not do any of the acts that I am talking about and that I call "wrong" when I say, "Kicking dogs is wrong." The same point applies to the counterfactual, "Even if we all approved of it, kicking dogs would still be wrong." The consequent is a judgment about acts in another possible world, not about attitudes in this world or that. Thus, even if Blackburn does capture one kind of mind-independence, it is different from the kind of mind-independence that realists find implicit in common moral thought and talk.

A related attempt to capture objectivity within an expressivist framework is made by Gibbard. Gibbard focuses on rationality instead of morality, but his points are supposed to apply to morality as well:

> When a person calls something rational, he seems to be doing more than simply expressing his own acceptance of a system of norms.... He claims the backing of considerations that, in some sense, "compel acceptance" of what he is saying. Perhaps he is wrong, but that is the claim he is making. Any account of his language that ignores this claim must be defective. (1990, 153; cf. Hare 1981, 208–9)

Gibbard later attempts to capture the relevant kind of objectivity with higher-order norms:

> To accept a norm as a requirement of rationality, we might say, is to accept it along with higher order norms that require its acceptance. To treat it as an existential commitment is to accept it along with higher order norms that permit it, but that permit accepting at least one incompatible alternative. (1990, 169; cf. 171)

For example, I can accept a norm against drinking alcohol without believing that other people must accept it as well, in which case I do not really believe that drinking is irrational (or immoral). In contrast, if I think that suicide is irrational (or immoral), then I must accept another second-order norm that binds everyone to accept this first-order norm.

However, the converse is not as clear. I do not accept a norm as a requirement of rationality or morality whenever I accept it as binding on everyone. Suppose I accept a first-order norm that forbids me to commit suicide, and I also accept a second-order norm that requires everyone else to accept this first-order norm (something like "Accept the norm, 'Don't commit suicide'"). I still might believe that my acceptance of this second-order norm is optional rather than required. Then I have what Gibbard calls an existential commitment to my second-order norm. In this case, I would not believe that my first-order norm is a requirement of rationality or morality. In order to believe that it really is irrational or immoral to commit suicide, I must also believe (or at least be disposed to believe) that everyone is rationally or morally required to accept not only the first-order norm not to commit suicide but also the second-order norm that requires everyone to accept the first-order norm.

Gibbard might respond by adding that rationality also requires a third-order norm that requires everyone to accept my second-order norm. But the same basic problem arises again at each higher stage. Why stop at the third-order? What if I have only an existential commitment to my third-order norms? Or fourth? Or fifth? Or sixth? It is hard to see why we should stop at any particular level. But if we do not stop, we never get a complete analysis of objectivity. I do not see how Gibbard can escape this infinite regress.[16] Consequently, Gibbard cannot adequately capture this aspect of common thought and talk within his expressivist framework.

For these reasons, I believe that minimal expressivists fail to capture the kinds of objectivity and mind-independence that are implicit in much common moral thought and talk. But that conclusion is not essential to my argument here. Sup-

---

16. Gibbard (1990, 169 note 12) tells us that his use of higher orders was influenced by Frankfurt (1971). A similar regress in Frankfurt's theory was pointed out by Watson (1975, sec. III).

pose that I am mistaken, and minimal expressivists can grant mind-independence and objectivity along with minimal moral truth, facts, correspondence, beliefs, assertions, propositions, and so on. Contemporary minimal expressivists admit that expressivism would be inadequate if it could not mimic *all* such realist aspects of common moral language and thought, so they go to great lengths to show that they can grant *everything* that moral realists would ever want to claim along these lines.[17]

Even if this strategy of accommodation works, it can backfire. For one thing, it becomes difficult to distinguish expressivism from realism. If these traditional rivals cannot be distinguished, then it is not clear that any real issues are at stake any more. (Cf. Dworkin 1996.)

Most important here is that expressivism no longer can support moral skepticism. If expressivists are happy to talk about moral truths, facts, beliefs, assertions, propositions, mind-independence, explanation, causation, and knowledge, then they can say all that they need to say in order to do moral epistemology in exactly the same way as a moral realist. Gibbard admits that moral judgments "can at least parallel the clearest and most literal cases of knowledge" (2003, 235). Blackburn adds examples: "I know that happiness is better than pain, that promises deserve some respect, and so on for countless, fairly unambitious, pros and cons that make up my practical stance to the world" (1998, 307). With all of this admitted, even if there still are some metaphysical differences between expressivism and realism, no form of moral skepticism will be supported by expressivism.

Expressivism also cannot create any problem for moral epistemology. Once expressivists admit that they *need* to mimic realists, they have only two options: either expressivists fail to capture all of the apparently realist elements in common moral language and thought, in which case expressivism is inadequate, or expressivists succeed in capturing all of the apparently realist elements, in which case expressivists can go on to do moral epistemology in exactly the same way as realists. Either way, expressivism will not undermine moral epistemology.

Consequently, we do not need to decide for or against expressivism before we go on to discuss moral epistemology and epistemological moral skepticism. I will speak freely of moral beliefs as true or false from now on. Expressivists can reinterpret that realist-sounding talk in their own terms, if they want.

---

17. Some expressivists did claim that moral facts can*not* enter into causal or explanatory relations (see Blackburn 1984, 244 and 257; and Gibbard 1990, 112), but now Blackburn admits even moral explanations and causes (see Blackburn 1993, 8 and 205–7). Blackburn (1996) even talks about reliability and knowledge of morality, as does Gibbard (2003). Once expressivists admit knowledge, their linguistic views cannot lead to epistemological moral skepticism.

3

Are Any Moral Beliefs True?

E ven if moral sentences and beliefs are truth-apt (that is, the kind of thing that *can* be true or false), that does not show that any moral sentence or belief *is* true. They still might all be false or, at least, not true. If no moral sentence or belief is true, then there cannot be any moral knowledge, since knowledge requires truth. Thus, in the terminology of section 1.3, moral error theories provide another route to Academic moral knowledge skepticism.

3.1. Error Theories

If moral sentences and beliefs are truth-apt, how could they all fail to be true? Here are two ways: A sentence or belief is *false* if it *claims* the existence of a fact that does not exist; so, if ordinary moral beliefs and assertions claim certain moral facts, but there are no such moral facts, then ordinary moral beliefs and sentences are false.[1] Alternatively, a sentence or belief is *neither true nor false* if it *presupposes* a fact that does not exist; so, if ordinary moral beliefs and assertions presuppose certain moral facts, but there are none, then ordinary moral beliefs and sentences are neither true nor false.[2]

The premise that ordinary moral beliefs and language claim or presuppose moral facts is often supported by the kind of objections to expressivism that were

---

1. Mackie (1977, 30–42) develops this type of error theory.

2. Joyce (2001, 6–9) develops this type of error theory. If a sentence ("He went off his diet") presupposes a fact (that he was on a diet), the sentence could be true or false if the fact did exist, so what keeps it from being true is external to the sentence itself. In contrast, expressivists claim that internal features of moral assertions and beliefs make them unable to be true or false, regardless of anything in the external world. Thus, even if moral assertions and beliefs lack truth-values because of failed presuppositions, as Joyce claims, they can still be truth-apt in the way that expressivists deny. They are still the kind of thing that *can* be true or false in appropriate external circumstances.

raised in section 2.2. However, the basic point can be put more simply and directly: When normal speakers assert that abortion is morally wrong, they usually are trying to do more than just express their emotions. They see themselves as stating a fact about abortion. They are trying to describe abortion by attributing a property to it. The nature of their claim is shown (or suggested) by the ways in which they talk and argue about abortion, press their views on opponents, and often commit their lives to a moral cause. None of this evidence is conclusive, but all of it together is supposed to fit better with the view that such common-language speakers are committed to moral facts and properties.

Speakers also commit themselves to moral facts less openly. When conservatives call abortion "baby murder," they commit themselves to a moral fact that abortion is morally wrong if they use "murder" to mean "morally wrongful killing." In contrast, they do not commit themselves in the same way to a moral fact if they say merely that abortion involves the killing of a fetus, as long as they use "killing" and "fetus" neutrally so that those terms do not entail any moral status for the act or the organism. More generally, moral facts include facts that something is morally wrong or morally obligatory, morally ought or ought not to be done, has a moral virtue or vice, or is morally good or bad, as well as every fact that entails any of these basic moral facts. In contrast, moral facts do *not* include other facts that are supposed to be morally relevant because they provide substantive reasons why acts are morally wrong, such as the fact that an act causes death or is an act of killing. Philosophers who deny that there are any moral facts do not deny that some doctors kill fetuses. What they deny is that there is any fact of the matter that such acts are morally wrong. To understand such denials, therefore, it is crucial to distinguish between moral facts and morally relevant facts.

The story gets even trickier for negative moral beliefs and assertions, such as that abortion is *not* morally wrong. Most speakers who assert this would also claim that opponents of abortions should not interfere with a woman seeking an abortion. Such speakers seem committed to the moral fact that such interference has the moral property of being what should not be done. In contrast, suppose Nancy asserts that abortion is not morally wrong, and all Nancy means is that it is not true that abortion is morally wrong. Unlike most speakers, Nancy has no belief and intends to make no claim about interference with abortion. She merely denies a moral fact or property. Similarly, suppose Candice asserts the conditional, "If abortion is wrong, so is contraception," or Donna asserts the disjunction, "Either abortion is wrong or euthanasia is not." These speakers do not assert that abortion is wrong, even though they use that claim as part of what they do say.

Are these speakers committed to the existence of moral facts or properties? That depends on what count as moral facts or properties. Some philosophers might postulate negative moral facts (such as the fact that abortion is not wrong) or conditional moral facts (such as that, if abortion is wrong, so is contraception) or disjunctive moral facts (such as that either abortion is wrong or euthanasia is not). Some might even countenance negative moral properties (such as the property of being not morally wrong) as well as conditional and disjunctive moral properties. If these count as moral facts and properties, then Nancy, Candice, and Donna are committed to the existence of some moral facts and properties.

This commitment might seem to undermine moral error theories. A moral error theorist denies the moral fact that abortion has the moral property of being wrong. This denial seems to imply the truth of Nancy's purely negative claim. Similarly, the falsity of "abortion is wrong" entails the truth of Candice's material conditional, "If abortion is wrong, so is contraception." So error theorists cannot avoid negative and conditional moral facts and truths.

Some error theorists try to avoid this problem by holding that moral sentences and beliefs presuppose (and do not claim) moral facts. The relevant notion of presupposition comes from Strawson (1950), who claimed that the statement "The present King of France is bald" is neither true nor false, because no present King of France exists. The presuppositions of a sentence are supposed be shared by the negation of that sentence, so "The present King of France is not bald" is also neither true nor false. Analogously, negative moral sentences are also neither true nor false, if moral sentences presuppose moral facts. However, this result fails when the negation takes the widest possible scope, as in "It is not the case that the present King of France is bald." This is true whenever "The present King of France is bald" is not true. Similarly, since Nancy's negation has the widest possible scope, even presuppositional error theorists must admit Nancy's claim as true. So the move to presuppositions cannot solve the basic problem for error theories.

Another possible response by error theorists is to deny either that negative and conditional facts are really facts or that negative and conditional moral facts are really moral facts. After all, denials of astrology do not assert astrological facts, and negative and conditional facts seem pretty weird. The metaphysical issues here are complex, disputed, and far from our main concern. Besides, even without negative moral facts, an error theorist would seem to endorse the truth of Nancy's negation and of Candice's conditional.

Luckily, another option is available. Error theorists can admit or remain neutral on negative, conditional, and disjunctive moral facts. They can still deny all *positive* moral facts. Then they need to define positive moral facts. One method is syntactic: a fact is negative if and only if it can be described by a sentence with a single widest-scope negation in a logic with only negation and conjunction. If it is not negative, then it is positive. On this account, conditional and disjunctive sentences do not describe positive facts, because "p⊃q" is equivalent to "~(p&~q)," and "(p∨q)" is equivalent to "~(~p&~q)," so each takes a single widest-scope negation when translated into a logic with only negation and conjunction.

This attempt runs into trouble with quantifiers. Error theorists presumably want to deny the truth of "All suicide is morally wrong." Do they also deny the truth of "All killing of centaurs is morally wrong"? This sentence seems true on the Boolean interpretation of quantifiers, where "No killing of centaurs exists" implies "All killing of centaurs is morally wrong" as well as "No killing of centaurs is morally wrong." Error theorists who deny the truth of these sentences could insist that universal quantifiers in moral claims range over all logically possible acts. Killing of centaurs is logically possible. Still, it is not logically possible to draw a square circle, so both "All square circle drawing is morally wrong" and "No square circle drawing is morally wrong" come out true even if their universal quantifiers range over all logically possible acts. But error theorists may simply admit that these universal generalizations are strange but trivially true for the same reasons as "All square circles are purple" and "No square circles are purple." If they admit this, then error theorists can define a moral fact as negative if it can be described by a sentence with a single widest-scope negation in a logic with only negation, conjunction, and existential quantification, where the domain of discourse includes all logically possible acts. If a moral fact is not negative, then it is positive.

Another problem arises from negative predicates. If "absent" means "not present," then "Tracy is absent" describes the same fact as "Tracy is not present," and "Tracy is present" describes the same fact as "Tracy is not absent." Which fact is positive? Many philosophers see this problem as devastating for any attempt to define positive facts in general. However, the problem might be soluble for the special case of positive *moral* facts. Both "It is morally wrong for Tracy to be present" and "It is morally wrong for Tracy to be absent" count as positive moral facts that error theorists deny. Thus, error theorists do not need to determine in general which predicates are positive. All they need to determine is which *moral* predicates and operators are positive. Here error theorists can simply list the ones that they want to deny. For example, an error theorist might deny that it is morally wrong to do any act, that it is morally wrong not to do any act, that anyone morally ought to do any act, that anyone morally ought not to do any act, that anything is morally good, that anything is morally bad, and so on. After the list of positive moral predicates is completed, error theorists can use the preceding definition of positive moral facts with the stipulation that supposed moral facts must be described in terms of predicates on the canonical list. It might not be easy to complete the list, but error theorists can at least include a great number of common moral predicates, and then they can deny positive moral sentences with those predicates. That will make their thesis very radical (and sufficiently radical for my arguments below). If someone comes up with a new moral predicate that is not on their list, then they can decide at that point whether or not to add that predicate to their list, thereby extending the number of moral facts that count as positive and that they deny.

If this syntactic approach to defining positive moral facts still seems inadequate, another possibility is to cite semantic entailments. Error theorists could define a supposed moral fact as positive when and only when its description entails any claim about what it is morally wrong to do or not to do, what anyone morally ought or ought not to do, what is morally good or bad, and so on. It might not be clear when such entailments hold, but error theorists can at least specify the range of moral claims that they want to deny and leave it open whether they might want to deny more later. Different error theorists might disagree about which claims they want to deny, but these differences will presumably be minor compared to their agreement in denying a very wide range of common moral beliefs.

The metaphysical thesis that there are no positive moral facts is, thus, logically coherent.[3] This thesis, together with the claim that moral sentences are true only if

---

3. Its semantic coherence will be shown in section 3.3, and its epistemic coherence will be addressed in chapter 10.

they correspond to moral facts, is enough to imply that no positive moral sentence or belief is true, so it is never true that anything is morally wrong or required, good or bad, and so on. This conclusion is probably all that error theorists want or need to claim anyway, so I will henceforth assume that this is all that they do claim. This claim still has important implications for moral epistemology, since it rules out all positive moral knowledge.

After limiting their denial to positive moral facts, error theorists still need to specify what facts are. Otherwise it's not clear what error theorists deny. Of course, different error theorists might use different notions of fact, but their view is less interesting if they deny an outrageous notion of fact that nobody accepts or needs to accept. The strongest kinds of moral error theories deny the weakest kinds of moral facts.

In section 2.2.4, I introduced a minimal notion of *fact* by stipulating that there is a fact that p if and only if "p" is true in a minimal way. A similarly minimal notion of *property* can be defined by saying that x has the property of being W if and only if "x is W" is true in a minimal way. These notions can be restricted to positive moral facts and properties by adding that "p" and "W" are positive in the relevant way. Then to deny that there are any positive moral facts is just to deny that any positive moral assertion or belief is true in the minimal way. Similarly, to deny that the moral property of being wrong is instantiated is just to deny that there is any x such that "x is wrong" is true in the minimal way. The issue of whether there are any moral facts or properties then comes down to the issue of whether any moral beliefs and sentences are true.

The reference to truth invokes a meta-language, but we can express the same basic idea in the object-language by saying simply that nothing is morally wrong or required, good or bad, and so on.[4] I will call this claim *moral nihilism*. This substantive claim has the same implications for moral knowledge: if nothing is morally wrong, then we cannot know of anything that it is morally wrong. Similarly for what is morally required, good, bad, and so on. Conversely, if moral nihilism is false, because some act is morally wrong, then it is (at least) minimally true that the act is morally wrong, and there is (at least) a minimal fact that the act is morally wrong. Thus, these three formulations—about moral facts, moral truths, and moral wrongness—stand or fall together.[5]

Whichever formulation is used, most moral nihilists embed their central claim within a larger theory. They argue for it or explain why so many people deny it so fervently. However, moral nihilism remains the same claim when moral nihilists

---

4. I use "and so on" for convenience because it would be grammatically unwieldy to add that moral nihilists deny that anything morally should or should not or ought or ought not to be done, that any person or act is morally virtuous or vicious, and that any act person or institution is morally decent or indecent or suboptimal or ideal or excellent or better or best.... I also want to leave the list open-ended so that it can cover a large variety of thick moral terms.

5. There could also be error theories and nihilisms about rationality, prudence, aesthetics, sin, epistemology, and other normative areas. However, such views in one normative area need not imply analogous views in other normative areas, although some reasons given for one kind of normative nihilism might extend to other kinds.

assert it without argument or admit that they cannot explain away the opposition. Moral nihilism still remains the same claim when opponents deny it or skeptics consider it as a possibility without asserting it or denying it. Whatever its surroundings, moral nihilism is the claim that there are no positive moral facts or truths, since nothing is morally wrong or required, good or bad, and so on.

3.2. Arguments Against Moral Facts

The next question asks whether we have any reason to believe any of this. Mackie (1977) tries to give several reasons.

3.2.1. *Relativity*

The most common argument against moral facts, which Mackie calls the argument from relativity, starts from the observation that moral disagreement is widespread. Of course, disagreement alone cannot show that there are no moral facts. A few people still believe that the earth is flat, and we disagree with them, but it is a fact that the earth is not flat and is round (or roughly spherical). So, facts do not ensure universal agreement.

This shapely dispute can be resolved, so opponents of moral facts still might argue that irresolvable disagreements rule out facts. But imagine that one person believes and another denies that the total number of dinosaurs was even. We have no way to resolve that dispute (even if there were no borderline dinosaurs), and yet there still seems to be either a fact that the number was even or a fact that the number was odd. Whichever it is, some fact exists in the face of irresolvable disagreement.

Probably nobody is crazy enough either to believe or to deny that the total number of dinosaurs was even. Yet scientists and historians do disagree on many issues that cannot be resolved by available evidence. They speculate on the basis of what evidence they have, even though they admit that they do not and cannot ever have enough evidence to settle the matter. Despite their epistemic limits, there can be a fact of the matter.

Such considerations undermine any deductive argument from moral disagreement against moral facts, so opponents of moral facts usually turn to inductive arguments, and they usually focus on patterns of disagreement instead of individual issues. For example, Mackie cites "the well-known variation in moral codes from one society to another and from one period to another, and also the differences in moral beliefs between different groups and classes within a complex community" (Mackie 1977, 36). These observations provide the basis for an inductive inference to the best explanation:

> The argument from relativity has some force simply because the actual variations in the moral codes are more readily explained by the hypothesis that they reflect ways of life than by the hypothesis that they reflect perceptions, most of them seriously inadequate and badly distorted, of objective values. (Mackie 1977, 37)

Mackie also dismisses the hypotheses that moral disagreement "results from speculative inferences or explanatory hypotheses based on inadequate evidence" (1977, 36) or from differing applications of "very general basic principles which are recognized at least implicitly to some extent in all society" (37). Mackie concludes that the best explanation is that the observed pattern of moral disagreements reflects ways of life. Since this explanation does not require any objective moral facts, there are no moral facts, according to Mackie.

Defenders of moral facts might question whether moral codes and beliefs really do vary as much as Mackie supposes. Some might even deny that any moral disagreements occur. This move seems unpromising, because radical variations in moral beliefs are well documented in many cases. (Cf. Gowans 2000.) Moral disputes between and within societies are (in)famous.

A more promising defense claims that, even though people disagree about many moral issues, they agree about some other moral issues. Perhaps everyone agrees that it is morally wrong to kill or deprive of freedom without an adequate reason. However, people still disagree about who is protected by such restrictions, what counts as life or freedom, and which reasons are adequate. If three people accept the rule "Don't kill," but one thinks that it protects only men, the second thinks that it protects all men and women (or only women), and the third thinks that it protects only members of a certain tribe, then they hardly agree in any way that supports moral facts. Similarly, suppose two people accept the rule "Don't deprive of freedom," but one thinks that imprisoning a person to improve them morally is a way of giving them what they really want, so it does not count as depriving of real freedom. The second person counts such imprisonment as deprivation of freedom and sees such deprivation as unjustified except to prevent very serious harms. The third person also counts such imprisonment as deprivation of freedom but thinks that it can be justified by minor benefits, including minor gains to other people. Again, these people hardly agree in any way that would undermine Mackie's argument. (See Snare 1980.)

Besides, some philosophers and non-philosophers espouse moral nihilism, moral egoism, and other radical positions that deny even the most widespread moral beliefs. Opponents might charge that these people do not understand the words they utter. Or maybe they are not sincere, so they don't really believe what they are saying. Or maybe they believe what they say, but they also believe what common folk say, although the two positions are incompatible. Or maybe they are just crazy. Such accounts are plausible in some cases, but I doubt that all radical positions can be explained as misunderstanding, insincerity, inconsistency, or insanity. (See section 3.3.) So I doubt that there is completely universal agreement about any positive moral claim.

Even if there is no disagreement at all about a few moral issues, Mackie could respond simply that the disagreements still need to be explained. If Mackie's "ways of life" (1977, 37) explanation works for the disagreements, and if he can provide related explanations of the widespread agreements (see section 3.2.2), then Mackie's overall account provides a more unified and, hence, better explanation than his objectivist rivals.

In response, Mackie's opponents often try to explain observed variations in ways that would not support Mackie's argument. One such hypothesis cites variations in non-moral beliefs and circumstances that affect moral beliefs. When Vikings killed their parents, they believed that this would help their parents in the after-life. When Eskimos killed their elderly, they might have seen this as the only way to save their families in the harsh weather. If we are neither Vikings nor Eskimos, our different situation and beliefs can then explain why killing our parents seems morally wrong for us. A current example is that our ignorance about whether capital punishment deters explains many disputes about the morality of capital punishment, even among people who accept the basic principle that punishment is justified by deterrence. However, other moral disagreements seem harder to explain by non-moral disagreement. Doctors who know almost all there is to know about fetal development often disagree on the moral issue of whether the fetus has rights. People also disagree about imaginary cases even after all of the relevant facts are stipulated. Admittedly, hidden ignorance, self-interest, or training always might distort people's beliefs in ways that explain their disagreement. The importance and complexity of morality make it hard to find any definitive example of a moral disagreement that cannot possibly be explained by any kind of bias or inadequate information. (See Brandt 1954.) Without any such decisive case, there seems to be no way for Mackie to refute the competing explanation of moral disagreements as "perceptions, most of them seriously inadequate and badly distorted, of objective values" (Mackie 1977, 37).

In any case, the most important response here is this: even if the pattern of moral disagreements were best explained by ways of life, that would show at most that those disputes reflect ways of life. It would not follow that there are no objective moral facts.

The first point is that Mackie's argument is about our *beliefs*, not about facts. Grant that the believer's way of life affects every moral belief. Still, some ways of life might distort moral beliefs, while other ways of life enable people to see the moral facts and form true moral beliefs. If so, differences among ways of life explain the pattern of moral disagreements, but this explanation of beliefs is compatible with moral facts.

Moreover, our ways of life might not affect *all* of our moral beliefs. Even if we need to cite ways of life to explain moral disagreements, we do not need to cite ways of life to explain moral beliefs when people agree. Mackie does not try to show that there is disagreement on every moral issue, so it is hard to see how his argument could support a universal denial of all moral facts. Moreover, there do seem to be many uniformities in moral belief. Almost everyone believes that it is morally wrong to torture babies just for fun, to break promises to peers just to gain advantages over them, to kill friends who cook you dinner (even if the dinner tastes bad), and so on. The agreement on these qualified claims might not be universal, because of moral nihilists, but the range of agreement is striking. Defenders of moral facts can claim that there are moral facts in these areas of agreement, even if not elsewhere.

They might even argue that moral facts are needed to explain such moral agreements. Many moral agreements can be explained by evolution (see section

3.2.2), but sometimes it might seem plausible to say that almost everyone agrees because the moral fact is so obvious. If that is ever the best explanation, then the moral agreements might provide evidence for a moral fact. Of course, all such explanations might fail, but my point is just that Mackie has not shown that yet.[6]

Even if moral facts are not needed to explain agreement or anything else, that shows at most that we cannot base our belief in moral facts on any inference to the best explanation. We still might have other kinds of reasons to believe in moral facts. Part II of this book will canvass a wide variety of arguments that purport to justify moral beliefs: naturalism, normativism, intuitionism, and coherentism. Each of these methods could be deployed in favor of moral facts, even if Mackie is right about the explanation of moral disagreement.

Finally, suppose that we do not have any reason to *believe* in moral facts. That still would not give us any reason to *deny* the existence of moral facts. Another option, instead of claiming or denying moral facts, is to suspend belief about whether or not there are any moral facts. We could refuse to take a stand one way or the other. Mackie's argument from disagreement by itself says nothing against such suspension of belief. Indeed, insofar as Mackie's argument claims that there is no explanatory reason to believe in moral facts but also gives us no reason to believe that there are no moral facts, these considerations seem to make it reasonable to suspend belief, at least until we find a better argument. So Mackie's own argument leads not to his moral nihilism but instead to a suspension of belief about moral facts.[7]

3.2.2. *Evolution*

A separate argument also attempts to explain moral beliefs without reference to moral facts, but now what gets explained is agreement rather than disagreement. What does the explaining is a kind of evolution by a process like natural selection. Such evolutionary explanations take many forms, but one general story is widely accepted.

Our environment is harsh, so individuals and groups compete for scarce resources and need to avoid many predators and dangers. Individuals do not survive or reproduce as often if their traits put them at a disadvantage. Thus, if traits somehow get passed to offspring, over many generations advantageous traits will become more common in the community or species. This kind of story explains physical traits such as wings of birds and large brains of humans. It also explains behaviors and emotions, such as why certain animals come out only at night and get scared by sudden noises. Similarly, if certain behaviors, emotions, or beliefs

---

6. Moral facts also might be needed to explain other observations, such as the fall of slavery in the United States, which some historians and philosophers explain by the fact that slavery got so much worse (morally) just before it fell. Such moral explanations will be discussed in section 8.1.

7. For more on the argument from moral disagreement, see Tolhurst 1987, Brink 1989, Sturgeon 1994, and Loeb 1998.

increase the chances of survival for humans, that benefit explains why so many humans share those traits.

One morally relevant trait, which is a kind of altruism, is a tendency to help close relatives who are in danger or need, even if the helper does not benefit. Human families whose members help each other in such circumstances will be more likely to survive and reproduce than other families whose members do not help each other in such circumstances. Even if individuals die while helping close relatives, if those relatives are likely to share that helping trait and pass it on, then the percentage of humans with the helping trait will grow over time.

Helping behavior also extends beyond families. To see why, consider three idealized "strategies" (from Dawkins 1976 via Mackie 1978). Suckers are pure altruists who help anyone in need. Cheaters are pure egoists who accept help from anyone but never help anyone else unless they benefit too. Grudgers are reciprocal altruists who help any stranger and anyone who helped them but refuse to help anyone who cheated them (that is, who refused to help them in return for having been helped), at least in their most recent interaction. Imagine a society with a mixture of Suckers, Cheaters, and Grudgers in a fairly harsh environment like ours. Cheaters will prey on Suckers, so Cheaters "will have more time and energy to spare for finding food, attracting mates, building nests, and so on" (Mackie 1978, 458). As a result, Suckers will die out, and Cheaters will spread. When Suckers die out, Cheaters run into trouble. Grudgers will help each other, but nobody will be left to help Cheaters. Without help, Cheaters will die out, assuming an environment that is harsh enough. In contrast, Grudgers can thrive alongside Suckers and Cheaters and also in a whole population. In common environments, therefore, a society with a mixture of Suckers, Cheaters, and Grudgers will evolve towards having a high percentage of Grudgers.

This spread of reciprocal altruism is promoted when organisms choose their partners. If Grudgers seek out and give preference to other Grudgers, especially by mating with Grudgers rather than with Cheaters (or Suckers), then reciprocal altruism will spread even more quickly (see Miller 2000). Verbally praising Grudgers can aid this process by enabling Grudgers to avoid mistaken interactions and locate other Grudgers with whom to interact and mate. Desires for esteem and for self-esteem also feed this tendency to do what gets us praise (see Brennan and Pettit 2004).

In addition to positive acts of praising, humans also tend to engage in negative acts of criticizing and ostracizing those who do not help in certain circumstances (such as when they alone can easily and safely avoid a serious harm to a nearby member of the same community). These tendencies arise partly because it costs so little to criticize. In our idealized example, if one Grudger warns another Grudger by privately calling someone else a Cheater, then the warning Grudger often suffers relatively little harm or danger, and the warned Grudger can avoid costly interactions with that Cheater. In addition, the warned Grudger will tend to reciprocate, so the act of criticizing benefits the warning Grudger. These Grudgers are cooperating at Cheater detection.

Other punishments can be more costly and dangerous than verbal warnings and criticisms, which explains why formal punishments are reserved for more extreme violations. Still, a system of punishment can sometimes be less costly than the harms that would fail to be prevented if Cheaters were not punished (see Sober and Wilson 1998, 142–49).

Other humans are not always able to detect and criticize or punish Cheaters, so the rate of cheating can be reduced further by a tendency for Cheaters to punish themselves. The emotion of guilt serves that purpose. Humans who tend to feel guilty after cheating will be less likely to cheat, so they will be less likely to get criticized, ostracized, or punished by Grudgers. This will increase their chances of survival and reproduction, so the tendency to feel guilt for cheating will slowly spread through the community.

In addition to emotions, moral beliefs can also reduce the rate of cheating and increase the rate of helping.[8] Humans who believe that they are morally required to help other humans in certain circumstances, even when it is not in their interest to do so, will be less likely to consider cheating. This moral belief will affect their deliberations and motivations in ways that make them more likely to help others. Notice that moral beliefs operate more reliably than mere desires (see Joyce 2001, 136–41; and Ruse 1998, 222). If someone wants to help others in need, this desire can be overcome by dislike for the needy person, weariness from a hard day's hunting, or a stronger desire for some more immediate gratification. These same obstructions will be less effective if the helper believes that people are morally required in some objective, categorical way that is independent of the agent's desires and moods (Mackie 1977, 42–46). Since such categorical moral beliefs lead to more helping, they also make helpers more likely to be helped by others with tendencies to reciprocity, so they make moral believers more likely to survive and reproduce. Thus, if moral beliefs get passed to offspring (by means of genes or culture), then these moral beliefs will slowly become more common throughout humanity. That is supposed to explain why so many people view reciprocal altruism as morally required.

Similar evolutionary tales can also explain other common moral beliefs, such as the beliefs that it is morally wrong to kill, disable, hurt, lie, and break promises (in the absence of strong defeaters). Humans with such moral beliefs will be less likely to kill, lie, etc. Thus, given the background tendency to reciprocity, they will be less likely to be killed, deceived, etc., so they will be more likely to survive and reproduce. Then, if these beliefs get passed to offspring, more and more humans will come to believe that it is morally wrong to kill, disable, hurt, lie, and break promises (in the absence of strong defeaters).

Sex is similar. Consider, for example, the widespread belief that brother-sister incest is morally wrong. Offspring of such incest are more likely to have genetic problems, but this fact is not known to many people who believe that such incest is immoral. So, what causes this belief? A plausible answer is that societies with incest prohibitions run into fewer genetic problems, so they are more likely to reproduce and survive than societies without incest prohibitions. These prohibitions might begin as feelings or emotions, but they become more effective when

---

8. Belief in a god who detects and punishes cheating can also reduce rates of cheating, so religious beliefs might also be explained by evolutionary pressures.

expressed in "incest taboos" or "cautionary myths against incest" and, eventually, beliefs that incest is morally wrong. The beliefs spread because they are the most effective way to prevent the incest that would decrease the chances of reproduction and survival (see Ruse and Wilson 1986).

These explanations are, admittedly, simplistic and incomplete. In particular, culture is needed to explain variations in moral beliefs, even if some general commonalities are explained biologically. Such explanations are also controversial and have been subjected to a variety of critiques. Luckily, the details are not essential here. If anything like this evolutionary story does explain common moral beliefs, then there is no need to postulate moral facts to explain those beliefs.

Evolutionary explanations are compatible with objective moral facts. (Cf. Nozick 1981, 346.) Indeed, some evolutionary ethicists claim that the usefulness of believing that reciprocal altruism is fair shows that it really is fair, because the point of morality is just to enable our society and species to survive. However, the general principle that moral beliefs are true only if they help society is at least questionable. Many utilitarians, such as Sidgwick (1907, 489–90), hold that utilitarianism is true even though widespread belief in utilitarianism would lead to abuses that would harm society. This position might be false, but it is at least coherent, so it seems inadequate merely to assume that moral truth depends on social survival value. Moreover, even if we *could* endorse such a general test of moral truth, there's no *need* to endorse any such moral view. The evolutionary explanations work even if there are no moral facts at all.

The same point could *not* be made about mathematical beliefs. People evolved to believe that $2+3=5$, because they would not have survived if they had believed that $2+3=4$, but the reason why they would not have survived then is that it is *true* that $2+3=5$. The same goes for the belief that wild animal bites hurt. In such cases, the truth of the belief explains why it is useful to believe it. In contrast, moral beliefs would be useful, so we would have evolved to believe them, even if they were not true. That is why the evolutionary explanation is supposed to undermine moral facts but not mathematical or medical facts.

This argument against moral facts still faces three main problems. First, it is not clear that this argument generalizes to all moral beliefs. Even if some moral beliefs can easily be explained by evolution, others pose harder problems. Consider, for example, the widespread belief that it is morally wrong to kill or neglect senile elderly people who cannot survive without great help and who cannot reciprocate adequately or have more children. It is not clear how this moral belief increased humans' chances for survival, at least in the bad old days when our moral beliefs evolved. Another example is the widespread doctrine of double effect, according to which it is harder to justify intentional harm than unintentional harm. (Cf. Quinn 1989b.) If the point of moral beliefs is to reduce harms, as the evolutionary explanation suggests, then it is not obvious why so many humans attach such importance to the question of whether a harm is intended as a means as opposed to being a mere side effect. The answer cannot be simply that people who aim at harms are more likely to cause those harms again, because the doctrine of double effect forbids causing harms as means even when the aim or end is good. So, the evolutionary explanation of this common moral belief remains a mystery.

Of course, such moral beliefs might have indirect evolutionary advantages or they might result from cultural variations. However, until some explanation is spelled out, it is not clear that evolutionary explanations work for all common moral beliefs. If not, then this evolutionary argument cannot rule out all moral facts.

Second, even if we do not need to postulate any moral facts to explain any common moral beliefs or anything else, that would rule out only inferences to the best explanation in favor of moral facts. Other kinds of arguments still might establish moral facts. Some candidates will be discussed in part II of this book. So moral nihilists cannot yet conclude that we have no reason to believe in moral facts.[9]

Joyce tries to support such a conclusion with an analogy: John is unjustified in believing that Sally is out to get him if John's belief results from paranoia, so John would have the same belief whether or not Sally really was out to get him. Similarly, Joyce claims, humans will evolve to believe in moral requirements both in a world where those requirements exist and also in a world where they do not exist, so "the process that generates moral judgments exhibits an independence between judgment and truth, and these judgments are thus unjustified" because they are "unreliable" (Joyce 2001, 162–63). This challenging argument conflates two kinds of reliability. A belief process is reliable *in the actual world* when it yields few, if any, false beliefs in the actual world. A belief process is reliable *in counterfactual worlds* when it would yield few, if any, false beliefs even in very different possible worlds. John's paranoia makes him unreliable in the actual world. Joyce's point about how evolution *would* work if there *were* no moral facts shows only that moral believers are unreliable in *counterfactual* worlds without moral facts. Joyce cannot show that moral believers are unreliable in the actual world without assuming that there are no moral facts in the actual world. But what Joyce needs to show is unreliability in the actual world. Even if reliability in the actual world is necessary for justified belief, it is much less clear that, or why, reliability in counterfactual worlds is necessary for justified belief in this world. If thermometers work in our world, we seem justified in trusting them here, even if they fail in other possible worlds. Similarly, if we live in a world with moral facts, and our moral beliefs are actually reliable in this world, then the fact that our moral beliefs would be false in a very different possible world without moral facts need not make our moral beliefs unjustified in this world.

The third problem for this argument against moral facts is most important here. Suppose that all moral beliefs can be explained by evolutionary pressures, so no moral facts are needed to explain any moral belief or anything else, and we have no other reason to believe in any moral facts. That still does not show that there are no moral facts. Metaphysical moral nihilism does not follow from epistemological moral skepticism. Indeed, the lack of any need to postulate moral facts would not even give us a reason to believe that there are no moral facts, since there might be moral facts that we do not need for any explanation. Thus, even if the

---

9. Evolution might explain why we hold some moral beliefs that are incoherent (see Greene, forthcoming). Their incoherence might then make these moral beliefs unjustified. But it is still not their evolutionary origins that make them unjustified. Besides, not all moral beliefs are incoherent in this way.

availability of evolutionary explanations for moral beliefs did undermine every reason to believe in moral facts, it would not give us any reason to deny moral facts. We might have no reason either to believe in or to deny moral facts.[10]

Opponents of moral facts often admit that evolutionary explanations "will not independently serve to show that moral judgments are probably false," but they still try to argue against moral facts by supplementing evolutionary explanations with additional premises.[11] One common move cites Ockham's razor, which says that entities should not be multiplied beyond necessity. This principle is supposed to imply that we should not believe in moral facts if we don't need to believe in them in order to explain some experience. But notice that the principle does *not* say that we should *deny* entities that are unnecessary. All it rules out is belief in unnecessary entities. It doesn't prescribe disbelief. We can also follow Ockham's advice by suspending belief in moral facts, that is, by withholding both belief and disbelief. The option of suspension is overlooked often when Ockham's razor is cited in support of denials. Such arguments work only if (a) there is adequate reason to believe that, if the denial weren't true, we would know that it wasn't true; (b) the best explanation implies the denial; or (c) there is independent reason for the denial, such as an argument from queerness. But none of this has been shown yet for moral facts. If such additional arguments were provided, then they would do all the work, and evolutionary explanations would have no role in arguing against moral facts (although they could still explain why we hold so many false moral beliefs). Thus, when Ockham's razor is added to evolutionary explanations of moral beliefs, the result still does not support any denial of moral facts. It supports at most a suspension of belief in moral facts.

Furthermore, what Ockham's razor shaves are *kinds* of entities, such as souls or phlogiston or universals, that are significantly different from the standard kinds of entities. Ockham's razor does not apply to moral facts if moral facts are not significantly different from standard entities. (Cf. Joyce 2001, 158.) Appeals to Ockham's razor, thus, depend on an assumption that moral facts are queer. Maybe they are, but the point here is that the real force of the argument from Ockham's razor comes from the queerness of moral facts. So we need to look at attempts to show how moral facts are queer.

3.2.3. *Epistemological Queerness*

Mackie gives three separate arguments from queerness. The first is epistemological: our ordinary ways of knowing include only "sensory perception or introspection or

---

10. The same point holds on the other side. Even if moral realists can explain moral nihilism (possibly as a reaction to parents or to bad moralizing) apart from the truth of moral nihilism, this explanation by itself does not show that moral nihilism is false or even that we have reason to believe that it is false.

11. Joyce 2001, 168. Joyce adds, "At best [his evolutionary explanation] shows [moral judgments] to be unjustified." This admission suggests that the proper conclusion from evolutionary arguments is epistemological rather than metaphysical, as I argue.

the framing and confirming of explanatory hypotheses or inferences or logical construction or conceptual analysis, or any combination of these." Objective moral values could not be known by any of these methods. Therefore, "if we were aware of [objective moral values], it would have to be by some special faculty of moral perception or intuition, utterly different from our ordinary ways of knowing everything else." But "it is indeed easy to point out [the] implausibilities" of special moral intuition (Mackie 1977, 39). Therefore, we could not know objective moral values if there were any.

Defenders of moral facts often look for "companions in guilt": it is also hard to figure out how we can know essences, causes, numbers, and so on, but most philosophers do not deny facts of those sorts. In response, Mackie cites his other works and says, "I can only state my belief that satisfactory accounts of most of these can be given in empirical terms" (Mackie 1977, 39). He seems happy to reject the other non-empirical facts along with moral facts. However, it remains to be determined whether investigations of these other areas will lead us to expand Mackie's list of ordinary ways of knowing.

Another response denies the second premise, that moral facts cannot be known by any ordinary ways of knowing. That claim will be discussed in part II of this book. So will Mackie's claim that positing moral intuition is implausible. (See chapter 9.) But that can wait.

For now the main point is just that these epistemological considerations do not yield Mackie's metaphysical conclusion. Even if we have no epistemic access to moral facts, that does not show that they do not exist. Maybe we should not believe in facts that we cannot know; but, if so, for the same reason, we also should not believe that such facts do *not* exist, if we cannot know that they do not exist. The only way to get from "no knowledge" to "no fact" is via a premise that we would be able to know moral facts if there were any. But Mackie gives us no reason to accept such a premise. So it seems reasonable to suspend belief until we find a better argument.

3.2.4. *Psychological Queerness*

Moral facts are also supposed to bear a queer relation to motives and reasons. As Mackie puts it, objective moral values would have a "power, when known, automatically to influence the will" (Mackie 1977, 40). His claim can't be that moral facts by themselves influence the will, since normally the fact that my act would be immoral cannot motivate me not to do it, if I don't have any awareness or access to that fact. Also, it doesn't matter whether the belief is justified or true. A false and unjustified belief in a moral fact would, presumably, motivate in the same way as if it were true and justified. So it seems to be beliefs rather than knowledge, truth, or facts that are supposed to have the queer relation to motivation.

How much motivation? In Plato's version: "The Form of the Good is such that it provides the knower with . . . an *overriding* motive" (Mackie 1977, 40; my emphasis). Since people act on their overriding motives, Plato's extreme position makes it hard to see how anyone could ever do what they know is bad or wrong. So it is more plausible to claim a relation between moral belief and *some* motivation, which might or might not be overriding.

Still, Mackie needs this motivation to follow "automatically" (1977, 40). If I believe that a car is coming at me, that will influence my choice to move out of the way. But it won't be conceptually necessary that everyone who believes that a car is coming at them will be motivated to move, since some people might want to be hit and hurt. Thus, moral beliefs differ from such non-moral beliefs only if the relation between moral beliefs and motivation is unusually tight, which here suggests conceptual necessity or something close to that.

With these clarifications, Mackie's argument can be reconstructed like this:

(1) It is conceptually necessary that everyone who believes that an act is immoral is at least somewhat motivated not to do it.
(2) No relation like this holds for non-moral beliefs.
(3) Thus, moral beliefs are "utterly different" from other kinds of beliefs.
(4) Thus, moral facts are "utterly different" from other kinds of facts.
(5) Thus, there are no moral facts.

One obvious problem is that (4) does not imply (5). Even if moral facts are different from other kinds of facts, it is not clear why this difference in power makes them suspect metaphysically. Magnets have a power of attraction that makes them different from anything else, but that does not lead us to deny the existence of magnets. We need some reason to believe in magnets or moral facts. Still, if we have such reasons, then the uniqueness of their powers hardly proves that they do not exist.

It is also not clear how (4) follows from (3). (4) is about moral facts. (3) is about moral beliefs. Maybe moral beliefs motivate automatically not because of anything in the moral facts that the beliefs are about but only because of something about the beliefs or their roles in our minds. If so, (4) can be false even if (3) is true.

Most importantly, it is questionable whether moral beliefs really are as closely tied to motivation as Mackie claims. Mackie never gives any argument for this premise, (1), other than to cite Plato, Clarke, and Hume.[12] Indeed, although many so-called internalists adopt similar positions, I know of no good argument for this assumption. Moreover, such claims seem subject to counterexamples. Some people seem not to care at all about cheating on their taxes even though they believe that such cheating is morally wrong. Their belief in the immorality of tax fraud is based on their recognition that anyone who is both rational and impartial would disapprove of tax fraud. Nonetheless, they are not and do not want to be impartial themselves, so they have no motivation to conform their conduct to the rules of other people who are impartial. Such tax-evaders might be morally bad, but they need not be irrational or ignorant or forgetful or weak-willed, so the counterexample cannot be evaded by limiting Mackie's claim to informed, rational

---

12. Elsewhere, Mackie (1980, 55) writes, "It is linguistically odd to use words like 'right' and 'wrong' with no prescriptive force." Even if so (what about past tense moral judgments?), any oddness can be explained by pragmatics of speech without implications for moral beliefs, much less truth.

belief. This example and others like it seem to refute premise (1). (See also Brink 1989, chap. 3.) Without that premise, Mackie's argument cannot get started.

A different argument might seem to bypass these problems. Instead of claiming that moral beliefs are tied to *motivation*, Mackie sometimes suggests that moral facts are tied to *reasons*. On his account (1977, 73–77), to say that I ought to do something implies that I have a reason to do it.[13] Following Kant (1785), Mackie (1977, 27–30) also holds that moral obligations are categorical in the sense that whether someone has a moral obligation to do something does not depend on whether that person wants to do it. But many philosophers hold that reasons depend on desires in some way. Another error theorist, Joyce (2001, 77), puts all of this together into the following argument:

(1) If *x* morally ought to ϕ, then *x* [morally] ought to ϕ regardless of what his desires and interests are.
(2) If *x* morally ought to ϕ, then *x* has a [moral] reason for ϕing.
(3) Therefore, if *x* morally ought to ϕ, then *x* has a [moral] reason for ϕing regardless of what his desires and interests are.
(4) But there is no sense to be made of such reasons.
(5) Therefore, *x* is never under a moral obligation.

The crucial premise, (4), denies the coherence of so-called "external" reasons. Joyce admits that some external reasons do make sense, but only if they are legitimated by rules of an actual institution, and he argues that moral reasons are not institutional in this way. He concludes that external *moral* reasons make no sense. That is enough to reach his conclusion, (5).

To argue for premise (4), Joyce invokes a principle that "reasons have to be able to explain action" (2001, 108; cf. Williams 1981). However, this premise is ambiguous in a crucial respect. To see the ambiguity, imagine that Dan drives his car through a puddle so as to splash dirty water all over three pedestrians and ruin their pretty clothes. Dan sees the puddle coming, could avoid it easily and safely, knows that driving through it would harm the pedestrians, and has nothing against these pedestrians; but he does not care at all about the pedestrians, and so he does not bother to avoid the puddle. Despite his indifference, it still seems that Dan ought to care and ought to avoid the puddle; so, on Mackie's analysis, Dan has a reason to avoid it. One reason might be a risk of negative repercussions to him, but there is very little risk, and he knows it. In any case, there also seems to be another reason for him to avoid the puddle, namely, that driving through it will harm the pedestrians. Dan has this reason insofar as he is aware of the fact that driving through the puddle will harm the pedestrians. However, neither the fact nor Dan's awareness of it can explain why Dan does drive through the puddle, as he does, since this reason is a reason for *not* driving though the puddle.

---

13. This implication is supposed to hold for prudential reasons as well, so Mackie's kind of argument might seem to suggest that there are no prudential facts. However, it is harder to specify how prudential reasons could hold "regardless of desires and interests."

Is this reason not to drive through the puddle "able to" explain any action? In one sense, yes. Suppose Dan avoids the puddle in order to avoid harming the pedestrians. Then Dan's awareness of the fact that driving through the puddle will harm the pedestrians, together with his concern for the pedestrians, would explain why he avoids the puddle. So this reason *is* able to explain his action *if* he has different desires and interests than he actually has and acts differently than he actually does. However, if we hold constant Dan's current desires and interests, including his indifference to the pedestrians, then we could not explain why he avoids the puddle by citing his awareness of the fact that driving through the puddle will harm the pedestrians. As long as he does not care what happens to them, no harm to them can explain his actions.

The crucial point here is that Dan still has a *reason* not to harm the pedestrians, even while he does not care about them or about this reason. The nature of this reason is not hard to see. As in the tax evasion case, if Dan were impartial and cared about anyone, then he would care about the pedestrians. Indeed, anyone who is both rational and impartial would, presumably, disapprove of harming the strangers. This counterfactual about what would happen if he or others were impartial seems to show what he ought to do and what he has a reason to do. Even if this reason cannot *explain* his action while he is not impartial, it can still perform another function, namely, it can *justify* an alternative action. In our example, if there were no pedestrians to splash and no other reason to avoid the puddle, but there were some risk in avoiding the puddle (say, a chance of swerving), then it would be irrational for Dan to avoid the puddle. In contrast, if we add the pedestrians, then harm to them can make it no longer irrational to avoid the puddle. This power to justify remains the same regardless of what [Dan's] desires and interests are, since, even while Dan does not care about the pedestrians, he still ought not to harm them, so he has a reason not to harm them. Other moral reasons are similar in this way. As long as people don't care about moral reasons, those reasons cannot explain their actions, but they can still justify actions as well as moral judgments of those actions.

Internalists might respond that, whenever there is a reason for an agent to do an act, that agent must be able to believe in that reason; but Dan cannot believe that he ought to avoid the puddle, because, if he believed this, and if he were fully rational, then he would have to be motivated to avoid the puddle (Smith 1994, 60–76). I grant that Dan is not motivated to avoid the puddle and that he is fully rational. He just doesn't care about the pedestrians. However, none of this shows that Dan cannot believe that he has a moral reason (and morally ought) to avoid the puddle. He can believe in this moral reason and not care about morality, because he is not impartial and does not care about being impartial. Hence, I am not committed to any reason for Dan that Dan could not believe in. Besides, even if Dan could not believe that he has any reason to avoid the puddle, there still could be a reason for him to avoid the puddle, he could have that reason insofar as he believes in the fact that constitutes the reason, and that reason could justify him in avoiding the puddle, even if it could not explain why he does what he does.

All of this shows that, contrary to Joyce's premise (4), there is "sense to be made of" external reasons as justifying reasons. So Joyce's argument fails, as did

Mackie's. There still might be no moral facts, as they claim, but this argument does not show that there are no moral facts.

3.2.5. *Metaphysical Queerness*

Mackie's final kind of queerness is metaphysical. His argument consists largely of questions:

> What is the connection between the natural fact that an action is a piece of deliberate cruelty—say, causing pain just for fun—and the moral fact that it is wrong? It cannot be an entailment, a logical or semantic necessity. Yet it is not merely that the two features occur together. The wrongness must somehow be "consequential" or "supervenient"; it is wrong because it is a piece of deliberate cruelty. But just what in the world is signified by this "because"? ... How much simpler and more comprehensible the situation would be if we could replace the moral quality with some sort of subjective response which could be causally related to the detection of the natural features on which the supposed quality is said to be consequential.[14]

Mackie seems to assume that defenders of moral facts will not be able to answer his questions. They are hard questions to answer. However, it is also hard to say exactly how biological facts are related to non-biological facts, such as facts from physics and psychology. That mystery does not lead us to deny biological facts. Our inability to understand relations among facts might be a reason to doubt those facts (or whether they are basic), but it is hardly a reason to deny that those facts exist.

Besides, it's not that hard to specify the relation between moral facts and non-moral facts. That relation is supervenience. Recent work on supervenience distinguishes several different relations. Defenders of moral facts do not all agree on which relation holds, but each has a favorite answer to Mackie's question: "What in the world is signified by this 'because'?" Even if they cannot justify their preference or explain why one relation holds rather than another, that is no reason to deny that moral facts exist and have some relation to non-moral facts.

To bolster his argument, Mackie needs to show either that no relation could possibly exist between moral and non-moral facts or, more plausibly, that the relation between moral beliefs and non-moral beliefs is better understood without bringing in moral facts at all. This latter move is developed by Blackburn (1985).

Blackburn interprets the claim that moral facts supervene on non-moral facts roughly as this: It is analytically necessary (AN) that, if some act (x) has a moral property (F) because it has a set of non-moral properties (G*) that underlie (U) moral property (F), then anything with those same non-moral properties (G*) will have the same moral property (F). In symbols:

---

14. Mackie 1977, 41. Mackie adds, "And how do we know the relation that it signifies . . . ?" but this is an extension of epistemological queerness, which I already discussed.

$(S_a) AN((\exists x)(Fx \ \& \ G^*x \ \&(G^*x \ U \ Fx)) \supset (y)(G^*y \supset Fy))$

Blackburn also follows Mackie in claiming that the relation "cannot be an entailment, a logical or semantic necessity" (Mackie 1977, 41), for reasons brought out by Moore's (1903) open question argument. This implies that it is analytically possible (AP) (or does not conflict with any analytic or semantic truths) that something has those same non-moral properties (G^*) without the same moral property (F):

$(P_a) AP(\exists x)(G^*x \ \& \sim Fx)^{15}$

The conjunction of (S_a) and (P_a) has strange implications for possible worlds. Assume that in the actual world (W) something (x) has a set of non-moral properties (G^*) that underlies a moral property (F). Then the antecedent of (S_a) is true in W, so we can infer that anything in W with those same non-moral properties (G^*) in W will have the same moral property (F) in W. Nothing in W is G^* but not F. But this holds only in W. (P_a) says that there is some other analytically possible world (W') where something (x) does have those non-moral properties (G^*) without the moral property (F). What's strange is that, although both worlds, W and W', are allowed by our assumptions, we cannot combine those worlds, because anything that has G^* but not F in W' would contradict the implication of (S_a) plus our assumptions in W. Blackburn calls this a "ban on mixed worlds" ([1985] 1993, 135).

Blackburn endorses the ban, but he argues that it is strange enough that it needs to be explained, and it cannot be explained by a defender of moral facts. Anyone who postulates facts that (S_a), that (P_a), and that G^* underlies F for some x in the actual world, W, will also have to claim that it is a fact that no mixed world is possible. But they can't say why this is impossible. Blackburn adds that, in contrast, expressivists can explain the ban in terms of how we coordinate morality. Even if he is wrong about that, the puzzle remains for defenders of real moral facts.

One possible response is that the ban on mixed worlds is a brute fact that does not need to be explained because it is not really so strange. After all, adding consistent worlds often yields inconsistency. Besides, what creates the strangeness in the ban on mixed worlds is the assumption that what underlies a moral property in one case underlies it everywhere within the same possible world but not in all other possible worlds. This problem can be avoided by restricting the "underlies" relation (U) to a relevant area (either within a single world or in a set of "nearby" possible worlds). This restriction gives up the universality of (S_a). With this restriction, the "underlies" relation need not extend to W' when W' is added to W. Moral relativists might even welcome this restriction, because it makes sense of their claim that moral properties vary from one area of the world to another.

A different response gives up (P_a). Defenders of moral facts might reject Moore's open question argument and argue that it is not even analytically possible

---

15. (S_a) and (P_a) come from Blackburn 1993, 137. My edition has "Fx" instead of "$\sim$Fx" in (P_a), but that must be a misprint.

for any act to have the same underlying properties (G*) and not have the super-vening moral property (F). If this position can be defended, then there would be no ban on mixed worlds to be explained.

I find other responses more plausible. One is championed by so-called Cornell realists (Boyd 1988; Brink 1989; Sturgeon 1984). In this view, the property of being water is necessarily constituted by the property of being H_2O, even though the term "water" does not have the same linguistic meaning as "H_2O," so it is analytically possible for something to be water without being H_2O. If moral properties are similarly constituted by non-moral properties, then it is not surprising that moral properties and non-moral properties co-vary in the way (S_a) specifies. Blackburn counters that Cornell realists have to give up the analytic necessity in (S_a) (Blackburn 1993, 147). However, this is not clear, because it might be analytic by virtue of the meaning of "underlies" even if not by virtue of the meaning of any moral term. It also might be analytically necessary which, if any, non-moral properties constitute moral properties. Anyway, even if such Cornell realists do need to drop the analyticity operator "A" from (S_a), the modified principle could still be a synthetic, a priori truth or an a posteriori necessity (Sinnott-Armstrong 1987). Blackburn never shows that supervenience must be analytic, and his argu-ment cannot work without that premise. Of course, the Cornell realists' claims of property constitution might run into other problems, but that is a separate issue. The point here is just that this argument from queerness cannot refute the kind of moral facts that Cornell realists envisage.

Yet another explanation of supervenience comes from Canberra moral realists, who see supervenience as analytic because it is one of a network of truisms that determine the meanings of moral terms. (E.g., Pettit 1997, 107; Jackson 1998, 130–31; cf. section 3.3.1.) What makes supervenience a truism is the function of moral talk: "It is part of our very understanding of ethical vocabulary that we use it to mark distinctions among the descriptive ways things are" (Jackson 1998, 125). We could not classify acts as morally right or wrong in the way that we do if there were no descriptive differences between acts that are morally right and those that are morally wrong. Moreover, we could not follow moral advice if we could not distinguish those acts that follow the advice from those that do not. We could not punish wrongdoers and avoid punishing the innocent if the terms "wrong" and "innocent" did not distinguish descriptive classes. Since the very purpose of moral language would be frustrated if it did not obey something like super-venience, supervenience is analytic, as (S_a) claims. Blackburn, of course, uses a similar kind of explanation from his expressivist perspective. The point here is that this type of explanation is available to at least some moral realists. Although moral realists claim that one function of moral language is to describe moral facts, moral realists need not deny that moral language also has other functions, such as ad-vising or guiding action. Blackburn's argument seems to overlook the possibility that moral language can have both functions, one of which (the action-guiding one) is enough to explain supervenience.

Finally, even if moral realists need to but cannot explain supervenience, that would hardly show that there are no moral facts. The most it would show is that moral realism is incomplete. There is still a mystery to be solved. To solve it, moral realists might need to add more to their theories. But taking away moral facts would not supply any explanation of supervenience. The only way to reach a negative verdict on moral facts would be to show that the only possible explanation of supervenience is incompatible with any and all moral facts. Blackburn does not even claim to have accomplished that much. So this argument, like the others, fails to reach the conclusion that there are no moral facts. At most, the mysteries of supervenience create doubts and reasons to suspend belief about moral facts.

3.3. Is Moral Nihilism Coherent?

Even if we have no good reason to believe that there are *no* positive moral facts, that does not give us any reason to believe that there are *some* positive moral facts. We might have no good reason for either belief. Those who believe in positive moral facts might, however, argue that they do not need any reason for their belief, since its denial is incoherent. To begin addressing this issue, I want to close this chapter with a few brief remarks about whether it is incoherent to deny all positive moral facts.

This denial is, as I said, equivalent to moral nihilism, which is the claim that nothing is morally wrong, required, bad, good, and so on, where "and so on" covers all positive moral properties. I will shift to this simpler formulation, because it will become important later (in section 4.3.2). So the issue here is whether moral nihilism is incoherent.[16]

That depends, of course, on what it means to call a claim incoherent. Some opponents of moral skepticism might go so far as to claim that moral nihilism is *meaningless*. That can't be correct. When a claim really is meaningless, such as "The square root of pine is tree," then its denial is meaningless too. But the denial of "Nothing is morally wrong" is "Something is morally wrong." The latter claim is not meaningless (even according to opponents of moral nihilism and skepticism), so neither is the former. The former is moral nihilism, so moral nihilism is meaningful.

Opponents still might hold that moral nihilism is syntactically *contradictory*. The denial of a contradiction is not a contradiction, and a contradiction is not meaningless (or else we could not tell that it is a contradiction). However, there is no way to derive a contradiction from the defining claim of moral nihilism alone, any more than from "Nothing is a witch." Just try. (See also section 3.1.)

A more plausible claim is that moral nihilism is semantically *incoherent* in the sense of being incompatible with the meanings of moral terms, just as it is incoherent (but not contradictory) to say that some cows are not mammals.[17] Anyone

16. Moral nihilists usually add to their central claim an explanation of common moral beliefs. Here I am not asking whether that explanation is coherent but only whether the central claim that defines moral nihilism is coherent.

17. Contrast logical coherence as discussed in section 3.1 and epistemic coherence as discussed in chapter 10.

who claims to have found a cow that is not a mammal must be confused about the meaning of "cow" or of "mammal." To determine whether moral nihilism is incoherent in this way, we need to consider how various theories of moral language apply to the defining claim of moral nihilism.

3.3.1. *Realism on Nihilism*

It might seem obvious that moral nihilism is semantically coherent according to moral realists. Moral realists hold that moral sentences and beliefs are about moral facts and have mind-independent truth-values. In this respect, they resemble assertions and beliefs about witches. Just as one can coherently deny that anything has the property of being a witch, so it must be coherent to deny that anything has the property of being morally wrong, and so on. This denial might be incorrect and implausible. Nonetheless, if moral realists are right about the meanings of moral terms, moral nihilism seems to make as much sense semantically and is as coherent as the opposite view that is held by most moral realists. In fact, some moral realists (such as Brink 1989, 34) see it as an advantage of their analysis that it allows and explains the coherence of moral nihilism.

However, there are distinct ways to develop moral realism, and they are not all equally friendly to the coherence of moral nihilism. Cornell moral realists (e.g., Sturgeon 1984, Boyd 1988, and Brink 1989) claim that moral properties are constituted by descriptive properties, but moral terms do not mean the same as any non-moral terms. They provide no analysis of basic moral language that could be used to show that moral nihilism is semantically incoherent.[18]

In contrast, Canberra moral realists (e.g., Jackson 1998 and Pettit 1997) do provide complex analyses of moral language. They give the meaning (or at least fix the reference) of a moral predicate by specifying its role in folk morality. Folk morality includes formal platitudes (such as "moral properties supervene on descriptive properties"), practical platitudes (such as "the judgment that an act is right is normally accompanied by at least some desire to perform the act"), internal platitudes (which link terms, such as "the best option is the right option"), and others. The crucial platitudes here are substantive. Common examples of substantive platitudes include "if an act is intentional killing, then normally it is wrong; pain is bad; 'I cut, you choose' is a fair procedure; and so on" (Jackson 1998, 130–31).[19] Since there are acts of intentional killing in normal circumstances, for example, these platitudes seem to imply that some acts are morally wrong. If a moral nihilist denies that these acts are morally wrong, then the moral nihilist

---

18. Some Cornell realists accept a causal theory on which moral terms refer to the natural properties that causally regulate their use, but that cannot make moral nihilism incoherent, since that general view leaves open the possibility that what regulates our use of moral terms is only our emotions and social settings rather than any property of the acts or agents being judged morally.

19. Pettit (1997, 107–8) gives a similar list. I have to add that "I cut, you choose" was not a fair procedure when my older daughter told my younger son to cut, because she knew that he could not cut pieces evenly.

cannot be using the term "morally wrong" according to the meaning that is specified by the network analysis in terms of folk morality. This might seem to show that moral nihilism is semantically incoherent.

But this is too quick. For one thing, moral nihilists can grant that the platitudes of folk morality are platitudes in the sense of common beliefs. All that moral nihilists deny is that the substantive folk beliefs are *true*. They can still use at least the non-substantive platitudes to specify the meanings of moral terms that they and common folk share. They just refuse to build substantial moral truths into the meanings of moral terms.

Moreover, "folk morality is currently under negotiation: its basic principles, and even many of its derived ones, are a matter of debate and are evolving as we argue about what to do" (Jackson 1998, 132). Changes in folk morality would change the meanings of moral terms, if those terms were defined by current folk morality. That is why Canberra moral realists must, instead, define moral terms by "mature folk morality, the theory on which current folk morality will converge under critical reflection" (Jackson 1998, 140; cf. 151). This qualification clears the way for moral nihilism. Jackson (1998, 137) claims, "It is part of current folk morality that convergence will or would occur," but he admits that "this may turn out to be, as a matter of fact, false." Similarly, Smith (1994, 189) argues that "we should . . . be quite optimistic" about convergence, but our moral beliefs "might" diverge irresolvably, and, "if that were to occur, then we might well quite justifiably come to think that Mackie was right after all, that there are no moral facts, though there would still be room for doubt." Insofar as there is a coherent possibility that our moral beliefs won't converge on any mature folk morality, then, moral nihilism is also a coherent possibility. Another possible outcome would also support moral nihilism. As we saw, moral nihilists give arguments to show that "under critical reflection" we will (or should) converge on the view that there are no positive moral facts, so nothing is morally wrong, etc. In short, mature folk morality might be nihilistic. Since this possibility is consistent with the kind of network analysis that Canberra moral realists favor, moral nihilism is semantically coherent on that view. (See also Zangwill 2000.)

A related but distinct kind of semantic theory, which is favored by some moral realists, still might seem to suggest that moral nihilism is incoherent. On this approach, the meanings of moral terms are given not by networks of general truisms but by similarity to particular paradigms.[20] "Morally wrong" just means "Something sufficiently like torture or terrorism or rape or. . . ." Moral nihilists deny that even these paradigm cases are morally wrong, so moral nihilism seems semantically incoherent on this view.

But compare a witch nihilist who denies that there are any real witches. A witch believer claims that Tituba is a paradigm witch, so the term "witch" just means "Someone sufficiently like Tituba or. . . ." This would hardly show that witch nihilism is incoherent. The witch nihilist could easily respond that Tituba

---

20. This view is associated with Wittgenstein and in ethics with Foot (1978). For a more detailed response, see Sinnott-Armstrong 1995a, 224–25.

lacks the properties that are supposed to make her a paradigm witch according to witch believers, so "witch" cannot properly be defined as "Someone sufficiently like Tituba or . . .." Analogously, a moral nihilist can respond that supposed moral paradigms lack the properties that are supposed to make them paradigm moral wrongs according to moral believers, so "morally wrong" cannot properly be defined as "Something sufficiently like torture or terrorism or rape or . . .." A better definition might be "Something sufficiently like torture or terrorism or rape or . . . , as common moralists take them to be." But then a moral nihilist can deny that any acts really have the properties that common moralists take them to have. Definitions by paradigms, therefore, cannot show that moral nihilism is any more incoherent than witch nihilism.

3.3.2. *Expressivism on Nihilism*

Next, consider whether nihilism is semantically coherent according to expressivism. As we saw in section 2.2, expressivists must grant minimal truth-aptness to explain how moral sentences can embed in unassertive contexts, including negation. If a positive claim like "Suicide is morally wrong" is truth-apt, then so is its negation, "Suicide is not morally wrong." Thus, expressivists must grant that some such moral negations could be true. Given that admission, nothing in expressivism makes it semantically incoherent to claim that all such moral negations are true and to deny that any positive moral assertion is true. Hence, moral nihilism comes out coherent within the semantic part of expressivism.

Expressivists also hold the pragmatic view that moral assertions express non-cognitive attitudes. It is not at all clear which attitudes are supposed to be expressed by negative moral assertions. However, if expressivists can specify the attitude that is expressed by negated moral assertions, the same analysis can be generalized to capture moral nihilism. For example, "Suicide is not morally wrong" might be analyzed in part as:

(i) Boo: Disapproval of suicide.
(ii) OK: Suicide.
(iii) Indifference: Suicide.
(iv) Non-Disapprove: Suicide.

It does not really matter which of these accounts wins out. Whichever it is, the same analysis can be generalized to capture moral nihilism. "Nothing is morally wrong" can be analyzed to the same extent as:

(i*) Boo: Disapproval of any act.
(ii*) OK: Any act.
(iii*) Indifference: Any act.
(iv*) Non-Disapprove: Any act.

These are unusual positions, but they are not incoherent, unless (i)–(iv) are also incoherent, in which case expressivism cannot be defended. Hence, any version of expressivism that is sophisticated enough to capture single negations would also seem to allow moral nihilism to be semantically coherent.

3.3.3. *Constructivism on Nihilism*

Instead of expressing non-cognitive attitudes, moral assertions make claims about attitudes, according to a third common approach to moral semantics. This view is called moral constructivism, because it suggests that moral truths and facts are somehow constructed out of some attitudes. Moral assertions don't seem to be claims about actual attitudes, since actual attitudes are often distorted by ignorance and partiality. Instead, most constructivists refer to attitudes in ideal circumstances. Such ideal constructivists claim that an act is morally wrong only if everyone under ideal circumstances would disapprove of doing it.[21]

In this view, an act is not morally wrong if not everyone in ideal circumstances would disapprove of it. Thus, if every act is such that, in ideal circumstances, some people would approve of it and others would disapprove of it, then nothing is morally wrong. If parallel points apply to other moral terms, then moral nihilism is true, according to ideal constructivism. Even if it seems unlikely, it is at least coherent to claim that people in ideal circumstances would disagree in their attitudes towards every act. It follows that moral nihilism is semantically coherent on this theory.

This argument depends on a specific feature of the analysis, that it refers to *all* members of the select group. But what is the alternative? Constructivists cannot analyze the meanings of moral words in terms of what *most* or even *almost* all ideal people would choose. Imagine the extreme case where one person disagrees with everyone else. If the lone dissident is ideal in all required ways, then moral constructivists have no reason to discount that person's reactions in any way that is relevant to morality. So moral constructivists have to refer to all members of a select group, and their universal quantifier is then enough to leave conceptual room for moral nihilism.

Constructivists might respond, next, that ideal disagreement is incoherent. But why? The only way to rule it out is to define ideal circumstances so as to ensure ideal agreement. There are many ways to do this. The most direct way is to require ideal persons to be informed about some moral truths, but that would be objectionably circular. A better way to obtain the same result indirectly is to require ideal persons to be impartial in some way that makes them favor certain moral views. This method is common. Harsanyi (1982) specifies conditions for rationality and impartiality in such a way as to ensure that all rational impartial people will choose utilitarianism. Rawls (1971, 111) specifies different conditions for rationality and impartiality so as to ensure universal ideal agreement on his principles of justice.[22] Gert (1998, 209) does the same for his moral system, using different notions of

---

21. Constructivism has been defined in many other ways, but nothing here hinges on the label. By ideal constructivism, I have in mind the most common and plausible versions under the definition by Brink (1989, 20). Notice also that my term "disapprove" is intended to cover not only feelings but also beliefs and choices, and ideal circumstances can include procedures as well as internal features of the disapprover, so my account of constructivism includes a variety of idealizing approaches to moral language.

22. Rawls writes only about justice, but his followers often try to extend his theory into a general moral theory. My points apply to this extension.

rationality and impartiality. The popularity of this method might seem to show its plausibility. However, the fact that there are incompatible ways to construct an analysis of this kind shows that no particular way can capture the shared meaning of "morally wrong" or of other moral terms. Harsanyi, Rawls, and Gert disagree substantively on many issues. They do not merely use the phrase "morally wrong" with different meanings. That phrase is flexible enough to allow all of their views to be coherent, even if some of their views are false. But if each of these views is coherent, then so is the denial of each view, and so is the denial of them all, for they do not exhaust the possibilities. Since none of these theories can be used to show that its non-nihilistic competitors are incoherent, none of their views can be used to show that moral nihilism is incoherent either.

I am not claiming that moral nihilism cannot be refuted by showing that all rational and impartial people would reject it. My only point here is that no analysis of the meanings of moral words in terms of the reactions of all rational impartial people can be used to show that moral nihilism is semantically incoherent. It still might be false or unjustified, but that is a separate issue that requires a separate argument (to be discussed in section 8.2).

Of course, there are other semantic analyses of moral language that might make moral nihilism semantically incoherent.[23] And there might be some way to argue that moral nihilism is semantically incoherent without depending on any semantic analysis.[24] However, it is hard to see how such an argument could succeed. In the absence of any good argument to the contrary, I conclude that moral nihilism is semantically coherent.

3.4. So Far

I am *not* a moral nihilist. I believe that many acts are morally wrong. I think that my positive moral beliefs are true and correspond to moral facts.

23. One neat alternative analyzes "x is morally wrong" roughly as "x violates a justified moral standard (or norm or prescription)." This style of analysis was presented first by Fogelin (1967) and developed recently by Copp (1995). Such analyses can explain unassertive embeddings as well as disagreement. However, "justified" is a normative term. If it is analyzed in accordance with expressivism or constructivism, then most of what I say about those views will apply to this alternative. If "justified" is analyzed according to realism and naturalism, then this style of analysis grants maximal truth values to moral assertions and can be seen as a version of moral realism. In any case, this alternative does not undermine moral epistemology or make moral nihilism incoherent.

24. Blackburn writes, "Possibilities are things that we allow and disallow," but the possibility of moral nihilism "only stifles and stultifies the rationale for argument," so "the pragmatics of the matter speak firmly against allowing this kind of radical global skepticism [or moral nihilism] as a possibility, for its effect can be nothing but paralysis" (1996, 94). However, it is not at all clear that whether one does or should allow or disallow a possibility determines what is possible. Moreover, the possibility of moral nihilism is compatible with strongly justified moral belief, as long as strongly justified beliefs can be false. At the very least, the possibility of moral nihilism does not stifle or stultify everyday argument, as we will see in chapter 6 on modestly justified moral belief, which does not require believers to rule out moral nihilism. So Blackburn's claims do not show that we should disallow the possibility (or coherence) of moral nihilism.

Nonetheless, I argued in section 3.3 that moral nihilism is semantically coherent. I did criticize the main arguments for moral nihilism in section 3.2, but I would never claim that my criticisms are all absolutely decisive. Some of the arguments for moral nihilism retain some force. They remain troubling. Several respectable philosophers, as well as many respectable non-philosophers, accept moral nihilism. Although these moral nihilists cannot prove their thesis, they do not adopt their position arbitrarily. They have *some* reason to accept moral nihilism.

Where, then, do we stand? Common sense accuses certain acts of being moral torts or wrongs. The grand jury of public opinion finds enough initial evidence to issue an indictment, so we go to trial. In our trial, the defense goes first (for a change) and gives the arguments for moral nihilism in section 3.2. These witnesses are cross-examined vigorously, but, even after criticism, the defense has given enough evidence that the plaintiff cannot simply rest. Some members of the jury remain unconvinced and not without reason. They and we need to hear something more positive in favor of moral facts and truths. The arguments for moral nihilism have enough force to give the other side what lawyers call "the burden of going forward." The judges—you and I—should not direct a verdict in favor of the plaintiff (or the defendant) at this early stage of the trial.

This legal analogy might seem stretched, but its point is simple: Moral nihilism deserves to be taken seriously. In other areas of inquiry, if enough intelligent and careful people really do believe a coherent position for some reason, then normally they should not be dismissed abruptly without argument. So moral nihilism also should not be dismissed without fair and careful consideration. This consideration will be given in the rest of this book, which will explore the epistemological importance of moral nihilism.

This chapter and its predecessor have also made another crucial point: there is no easy road to moral skepticism. More precisely, common arguments for Academic moral knowledge skepticism from skepticism about moral truth are inconclusive at best. There might be better arguments that focus on moral truth, but I can't find any. So I will turn to a different set of arguments for moral skepticism that focus on justified moral belief.

4

Are Any Moral Beliefs Justified?

A separate group of arguments for Academic skepticism about moral knowledge focuses on another requirement for knowledge, namely, justified belief. As before, the basic argument is simple: Knowledge requires justified belief. No moral belief is justified. Therefore, no moral belief is knowledge. Also as before, each premise needs clarification. The first is a very good place to start.

4.1. Does Knowledge Require Justified Belief?

Almost everyone (except Sartwell 1991, 1992; and Levi 1980) agrees that belief and truth are not sufficient for knowledge. To see why, suppose someone asks you how many sons Abraham Lincoln had. You are certain that you have never heard or read the answer. For no apparent reason, you guess that Lincoln had four sons, and you come to believe your guess because you repeat it over and over to yourself. (Many people are surprisingly susceptible to this process.) You are lucky, for Lincoln truly did have four sons. Still, you don't *know* that Lincoln had four sons.

You also don't have knowledge if some joker convinces you with a silly argument, such as that Lincoln was married for four years, and married couples in Lincoln's day always had one child each year. Both premises are false, and the conclusion doesn't follow anyway. Arguments this bad cannot be the basis for knowledge, even if their conclusions happen to be true.

To exclude such lucky guesses and bad arguments, many philosophers (supposedly following Plato 1997a, 98a; and 1997b, 201d) claim that a true belief must also be justified to count as knowledge. This third necessary condition for knowledge avoids the above counterexamples, because a belief is not justified if it depends on a lucky guess or a bad argument.

Other cases, however, have convinced some philosophers that justified belief is *not* necessary for knowledge. One popular example cites a chicken sexer, who can separate male from female chicks right out of the egg, even though the chicken sexer himself cannot identify any feature of the chick that he uses to make the classification.[1] The chicken sexer is not just guessing and not just lucky, because he uses a reliable method that works again and again. His belief also isn't based on a bad argument, if he uses no argument at all; he simply looks the chick over without formulating any argument explicitly. Since this chicken sexer's belief is based on neither a lucky guess nor a bad argument, these common problems cannot show that he lacks knowledge. Many commentators conclude that he does know the chick's sex. Some of these commentators also argue that the chicken sexer is not justified in believing that the chick is male (or female), because he cannot point to anything about the chick that makes him believe that it is male (or female). This example is, thus, supposed to refute the principle that knowledge requires justified belief.

Defenders of the principle have two options. They can argue that the chicken sexer is justified. Or they can deny that he has knowledge (of the relevant kind). Their best strategy is probably to use different responses in different cases. A chicken sexer seems justified if he has often checked adult chickens and found that he correctly identified their sex when they were chicks. In contrast, if a chicken sexer has never confirmed that he (or anybody else) has ever correctly identified the sex of a chick, then defenders of the principle that knowledge implies justification can deny that the chicken sexer really knows the chick's sex, even if he does reliably get it right.[2]

I take no stand on whether any such response succeeds. Most defenders of the principle that knowledge implies justified belief seem to find it obvious that the reliable but unconfirmed chicken sexer does not have knowledge. However, some reliabilists (and other externalists) seem to find it just as obvious that the unconfirmed but reliable chicken sexer does have knowledge. I see no way to resolve this clash of intuitions in general epistemology.[3]

The principle still might hold within moral epistemology if "S knows that X is immoral" implies "S is justified in believing that X is immoral." Moral knowledge might require justified belief, even if knowledge in some other areas (such as chicken sexing) does not.[4]

---

1. It is not clear where this example first appeared and whether real chicken sexing fits the supposed pattern. Clairvoyants and idiot savants are used to make similar points in Audi 1998, 229–31. A more realistic example would be our ability to tell male from female faces without knowing which facial features tip us off.

2. Another move distinguishes knowing an answer from knowing that the answer is correct. Even if the former does not imply justified belief, the latter still might imply justified belief. See Lehrer 1990, 30.

3. It seems likely that the two sides of this debate are using different concepts of knowledge. See Sosa 2004.

4. Maybe because morality is interpersonal and prohibitive. When one person believes that another person's action is morally wrong, the believer judges, affects, and restricts a separate individual. If the judger has no justification or ground for the negative judgment, then to hold that belief anyway evinces a kind of disrespect towards the person whose action is judged. Nothing like that happens when a chicken sexer gives an answer that is not known to be correct. Even if it is enough just to give a correct answer in such other contexts, in morality we want and need some ground for believing that our answers are correct. Otherwise our moral beliefs do not deserve the commendation "knowledge." I am attracted to this view, but I will not rely on it here.

In any case, there is a crucial difference between moral believers and chicken sexers. It is easy to determine whether the chicken sexer is correct. Just wait until the chick grows up. Confirmation is not so easy for moral beliefs, especially if Academic moral skeptics are correct that no moral belief is justified. More precisely, we can distinguish two versions of the principle that knowledge requires justified belief:

(KJ)   If S now knows that x, then S now is justified in believing that x.

(KJ*)   If S now knows that x, then it is possible for someone at some time to be justified in believing that x.

The consequents in these versions differ in three ways: The consequent of (KJ) is only about S, whereas the consequent of (KJ*) refers to *someone* (not necessarily S). The consequent of (KJ) is only about the present time, whereas the consequent of (KJ*) refers to *some time*. And the consequent of (KJ) concerns who is actually justified, whereas the consequent of (KJ*) refers to what is *possible*. It is not clear which of these differences is crucial, but that does not matter here. The chicken sexer counterexample is directed only against (KJ). It has no force at all against the weaker principle, (KJ*), because it is possible for other people years later to be justified in believing that the chicken sexer's answer was correct. They just have to see the adult chicken.

The weaker principle, (KJ*), is enough for most Academic moral skeptics. As I said in section 1.3, some Academic moral skeptics might deny only the actuality and not the possibility of moral knowledge or justified moral belief. But a stronger position is more common. Most Academic skeptics about justified moral belief deny that it is possible for anyone at any time to be justified in holding any moral belief. From this claim plus the weaker principle, (KJ*), it follows that no moral belief is known.[5] Thus, these skeptics' argument against moral knowledge cannot be avoided simply by denying (KJ).

Nonetheless, other examples and arguments might raise other doubts about even the weak version, (KJ*). Many respected and careful epistemologists seem to deny this claim (Nozick 1981; Goldman 1986). So I do not want my arguments to depend on even this weak assumption.

To sidestep this controversy, I will concentrate on justified belief instead of knowledge. Any argument for moral skepticism about justified belief will also support moral skepticism about knowledge, if knowledge implies justified belief, even in the weak way specified in (KJ*). Besides, even if knowledge does not require justified belief, justified belief still remains a distinct and important issue for general epistemology. (See BonJour 2002, 49; and Kvanvig 2003.) Justified belief is especially important in moral epistemology because most people are concerned not to call other people's acts morally wrong unless they are at least justified in believing that those acts are morally wrong. So, little is lost by focusing on justified belief. And something

---

5. That conclusion also follows from a stronger variation on (KJ*) without "possible" in its consequent plus the claim of Academic moral skeptics that nobody at any time is justified in any moral belief.

is gained. Many philosophers remain devoted externalists about knowledge, but externalism seems much less plausible for justification and justified belief.[6] Thus, by discussing justified belief, I can direct attention to the internal issues, which bear more directly on how we should choose among moral beliefs in real life.

For such reasons, I will henceforth restrict my attention to whether and how moral beliefs can be justified. Still, the kind of justifiedness that will concern me is the kind that was traditionally supposed to turn true belief into knowledge. It is crucial, then, to specify precisely which kind of justified belief can play that role.

4.2. Ways to Be Justified

When someone asks us whether a belief is justified, we often find ourselves wanting to answer both "Yes" and "No," even when all other facts are settled. This ambivalence is a signal that we need to distinguish different ways in which a belief may be said to be justified. These distinctions are often overlooked, but the failure to draw them creates countless confusions in moral epistemology and in everyday life. Let's try to do better.

4.2.1. *Instrumentally versus Epistemically Justified*

One simple distinction that is overlooked surprisingly often, at least in moral epistemology, is between instrumentally justified beliefs and epistemically justified beliefs. (Cf. Copp 1991.) To grasp this distinction, imagine that a benefactor will give me ten million dollars if I believe that there are aardvarks on Mars. I have a drug that (or a hypnotist who) will make me believe this. I am justified in taking the drug, so I am justified in making myself believe that there are aardvarks on Mars, so I am justified in being in this belief state, and my belief seems justified at least derivatively in one way. Nevertheless, even after I take the drug, I have no evidence or grounds for the content of my belief, that is, for what I believe. In cases like this, I will say that the believer is *instrumentally* justified but is not *epistemically* justified in holding the belief.

Instrumental justification of this kind depends only on the beneficial *effects* of the mental *state* of belief.[7] It is being in the state of believing in aardvarks

---

6. See Audi 1998, 237–38; and 2002. To see why externalism has problems with justified belief, consider its most popular version, reliabilism. In addition to the unconfirmed chicken sexer, consider a gambler who believes that a coin will come up heads on its next flip because heads is lucky for him. This gambler has no evidence either that heads is lucky or that it is not, but he believes that it is. And it is! Although the gambler has no way to tell in advance, this coin has heads on both sides, so it will in fact come up heads every time. The gambler's process of belief formation is then reliable in these peculiar circumstances. Nonetheless, the gambler is not justified in believing that the coin will come up heads. Therefore, reliability is not sufficient for justified belief.

7. In conversation, Jon Tresan pointed out that one might call a belief justified because a belief state has value in itself apart from its effects. Robert Audi mentioned that the process of coming to believe might have benefits when the resulting belief state itself has no good effects. These kinds of justification do not make beliefs instrumentally justified on my account, but they also do not provide evidence or grounds for the truth of the belief, so they are not epistemic.

on Mars that gets me ten million dollars. There is also a way in which its content matters, since I do not get ten million dollars unless I have a belief with the desired content. Nonetheless, it does *not* matter whether the content of the belief is *true* or even probable. After all, it is just as easy to imagine that my benefactor will give me ten million dollars for believing the opposite or for believing anything else. In general, instrumental justifiedness depends on the effects of a belief state, and the effects of a belief state do not affect the truth or probability of the belief's content,[8] so instrumental justifiedness is not tied to truth even probabilistically.

In contrast, epistemic justifiedness is tied to truth. That is what makes it epistemic. The tie need not be foolproof, since misleading evidence can make a believer epistemically justified in believing a falsehood. Nonetheless, evidence raises the probability of the truth of the belief for which it is evidence.[9] More technically, an observation is evidence for a hypothesis only if the conditional probability of the hypothesis on the evidence is greater than the conditional probability of the hypothesis on the negation of the evidence.[10] The probability of aardvarks on Mars, given observations of aardvark tracks on Mars, is greater than the probability of aardvarks on Mars given no observations of aardvark tracks on Mars. That is why observations of aardvark tracks on Mars can be evidence for aardvarks on Mars.

Although this example refers to evidence, it is controversial whether evidence is always necessary for epistemically justified belief. I do not want or need to prejudge that issue here. Still, if some believers really are epistemically justified without evidence, then their status as epistemically justified is the same status that they would have if their beliefs were, instead, based on evidence. It is also the same status that other believers have when they hold the same belief on the basis of evidence. Since evidence must be related to truth, non-evidential grounds must also be related to truth in order to confer the same epistemic status. Thus, whatever it is that makes any belief epistemically justified, it must have some relation to truth. It remains to be seen exactly what kind of relation to truth is necessary, and

8. There are exceptions, such as that it is more likely that one will be happy if one believes that one will be happy. See James 1896. Such special cases do not include moral beliefs since moral beliefs are not about their own effects.

9. A belief is true only if its content is true, and a belief content is justified when there is evidence for that content. However, a believer can be unjustified in believing a content that is itself justified by evidence that this believer lacks (and others have). Instead of asking whether belief contents are justified in this impersonal way, I will be concerned with whether believers are epistemically justified in forming or retaining belief states with certain contents. It is then primarily the believer who is justified. I will sometimes for simplicity describe beliefs as justified, in which case I will be referring to belief states of certain believers, not to belief contents, unless otherwise indicated.

10. This requirement on evidence has been questioned (e.g., Achinstein 2001) but not in cases that matter here. Still, I do not claim that evidence can be reduced to probability because the probability of any proposition is one minus the probability of its negation, but a believer can have very little evidence that a certain proposition is true and also very little evidence that that proposition is false. Just consider a fair coin flip, where we know that the probabilities of heads and of tails are each 0.5, but we have no evidence at all for heads or for tails.

which grounds have the right relation to truth,[11] but the required relation is clearly missing from the ten million dollar bribe, so that case is enough to show that instrumental justifiedness is different from epistemic justifiedness.

This same distinction applies as well to moral beliefs. If a benefactor (who makes his money by selling clothes that were made in sweat shops) will give me ten million dollars to believe that sweat shops are not morally wrong, and if I have a drug that (or hypnotist who) will make me believe this, then I might be instrumentally justified in getting and being in the mental state of believing that sweat shops are not morally wrong. Nonetheless, my being instrumentally justified does not show that the content of this belief is true or even likely to be true, any more than in the non-moral case.[12] The benefactor has not given me any grounds that could make me epistemically justified in believing that sweatshops are not morally wrong.

These examples should make it clear that the epistemic way of being justified is the topic in epistemology and moral epistemology. Drug-induced beliefs in response to bribes are not knowledge, so they are not justified in the way that concerns epistemologists, scientists, juries, or most everyday people. Moral naturalists, intuitionists, and coherentists do not cite good effects of belief states as reasons to hold those beliefs. (See chapters 7, 9, and 10.) Some contractarians and contractualists do refer to effects of belief states, but even contractarians usually deny that their theories provide only instrumental justifiedness of the kind defined here. (See chapter 8.) Moreover, many moral skeptics see morality as a useful illusion that we are instrumentally justified in adopting (e.g., Mackie 1977, chap. 5; and Joyce 2001, chaps. 6–8), so they do not deny that believers are instrumentally justified in holding moral beliefs. Thus, if any moral epistemology is to respond to moral skepticism, it will have to show that some moral beliefs are justified epistemically and not just instrumentally.

For these reasons, when discussing whether believers and beliefs are justified, I will henceforth refer to epistemic justifiedness, unless otherwise indicated.

4.2.2. *Permissively versus Positively Justified*

While focusing on epistemically justified belief, some people sometimes use the word "justified" in a very weak way. (Cf. Sayre-McCord 1996, 159.) When they say

---

11. Although it is not clear what is required, some relations are inadequate. For example, Audi (1993, 320) writes, "Justification does not necessarily imply truth or (objective) probability of truth; yet it is necessary that the process of justification 'aim' at truth." The point is not that the believer must personally aim at truth but, instead, that the purpose or function of the process must be to gain truth. However, the purpose of gazing into crystal balls is to gain true beliefs about the future. That hardly seems enough to show that gazing into crystal balls provides evidence or grounds in any sense that is important in epistemology, since that process does not increase the probability of success. Moreover, skeptics who deny that any belief is epistemically justified need not deny that many methods (and people) *aim* at truth. Thus, if any view in epistemology or moral epistemology is to respond to skepticism, it will have to show that some beliefs are justified in some way that does not just aim at truth.

12. Such epistemic justifiedness could not apply to moral beliefs if they could not be true even minimally, but I already argued for minimal moral truth-aptness in section 2.2.2.

that someone is justified in believing something, all they mean is that, epistemically, it is *not wrong* for her to believe what she does, so she is *permitted* to believe what she does. This permissive use of "justified" occurs, for instance, when religious believers claim that their beliefs in God are justified by faith alone, if they mean that their beliefs are justified without any positive ground that is independent of the beliefs themselves.[13] They presumably deny that their beliefs are refuted, irrational, or irresponsible, and these negative points are all that is needed for their beliefs to be justified in this permissive way.

Even if such faith is permissively justified, it need not be positively justified. A belief is *positively* justified only when the believer has some positive ground for believing it as opposed to withholding belief. (Cf. Chisholm 1989, 11.) Suppose you have no reason to believe that there is a planet revolving around a certain star. If you also have no reason to deny such a planet, you might be epistemically permitted to believe in such a planet.[14] However, you are not positively justified unless you have some positive ground for holding your belief instead of suspending belief and taking no position on whether or not there is such a planet.

What kind of ground is needed to make a belief positively justified? The ground must be related to truth in order for the belief to be justified epistemically (as opposed to instrumentally). Beyond this, however, I do not assume any restrictions on the kinds of grounds that can make a belief positively, epistemically justified. Competing theories claim that different features are necessary or sufficient for a belief to be justified in this way. Some epistemologists claim that every justified belief must be grounded in an inference from another belief. Others claim that some justified beliefs can be grounded in experiences independent of any belief or inference. Still others claim that a belief is justified when it results from a method that is in fact reliable, regardless of any experience, inference, or belief about its reliability. All of these substantive epistemological theories agree that *something* more than the mere absence of conflicting reasons is necessary for a belief to be justified, so they can all accept the distinction between being positively justified and being permissively justified.

This neutrality among competing theories is possible because to call a believer or belief positively justified is to refer to a status, not necessarily to any process or procedure. Believers need not go through any particular procedure or process to be positively justified. They need not even be conscious of the grounds that make their beliefs positively justified. Even if some contexts call for explicit arguments, in other cases good grounds might not be beliefs or experiences or any kind of

---

13. Some religious believers mean more than this by "justified by faith alone," but I am referring to those who claim only epistemic permission.

14. Atheists and agnostics often cite Clifford's dictum: "It is wrong always, everywhere, and for anyone to believe anything upon insufficient evidence" (1879, v. 2, 186). If so, a belief is permissively justified only if it is positively justified. However, even if Clifford's dictum is true, it is logically, semantically, and conceptually consistent to deny it and hold that, although there is nothing epistemically wrong or bad about a certain belief, there is also nothing epistemically right or good about that belief. This possibility is enough to show that being permissively justified is distinct from being positively justified.

conscious mental state. Although *some* positive ground is needed to make a believer justified positively, the mere concept of positive epistemic support or grounds does not place any hidden restrictions on the kind of ground that could make a belief justified positively.

Epistemologists could study either permissively or positively justified belief, but the most interesting and important questions in epistemology ask when and how beliefs are justified positively. One reason is that you cannot know that a coin will come up heads if you are permissively but not positively justified in believing that the coin will come up heads. This connection to knowledge explains why positive rather than permissive justifiedness has been the main topic in general epistemology. Moreover, as we will see in chapters 7–10, most theories in moral epistemology propose conditions for beliefs to be justified positively rather than merely permissively. When moral coherentists claim that a moral belief can be justified because of how it coheres with other beliefs, they are not claiming only that nothing is wrong with beliefs that cohere. They are claiming that something is positively right about beliefs that cohere. Similarly, when moral intuitionists claim that some moral beliefs are justified non-inferentially, they are claiming that moral intuitions provide positive support for moral beliefs. And when moral skeptics deny that any moral belief is justified, they need not claim that there is overriding reason to believe the opposite or that people should change or give up all of their moral beliefs. Thus, the main debates within moral epistemology about justified moral belief are about some positive way of being justified.

For these reasons, when discussing whether beliefs are justified, I will henceforth be talking about whether any moral beliefs are justified positively and epistemically, unless otherwise indicated.

4.2.3. *Slightly versus Adequately Justified*

Although having some ground is necessary for a belief to be justified in the relevant way, merely having some ground is not sufficient, because grounds can conflict, and some grounds are not strong enough. Consider a non-moral example from everyday life. A murder was committed in the library. The only people known to be near the building at the time were Colonel Mustard, Professor Plum, and Miss Scarlet. A detective finds a bloody size-thirteen boot print in the library. Colonel Mustard wears size-thirteen boots. This observation seems at first sight to be some reason to suspect that the Colonel committed the murder.

However, if Professor Plum also wears size-thirteen boots, then the bloody boot print is not really any reason at all to believe that the murder was committed by Colonel Mustard instead of by Professor Plum. When an observation (the bloody boot print) can be explained just as well by either of two hypotheses (that Colonel Mustard did it and that Professor Plum did it), then the observation is no good as evidence for one hypothesis as opposed to the other. So let's suppose that Professor Plum wears much smaller shoes, as does Miss Scarlet.

But now suppose that we find Colonel Mustard's boots. They are still dirty, so they have not been cleaned recently, but there is no trace of blood. Moreover, we find a bloody pair of size-thirteen boots in the woods outside the murder scene.

This new information undermines the epistemic force of the bloody boot print in fingering Colonel Mustard. That print now fails to provide a good reason to believe that Colonel Mustard committed the murder.

These discoveries still might not halt the investigation. Suppose that an overeager detective argues that a Colonel committed the murder, and Colonel Mustard was the only Colonel, so he must have done it. Mustard's defenders will, of course, ask, "How do you know that a Colonel did it?" The detective's only answer is that Colonel Mustard did it, and he is a Colonel, so a Colonel did it. This short chain of arguments clearly begs the question, so it provides no good reason or ground for the belief that Colonel Mustard did it.

This little story brings out several essential features of grounds. For a believer to have positive epistemic support for her belief, she must have some ground that is (a) not neutral between competing beliefs (as when Plum and Mustard wear the same size boots); and also (b) not undermined (as when the bloody boots are discovered); and also (c) not question-begging (as in the detective's argument). These three conditions must all be met for any apparent ground to be a real ground for a belief. There might be other conditions as well, but these three conditions are all necessary for a ground to provide any positive epistemic support.

Still, merely having some ground is not sufficient to make a belief justified in the relevant way. Even if there is some reason to believe that Colonel Mustard did do it, there might be stronger reason to believe that he did not do it. For example, if Miss Scarlet is very trustworthy and testifies that she saw Professor Plum commit the murder alone, and Professor Plum himself confesses, then together this is enough to defeat the bloody boot print as evidence against Colonel Mustard. If the detective had this new evidence but continued to believe that Mustard did it solely on the basis of the bloody boot print, then the detective's belief would not be adequately supported, and he ought not to believe that Mustard did it, because he would have better reason to believe that Plum did it alone. Defeaters like this will be called *overriders*. One ground or reason *conflicts* with another when the former provides a ground or reason to believe something to the contrary. One ground or reason *overrides* another when both they conflict and the former is stronger.

Overriders are crucially different from the defeaters discussed before. The discovery that Professor Plum also wears size-thirteen boots shows that the bloody boot print provides no reason to believe that the murder was committed by Colonel Mustard instead of Professor Plum. Still, Plum's boot size is not any reason to believe that Plum committed the murder (as opposed to Mustard) or that Mustard did not commit the murder. Similarly, the bloody boots in the woods undermine the evidential force of the bloody boot print as a reason to believe that Colonel Mustard did it without providing any reason to believe that anyone else did it or that Mustard did not do it (since anyone might have worn and discarded those boots). Defeaters like this will be called *underminers*. One reason *undermines* another when the former does not provide any reason to believe anything to the contrary but still does make the conflicting reason inadequate for justified belief.

Even if a ground is neither undermined nor overridden, it still might not be strong enough to justify belief. If the only evidence for or against Colonel Mustard's guilt is the bloody boot print, it is not *enough* to show that a jury *ought* to believe that the Colonel is guilty. The positive support from the boot print is, then, not *adequate* by itself for justified belief in these circumstances. There might also not be adequate reason to believe that Mustard did not do it, so maybe observers ought to suspend belief, that is, withhold belief from both the claim and its denial. Anyway, to be adequate, positive support must be strong enough that one ought to believe rather than either disbelieving or suspending belief.[15]

How strong is strong enough? That seems to depend on the context and, especially, on what is at stake in the belief. Context also might affect what counts as support at all. How this works and how much support is required are controversial, and I will not prejudge these issues. I will not build any specific view about when or how much support is adequate into the concept of adequately justified belief.

In particular, nothing I say depends on any extreme view about how much support a belief needs in order to be justified adequately. Many critics dismiss skepticism out of hand because they think that it requires certainty for justified belief (or knowledge). Although I will defend a limited version of moral skepticism, my arguments definitely will not require certainty for justified belief (or for knowledge). Indeed, my arguments will not require any unusual degree of support for anything. The support need only be adequate according to normal standards as revealed in everyday examples like that of Colonel Mustard.

Keeping these qualifications in mind, some technical terminology will help: A feature is a *prima facie* reason or ground when it appears to be a reason or ground but still might be completely undermined or neutral or question-begging. When it *is* completely undermined or neutral or question-begging, then the prima facie reason is *merely* prima facie. A merely prima facie reason has no epistemic force, so it is not a real reason at all but at most the misleading appearance of a reason. In contrast, a reason that is not merely prima facie is a *pro tanto* reason (or a *good* reason). Pro tanto reasons can be overridden, in which case they are *merely* pro tanto reasons, but they still have some epistemic force. If a reason is neither undermined nor overridden, then it is a *non-overridden* reason. A non-overridden reason that also overrides all conflicting reasons, if any, is an *overriding* reason. If an overriding reason is strong enough that one ought to believe what it supports as opposed to suspending belief, then it is an *adequate* reason for belief. Adequate reasons for belief are still *defeasible* in the sense that they *might* be either overridden or completely undermined in the future, but at least for now they are neither merely pro tanto nor merely prima facie.

It is often unclear which of these kinds of grounds and justifiedness are at issue in various theories in epistemology and moral epistemology. Some moral intuitionists say that their theories are about when beliefs are justified prima facie, although it is not clear whether they see prima facie justifiedness as compatible

---

15. A reason that is inadequate for belief might be adequate for a good guess. If I can win a prize by picking the month of Jim's wedding anniversary, and I know that more people are married in June than in any other month, then I seem to have an adequate reason to guess that Jim's anniversary is in June. I am still not justified in *believing* that Jim's anniversary is in June.

with undermining and, hence, with no real justification at all. These and other moral epistemologists really seem to be interested in whether certain factors make moral beliefs pro tanto justified by providing positive support that is not undermined. However, pro tanto grounds can be overridden and, hence, inadequate. Inadequately justified belief, even when true, is not enough for knowledge. Thus, if moral epistemologists want to show that moral beliefs are justified in the way that is traditionally required for knowledge, then they need moral beliefs to be more than merely pro tanto justified. Moreover, the weak thesis that some moral beliefs are pro tanto justified is compatible with the skeptical view that support for moral beliefs is always defeated in some way or other, so no moral belief is ever justified adequately, and we never ought to believe any moral claim. To capture the debate between such skeptics and their opponents, I will henceforth call a (moral or non-moral) belief justified only when it is adequately justified, unless otherwise indicated. Our topic, then, will be adequate positive epistemic justifiedness.

4.2.4. *Personally versus Impersonally versus Wholly Justified*

Yet another distinction arises from what are known as Gettier examples. Since Plato, most philosophers have believed that justified true belief is sufficient for knowledge. Over 2000 years after Plato, this traditional definition was famously denied by Bertrand Russell (1948) and Edmund Gettier (1963), who described examples where justified true belief does not seem sufficient for knowledge. In one example (modified from Russell), a clock stops at 8:00. Twelve hours later Bethany glances at the stopped clock; it reads 8:00, so she believes that the time is 8:00. This belief is true. The clock has never stopped in years, and there is no way to tell that it is not working now (except to wait long enough), so the believer seems justified in believing that the clock is working and that it is 8:00. But Bethany still does not seem to *know* that it is 8:00. So she seems to have justified true belief without knowledge.

It is worth noting that Gettier problems can also arise when *moral* beliefs are based on "broken" sources. Imagine that, on the basis of a new statistical study, Jeremy believes that executions do not deter murder but actually increase the rate of murder; so he concludes that capital punishment is morally wrong. Now add that the data was fabricated, and the study is incorrect: executions do deter murder. Jeremy's conclusion still might be justified, if he has no way of telling that the study is faulty. Jeremy's conclusion also might be true, if capital punishment is morally wrong for some other reason, such as that capital punishment is inhumane or discriminatory, which Jeremy never considers. Jeremy's belief is then analogous to Bethany's belief that the time is 8:00, and Jeremy's study is analogous to Bethany's clock. Since both sources of belief are problematic, Jeremy seems to lack knowledge for the same reasons as Bethany.

Defenders of capital punishment might respond that Jeremy's belief can't be justified true belief because it can't be true, since capital punishment is not immoral. However, the example can easily be modified to fit this moral claim.

Suppose that a new statistical study convinces Jeremy that executions do deter murder, so capital punishment is not immoral. Now add that the study is incorrect, and executions do not deter murder. Jeremy's conclusion still might be justified and true, if what makes it true is something separate, such as that capital punishment is required for just retribution. Here again Jeremy lacks knowledge because his moral belief is based on a problematic source. So Gettier examples can arise for some moral beliefs regardless of which moral beliefs are true.

Despite the persuasiveness and pervasiveness of Gettier examples, epistemologists do not agree about precisely how to diagnose or cure their ills. In the clock example, some say that Bethany lacks knowledge that it is 8:00 because her belief is based on a false belief that the clock works. Others say that Bethany lacks knowledge because her basis for belief is not reliable in the circumstances. Yet others say that she lacks knowledge because what makes it 8:00 is independent of what causes Bethany to believe that it is 8:00, or because of this counterfactual: Bethany would still believe that it is 8:00 if it were not 8:00. And so on. These competing diagnoses lead to a wide variety of proposals for fixing the traditional analysis of knowledge. (Cf. Shope 1983; and Fogelin 1994, chaps. 1–4.)

What matters for my purposes here is not the analysis of knowledge but whether Bethany is justified in believing that it is 8:00. She does seem justified in one way. Bethany has strong grounds for believing that it is 8:00, and her grounds are neither overridden nor undermined by any information that she possesses. Bethany does base her belief in the time on a false belief about the clock, but she lacks any information that should make her suspect that the clock stopped. Let's imagine that she also lacks any easy access to such information, since she is in a hurry and has time only for a quick glance. She is not just lazy or careless. (We could add that the clock runs intermittently and happens to be running as Bethany waits to check whether it is running.) Thus, careful, rational people who are limited to the same experiences, information, and access as Bethany would use the same process or procedure to reach the same belief. They would also recommend that others form the same belief on the same basis. That makes Bethany seem justified in one way.

The problem is that we, as more informed observers, know that Bethany is lucky. We know that Bethany bases her belief in the time on a false belief about the clock. Because of this, rational people who possess the additional information would not endorse Bethany's grounds as adequate in these circumstances. So Bethany seems not justified in this other way.

The epistemic status that Bethany lacks concerns the relation between her grounds and her belief. We informed observers know that this relation is inadequate, even if Bethany has no way (for the moment) of discovering its deficiency. This defect does not show that there is anything wrong with Bethany as a believer. She is still as trustworthy in general as other believers. There is also nothing wrong with her procedure in general. Normally, looking at a clock that has worked for years is a reliable way to tell the time. Nonetheless, if we concentrate on the particular circumstances and on the relation between Bethany's grounds and her belief independently of her procedure and of her as a believer, then our assessment of that relation is negative, because we informed observers know that the clock is broken.[16]

Accordingly, we can contrast two ways to be justified:[17]

A believer is *personally justified* if and only if the believer's grounds are adequate, given the information that is available to that believer.

A believer is *impersonally justified* if and only if the believer's grounds are adequate, given full and accurate information.

To be impersonally justified, a believer need not actually have full information. All that is required is a *counterfactual*: If someone did have full information, then that person would properly assess the believer's grounds as adequate. The definition refers to *full* information, because partial additional information can make the believer's grounds seem inadequate, when even more information would make those grounds seem adequate again, and so on. The only definitely stable resting point is full information. The reference to full information then makes the notion *impersonal*, for it does not matter which person has which information, if the grounds must be adequate from the perspective of full information. Since no higher standard applies, it would make little difference here if, instead of referring to full information, I said simply that a believer is impersonally justified if and only if the believer's grounds are adequate.[18]

Bethany illustrates this distinction. If Bethany had full information, she would know that other clocks all over town also read 8:00. Then she would have adequate grounds for believing that it is 8:00. But Bethany still would not take her original grounds—her belief that the particular clock in her office works—as adequate to make

16. A parallel distinction applies to actions. Suppose Suzy struggles as Paul pushes her into a car. Oliver observes their struggle and believes Paul is kidnapping Suzy, so he runs over and pounds Paul to save Suzy. Unbeknownst to Oliver, Paul is a plain-clothes police officer who is arresting Suzy for murder. Was Oliver justified in interfering? Yes, in one way; but no, in another. An informed rational impartial observer would advise Oliver not to interfere (assuming that Suzy's arrest is proper), but a rational impartial observer with access only to Oliver's information might advise Oliver to do just what he did (assuming that Oliver's mistake is reasonable). In such cases, many (though not all) legal systems say that Oliver has an excuse but no justification. (Cf. *People v. Young* 1962; and Austin 1961.) We can also say that, even though Oliver's act is wrong, he is not responsible, and it is not his fault, so his act does not show anything bad about his reason or motive or about him as a person. Analogously, Bethany is not responsible for her false belief about the clock. Who would have suspected that it was broken? It is not her fault, and Bethany is not blameworthy or irresponsible as a believer. Why not? Because, like Oliver, Bethany has an excuse, even if she lacks any adequate grounds.

17. Fogelin (1994, 17–21) uses a similar distinction to solve Gettier problems. Compare Lehrer's (1990, 115 and 135) distinctions among personally, verifically, and completely justified. My discussion owes a great deal to both of these sources.

18. To be justified impersonally is to be justified objectively, so what is justified personally might seem to be justified subjectively. Unfortunately, the term "subjective" is ambiguous and misleading. A believer seems to be justified subjectively if the believer has grounds and sees those grounds as adequate. Such a subjectively justified believer still might not be personally justified if those grounds or that assessment of those grounds conflicts or does not cohere with the believer's other beliefs. That is why I contrast personal and impersonal instead of subjective and objective justifiedness.

her justified in believing that it is 8:00. She and other informed rational people would reject those original grounds as inadequate, because they know that this particular clock stopped. Thus, Bethany is personally justified but not impersonally justified.

Critics might insist that Bethany is justified in the *normal* sense of that term. The important point, however, is that Bethany's grounds can be assessed from several perspectives. Her grounds are adequate from her personal perspective. They are not adequate from a fully informed impersonal perspective. The distinction is what matters here, not the word.

It still might not seem obvious which of these ways of being justified is at issue in various debates in epistemology. Part of the goal in that field seems to be personal justifiedness. Most people want to avoid being irresponsible or at fault epistemically (as well as morally). Maybe that is all that some people want. However, most epistemologists would not be satisfied if their theories showed how people can be personally justified but did not show how anyone could ever be impersonally justified. To be personally justified is, after all, compatible with being ignorant in the same way as Bethany in our Gettier example. Surely, most foundationalists, coherentists, naturalists, and externalists want more than that. They don't want to rely on broken clocks. Moreover, most skeptics are not trying to show that believers are irresponsible or at fault or bad as believers, so they would be satisfied if they could show that believers are never impersonally justified. This makes the status of being impersonally justified an essential topic in epistemology.

Since non-skeptics want to be both personally and impersonally justified, the total topic can be captured by a conjunctive concept:

> A believer is *wholly justified* if and only if the believer is justified both personally and impersonally.

To be wholly justified, then, a believer needs grounds that are adequate from the perspective of the believer's information and also adequate from the perspective of full information.

Consequently, I will henceforth call a (moral or non-moral) belief justified only when it is wholly justified, unless otherwise indicated. Our topic, then, will be whether and how moral beliefs can be wholly, adequately, positively, and epistemically justified.

One more crucial distinction needs to be drawn, but, before I get to that distinction (in chapter 5), it needs to be motivated by introducing some arguments for Academic moral skepticism. That is the task of the next section.

4.3. Arguments Against Justified Moral Belief

Epistemological moral skeptics offer a variety of arguments for their position. Here I will focus on two arguments for Academic skepticism about justified moral belief, but these arguments could be reformulated to support skepticism about moral knowledge. I will return to Pyrrhonian moral skepticism in chapters 5–6. In the current section, 4.3, whenever I refer to moral skepticism, I will have in mind Academic skepticism about justified moral belief.

The arguments to be discussed here are versions of well-known arguments for Academic skepticism about all beliefs of any kind, but Academic moral skeptics apply these arguments to morality in particular. Although these arguments can also be used outside morality, they should not be dismissed simply because they are general. If the problems raised by these arguments cannot be solved at least in morality, then we cannot be justified in believing any moral claims, so Academic moral skepticism is true.

Moreover, I will argue below that these skeptical arguments have special force within morality. One reason is that special problems with moral beliefs create a greater need for inferential confirmation. (See section 9.4.) Also, many smart people actually do believe and have some reason to believe in the skeptical hypothesis of moral nihilism. (Recall chapter 3.) The role of these differences between moral beliefs and other beliefs will come out as we outline the skeptical arguments.

4.3.1. A Regress Argument

The first featured argument is a regress argument, which derives from Sextus Empiricus (1996, book I, chap. XV). Arguments of this kind sometimes concern knowledge, but the version here will focus on justified belief. Its goal is to lay out all of the ways in which a person might be justified in believing something and then to argue that none of them works.

The first premise denies that any moral belief can be justified non-inferentially (that is, independently of the believer's ability to infer that belief):

> (1) If any person S is ever justified in believing any moral claim that p, then S must be able to infer p from some other beliefs of S.

In short, any justified moral belief must be justified by some inference.[19]

Premise (1) is often supported by examples of moral disagreements and of moral beliefs that are distorted by cultural and psychological forces. (See sections 3.2.1 and 9.4.) When moral believers disagree, both believers might be permissively or instrumentally or somewhat or personally justified, but it is hard to see how both conflicting moral beliefs could be positively, epistemically, adequately, and impersonally justified apart from any inference at all. To claim to be so justified in the face of disagreement without being able to give any reason that could be expressed in any inference would seem dogmatic, arrogant, and disrespectful of those with whom one disagrees. Even if some moral beliefs are not subject to disagreement, moral disagreements and distortions are widespread enough to make all of morality an area where inferential justification is needed, according to moral skeptics. (See section 9.5.1.) This need is registered in premise (1).

---

19. To be justified by an inference is to be justified by either an actual inference or a potential inference that the believer could but does not draw. Thus, believers are justified by an inference when an ability to infer is required for them to be justified.

Once inference is required, there are only three options:

(2) Any inference must have either (a) no normative premises or (b) some normative premises but no moral premises or (c) some moral premises.

Option (a) might seem to have advantages if non-normative premises are easier to justify than normative premises. This is why some naturalists try to derive morality from science.

However, moral skeptics deny that non-normative premises alone could ever be enough to justify conclusions that are moral and, hence, normative:

(3) No person S is ever justified in believing any moral claim that p by an inference with no normative premises.

If an inference has no normative premises at all, but its conclusion is that an act is morally wrong, then the inference seems to depend on a suppressed premise that all acts with certain non-normative features are morally wrong. Such suppressed premises seem moral and, hence, normative. But then the crucial inference does not really work without any normative premises. So premise (3) seems safe.

The next possibility is to justify a moral conclusion with an inference whose premises are not moral but still are normative in some other way. The most popular variety within this approach is contractarianism. Such contractarians start with supposedly non-moral premises about who is rational and sometimes also about who is impartial. Then they argue that rational impartial people would agree to certain moral rules (or norms or standards), so the corresponding moral beliefs are true or justified. A basic problem with this approach is that inferences like these assume that an act is morally wrong if it violates a rule that would be accepted by all people who are rational and impartial in the specified ways. This bridge principle might seem innocuous at first, because it has little content until "rational" and "impartial" are defined. Once these terms are defined, however, the bridge principle ceases to be morally neutral. This becomes clear when different contractarians use different notions of rationality and impartiality to reach conflicting moral conclusions.

There are other arguments from non-moral norms to moral conclusions, but they run into similar problems.[20] Moral skeptics generalize to the conclusion that:

(4) No person S is ever justified in believing any moral claim that p by an inference with some normative premises but no moral premises.

Premises (1)–(4) together imply that moral beliefs must be justified by actual or potential inferences from moral beliefs.

This creates a problem. Although the justifying premises must include some moral beliefs, not just any moral beliefs will do:

(5) No person S is ever justified in believing a moral claim that p by an inference with a moral premise unless S is also justified in believing that moral premise itself.

---

20. Premises (3) and (4) are also often supported by the general doctrine that logic is conservative in the sense that all of the content of a valid argument must be contained somewhere in the premises, so you can't get out what you didn't put in. See, for example, Pigden 1991, 423.

Premise (5) is denied by some contextualists (Wellman 1971; Annis 1978; Timmons 1998), who claim that, even if a moral belief is not itself justified, if it is shared within a certain social context without being questioned, then it can be used to justify other moral beliefs. However, the fact that a moral belief happens to be held without question by everyone in a social group is not sufficient to make anyone justified in believing it or what follows from it. To see this, suppose that everyone in a small town believes without question that it is immoral for a black person to marry a white person. They infer that it is immoral for Ray, who is black, to marry Terry, who is white. This conclusion is not justified, because the general belief is not justified (since it should be questioned, even if it isn't). Indeed, every belief would be justified if a belief could be justified simply by inferring it from an unjustified belief, since every belief can be validly inferred from itself. The only way to avoid such absurd results, according to moral skeptics, is to accept (5).

But then how can the needed moral premises be justified? The only remaining alternative is to infer the moral premises from still other moral beliefs which must also be justified by inferring them from still other moral beliefs, and so on. To justify a moral belief thus requires a chain (or branching tree) of justifying beliefs or premises. This justifying chain can take only two forms, so:

> (6) No person S is justified in believing any moral claim that p by an infer-
> ence from moral premises unless S is justified by a chain of inferences that
> either goes on infinitely or includes p itself as an essential premise.

The latter kind of chain is usually described as circular, although its structure is more complex than a simple circle.

Moral skeptics deny that either kind of chain can justify any moral belief. First:

> (7) No person S is ever justified in believing any moral claim that p by a chain
> of inferences that includes p as an essential premise.

Any argument that includes its conclusion as a premise will be valid and will remain valid if other premises are added. However, anyone who doubts the conclusion will have just as much reason to doubt the premise. So, skeptics claim that nothing is gained when a premise just restates the belief to be justified.

Premise (7) is opposed by moral coherentists. Recent coherentists have emphasized that they are not inferring a belief from itself in a linear way. Instead, a moral belief is supposed to be justified because it coheres in some way with a body of beliefs that is coherent in some way. Still, moral skeptics deny that coherence is enough for justification. One reason is that the internal coherence of a set of beliefs is not evidence of any relation to anything outside of the beliefs. Moreover, every belief—no matter how ridiculous—can cohere with some body of beliefs that is internally coherent. Such possibilities are supposed to show why coherence is not enough to justify moral beliefs and why premise (7) holds.

The final possible form of justification is an infinite chain. Moral skeptics, of course, claim that:

(8) No person S is ever justified in believing any moral claim that *p* by a chain of inferences that goes on infinitely.

Someone who denied this premise could be called a moral infinitist, but nobody clearly develops this approach (though suggestions can be found in Peirce 1934, 154–55, 158, and 186; Brink 1989, appendix 1; and Sanford 1984).

Now moral skeptics can draw a final conclusion. (1)–(8) together imply:

(9) No person is ever justified in believing any moral claim.

This is Academic skepticism about justified moral belief. It might seem implausible, but the regress argument is valid, so its conclusion can be escaped only by denying one or more of its premises.

Different premises are denied by different opponents of moral skepticism. Moral intuitionists deny premise (1). Moral naturalists deny premise (3). Moral normativists deny premise (4). Moral contextualists deny premise (5). Moral coherentists deny premise (7). And moral infinitists would deny premise (8). The regress argument, thus, provides a useful way to classify theories in moral epistemology, regardless of whether it establishes moral skepticism.

The most important question, however, is whether the regress argument shows that Academic moral skepticism is true. I have tried to say enough to give some initial plausibility to the premises of the regress argument, but each premise deserves much more careful attention. I will discuss premise (3) and naturalism in chapter 7, premise (4) and normativism in chapter 8, premise (1) and intuitionism in chapter 9, and premise (7) and coherentism in chapter 10. I will return to a different form of contextualism and premise (5) in sections 5.3 and 6.5–6.6. There is much to be said on both sides of this regress argument for Academic moral skepticism. That is one reason why Pyrrhonian moral skeptics end up suspending belief about its conclusion.

4.3.2. *A Skeptical Hypothesis Argument*

The second featured argument, which derives from René Descartes (1641), starts from the common experience of being deceived. For example, yesterday I was driving down a strange road. I thought I saw a lake in the distance. My wife thought and said that it was really a river, not a lake. We were in a hurry, so we did not check it out, but I still believe that it was a lake. Is my belief justified? Not if my experience was compatible with its being either a lake or a river and I have no other ground for believing that my wife was incorrect. My belief that it is a lake also cannot be justified if I cannot rule out the possibility that it was a bay or a bayou, even if I can rule out the possibility of a river. Such everyday examples suggest the general principle that I am not justified in believing something if there is any contrary hypothesis that I cannot rule out.

This does not mean that I must self-consciously think about every other possibility and run through an argument to rule out each one. If I don't think about the possibility of an inlet off the ocean, I still can rule out that possibility if I possess the background information that we are in Kansas, which is nowhere near any ocean, assuming that I have the minimal intelligence needed to use this information. As long as I possess that information and intelligence, I am able to rule out the hypothesis of an inlet off the ocean, even if I never actually bother to use that information to rule out that possibility. However, if I have no information from any source that could be used to rule out the possibility of an inlet, then I cannot rule out that possibility. The same goes for the possibilities of a bay and a bayou. If I cannot rule out any one of the contrary hypotheses, then I am not justified in believing that what I see is a lake. This is supposed to be a common standard for justified belief.

When this supposedly common sense principle is applied thoroughly, it leads to skepticism. All that skeptics need to show is that, for each belief, there is some contrary hypothesis that cannot be ruled out. It need not be the same hypothesis contrary to every belief. However, skeptics usually buy wholesale instead of retail, so they seek a single hypothesis that is contrary to all or very many common beliefs and which cannot be ruled out in any way.

The famous Cartesian hypothesis is of a demon who deceives me in all of my beliefs about the external world while also ensuring that my beliefs are completely coherent. If there is such a deceiving demon, then there really is no lake when I think that I see one. Nobody claims that such a deceiving demon actually exists, but that is not needed for the argument. All the argument needs is that a deceiving demon is possible. Descartes' deceiving demon does seem possible.[21] In addition, this possibility cannot be ruled out by any experiences or beliefs of any kind, because of how the deceiving demon is defined. Whatever I seem to see, feel, hear, smell, or taste, my sensations might all be caused by a deceiving demon. The deceiving demon hypothesis is contrary to many of my beliefs, but that is just what one would expect if there were a deceiving demon. Since there is no way to rule out this skeptical hypothesis, my beliefs about the lake are not justified, according to the above principle. Moreover, there is nothing special about my beliefs about the lake. Everything I believe about the external world (or even mathematics) is incompatible with the deceiving demon hypothesis. Skeptics conclude that no such belief is justified.

This kind of argument can be applied to moral beliefs in several ways. First, another demon might deceive us about morality (either alone or in addition to other topics). Almost everyone believes that it is morally wrong to torture babies just for fun, but we might be deceived in our beliefs that babies feel pain or that they have moral rights. A demon might make us believe that some creatures have moral rights when really they do not, although other things do; or a demon might make us believe that some creatures have moral rights when really nothing does (just as a demon might deceive us into believing that some women are witches

---

21. Despite arguments often attributed to Putnam (1981, chap. 1). For responses to Putnam, see DeRose and Warfield 1999, part one.

when really none are). Such a deceiving demon seems possible and cannot be ruled out by the fact that it seems obvious that babies have moral rights, any more than Descartes' deceiving demon could be ruled out by the fact that it seems obvious to me when I am swimming in water. Such responses would beg the question.

Some philosophers (e.g., Peirce 1934) object to such deception scenarios on the grounds that nobody really does believe in such deceiving demons and nobody could have any reason to believe in them, so skeptical hypotheses like these are idle and do not express real doubts. I do not see why this matters, so this response strikes me as inadequate. However, I do not want my argument to depend on this assumption, so I will avoid this objection by discussing a different skeptical scenario.

The same kind of argument can be constructed with a skeptical hypothesis that people really do believe and give reasons to believe.[22] We already discussed this one:

Moral Nihilism = Nothing is morally wrong, required, bad, good, etc.[23]

This hypothesis is constructed so as to leave no way to rule it out. Since moral nihilists question all of our beliefs that anything is morally wrong, and so on, they leave us with no moral starting points on which to base arguments against them without begging the question at issue. If we cannot start from moral premises, then the only way to refute moral nihilism is to derive moral conclusions from morally neutral premises, but all such attempts are subject to strong criticisms from many philosophers, not only moral skeptics. So there seems to be no way to rule out moral nihilism. (See part II.) Thus, this hypothesis fits perfectly into a skeptical argument.

The skeptical hypothesis argument is clearest when applied to an example. Moral nihilism implies that it is not morally wrong to torture babies just for fun. So, according to the general principle above, one must be able to rule out moral nihilism in order to be justified in believing that torturing babies just for fun is morally wrong. Moral skeptics conclude that this moral belief is not justified. More precisely:

(i) I am not justified in believing that moral nihilism is false.
(ii) I am justified in believing that (*p*) "It is morally wrong to torture babies just for fun" entails (*q*) "Moral nihilism is false."

---

22. Defenders of something like moral nihilism include Mackie (1946, 1977), Robinson (1948), J. P. Burgess (1979), Hinckfuss (1987), Garner (1994), J. A. Burgess (1998), Joyce (2001), and Greene (forthcoming). Parallel arguments could be constructed with other coherent but extreme hypotheses, such as moral egoism (see Rachels 1971), relativism Harman (1977), and so on, which people really do believe and give reasons to believe. However, I will focus on moral nihilism.

23. This hypothesis is normally embedded in a larger theory that explains why most people deny it. I will focus on the hypothesis alone when its logical relations are what matter, but it should be remembered that moral nihilists also try to explain away contrary appearances and beliefs, so their overall theory is more complex than this central claim in isolation.

(iii) If I am justified in believing that p, and I am justified in believing that p entails q,[24] then I am justified in believing that q.

(iv) Therefore, I am not justified in believing that (p) it is morally wrong to torture babies just for fun.

This moral belief (p) is not especially problematic in any way. Indeed, it seems as obvious as any definite moral belief.[25] Hence, the argument can be generalized to cover any moral belief. Moral skeptics conclude that no moral belief is justified.[26]

There are two main ways to respond to such skeptical arguments. First, some anti-skeptics deny (i) and claim that skeptical hypotheses can be ruled out somehow. They might argue that moral nihilism can be ruled out by logic and semantics alone, because it is inconsistent or meaningless or semantically incoherent. I already countered this move in section 3.3. Other attempts to rule out moral nihilism are made by naturalists, normativists, intuitionists, and coherentists. These attempts mirror the stages of the regress argument in the preceding Section (4.3.1) and will be discussed in detail in chapters 7–10, respectively. The basic dilemma is clear: moral nihilism cannot be ruled out without at least some moral assumptions, but any moral assumptions beg the question against moral nihilism, no matter how obvious they might seem to us. If there is no way around or out of this dilemma, then there is no way to rule out moral nihilism, as premise (i) claims.

Another response, which has gained popularity recently (DeRose and Warfield 1999, part two), is to deny premise (iii). This is often described as a principle of *closure*. Since a belief entails the denial of every contrary hypothesis, this closure principle in effect says that I cannot be justified in believing p unless I am justified in denying every hypothesis contrary to p, that is, unless I can rule out *all* contrary hypotheses. This principle has been denied by relevant alternative theorists, who claim instead that only relevant hypotheses need to be ruled out. On this theory, if skeptical hypotheses are not relevant, then a belief that it is morally wrong to torture babies just for fun can be justified, even if the believer cannot rule out moral nihilism.

For this response to have force, however, opponents of moral skepticism need to say why moral nihilism is irrelevant. It certainly seems relevant, for the simple reason that it is coherent, believed, supported by arguments, and directly contrary to

24. Some might want to add that it must also be true that p entails q, or that I am justified in believing the conjunction of p and (p entails q), but these additions would not affect the main points here.

25. Disjunctions might seem more obvious, such as: it is morally wrong either to torture babies just for fun or to commit genocide or to cheat just to win a game against a friend or.... The disjunction could go on; and the longer it is, the more chance that at least one of its disjuncts is true. Long disjunctions could be avoided by existential quantifiers. It might seem even more obvious that *some* act is morally wrong. However, to use that claim against moral nihilists is like saying "Surely, something is a sin" to those who deny (the religious notion of) sins or "Surely, someone is a witch" to refute those who deny witches.

26. The argument could also be run against moral knowledge: I do not know that moral nihilism is not true; but I do know that "It is morally wrong to torture babies just for fun" entails "Moral nihilism is not true"; and, if I know that p, and I know that p entails q, then I know that q; so I do not know that it is morally wrong to torture babies just for fun. However, I will focus on justified moral belief.

the moral belief that is supposed to be justified. Compare Curly, who gets a sealed letter from Larry. Curly believes that the letter is a dinner invitation, but Moe thinks that the letter is a request for a favor. Each has some reason for his belief, each tells the other, and their reasons are equally strong. In these circumstances, before reading the letter, Curly does not seem epistemically justified in believing that the letter is a dinner invitation unless he can rule out Moe's contrary hypothesis that it is a request for a favor. That hypothesis cannot be dismissed as irrelevant as long as it is coherent and believed for some reason. The same standards suggest that the hypothesis of moral nihilism also cannot be dismissed as irrelevant as long as it is coherent and believed for some reason. Just as Curly needs to open the letter to rule out Moe's hypothesis before he can be justified in believing his contrary hypothesis, so opponents of moral nihilism need to find some way to rule out moral nihilism before they can be epistemically justified in their positive moral beliefs.

This point holds even if it is legitimate to dismiss skeptical hypotheses that nobody believes or has any reason to believe. The hypothesis of moral nihilism is coherent, some intelligent people believe it, and they give reasons to believe it. In addition to those already discussed in section 3.2, some people are led to moral nihilism because they cannot find any defensible moral theory. If consequentialism is indefensible (as its critics argue), and if deontological restrictions and permissions are mysterious and unfounded (as their critics argue), then some people might believe moral nihilism because they rule out the alternatives. The point is not that such reasons for moral nihilism are adequate. The point here is only that there is enough reason to believe moral nihilism that it cannot baldly be dismissed as irrelevant on this basis (See also section 6.5.)

If moral nihilism is relevant, and if closure holds for all or relevant alternatives, and if moral nihilism cannot be ruled out in any way, then moral skepticism follows. That's a lot of "ifs." Each will be discussed in more detail later (chapters 5–6). The point here is just that moral nihilism poses a serious challenge that leads some toward Academic moral skepticism.

4.3.3. *Relations between the Arguments*

These two arguments for Academic moral skepticism differ in many ways. Some commentators claim that these two arguments are so different that they do not really support the same position. But that claim is misleading. The conclusions are the same. Both arguments try to show that no moral believer is justified in the relevant way—wholly, adequately, positively, and epistemically.

Moreover, the arguments are mutually supportive. One crucial premise in the skeptical hypothesis argument claims that nothing can rule out moral nihilism. The most common and the best way to support that premise is to criticize each method for ruling out moral nihilism. That is just one instance of what the regress argument does more generally. Thus, if the regress argument works, it supports the skeptical hypothesis argument by establishing its crucial premise.

Conversely, one crucial premise, (1), in the regress argument claims that no moral belief can be justified non-inferentially, so moral beliefs need inferential justification. The need for such justification could be established in several ways, but one way is to point out a contrary belief that has not been ruled out. That is what the skeptical hypothesis argument does. Thus, if the skeptical hypothesis argument works, it supports the regress argument by establishing a crucial premise.

To Academic moral skeptics, this relation of mutual support might seem to make both arguments better. However, to anti-skeptics, this mutual support might seem to make the two arguments circular (jointly or separately). In the end, the force of the arguments depends on the defensibility of non-skeptical views in moral epistemology. If naturalism, normativism, intuitionism, or coherentism works to justify some moral beliefs and/or to rule out moral nihilism, then this will undermine crucial premises in both arguments for Academic moral skepticism. That is why we need to look carefully at the alternatives in chapters 7–10 before we can fully assess these arguments for Academic moral skepticism.

It should be clear already that these arguments pose a kind of dilemma. The arguments for Academic moral skepticism seem strong. Yet most people reject their conclusion. Even after working through these arguments, most people still think that they are justified in believing some moral claims, such as that it is morally wrong to torture babies just for fun. Moreover, such moral beliefs do have a lot going for them. They seem obvious to many people who seem impartial and informed. These moral beliefs also connect well with other beliefs, both moral and non-moral. So some moral beliefs seem justified to some extent. Nonetheless, this appearance does not refute or even undermine the arguments for moral skepticism. Arguments cannot be refuted or undermined simply by denying their conclusions. Moreover, moral skeptics would predict that and could explain why most people deny their conclusion. Besides, there seems to be something right in the skeptics' arguments insofar as their premises rest on general principles that seem plausible in many examples that are independent of the issues at stake in moral skepticism. So both sides seem to contain some truth.

The problem is to see how this is possible. How can both sides be right when one denies the other? To see how, and to help assess the arguments for moral skepticism, we need to draw one more distinction between ways in which a moral belief can be justified. That is the task of chapters 5 and 6.

5

In Contrast with What?

A cademic moral skepticism strikes most people as implausible, but the arguments for it are hard to refute. That is why many people seek a compromise between academic moral skeptics and their detractors. In my view, the key to compromise lies in contrast classes. This concept is technical and will need to be handled carefully, but it can be introduced with a simple everyday example.

Are jumbo shrimp large? An answer of "Yes" or "No" would be too simple. Jumbo shrimp are large for shrimp, but they are not large for edible marine crustaceans. Whether one sees jumbo shrimp as large or not depends on whether one contrasts jumbo shrimp with other shrimp or with lobsters and crabs. Speakers need not have a fully specified contrast class in mind, but it is silly to argue about whether jumbo shrimp are large if the arguers have in mind very different contrast classes.

This is just one example of a pervasive phenomenon. The same question might be difficult for an introductory course but easy for a graduate seminar. The same temperature on a summer day might be hot for Hanover but cool for Tucson.

When no contrast class is mentioned, claims about what is large, easy, or hot can be indeterminate. Such inspecificity is innocuous when the exact contrast class doesn't matter or when the context makes the contrast class clear enough. However, variation in contrast classes can become important when imprecision creates misunderstanding, as in many philosophical debates.

Contrast classes have proven useful in various areas of philosophy. One example is explanation. (Cf. Van Fraassen 1980, chap. 5.) A high humidity level can explain why it rains rather than not precipitating at all, but humidity cannot explain why it rains rather than snows. Temperature is what explains rain in contrast with snow.

Reasons for action are also relative to contrast classes: our friendship can be a reason for me to bake you a chocolate birthday cake rather than no cake at all, but our friendship is not a reason for me to bake you a chocolate birthday cake instead of a lemon birthday cake, if you and I have no preference between those flavors. Similarly for moral reasons: if I promise to pay you five dollars by Wednesday, then I can have an overriding moral obligation to pay you five dollars on Wednesday instead of Thursday, even if I have no moral reason at all to pay you five dollars on Wednesday instead of Tuesday, or to pay to you with a five dollar bill instead of five one dollar bills (although five hundred pennies might be insulting).

A survey of such cases makes me suspect that all reasons (whether explanatory or justificatory, for acts or for beliefs) are relative to contrast classes in that they are reasons for *x* as opposed to *y* rather than simply for *x*. If so, that universal claim about all reasons would support my position here on epistemic reasons. However, that broader thesis is not necessary for my main views on moral epistemology, so I won't rely on it.

5.1. Contrast Classes in Epistemology

What matters here is the use of contrast classes in epistemology. (Cf. Dretske 1970; and Goldman 1976.) In section 4.2.3, we saw that, if both Colonel Mustard and Professor Plum wear size-thirteen boots, but Miss Scarlet has much smaller feet, then a size-thirteen bloody boot print can provide a reason to believe that the murderer was Colonel Mustard instead of Miss Scarlet without providing any reason to believe that the murderer was Colonel Mustard as opposed to Professor Plum. Similarly for reasons from other sources. Hearing can give you strong reason to believe that a piece of music is by Mozart as opposed to Bob Dylan, even if you have no reason to believe that it is by Mozart as opposed to Salieri. Memory can provide reason to believe that President Kennedy was shot in 1963 as opposed to 1973, even if you can't remember whether it was 1963 or 1962. Testimony by top scientists can supply a reason to believe that the earth in the next century will get warmer rather than colder, even if the scientists do not say whether it will warm by more than three degrees instead of less than three degrees. And so on.

In all such cases, the believer's reasons are relative to contrast classes. These reasons then determine whether the believer is justified. Hence, justified belief will also be relative to contrast classes. These cases thus illustrate the general point that believers are often justified in believing a claim as opposed to other members of one contrast class without being justified in believing the same claim as opposed to other members of a different contrast class.

The fact that such a wide variety of beliefs can be justified relative to some but not all alternatives points towards the position that all justified beliefs are justified only relative to contrast classes. My examples involve explicit evidence that rules out some alternatives without ruling out others. Some externalists might object that other beliefs are justified without explicit evidence, and these beliefs might be justified independent of any contrast class.[1] However, these other beliefs are

---

1. I doubt that reliabilists can avoid contrast classes because the reliability of a process is relative to contrast classes. In certain lighting my vision can reliably tell blue from orange but cannot reliably tell

supposed to be justified in the same sense as beliefs that are justified by evidence. Since so many different kinds of beliefs are justified relative to contrast classes, one would need a special reason to hold that other beliefs are justified independent of any contrast class. There is no such special reason, as far as I can tell, so I conclude that all beliefs are justified (or not) only relative to contrast classes.[2]

What is a contrast class? It is merely a set of propositions, which are potential belief contents,[3] but the members of a contrast class must meet certain restrictions: First, a contrast class must include the belief at issue; otherwise, a believer could not believe it *out of* the class. Second, every contrast class must include at least one other belief; otherwise, there could be nothing to contrast *with*. Third, members of contrast classes must conflict in some way; otherwise, there would be no *contrast*. Specifically, I will assume that members of a contrast class must be contraries in the sense that both cannot be true.[4]

Wouldn't it be simpler to say that a contrast class consists only of a proposition and its negation? Yes, it would be simpler, but this formulation would hide something important: the domain of discourse. If I have a reason to believe that a bird is a crow as opposed to not a crow, this must be a reason to believe that it is a crow as opposed to anything that is not a crow. The quantifier "anything" is indeterminate without a domain of discourse, as logicians recognize. Normally, when we say "anything that is not a crow," we mean something like "any kind of bird that is not a crow." Then to claim a reason to believe that something is a crow as opposed to not a crow is to claim a reason to believe that it is a crow as opposed to any other kind of bird. However, this reason still might not be a reason to believe that it is a crow as opposed to a robot replica of a crow or a perfect image of a crow created in our minds by a mad scientist on Alpha Centauri. Admittedly, when we claim to have a reason to believe that it is a crow, we often claim a reason to believe that it is a crow as opposed to anything else at all, including robots and images. But then what we claim is a reason to believe out of the unlimited contrast

---

blue from green. Other externalists hold that whether S is justified in believing P depends on counterfactuals, such as that S would not believe P if P were not true. On a standard analysis, this counterfactual depends on which possible worlds are "nearby," and contrast classes are needed to specify which worlds are "nearby" by spelling out which alternatives exist in "nearby" worlds. Externalists of these kinds should, therefore, accept my claim that justified belief is relative to contrast classes.

2. I do not claim to have proven this conclusion conclusively. My arguments are only supposed to suggest why a contrastive approach to epistemology is coherent and fruitful. For further arguments, see Schaffer 2004; and Karjalainen and Morton 2003.

3. My framework does not depend on any theory of the nature or identity conditions of propositions. A proposition is whatever it is that can be believed. This loose use sidesteps metaphysical suspicions about propositions.

4. It would not affect my position much if members of contrast classes could conflict merely epistemically in the sense that one provides epistemic reason to doubt the other. Cf. Lipton 1991b, 36–37; and Lehrer 1990, 117–18; on competition. On this broader notion of conflict, "The bird that I see is black" contrasts with "It is so dark that every bird looks black." Such epistemological conflicts seem relevant when discussing whether beliefs are justified epistemically, but, for simplicity, I will stick with examples where the alternatives are logical or semantic contraries.

class. The unlimited contrast class is still a contrast class, so the claimed reason is still relative to a contrast class.

Once a contrast class is specified, believers need to decide which member of that contrast class to believe. Whether a believer ought to believe a certain member in contrast with the other members then depends on how that believer's grounds relate to members of the contrast class. More precisely:

> Someone, S, is justified in believing a proposition, P, out of a contrast class, C, when and only when S is able to rule out all other members of C but is not able to rule out P.[5]

I will express this idea variously by saying that someone is justified in believing something out of a class, or relative to a class, or rather than, in contrast with, instead of, or as opposed to other members of a class. The basic idea remains the same: if there is any other member of the class that the believer is unable to rule out, then the believer is not justified in believing any member out of that class.[6]

For example, if a birdwatcher sees a bird and is able to tell that it is not a cardinal or blue jay or seagull or parrot, then this experience and ability can make the birdwatcher justified in believing that it is a crow out of the contrast class {crow, cardinal, blue jay, seagull, parrot}.[7] That is an accomplishment and an epistemic one, but it is not enough to make the birdwatcher justified in believing that the bird is a crow out of any contrast class that includes ravens, such as {crow, cardinal, blue jay, seagull, parrot, raven}. To be justified relative to that larger

---

5. It might seem that S also needs some positive ground for believing P out of C. Without that requirement, I would be justified in believing that Queen Elizabeth committed a certain murder out of the contrast class {Q, X, Y, Z} whenever I can rule out X, Y, and Z, but I cannot rule out Q, maybe just because I have no idea where the Queen was at the time. The mere fact that I cannot rule out the Queen when I have no positive reason to suspect her might not seem enough to justify me in believing that the Queen did it, even out of a small contrast class. However, two responses are available. First, normally I *can* rule out people like Queen Elizabeth, because it is so unlikely that she would have committed this murder. She had no motive, and she's not the type. Second, even if I could not rule her out, the oddness of calling my belief justified could be explained away: it sounds strange to call my belief justified out of the small contrast class, simply because such small contrast classes don't matter. Nonetheless, it can still be *true* that I am justified out of this small contrast class. Of course, these responses will not satisfy all readers. If such odd implications are too much for you to stomach, feel free to add a clause requiring positive grounds for P in the above account of when a believer is justified. The grounds can still be relative to C. This addition will not affect my main arguments.

6. More precisely, a justified believer must be able to rule out the disjunction of the other members of the contrast class. To see why, imagine a fair lottery with 1000 tickets. I own two tickets, and 998 people own one ticket each. Each of them has a probability of only 0.001 of winning; I have more chance than anyone else, and I know all of this. Does this justify me in believing that I will win as opposed to believing contestant #2 will win, contestant #3 will win, and so on? It seems not, because it is less likely that I will win than that one *or* the other of them will win. Generalizing, I must be able to rule out the disjunction of other members of the contrast class in order to be justified in believing that I will win. I will usually drop this qualification, but this simplification will not affect my arguments.

7. Since members of contrast classes are propositions, each name on this list strictly should be preceded by "it is a . . . ." For simplicity, I will often drop the repetitious "it is a . . ." and refer to members of contrast classes by names. I will also often call members of contrast classes "alternatives."

contrast class, the birdwatcher also needs some ground for believing that the bird is not a raven, that is, for ruling out that last member of the larger contrast class.

The point is *not* that the proposition that is believed must be qualified by a contrast class. If the proposition itself changed with the contrast class, then a birdwatcher who believes that the bird is a crow but never considers ravens could not be contradicted by a more discriminating birdwatcher who knows it is a raven and believes it is not a crow. The proposition must stay constant to explain such disagreements. Instead of propositions, it is reasons or grounds that are relative to contrast classes because different kinds of grounds rule out different alternatives.

It might seem circular to explain one epistemic notion ("justified") in terms of others ("grounds" and "ruling out"). However, the point is *not* to reduce justified belief to non-epistemic notions. It is only to specify how grounds of different sorts for or against different propositions need to fit together in order to make believers justified.

The grounds that make a believer justified out of a certain contrast class are also relative to that same contrast class. A visual experience that is incompatible with the bird being a normal cardinal, blue jay, seagull, or parrot but compatible with the bird being a crow can be enough to make a believer justified out of the contrast class {crow, cardinal, blue jay, seagull, parrot}. However, that same visual experience is not enough to rule out cardinals or seagulls if the contrast class includes mutant cardinals or painted seagulls that look just like crows. Thus, the notions of grounds and ruling out have to be relativized to the same contrast class, C, out of which the believer is supposed to be justified.[8]

It is also important that the notions of grounds and ruling out are broad. In particular, no explicit argument is necessary. To require an explicit argument or any other actual process would be unreasonable because it would make it impossible for anyone ever to be justified in believing anything out of an infinite contrast class. My principle requires only that the believer be *able* to rule out the other alternatives. This ability need not be exercised at the time of belief. The believer would not have this ability without some grounds that would rule out the alternatives, but the believer need not consciously think about these grounds or use them in any procedure in order to be able to rule the alternatives.[9]

Moreover, grounds can rule out alternatives without being conclusive. They can be fallible and defeasible, uncertain and incomplete. Grounds also need not be deductive in form. Inductive grounds are fine, since grounds can rule out a member of a contrast class without entailing that the member is false. The needed grounds might include perception, memory, introspection, reflection, testimony, or any kind of justificatory procedure, which could use any kind of evidence or

8. When I define a contrast class in terms of cardinals, for example, I will mean normal cardinals, except when something else in the contrast class or situation indicates some funny business.

9. I am not able to rule out the hypothesis that I have ten coins in my pocket just because I am able to pull all of the coins out of my pocket and count them. To be able to rule out the hypothesis now, I must be able to rule it out using just the information that I have now. The fact that I am able to get more information *later* cannot make me justified *now*.

only an externally reliable method. This flexibility is what enables my framework to apply to so many different kinds of belief.

This flexibility is also crucial because skeptics are often accused of gaining their conclusions by placing overly stringent restrictions on which grounds are adequate. Nothing like that is going on here. Even non-skeptics need this abstract framework with contrast classes, and skeptics don't need any peculiar limits on the strength of the grounds that can succeed in ruling out an alternative.

All that skeptics need is an alternative that cannot be ruled out by any adequate ground. Descartes' deceiving demon is supposed to accomplish this goal because all our common grounds appear just as we would expect them to appear if we were deceived by Descartes' demon. Hence, it seems to beg the question to use any of those grounds to rule out Descartes' demon. This point applies to all such grounds regardless of strength, so skeptics who cite such skeptical scenarios need not put any special restrictions on the strength of grounds.

Some externalists respond that skeptical scenarios can be ruled out by a certain kind of evidence. In Williamson's version (2000), S's evidence is everything S knows. If S knows that S has hands, this known proposition is evidence that rules out the hypothesis of Descartes' demon because S would not have hands if S were deceived by such a demon (or if S were a brain in a vat). However, to claim that S has such knowledge and, hence, evidence begs the question against a skeptic who is raising the very question of whether S has any knowledge or evidence.[10] Thus, again, all that skeptics need is a rule against begging the question.[11] Beyond that, they need not put any special restrictions on the kinds of grounds that can be used to rule out alternatives.

Indeed, skeptics need not even go so far as to postulate a deceiving demon (Vogel 1990; Fogelin 1994, 193; Hawthorne 2004). An expert birdwatcher who gets a good look at a bird and classifies it as a crow still normally cannot rule out the possibility that it is a mutant raven or a robot that looks just like a crow. The birdwatcher is then not justified in believing that it is a crow as opposed to such uneliminated possibilities, even though these alternatives are eliminable in principle, unlike deceiving demons and other skeptical scenarios. Hence, skeptics don't need their skeptical scenarios to be uneliminable in principle. Nonetheless, for the

10. If any readers still deny that such evidence begs the question, I can add a place in my analysis for kinds of evidence (or grounds): S is justified on evidence of kind K in believing P out of contrast class C if and only if S has evidence of kind K that rules out all members of C except P. Call evidence *internal* when it is restricted to non-factive internal states, such as that I seem to see X and I seem to remember X. Call evidence *external* when it includes factive states or known propositions about the external world, such as that I have hands. If S can rule out skeptical hypotheses with external evidence but not with internal evidence alone, then S *can* be justified in believing commonsense as opposed to skeptical hypotheses on the basis of external evidence, but S still *cannot* be justified in denying skeptical hypotheses or believing commonsense as opposed to skeptical hypotheses on the basis of internal evidence alone. Since skeptics are concerned with internal evidence, I will usually restrict my attention to internal evidence and grounds.

11. It might also beg the question to assume that S has *no* knowledge or evidence against skeptical scenarios, but Pyrrhonian skeptics need not make that assumption, even if Academic skeptics do.

sake of simplicity and tradition, I will focus on skeptical scenarios that are systematically uneliminable.

More formally, we can distinguish two rough sets of alternatives:

The Extreme Contrast Class for P = all propositions contrary to P, including skeptical scenarios that are systematically uneliminable.
The Modest Contrast Class for P = all propositions contrary to P that need to be eliminated in order to meet the usual epistemic standards.

Deceiving demons (and brain-in-vat scenarios) are systematically uneliminable, so they are included in the extreme contrast class but not in the modest contrast class, assuming that the usual epistemic standards do not require believers to be able to eliminate those possibilities. Robins and ravens are in the modest contrast class as well as the extreme contrast class. Many more classes could be defined,[12] and the boundaries and members of these classes could be specified in more detail, but my argument will not depend on details of these classes.

In particular, although the modest contrast class is defined in terms of "the usual epistemic standards,"[13] this formula is just a convenient replacement for a long list of alternatives. The usual standards are no more than the standards that people usually apply. We can determine whether a proposition is in this modest class simply by doing a survey to determine whether most people think it must be ruled out for a belief to be justified. When I describe this modest class in this way, I am not endorsing these standards. I am merely specifying what is in the modest class.

These contrast classes enable us to distinguish levels of justified belief. Imagine that Newt is a novice birdwatcher who sees a bird quickly from faraway. Ellen is an expert birdwatcher who gets a long close look at the same bird, although she never dissects it. Both believe it is a crow. Now consider these judgments:

(1) Newt is justified in believing that it is a crow out of the modest contrast class.
(2) Ellen is justified in believing that it is a crow out of the modest contrast class.
(3) Ellen is justified in believing that it is a crow out of the extreme contrast class.

In this situation, (1) is false, assuming Newt's evidence rules out robins but not ravens, and ravens are in the modest contrast class. Still, (2) is true, assuming Ellen's evidence rules out ravens along with all other members of the modest contrast class,

---

12. Also important is the Rigorous Contrast Class for P, which includes all propositions contrary to P that could somehow be eliminated, even if doing so is not needed in order to meet normal epistemic standards. I discuss this class in Sinnott-Armstrong 2004a, but it seems less important for moral epistemology.

13. The standards to which I refer here do not govern strength or kinds of grounds. They govern only which alternatives need to be ruled out for a belief to be justified.

even if it does not rule out deceiving demons, mutant crows, or robot replicas, since they are not in the modest contrast class. Finally, (3) is false, assuming Ellen cannot rule out such demons, mutants, and robots.

Notice that (3) implies (2), but not conversely, because the extreme contrast class properly includes the modest contrast class. Also notice that the truth-values of (1)–(3) do *not* vary with the speaker's context. (3) is false if asserted in an everyday context, and (2) is true if asserted in a philosophy course, even if saying so seems odd in those contexts. Finally, notice that a speaker who asserts (3) does *not* say that the extreme contrast class is more appropriate than the others or that Ellen ought to eliminate all members of the extreme contrast class before claiming to be justified. Thus, claim (3) is non-normative insofar as it is neutral on the value of the contrast class that it uses.[14] Similarly for (1)–(2).

The same judgments can be expressed more concisely with adverbs:

> A believer is *modestly justified* when and only when the believer is justified out of the modest contrast class.
> A believer is *extremely justified* when and only when the believer is justified out of the extreme contrast class.

Thus, Ellen can be modestly justified even while she is not extremely justified.

5.2. Unqualified Epistemic Judgments

These technical locutions are not common language. Normal speakers usually call a belief justified (or not) without mentioning any contrast class, as in:

> (4) Ellen is justified in believing that it is a crow.

(Actual speakers are more likely to say something like "She can tell it's a crow," but let's play along with the philosophical usage.) Such unrelativized claims assert that believers are justified (simply, simpliciter, plainly, period, full stop, without qualification). In many contexts, we can understand such unqualified claims in the same way as we understand someone who says only, "Those jumbo shrimp are large." If we think that the speaker has in mind other shrimp and is probably not thinking about lobsters or crabs, then we interpret the statement with only shrimp in the contrast class. Similarly, when Ellen claims to be sure that it is a crow, we normally assume that she has in mind robins, ravens, and other common birds, and that she would dismiss deceiving demons, mutants, or robots as outlandish or

---

14. (1)–(3) might seem normative conditionally in much the same way as "This tomato is good for the winter." However, although this sentence could be used to recommend that tomato during the winter, an utterance of the same sentence during the late summer would not recommend it (even if the sentence referred to the same tomato in the same condition). Thus, this sentence is not *essentially* normative, even if it can be used to make recommendations in some circumstances. The same goes for (1)–(3): they cannot be used to recommend belief without presupposing that the mentioned contrast class is appropriate or relevant, but (1)–(3) by themselves make no such normative claim about the mentioned contrast class. That is all I mean by calling them non-normative.

irrelevant to her claim, so we interpret Ellen's statement in terms of the modest contrast class.

It is harder to say exactly what unqualified sentences like (4) mean in the abstract outside of particular contexts. One common suggestion is that (4) means the same as (3), since no belief is justified (without qualification) unless it is justified relative to an unlimited contrast class, which is the extreme contrast class. That hypothesis creates problems. In at least some cases, there is no end to the process of refinement. By looking, asking, and measuring, I can be justified in believing that Joel is six feet tall as opposed to six feet and one inch, but I still need not be justified in believing that Joel is six feet tall as opposed to six feet and one-tenth or one-hundredth of an inch. There is no limit to levels of precision, so there is no upper limit to the increases in the contrast class with respect to which my belief might be justified. That entails that, if the contrast class is not limited in some way, I can never be justified in believing that Joel is six feet tall. Common speakers are rarely so restrictive in calling beliefs justified.

The same point arises even when precision is not at issue. When Ellen classifies the bird as a crow, most people would see Ellen as justified in believing that it is a crow, even if Ellen did not consider and could not rule out deceiving demons, mutant ravens, robot replicas, and so on. Common speakers often call a belief justified when they know that the believer could not rule out all incompatible alternatives in the extreme contrast class (see Fogelin 1994, 93–94).

This feature of common usage motivates a second interpretation of (4), on which it means (2). This account implies that Ellen and other believers can be justified (without qualification) when they cannot rule out skeptical scenarios or even potentially eliminable alternatives, like mutants and robots, as long as the believers can rule out all alternatives in the modest contrast class, which must be ruled out according to normal epistemic standards. One problem with this view, however, is that normal epistemic standards may be, and often are, questioned. Normally there seems to be no need for Ellen to rule out mutant ravens or robot mimics. However, if mutant ravens invaded the neighborhood, and Ellen is unaware of this news and cannot tell mutant ravens from crows, then many people who are aware of this background would be reluctant to say that Ellen is justified in believing that the black bird she sees is a crow. At least, it makes linguistic sense to deny that she is justified (without qualification), as (4) claims, even though she is justified out of the modest contrast class, as (2) claims. So (4) and (2) cannot mean the same thing.

To equate (4) with (2) would also make nonsense out of Academic skepticism. When Academic skeptics deny that a believer is justified because the believer cannot rule out a deceiving demon or a robot mimic, these skeptics might be wrong, but their claim seems to make sense linguistically. However, such skeptical claims and arguments would be nonsense if to call a believer justified (without qualification) were to say that the believer is justified out of the modest contrast class.

Similar problems arise if (4) is interpreted by the contrast class of the person who is judged to be justified or not, like this:

(5) Ellen is justified in believing that it is a crow out of the contrast class that Ellen is considering.

In a normal situation, Ellen considers only the modest contrast class. But suppose that she, like Newt, forgets to consider ravens. Surely, not just skeptics but any third party can deny that Ellen has considered all of the alternatives that she ought to have considered. That criticism could not be expressed by denying that Ellen is justified, if (4) were equated with (5). If believers could be judged only by the contrast classes that they actually use, then epistemic assessments would lose much of their critical edge.

This problem might seem to be solved if (4) is interpreted, instead, by the contrast class of the person judging the believer. Then (4) means something like:

(6) Ellen is justified in believing that it is a crow out of the contrast class that I am (the speaker is) considering.

However, this proposal runs into the same problem as its predecessor. Both proposals make epistemic judgments lose their critical edge. Just as believers can be criticized for using a contrast class that is too small (or too large), so speakers can also be criticized for using an improper contrast class when they assert epistemic judgments like (4). When a speaker asserts (4), but I think the speaker is using a contrast class that is too small, then I can call that speaker's assertion false. Such criticism would make no sense if (4) meant (6).

Another problem involves the ascription of beliefs about justified belief. Suppose that Newt has never heard of ravens or rooks. Ellen knows this and also knows about ravens and rooks. When they see a black bird, Ellen says, "Newt believes that he is justified in believing it is a crow." Ellen is the speaker, so the proposal that (4) means (6) suggests that the epistemic term here should be interpreted in light of Ellen's contrast class. Then Ellen is saying, "Newt believes that he is justified in believing it is a crow as opposed to a rook, a raven, and so on." But that can't be what she is saying, since Ellen knows that Newt would never put rooks or ravens in his contrast class. Hence, (4) cannot mean (6).[15]

Third, those who interpret (4) as (6) cannot explain the disagreement between skeptics and their opponents. On this view, when academic skeptics deny that believers are justified, they are considering the extreme contrast class. Thus, such skeptical claims make sense and even come out true, if believers cannot be justified out of the extreme contrast class. Moreover, when opponents of skepticism insist that believers are justified (without qualification), they are considering the modest contrast class, so their claims are true, too. The problem is that they disagree with skeptics, when they assert (4) and skeptics deny (4). On the current proposal, they are both right, so they do not really disagree. An important aspect of common language would, thus, be lost by equating (4) with (6).

---

15. Similarly, if (4) meant (6), a skeptical zoo visitor who thinks that mutants and robots are relevant would have to say, "The zoo keepers don't believe that they are justified in their beliefs about which animals are in which cages."

Normative epistemic terms contrast in this respect with other examples of contrast classes. "Those jumbo shrimp are large" might be analyzed as "Those jumbo shrimp are larger than most members of the contrast class that the speaker is considering." To see why, suppose that, while shopping in a fish market for crustaceans, Paul says, "Those jumbo shrimp are large," while considering other shrimp as a contrast class. Then Peter says, "No, they're not large. They are much smaller than lobsters and crabs." A natural response for Paul would be conciliatory: "Fine, but that's not what I was saying. Shrimp aren't usually as big as these." This response seems natural, because Peter is not really denying what Paul said. In contrast, imagine Newt says, "I can't tell whether it is a crow or a raven, because I am not expert or close enough; but Ellen is an expert, and she is close, so she is justified in believing it is a crow." Newt and Ellen are using the same modest contrast class. Then an Academic skeptic responds, "No, she's not justified, because Ellen cannot rule out robot mimics or deceiving demons." In a normal situation, Newt might respond: "Give me a break! She's as justified as she needs to be. Deceiving demons and robot mimics are irrelevant." Here the skeptic and the birdwatcher really do disagree. In particular, they disagree about which alternatives must be ruled out in order for a believer to be justified. Newt, like most common people, does not take deceiving demons or robot mimics seriously, but the skeptic insists on considering a wider range of alternatives. They disagree about the proper epistemic standards, not regarding the kind or degree of evidence that is required, but regarding which contrast class is relevant.

To capture this disagreement, we need to build the notion of relevance into an analysis of (4). We also need to distinguish sentence-meaning from speaker-meaning.[16] For example, when two fathers tell their respective children, "Don't do anything dangerous while I am gone," this sentence can have the same meaning in both utterances, even if the two speakers mean different things by it because they would count different activities as dangerous. Similarly, if I am discussing only shrimp, and you are discussing all kinds of crustaceans (so you would consider lobsters and crabs to be relevant), but we both say, "Those jumbo shrimp are large," then our utterances can have the same sentence-meaning but different speaker-meanings. The speaker-meaning of my utterance is something like "Those jumbo shrimp are larger than most shrimp," whereas the speaker-meaning of yours is something like "Those jumbo shrimp are larger than most crustaceans."

The same dichotomy applies to justified belief. Suppose you and I both utter the unqualified sentence (4). Add that I have considered the possibilities of mutant ravens, robot replicas, and deceiving demons, and I would not utter (4) if I did not believe that Ellen has grounds that rule out such mutants, robots, and demons. In contrast, you have not thought of mutants, robots, demons, or anything beyond the modest contrast class, and you would dismiss such remote possibilities as

16. In Sinnott-Armstrong 2004a, I used the distinction between character and content from Kaplan 1989. Jonathan Schaffer showed me problems with that model. Then Antti Karjalainen and Christie Thomas convinced me that sentence-meaning and speaker-meaning provide a better model of what I had in mind. Thanks.

outlandish and irrelevant if someone did raise them (and you know all of this). In these circumstances, our utterances have the same sentence-meaning but different speaker-meanings. Roughly, part of the speaker-meaning of your utterance is (2), whereas part of the speaker-meaning of my utterance is (3). The speaker-meanings of most actual utterances are not this precise, so it might be better represented in terms of a class of classes or supervaluation. Nonetheless, the relativized claims (2)–(3) do help to locate that aspect of speaker-meaning that is important here.

This still does not tell us the sentence-meaning of (4). Since the speaker-meaning of utterances of (4) varies, the sentence-meaning of (4) must be represented by something that allows room for those variations. It also needs a normative term to give a critical edge to epistemic judgments and to account for disagreements about contrast classes. I will use the term "relevant," as an allusion to "relevant alternatives" theories, although I could substitute "pertinent," "appropriate," "proper," "apt," "suitable," "important," "crucial," "correct," or "legitimate." What matters is that to call an alternative relevant to a particular belief is to say that a believer needs to be able to rule out that alternative in order to be justified without qualification in holding that particular belief. A contrast class is then relevant when and only when all of its members are relevant. The relevant contrast class is the one that includes all and only relevant alternatives. Since to call a class or its members relevant is to specify what is needed in order to be justified without qualification, and the term "justified" is normative, the term "relevant" is also normative, as it must be to capture the normative force of (4).

Using this terminology, the sentence-meaning of (4) can be represented roughly as:

(7) Ellen is justified in believing that it is a crow out of the relevant contrast class.[17]

The idea is *not* that, when someone says, "S is justified in believing P," the speaker must be consciously thinking in terms of relevance or a specific contrast class. Overt formulation is not necessary. Instead, this analysis merely makes it explicit that the speaker would be bothered if he could not rule out a certain range of alternatives but would refuse to take other alternatives seriously. In third-person judgments, the speaker would disapprove of those who claim that S is justified without qualification while S is not able to rule out a certain range of alternatives or who claim that S is not justified simply because S cannot rule out some alternative outside that range. In this sense, speakers who assert (7) are implicitly committing themselves to the claim that some contrast class (or set of contrast classes) is really relevant.

---

17. This formulation is intentionally neutral on the issue of whether (7) entails or, instead, presupposes that a certain class is the relevant contrast class. The presupposition interpretation comes out when (7) is read as (7p) "Ellen is justified out of a contrast class, which is the relevant one, in believing that it is a crow," assuming such dependent clauses introduce presuppositions. The difference between the presupposition and entailment readings will be discussed in a few paragraphs.

Since (7) gives the sentence-meaning of (4), (2)–(3) cannot give the *whole* speaker-meaning of (4). (4) and (7) are normative in a way that (2)–(3) are not. Hence, we need to add something to (2)–(3) to capture that normativity. What needs to be added? Relevance, of course, but how exactly does relevance fit in?

One temptingly simple way to make (2)–(3) normative is to add a relevance claim as a conjunct, so that (2)–(3) become:

(2*) Ellen is justified in believing that it is a crow out of the modest contrast class, and this is the relevant contrast class.

(3*) Ellen is justified in believing that it is a crow out of the extreme contrast class, and this is the relevant contrast class.

This whole conjunction is false whenever the added conjunct about relevance is false. That implication creates problems when one person thinks that another person uses a contrast class that is too large. For example, imagine that Fred asserts (4) and takes the relevant contrast class to include mutant ravens and robot mimics in addition to the modest contrast class. Call this a supplemented modest contrast class. On the current proposal, the speaker meaning of Fred's claim is then "Ellen is justified in believing that it is a crow out of a supplemented modest contrast class, and this is the relevant one." Suppose you agree that Ellen can rule out everything in the modest contrast class, and you also agree that Ellen can rule out mutant ravens and robot mimics (because she has done genetic tests). Still, you think that mutant ravens and robot mimics are not really relevant, so the modest contrast class is the relevant one. In this situation, you think that Fred's speaker meaning on the conjunctive analysis is false, because its second conjunct ("...this is the relevant one") is false. However, you do not think that (4) is false, whether uttered by Fred or by you, since you know that Ellen can rule out everything in both of the different classes that you and Fred take to be relevant. In this situation, it would be at least misleading for you to deny Fred's assertion. Yet this misleading statement comes out true if the speaker-meaning of (4) is analyzed by conjoining a claim about relevance as in (2*)–(3*).[18]

That odd implication can be avoided by deploying a kind of presupposition. If "Bob stopped talking" presupposes "Bob had been talking," then people who doubt or deny that presupposition would not assert "Bob stopped talking," but they also wouldn't deny it—that is, they would not assert, "Bob did not stop talking." (Cf. Strawson 1950; and section 3.1.) Similarly, when Fred asserts (4) using a contrast class that we do not take to be relevant, we would not accept Fred's assertion but we would also not deny it—that is, we would not assert "Ellen is not justified." Using dependent "which" clauses to signal presuppositions, we can represent the complete speaker-meaning of an utterance of (4) as something like:

18. Another possibility is that "S is justified out of contrast class C" normally conversationally implies "The relevant contrast class is C." And this implication might seem cancellable. However, this pragmatic interpretation cannot adequately explain why people continue to argue vociferously about whether someone is really justified even after they realize that they are using different contrast classes. That is why relevance needs to be built into the semantics (including presuppositions) of (4).

(2+) Ellen is justified in believing that it is a crow out of the modest contrast class, which is the relevant contrast class.[19]

(3+) Ellen is justified in believing that it is a crow out of the extreme contrast class, which is the relevant contrast class.

Which of these gives the speaker-meaning of a particular utterance depends on which possibilities the speaker would take seriously, as previously discussed.

This analysis of the speaker-meaning of (4) explains your reluctance to deny or agree with Fred's utterance of (4) two paragraphs back. It also explains why common speakers say that Ellen is justified in believing that the bird is a crow, even though she cannot rule out the possibility of a mutant raven or robot replica, if they see such alternatives as outlandish and, hence, irrelevant. And it explains why I am justified in believing that Joel is six feet tall, even though I cannot rule out six feet and one-tenth of an inch, if increments less than one inch are seen as too picky and, hence, irrelevant. So this analysis in terms of relevance fits the cases well.

Extreme invariantists still might insist that, even if some speakers use the term "justified" according to some relevance analysis, this is just loose talk; and nobody can ever really be justified in believing anything unless the believer can rule out every alternative. However, these invariantists can be understood as claiming that every incompatible alternative is always relevant. This claim is not implied by my analysis, but neither is it excluded. My analysis takes no stand on which, if any, contrast classes are relevant. This neutrality should make my analysis acceptable to such extreme invariantists. Similarly, modest invariantists might hold that the modest contrast class is always the relevant one, so skeptical hypotheses are never relevant. Their position can also be accommodated by my analysis, since modest invariantists call believers justified when the believers can rule out all other members of the modest contrast class. A third possibility is contextualism, which holds that the modest contrast class is relevant in some contexts and the extreme contrast class is relevant in other contexts. When such contextualists call a belief justified, the sentence-meaning and speaker-meaning of their claims fit perfectly into my analysis. Thus, my analysis captures all sides in these debates.

Since it fits both the cases and the theories, I will henceforth assume this analysis, unless otherwise indicated. This framework does not imply that any contrast class or any alternative is relevant, so it would be badly misleading to classify it as a "relevant alternatives" view. A better description would be "neutral alternatives," because it is neutral about which, if any, contrast class is relevant, even in a particular context. It can also be seen as a form of contrastivism (Schaffer 2004; Sinnott-Armstrong forthcoming).

My analysis could be supplemented by introducing a similar relativity to standards for ruling out alternatives. These standards might concern the strength of

---

19. Readers who deny that dependent "which" clauses create presuppositions may reformulate (2+) as "Ellen justified in believing that it is a crow out of the modest contrast class, presupposing that this is the relevant one."

grounds required to rule out an alternative. For example, an expert who closely inspects and dissects a bird has much stronger evidence that it is not a raven than a novice who can usually tell crows from ravens, but who sees this bird only for a few seconds across a field. Does this show that the novice is not justified in believing that the bird is a crow instead of a raven? Again, we need to distinguish levels: the expert is strongly justified, and the novice is weakly justified, in believing that the bird is a crow instead of a raven. The claim that the novice is justified (without qualification) out of a given contrast class can then be analyzed in terms of whether the novice's grounds meet the relevant standards of strength for ruling out other members of the contrast class. The novice, for example, is not justified if the relevant standards require more than a quick glance from a distance. This issue about which grounds are strong enough is separate from the issue about which contrast class is relevant, since the issue about strength arises even for a single contrast class, as in our example where the beliefs of the novice and the expert are evaluated with respect to the same contrast class, {crow, raven}.

Another aspect of standards concerns not strength but the kinds of grounds that may be used to rule out an alternative. Williamson (2000) claims that knowledge is evidence. If so, and if I know that I have hands, then I have evidence against the skeptical hypothesis that I am a brain in a vat. This might seem to be enough to rule out that hypothesis. However, if the kinds of grounds that may be used to rule out the skeptical hypothesis are restricted to non-factive internal states, such as perceptual and memorial seemings, then believers will not be able to rule out skeptical hypotheses on the basis of such internal evidence alone. To capture this situation, one could add relativity to kinds of evidence and say that a believer might be justified in believing commonsense claims as opposed to skeptical alternatives based on external evidence but cannot be justified in believing commonsense claims as opposed to skeptical alternatives based on internal evidence alone.

Although this additional relativity is interesting and important in many ways, I will usually omit reference to alternative standards governing both strength and kinds of grounds. I will limit my claims to internal grounds in order to avoid begging the question against skeptics. I will assume common, loose standards of strength for ruling out alternatives in order to avoid begging the question against opponents of skepticism.[20] This strategy will enable us to focus, instead, on the issues raised by contrast classes themselves.

5.3. Problems for Relevance

One crucial issue concerns which, if any, contrast class is relevant. My abstract framework is compatible with various views on this issue. As I said, it can accommodate extreme invariantists who claim that the extreme contrast class is always the

---

20. I am not assuming that these standards are correct. I am merely choosing to talk about whether and how believers can meet these common standards for ruling out.

relevant one, modest invariantists who reply that the modest contrast class is always the relevant one, and contextualists who hold that the relevant contrast class varies so that the modest contrast class is relevant in some contexts, but the extreme contrast class is relevant in other contexts.

Still, I see no adequate reason to adopt one of these views as opposed to the others. Moreover, each of these positions faces profound problems. These problems are serious enough to make me unwilling to assert any of these theories, but they are not so devastating that I would deny any of them. Instead, in line with Pyrrhonism, I suspend belief among these theories. My Pyrrhonism also extends beyond theories to cases: I suspend belief about which alternatives and which contrast classes are really relevant, even in a particular context. In some contexts, a certain contrast class might *seem* relevant, and almost everyone might find it natural to *treat* that contrast class as relevant, but that is usually because of *practical* concerns and not because that class really is relevant *epistemically*. The same conflation recurs when contrast classes appear irrelevant. It is not clear whether or not any such appearance reflects reality regarding relevance or irrelevance. Hence, I avoid committing myself to any claim that any alternative really is or is not relevant epistemically.

This meta-skepticism about real relevance is another way in which my position is not a "relevant alternatives" view. Relevant alternatives theorists assume that some alternatives are relevant and others are not. I shun that assumption as well as its denial.

My main reason for suspending belief about real relevance is, as I said, that deep problems arise for every attempt to specify which contrast class is the one that is really relevant. I already discussed problems for the main versions of invariantism.

Extreme invariantists claim that the extreme contrast class is always relevant. Since that claim implies that all contrary propositions are always relevant, it conflicts with the common practice of dismissing some outlandish skeptical alternatives as irrelevant. On the other hand, the modest invariantist claim that the modest contrast class is always the relevant one conflicts with the common practice of recognizing that some alternatives which we had not previously recognized as relevant are relevant after all. There is no reason to assume that our current standards already include everything that is really relevant, so they cannot be improved. Thus, neither variation on invariantism in compatible with our common epistemic practices. Of course, our common practices might be confused or wrong, but it is hard to find any adequate reason to dismiss them. Hence, there are reasons to doubt both extreme and modest invariantism. It is possible that some third contrast class other than the extreme contrast class and the modest contrast class is always the relevant one, but it is hard to imagine what it would be. For these reasons, we should not endorse invariantism.

The remaining option is contextualism, which claims that which contrast class is really relevant varies from context to context. This approach promises to explain both aspects of our common practices that undermine invariantism. Unfortunately, contextualism also runs into troubles of its own when its details are spelled out.

One problem is that there is no way to formulate plausible rules about which contrast classes are relevant in which contexts. David Lewis makes the most valiant effort to provide such rules, but consider his rule of attention: "No matter how far-fetched a certain possibility is, no matter how properly we might have ignored it in some other context, if in *this* context we are not in fact ignoring it but attending to it, then for us now it is a relevant alternative."[21] This rule leads us astray when a desperate defense attorney argues, "Perhaps all of the witnesses (and all of us) were deceived by a demon." The jury is required by law to pay attention to what the defense says, so Lewis's rule of attention implies that the deceiving demon hypothesis becomes relevant as soon as the defense mentions it. Since the jury cannot rule it out, Lewis's contextualism implies that the jury members are not justified in believing that the defendant is guilty. But then they should not find the defendant guilty. This seems absurd. It seems that the jury could attend to the defense ploy and yet properly ignore it by not letting it affect their belief in the defendant's guilt or their epistemic assessment of themselves as justified in believing in the defendant's guilt. Examples like these suggest that Lewis's rule of attention is dubious at best.[22]

A more general problem arises from the indeterminacy of the modest contrast class. I specified it loosely as those alternatives that need to be eliminated in order to meet the usual epistemic standards. This description hardly picks out a determinate set. Imagine a customer in a restaurant. The waiter walks up and pronounces his name, so the customer believes and seems justified in believing that her waiter is named "Jeff." She could not, of course, list all the names that she needs to be able to rule out in order to be justified in believing that the waiter's name is "Jeff." Few of us could give more than a small percentage of the names other than "Jeff." This limitation puts contextualists in the odd position of claiming that there is one and only one contrast class that is really relevant in this context, but neither they nor the justified believer can specify the members of that contrast class.

The deeper problem is not just about size. It is not even clear whether the relevant contrast class includes all names or only male names. Either way, different people would give different lists because some people know some names that others do not know. Moreover, some names are neither clearly inside nor clearly outside the supposedly relevant contrast class. Consider "Geoff," which is spelled differently but pronounced the same as the waiter's name.[23] These names are

21. Lewis 1996, 559. Lewis's theory is about knowledge, but I will extend his rule of attention to my topic, justified belief. Lewis's other rules are also questionable, but I will discuss only the rule of attention as an example. For more criticisms of Lewis's rules, see Hawthorne 2004, 61–68.

22. Roy Sorensen gave another counterexample: When asked to evaluate a Descartes scholar, a recommender might say, "He knows a lot about Descartes' deceiving demon argument." This recommender and the scholar both attend to the possibility of a deceiving demon, but it still seems proper for them to ignore that possibility while forming beliefs about the scholar or about Descartes. Since Descartes scholars take the demon hypothesis seriously, this example also refutes a related rule in Timmons 1998, 220: "Once skeptical challenges are taken seriously, then the context has been switched (in the sense that the relevant social group or community crucial for epistemic evaluation is the group of skeptics)."

23. The same points could, of course, be made with names that are spelled the same but pronounced differently, such as "Ralph" pronounced the American way (so that it rhymes with "Alf") or as by some British speakers (so that it rhymes with "safe").

different, since the customer might ask the waiter whether his name is "Jeff" or "Geoff." They are also contraries insofar as the waiter's first name cannot be "Jeff" if his first name is "Geoff." However, the customer only heard the waiter's name spoken, so she cannot rule out that his name is "Geoff." Hence, the customer has no justified belief in the waiter's name, if "Geoff" is a relevant alternative. But is it relevant? You could call it relevant if you wanted to conclude that the customer's belief is not justified. But you could just as easily call it irrelevant if you wanted to conclude that the customer's belief is justified. I see no solid basis for deciding between these positions. There is no way to determine whether this alternative is or is not really relevant.[24]

Contextualists might respond that the context includes the purpose of the believer or the epistemic judge. A general problem for this response is that it seems to conflate instrumental reasons with epistemic reasons. What serves the customer's or the judge's purposes should be separated from what provides an epistemic reason for belief, since epistemic reasons are tied to truth in a way that purposes are not. (See section 4.2.1.)

Other problems arise when contextualists try to specify details of their appeal to purposes. First consider the view that the *customer's* purpose determines the relevant contrast class. Then, if the customer cares only about being able to get the waiter's attention by calling his name, differences in spelling do not matter, so "Geoff" is not in the contrast class, and the customer is justified in believing that the waiter's name is "Jeff." However, the customer might care about being able to write a note to the manager about the waiter, in which case spelling does matter, so "Geoff" is in the relevant contrast class, and the customer is not justified in believing that the waiter's name is "Jeff." Thus, we need to determine which purpose the customer has in order to determine which beliefs are justified. But the customer might have no specific purpose. After all, the waiter just came up and announced his name. The customer did not even ask. Since the customer has no specific purpose while being told the waiter's name, at that time there is no purpose that could determine whether "Geoff" is a relevant alternative to "Jeff."

Moreover, there might be several customers at the table with different and even conflicting purposes. In addition to our customer with no purpose, a second customer might only want to be able to call out the waiter's name, and a third customer might already want to be able to write a note to the manager. It would be implausible to hold that the first two are justified, but the third is not justified, in believing that the waiter's name is "Jeff." There is also no basis for declaring that one of their purposes is the one that determines which beliefs are justified in this context. Contextualists might hold that these customers are in different contexts, but this proliferation of contexts quickly becomes too profligate. If different purposes put different people in different contexts, the same purposes within a single person would put that person in several contexts at once. That would make it

---

24. Contextualists might claim that the customer is justified in believing (a) the waiter's name is pronounced like "Jeff" but not (b) the waiter's name is spelled like "Jeff." However, this move won't solve the problem, which concerns the distinct belief that (c) the waiter's name is "Jeff."

impossible to say whether this person is justified or whether an alternative is relevant to that person's belief. Hence, the believer's purpose cannot be used to determine which contrast class is really relevant.

Contextualists might, instead, refer to the purpose of the epistemic judge who assesses whether the customer is justified. Most contextualists go this way. A focus on the context of the epistemic judge is sometimes even built into the definition of contextualism (DeRose 1999, 190–91). However, as with believers, judges can have multiple purposes with contrary implications for membership in the relevant contrast class. Moreover, even if each judge has only one purpose, there can be a multitude of judges with different purposes. One judge might have a purpose for which spelling is relevant. To this judge, "Geoff" will seem relevant as an alternative to "Jeff." Another judge might have no purpose for which spelling is relevant, so this judge might hold that "Geoff" is not really a relevant alternative to "Jeff." It is hard to believe that both of these views are correct,[25] but there is no basis for saying which one is correct.

Contextualists might respond that an alternative is relevant if it is relevant to *any* purpose at all (even if it is irrelevant to all other purposes). But then the widest contrast class is always the relevant one, so the customer is not justified in believing that the waiter is named "Jeff" right after being told, even if the customer and the epistemic judge do not care about spelling. Another move holds that an alternative is relevant only if it is relevant to *all* purposes (and irrelevant to none). But then a very narrow contrast class is always the relevant one, and a customer is justified in believing that the waiter is named "Jeff" even if spelling matters to both the customer and the judge, and the customer cannot rule out the alternative spelling "Geoff." Since neither option is attractive, contextualism cannot be saved by quantifying over purposes (as supervaluationists might suggest). Similar problems arise if contextualists quantify, instead, over contrast classes.

These difficulties might seem to be due to peculiarities of naming, but the point is much more widespread than contextualists assume. In almost every situation there will be alternatives that are not clearly relevant and also not clearly irrelevant. Another example is a young girl who believes that her pet is a dog but has never heard of wolves, coyotes, jackals, or dingos, so she cannot rule out the possibility that her pet is a wolf, coyote, jackal, or dingo rather than a dog. Are wolves, coyotes, jackals, and dingos in the relevant contrast class for determining whether she is justified (without qualification)? I see no grounds for excluding them, and yet including them as relevant will imply that many children are not justified (without qualification) in believing that their pets are dogs. It is more fruitful to avoid arguing about which class is relevant and say only that this girl is justified in believing that her pet is a dog rather than a cat or a snake, even though she is not justified in believing that her pet is a dog rather than a wolf, coyote, jackal, or dingo.

25. It can be true that spelling does not matter to one judge but does matter to a different judge. What cannot be true is that "Geoff" really is and really is not a relevant alternative to "Jeff."

Contextualists have not supplied any way to determine which alternatives are relevant, and I do not see how to begin to decide this issue. The issue of what is in the relevant contrast class is crucial for determining whether someone is justified, according to contextualism. Without solving this problem, contextualists cannot specify what is necessary for a believer to be justified on their view.

None of this poses any problem for those of us who eschew the notion of real relevance and suspend belief in all claims that any contrast class is or is not the relevant one. If the believer can rule out every other name on a long list, then the believer can be justified out of that contrast class. If somebody later comes along with a longer list, and if the believer cannot rule out every other name on that longer list, then the believer cannot be justified out of that larger contrast class. Generally, if someone asks whether the believer is justified out of a particular class, we can answer. However, if someone asks, "But which contrast class really is the relevant one for determining whether this believer is justified (without qualification)?" then our response should be, "Maybe none. Maybe all. Maybe one. We see no way to tell." Moreover, if someone asks, "Which is the modest class, that is, the one that is relevant according to usual epistemic standards?" then our answer should be, "The usual epistemic standards are indeterminate, but it does not matter as long as those usual epistemic standards are not supposed to capture any fact of the matter about whether someone really is justified (without qualification)." Such meta-skepticism about relevance thereby avoids a serious problem for contextualism.

And there are more problems: most contextualists seem to agree that, if there are lots of fake barns in the neighborhood of a barn that I see from the road, and if I should know this and could know this, then I am not justified in believing that what I see is a barn, even if it is (Goldman 1976, 772–73). The presence of fake barns changes the context. But how many barns must there be? How close must they be? What if the fake barns are in the next town or the next county or the next state or the next country? When do fake barns become relevant or members of the relevant contrast class? Such questions seem impossible to answer non-arbitrarily, so it is useful to avoid them by suspending belief about whether any contrast class really is the relevant one.

Yet another problem arises when epistemic judgments cross contexts. Most contextualists focus on first-person claims ("I am justified . . ."), but any adequate epistemology also needs to handle problems that arise when third-person claims ("He is justified . . .") cross contexts. Suppose a philosopher teaching a course about the problem of other minds asks a student whether a certain doctor in a hospital is justified in believing that a certain patient is in pain. These three people (the philosopher, the student, and the doctor) play different roles: the philosopher assesses the student's judgment about whether the doctor's belief is justified. Now, if a larger extreme contrast class is relevant in the philosopher's context, but a smaller modest contrast class is relevant in the doctor's context, then contextualists have no non-arbitrary way of telling which context or contrast class determines how the philosophy student should assess the doctor's belief. The only way to handle such cross-context judgments is to say that the doctor is justified out of one contrast class but not another and then refuse to pick one contrast class as the relevant one or to say whether the doctor is justified (without qualification).

For all of these reasons (and others to be given in sections 6.5–6.6), I give up the notion of real relevance and suspend belief about whether or not any contrast class is really relevant or the relevant one. This might seem to undermine my analysis of the sentence-meaning of (4) "Ellen is justified in believing it is a crow" as (7) "Ellen is justified in believing it is a crow out of the relevant contrast class" in section 5.2. However, even if we give up on real relevance, we can still accept that (4) is equivalent to (7), and that to say (4) is to say (7). Just as historians can analyze "witch" as implying "woman with supernatural powers" without committing themselves to supernatural powers, so epistemologists who analyze (4) as (7) are not thereby committed to any contrast class being really relevant. They would become committed to real relevance if they went on to assert (4) or (7). However, those who doubt that any contrast class is ever really relevant can accept (7) as the sentence-meaning of (4) as long as they never go on to claim anything with the form of (4) or (7), at least while they are doing serious constructive epistemology.

5.4. Classy Pyrrhonism

This meta-skepticism about relevance illuminates the difference between Academic and Pyrrhonian skepticism about justified belief. Academic skeptics about justified belief claim this:

(8) Nobody is justified in believing anything.

On my analysis, the sentence-meaning of (8) is this:

(9) Nobody is justified in believing anything out of the relevant contrast class.

Academic skeptics who assert (8) cite skeptical scenarios and treat those scenarios as relevant, so they seem to use the extreme contrast class. Thus, the speaker-meaning of their assertions of (8) is this:

(10+) Nobody is justified in believing anything out of the extreme contrast class, which is the relevant contrast class.

Academic skeptics also apply this general claim to specific cases. If they think about Ellen, they claim these:

(11) Ellen is not justified in believing that it is a crow.
(12) Ellen is not justified in believing that it is a crow out of the relevant contrast class.
(13+) Ellen is not justified in believing that it is a crow out of the extreme contrast class, which is the relevant contrast class.

In other words, Academic skeptics deny (4), (7), and (3+).

In contrast, Pyrrhonian skeptics suspend belief about such claims. Why? Because they are meta-skeptics about relevance. Meta-skeptics about relevance want to avoid committing themselves to the claim that the extreme contrast class is the relevant contrast class for Ellen's belief (or any other belief). Hence, they neither assert nor deny (13+). If (13+) gives the speaker-meaning of (11), whose sentence-meaning is (12), as I argued, then meta-skeptics about relevance will also neither assert nor deny (11)–(12). Moreover, meta-skeptics about relevance would not assert even the wide-scope negation versions:

(11w) It is not the case that Ellen is justified in believing it is a crow.
(12w) It is not the case that Ellen is justified in believing it is a crow out of the relevant contrast class.
(13+w) It is not the case that Ellen is justified in believing it is a crow out of the extreme contrast class, which is the relevant contrast class.

For example, (11w) means that (4) is either (a) false or (b) neither true nor false. Meta-skeptics about relevance want to avoid committing themselves to either (a) or (b). They do not claim that (4) is false because they do not *assert* its presupposition. They also do not claim that "S is justified in believing P" is neither true nor false because they do not *deny* its presupposition. Hence, they do not assert or imply (11w). Similarly for (12w) and (13+w).

The same goes for generalizations (8)–(10+). Presuppositions carry over to generalizations. If "Sammy could not hit Rocket's fast ball, which was his best pitch," presupposes "Rocket's fast ball was his best pitch," then "Nobody could hit Rocket's fast ball, which was his best pitch" shares the same presupposition. Similarly, since "S is not justified in believing P out of contrast class C, which is the relevant one" presupposes "Contrast class C is the relevant one," then "Nobody is justified in believing P out of contrast class C, which is the relevant one" shares the same presupposition. Hence, (8)–(10+) all presuppose that some contrast class is the relevant one. Meta-skeptics about relevance suspend belief about that presupposed claim, so they also suspend belief about (8)–(10+). They neither assert nor deny such generalizations.

Of course, meta-skeptics about relevance also do not assert the affirmative claims that correspond to (8)–(10+) and (11)–(13+). They do not claim that Ellen or anyone *is* justified in believing anything (without qualification or out of the relevant contrast class or out of the extreme contrast class, which is the relevant one). Meta-skeptics about relevance avoid the whole language game of relevance, so they neither assert nor deny any claims that presuppose relevance. Thus, they suspend belief about Academic skepticism. That makes them Pyrrhonian skeptics.

The notion of presupposition might seem questionable to some readers, so it is worth exploring how Pyrrhonian skepticism would look without that notion. Suppose that (10+) is read instead as a conjunction:

(10*) Nobody is justified in believing anything out of the extreme contrast class, and this is the relevant contrast class.

This claim contains a scope ambiguity. One way to read (10*) is this:

(10.1*) $(x)(p)\sim(JBxpe\ \&\ Re)$

where "JBxpe" means "x is justified in believing p out of e (the extreme contrast class)," and "Re" means "e (the extreme contrast class) is the relevant contrast class." However, (10*) could also be read like this:

(10.2*) (x)(p)(~JBxpe & Re)

Academic skeptics who assert (10*) must intend (10.2*) because such skeptics use (10*) to derive (11) "Ellen is not justified in believing that it is a crow." Without presupposition, an utterance of (11) by such a skeptic would have this speaker-meaning:

(13*) Ellen is not justified in believing that it is a crow out of the extreme contrast class, and this is the relevant contrast class.

This would not follow from (10*) if (10*) were read as (10.1*), but it would follow if (10*) were read as (10.2*). Hence, Academic skeptics must assert (10.2*).

In contrast, Pyrrhonian skeptics who are meta-skeptics about relevance do not assert (10.2*) because (10.2*) implies "Re." Meta-skeptics about relevance suspend belief about "Re." Hence, they also suspend belief about (10.2*). They still might make claims that do not assert or presuppose relevance. This includes "(x)(p) ~ JBxpe," which implies (10.1*) in normal logics. Hence, Pyrrhonian skeptics who do not use presupposition might end up committed to (10.1*), even if they are meta-skeptics about relevance. Nonetheless, they assert (10.1*) for different reasons than Academic skeptics. Moreover, what Pyrrhonian skeptics assert would still be weaker than what Academic skeptics assert—namely, (10.2*). And Pyrrhonian skeptics still do not derive (11), (12), or (13*), as Academic skeptics do. So these kinds of skepticism remain distinct.

Although Pyrrhonian skepticism is distinguished from Academic skepticism by what it does not claim, it is also important to realize that Pyrrhonians who are meta-skeptics about relevance can still make other epistemic claims without that questionable presupposition (or conjunct). It seems plausible (and natural for Pyrrhonians) to deny:

(14) Nobody is justified in believing anything out of the modest contrast class.

and yet assert:

(15) Nobody is justified in believing anything out of the extreme contrast class.

(14) will be called *skepticism about modestly justified belief*, and (15) will be called *skepticism about extremely justified belief*. The position that denies (14) but claims (15) will be called *moderate skepticism about justified belief*. Such moderate skepticism is about relativized epistemic judgments, whereas Pyrrhonian skeptics suspend belief in non-relativized epistemic judgments, so moderate skepticism is logically independent of Pyrrhonian skepticism. Thus, although Pyrrhonian skeptics neither assert nor deny Academic skepticism, that is, (8)–(10+),

Pyrrhonians can still assert moderate skepticism about justified belief, which is (15) plus the denial of (14).[26] I will call this combination *moderate Pyrrhonian skepticism*.[27]

Moderate skepticism allows my Pyrrhonian skepticism to be more urbane by preserving a central part of common epistemic language. My brand of Pyrrhonism suspends beliefs even about common epistemic claims like (4) "Ellen is justified in believing it is a crow," which presuppose relevance and do not mention contrast classes. Nonetheless, a moderate Pyrrhonian skeptic can accept nearby cousins of (4), including (2) "Ellen is justified in believing it is a crow out of the modest contrast class," which does not presuppose relevance and does mention a contrast class. Moderate Pyrrhonians thereby explain why claims like (4) seem so plausible, namely, because they are so close to true claims like (2). The relevance clause is needed to capture disagreements and the critical edge in common epistemic assessments. That clause creates doubts, so not all of common language can be preserved. Still, this doubtful part can be separated off to reveal the truth within common language. Thus, although moderate Pyrrhonism finds a fundamental problem in common epistemic assessments, it is still able to explain how that dubious element could go unnoticed and remain widespread.

To support this compromise, Pyrrhonian skeptics still need to argue that nobody can rule out skeptical scenarios, which makes (15) true, and that some believers can rule out every alternative in the modest contrast class, which makes (14) false. Remember that I am considering only internal evidence and not external evidence. This should make it plausible, at least, that nobody can rule out skeptical scenarios, so nobody can be justified out of the extreme contrast class (based on internal evidence). In any case, I will not argue for these claims apart from morality. (For general arguments, see Fogelin 1994 and Sinnott-Armstrong 2004a.) Instead, in part II, I will argue for their analogs about moral belief, that is, that moral beliefs can be justified modestly but not extremely. My arguments there about moral beliefs will, I hope, suggest how similar conclusions might be reached about non-moral beliefs. In any case, so far I can conclude only conditionally: if no believers can rule out all skeptical scenarios, but some believers can rule out all modest alternatives, then moderate Pyrrhonian skepticism follows from my analysis plus my meta-skepticism about relevance.

26. It might seem unhistorical to call this view Pyrrhonism, since Pyrrho is often represented as eschewing all assertions or at least all philosophical assertions, whereas my moderate Pyrrhonist makes relativized epistemic claims. Still, my Pyrrhonist does refuse to make any unrelativized epistemic claims, and traditional epistemology trades in such unrelativized claims, so my Pyrrhonist does refuse to make such traditional philosophical claims. For more on the relation between my views and traditional Pyrrhonism, see the last section of Sinnott-Armstrong 2004a.

27. It might seem odd to call this position skepticism, since it includes no active doubt but only suspension of belief about unrelativized epistemic judgments, and it admits that some beliefs are modestly justified. However, this only shows why it is not Academic skepticism. It can still be Pyrrhonian skepticism. Anyway, it does not matter much whether the position gets classified as skepticism as long as it is clear.

5.5. Objections

Several objections might be raised against my use of contrast classes. My goal is to understand the truth behind skepticism while also recognizing that some beliefs can be justified in modest ways. I want to have my cake and eat it, too. Critics will argue that I can't.

5.5.1. *Are Relativized Judgments Epistemic?*

A common complaint is that the relativized judgments that moderate Pyrrhonists accept are too modest to be epistemic. One reason might be that epistemic judgments, including judgments about what is justified (without qualification), are normative; but there is no normative force to the claim that a belief is justified out of a limited contrast class. If an astrologer simply refuses to consider anything but various astrological theories, the astrologer does not seem really justified in any way with any epistemic value.

But consider tomatoes in winter. Although they are not good compared to summer tomatoes, if it is winter, and I need to make a salad tonight, it can be important to find the best tomatoes among those that are available here now. Analogously, even if certain believers consider only a narrow range of options, they can still do a good job of determining which option is best among the options that are considered. Moreover, they can still have good grounds, and it can matter whether their grounds are good enough to support their belief and rule out other options within the specified contrast class. We as observers might wish that they as believers had considered other alternatives, and they would have had a higher epistemic status if they had considered and ruled out more alternatives. Nonetheless, their belief still might have more epistemic value than any other belief inside the contrast class that they did consider. That is enough for the notion of being justified out of a limited contrast class to be normative enough to be epistemic even though it is not normative in the stronger sense of favoring a certain contrast class as relevant.

Such relativized judgments would still not be *epistemic* if they could not depend on evidence or be tied to truth. But they can. To see how, consider an office betting pool where each worker picks one out of the ten horses in a race. Four horses have already been chosen, and the remaining six include a horse named Playboy. Playboy is better in the mud than the five other remaining horses, and rain is forecast for race day. This evidence can make you justified in believing that Playboy will win, assuming that one of the remaining six horses will win. Nonetheless, if you know nothing about the four previously chosen horses, or if you know that one of them is an even better mudder than Playboy, then you are not evidentially justified in believing that Playboy will win out of all ten horses. Thus, one can be evidentially justified in holding a belief out of a limited contrast class. Similarly, if only one astrological theory is consistent with certain observations, then those observations are evidence that this astrological theory is true, given the assumption that some astrological theory is true. That can make an astrologer evidentially justified in believing this theory out of the limited contrast class of astrological theories. Relativized judgments like these are needed to make sense out of what astrologers say and do, regardless of how reluctant non-astrologers are to call such beliefs justified without qualification.

5.5.2. *Closure*

Other critics charge that moderate skeptics cannot argue for skepticism, because contrast classes undermine a crucial premise in skeptical hypothesis arguments (section 4.3.2), specifically:

> (Closure) If I am justified in believing that p, and I am justified in believing that p entails q, then I am justified in believing that q.

Closure is supposed to fail in cases like this one by Dretske:

> You take your son to the zoo, see several zebras and, when questioned by your son, tell him they are zebras. Do you know they are zebras? Well, most of us would have little hesitation in saying that we did know this.... Yet something's being a zebra implies that it is not a mule and, in particular, not a mule cleverly disguised ... to look like a zebra. (1970, 1015–16)

This case is a counterexample to Closure if (i) I am justified in believing that the animals are zebras; (ii) I am justified in believing that: "the animals are zebras" entails "The animals are not cleverly disguised mules"; and (iii) I am not justified in believing that the animals are not cleverly disguised mules. The description of the example makes (ii) true. (iii) is also true because, if I depend totally on vision from far away, I have no (internal) evidence that could rule out the possibility of a mule cleverly disguised to look just like a zebra. Dretske then claims that (i) is true because "most of us would have little hesitation in saying that we did know this," which implies, if knowledge implies justified belief, that we are justified in believing this.

But out of which contrast class? When we say that we are justified in believing that the animals are zebras, our lack of hesitation suggests that we presuppose that a modest contrast class is relevant. Our utterance then claims something like "We are justified in believing that the animals are zebras as opposed to horses or tigers or any other animals that normally appear in zoos, which is the relevant contrast class." Cleverly disguised mules do not normally appear in zoos, so they are not in the contrast class that we assume to be relevant. If cleverly disguised mules were in our contrast class, then we would not say without hesitation that "We are justified in believing that the animals are zebras," because then we could not rule out some of the alternatives in the supposedly relevant contrast class.

The situation is different when we claim that I am not justified in believing that the animals are not cleverly disguised mules. The presupposed contrast class here must include cleverly disguised mules for this claim to make sense. The contrast class with respect to which a proposition is said to be justified or not justified must always include that proposition itself. Otherwise there would be no issue about whether it is justified *out of* that contrast class.

Thus, Dretske's example seems to work because the antecedent of closure presupposes a narrower contrast class than does the consequent of closure. This would refute any version of closure that places no restriction on contrast classes. However, a qualified closure principle does restrict the contrast classes:

> (Qualified Closure) If I am justified in believing that *p* out of contrast class *C*, and I am justified in believing that *p* entails *q*, then I am justified in believing that *q* out of contrast class *C*. (Cf. Stine 1976.)

The antecedent of this principle is not true for any contrast class that includes disguised mules. Its consequent is not false for any contrast class that does not include disguised mules or other oddities. (Admittedly, the consequent is also not true for any contrast class that does not include disguised mules, since, as I said, the contrast class with respect to which a proposition is said to be not justified must include that proposition itself. Still, at least that consequent is not false.) So Dretske's example does not refute the qualified closure principle. Neither does any other example. There seems to be no situation in which the qualified closure principle has a true antecedent and a false consequent. (See Vogel 1990; and Hawthorne 2004.)

Moreover, the qualified closure principle is all that is needed when the skeptical scenario argument is used to support skepticism about extremely justified belief. Its first premise claims that I am not justified in believing that a skeptical scenario is not true. To make sense, this premise must presuppose a contrast class that includes the skeptical scenario. So the closure principle must also refer throughout to a contrast class that includes the skeptical scenario. If the skeptical scenario cannot be ruled out, it follows that I am not justified in believing that I have hands as opposed to the skeptical scenario or out of the extreme contrast class. Since there is nothing special about this belief, we can generalize to the conclusion that no belief is extremely justified. This is skepticism about extremely justified moral belief.

The same argument cannot be used to support skepticism about modestly justified belief, because the modest contrast class makes nonsense out of the first premise of the skeptical scenario argument, namely, that we are not justified (modestly!?) in denying the skeptical scenario. This judgment makes no sense, because the skeptical scenario is not a member of the modest contrast class. This does not, of course, show that any belief can be modestly justified. To determine that, we will need to determine whether believers can ever rule out all other alternatives in the modest contrast class. If so, the conclusion will be moderate skepticism, which combines skepticism about extremely justified belief with non-skepticism about modestly justified belief.

5.5.3. *Relations among Contrast Classes*

Another common objection to my general approach is that separating contrast classes makes it unclear how being justified out of one contrast class is related to being justified out of a larger contrast class. If these ways of being justified are different kinds of the same thing, then there should be some relation between them. What is that relation?

This answer might seem tempting:

> S is modestly justified in believing P if and only if the following conditional is true: if skeptical scenarios are false, S is extremely justified in believing P.

This account cannot be right, since, if it were, one could detach "S is extremely justified in believing P" when skeptical scenarios are false and S is modestly justified. That would mean that, in every possible world where skeptical scenarios are false, anyone who is modestly justified is also extremely justified. That would leave no room for skepticism about extremely justified belief without skepticism about modestly justified belief.

This problem might be solved by widening the scope of the epistemic operator to get this:

> S is modestly justified in believing p if and only if S is extremely justified in believing the conditional: if all skeptical scenarios are false, then p.

This proposal fails, too, because the crucial conditional is material, so it is true if and only if either its antecedent is false or its consequent is true. Since this crucial conditional is not true by virtue of its form, if one cannot be extremely justified in believing that its antecedent is false (that is, that a skeptical scenario is true), then one could be extremely justified in believing the crucial conditional only if one could be extremely justified in believing its consequent, which is p. This condition is never satisfied, according to skeptics about extreme justification; so such skepticism would imply skepticism about modestly justified belief. This problem would disappear if one could be extremely justified in believing in a skeptical scenario, like Descartes' deceiving demon; but then one would be extremely justified in believing that the crucial conditional is true by falsity of antecedent. The present proposal then implies that I am modestly justified in believing p and also modestly justified in believing ~p, for any p. That result is not what moderate skeptics want.

Such difficulties suggest that the relation between extremely and modestly justified belief needs to be explained by a special operator:

> S is modestly justified in believing p if and only if S is extremely justified in believing p, *given that* skeptical hypotheses are false.[28]

The idea is analogous to conditional probability. The non-conditional probability of picking an ace out of a standard deck is 4/52. The conditional probability of picking a second ace given that an ace was picked the first time and not returned to

---

28. This principle can be generalized to cover other contrast classes as well: S is justified in believing P out of contrast class C if and only if S is justified in believing that (P given C) out of an appropriate larger contrast class. To believe P given C is to believe P given the disjunction of the members of C, that is, given that some member of C is true. The generalized principle refers to "an appropriate larger contrast class" because the appropriate larger class for moral beliefs might not be as large as the appropriate larger class for all beliefs, including non-moral beliefs.

the deck is 3/51. This is much less than the probability of the material conditional "If I pick an ace the first time, then I pick an ace the second time," since this conditional is true whenever I do not pick an ace the first time. In contrast with the probability of a conditional, the conditional probability need not be high when the probability of the antecedent is low. Instead, we determine the conditional probability by assuming that the antecedent is true and then calculating the probability of the consequent in those assumed circumstances. Analogously, the idea behind modest justifiedness is to locate a way of being justified that can be independent of whether skeptical hypotheses are true or whether they can be ruled out epistemically. That idea is captured if we assume that skeptical hypotheses are false, and then figure out which alternative among the remaining modest alternatives is best supported by the believer's epistemic grounds. This is what the above principle is meant to capture.[29]

Other principles governing contrast classes and their interaction could be developed. However, I hope I have said enough to suggest the usefulness of contrast classes and the plausibility of moderate Pyrrhonian skepticism in general epistemology. It remains to be seen how this approach applies to moral beliefs. That will be the task of chapter 6.

29. My analogy with conditional probability leads to an objection by Bird (2001). I respond in Sinnott-Armstrong 2002a.

Classy Moral Pyrrhonism

So far contrast classes have been introduced without mentioning morality in particular. The next step is to show how naturally this general framework applies to epistemic grounds for moral beliefs.

6.1. Moral Contrast Classes

Moral beliefs can be contrasted at various levels. The alternatives might be general moral theories, more specific moral judgments, or actions.

6.1.1. Contrasting Moral Theories

Moral philosophers have produced many moral systems, but the first two that are taught to students are often these:

(AU) Act Utilitarianism = An act is morally wrong if and only if that act fails to maximize the good for all.

(KD) Kantian Deontology = An act is morally wrong if and only if that act (or its agent) treats some person as a means only or fails to treat some person as an end (even if doing so maximizes the good for all).[1]

After defining these positions, teachers usually describe some counterexample to act utilitarianism, such as a doctor cutting up one healthy innocent person and distributing his organs to five unrelated people who would die without these

---

1. Some scholars argue that Kant allowed some exceptions or that he was concerned with intentions or character as opposed to actions, but (KD) is a view that is often ascribed to Kant. It does not matter for my purposes whether that common interpretation is correct.

transplants. If this doctor's act is morally wrong, and if Kantian deontology implies that this act is morally wrong, and if act utilitarianism implies otherwise, then students who are justified in believing these premises and have no separate reason to prefer (AU) to (KD) are justified in believing Kantian deontology as opposed to act utilitarianism.

Even if this transplant example does show this much (which could be questioned), it still might not justify anyone in believing in Kantian deontology as opposed to some other moral system, such as:

(GU) General Rule Utilitarianism = An act is morally wrong if and only if it would be disastrous for everyone to do acts of that kind.

This moral system can explain why it is morally wrong for a doctor to cut up one person to save five, if it would be disastrous for every doctor to perform similar transplants for similar reasons in similar situations (as far as they can tell). This seems likely, since doctors would make many mistakes in cutting up so many people; but my point here does not depend on that being true. My point is only that, if generalizing such transplants would be disastrous, then the transplant example alone would provide no basis for choosing between Kantian deontology and general rule utilitarianism. As with non-moral beliefs, to be justified in believing one member out of a contrast class, one must be able to rule out all other members of that class. The transplant example does not rule out (GU), so this example might make some believers justified in believing moral system (KD) out of the contrast class {AU, KD} without being justified in believing (KD) out of the larger contrast class {AU, KD, GU}.

Other counterexamples might later rule out (GU): it would be disastrous if everyone stood on his or her head all day, but there is nothing morally wrong with one person doing so.[2] The reason seems to be that few people can or want to stand on their heads all day, so no problem would arise if everyone were publicly allowed to do such acts. Thus, this counterexample is avoided by:

(PU) Public Rule Utilitarianism = An act is morally wrong if and only if it would cause more harm than benefit for everyone to know that everyone is allowed to do any act of that kind.

These are standard views, and they face standard problems. The point here is only that different positions can handle different examples. If Ann thinks up only the transplant example, but not the head-standing example, then Ann might be justified in believing (KD) out of {AU, KD} but not out of {AU, KD, GU}. In contrast, if Betty also thinks up the head-standing example, she might be justified in believing (KD) out of {AU, KD} and also out of {AU, KD, GU} but still not justified in believing (KD) out of {AU, KD, GU, PU}. As more counterexamples and other kinds of arguments are constructed, people can become justified in holding their moral beliefs out of larger and larger contrast classes. This is one way in which moral inquiry progresses.

---

2. This example comes from Gert 1998, 121. Gert endorses a version of (PU), as I explain in Sinnott-Armstrong 2002b.

These theoretical alternatives have been described in very general terms that allow variations. Within the framework of public rule utilitarianism, for example, people will disagree about what counts as a harm or a benefit, how harms and benefits are to be compared, who counts under "everyone," what it means to be allowed, what constitutes knowing that others are allowed, and which features of the act are morally relevant in a way that makes two acts instances of the same kind. Different versions of public rule utilitarianism can be distinguished by their different answers to these questions. To justify a belief in one particular version as opposed to another, the believer would need some reason to rule out each of the other versions. These details make a difference only at the margins. At the margins, arguments will be scarce and weak. Moral intuitions will not be as clear. This makes it hard for anyone to be justified in picking one precise version of public rule utilitarianism as opposed to every other moral system, including other versions of public rule utilitarianism that differ from this one only in minor details. Similar remarks apply to other moral systems, such as Kantian deontology and act utilitarianism. We might be able to get pretty far along the process of refinement, but it is hard to see how we could ever have enough reasons and arguments to nail down every detail. That is one problem that seems to lead to skepticism about justified belief in any moral theory.

6.1.2. *Contrasting Moral Statuses*

A similar process of refinement can occur when people debate the moral status of a single act or kind of act. Suppose that a serious famine or disease threatens the lives of millions of poor people in Africa. A rich American named Bill could save the lives of thousands of these people by donating 10% of his income to a charity, such as Oxfam. Someone named Peter, who happens to be an act utilitarian, claims that:

(R) Bill is morally required to give 10% to Oxfam.

This implies:

(W~) It is morally wrong for Bill *not* to give 10% to Oxfam.

A friend named Garrett responds that donations like this actually end up hurting more people than they help because the population will grow unchecked and then there will be even more people to be hurt in inevitable future famines. On this basis, Garrett concludes that:

(W) It is morally wrong for Bill to give 10% to Oxfam.

(W) is incompatible with (R), assuming "wrong" is used so that it cannot be both wrong for Bill to give and also wrong for Bill not to give 10% to Oxfam.[3] Now suppose that Peter can and does show that Garrett's non-moral claims about the

---

3. The term "wrong" need not always be used in this exclusive way. See Sinnott-Armstrong 1996b.

effects of famine relief are factually inaccurate. Then Peter might be justified in believing (R) out of {R, W}.

Enter a compromiser. Susan invokes the classic category of supererogation and claims that:

> (G) It is morally good for Bill to give 10% to Oxfam, but neither giving nor not giving is morally wrong.

Her argument might not be about non-moral facts, but rather about the conceptual difference between what is morally good and what is morally required. She might argue that an act is morally wrong only if it is better overall for society to punish people for doing such acts. On this view, if it is better overall for society to punish people neither for giving nor for refusing to give to charity, then she can rule out (R) and (W), if she can justify her assumptions. In any case, if she can rule out these other options, then she can be justified in believing (G) out of {R, W, G}. If she is also convinced by Peter's arguments against Garrett, then she might still be justified in believing (R) out of {R, W} even though she eventually rejects (R) on other grounds.

There are many more possibilities, but the basic point should be clear: we cannot understand the force of various arguments in cases like these unless we get straight about which kinds of moral status—such as required, wrong, and good—are being contrasted.

6.1.3. *Contrasting Options*

A third kind of contrast is among alternative actions. Consider Candice, who has cancer. There is no significant chance that she will live more than a month, but strong medications and life-support machines can keep her alive for more than two weeks. She is in great physical pain, which can be relieved but not stopped without making her unconscious. She asks her doctor to kill her now, and she refuses to discuss other options. Her doctor asks the medical ethics committee what he should do. Their job is not to determine what the law is. Their job is to determine what the morally right act is.

A new member of the committee, considering that Candice is competent and asked for it, claims that:

> (AE) The doctor morally ought to perform active euthanasia by administering a massive dose of some drug that is known to be almost certainly lethal.

Everyone else on the committee quickly dismisses this view as so outrageous that they cannot bring themselves to stoop so low as to dignify it with a response. After facing the committee's scorn, the member who proposed active euthanasia storms out in disgust or slinks out in disgrace.

The remaining members then propose other options. Some think that:

> (KA) The doctor morally ought to keep Candice alive with medications and machines as long as possible while relieving her pain as much as possible without making her unconscious.

This is the option of *keeping her alive*.

Despite the anesthesia, Candice will feel some physical pain and much mental distress during her remaining weeks. For this reason, other members propose that:

> (PE) The doctor morally ought to do nothing to prolong Candice's life except to give her food and fluids, while relieving her pain as much as possible without making her unconscious.

This option will be called *passive euthanasia* (although it is only one kind of passive euthanasia).

The committee discusses the pros and cons of these options. They rule out keeping Candice alive on the grounds that life support wastes resources and is contrary to the patient's competent refusal, so it violates the patient's right not to be treated without consent. Passive euthanasia avoids these problems and is closer to what Candice requested. On this basis, the committee concludes that passive euthanasia is what the doctor morally ought to do, as (PE) says. If the committee has good enough grounds to rule out keeping her alive but not to rule out passive euthanasia, then the committee is justified in believing (PE) out of {PE, KA}.

At this point, another member argues that withdrawing medication and machines is not enough. Instead of (PE), this member argues that:

> (WF) The doctor morally ought to withdraw food and fluids, as well as medications and machines, while relieving her pain as much as possible without making her unconscious.

With this option, Candice will die more quickly and less painfully than with the kind of passive euthanasia prescribed in (PE). Candice also might seem to have a moral right not to have food and fluids forced into her after she explicitly refuses to grant permission for these invasions. If so, the committee might not be justified in believing (PE) out of the larger contrast class {PE, KA, WF}. Indeed, the committee might become justified in believing (WF) out of {PE, KA, WF}.

Of course, this example is oversimplified. It is not clear which option is best until many more details are spelled out. The patient's competence and mental state, preferences of family members, local laws, and hospital policies might be crucial. There also might be other options to consider, including "terminal sedation," which is sedating the patient into unconsciousness while withdrawing food and fluids. The point here is just that a person can be justified in holding a particular moral belief about a specific action (such as passive euthanasia) when that action is contrasted with a small set of alternatives (not including withdrawing food and fluids) even if that same person would not be justified in that same moral belief out of a larger contrast class (that does include withdrawing food and fluids).

The same relativity arises when options are dismissed as irrelevant. Recall that Candice asks to be killed, but the ethics committee dismisses this option with much scorn. Of course, the fact that they don't respond does not show that they can't respond. So let's add that they cannot bring themselves to consider this option seriously. Furthermore, even if they did argue against active euthanasia, they could only cite their background belief that doctors should never kill their patients intentionally (and that active euthanasia involves such intentional killing). This background belief provides no good ground to rule out active euthanasia because it begs the question against anyone who favors active euthanasia, and the committee could not provide any independent justification for their background belief. We can also imagine that the committee members do or would recognize many exceptions to the general prohibition on doctors killing patients intentionally, and they do not and could not figure out how to refine that principle so as to make it defensible, even to themselves. Moreover, they have reasons to doubt their own impartiality, since they know that they would find it very disturbing to have to face the choice of whether to commit active euthanasia. In these circumstances, the committee cannot rule out (AE) with either a first-order or a second-order reason, so the committee is not justified in believing (WF) out of {PE, KA, WF, AE}. Nonetheless, the committee can still be justified in believing (WF) out of the smaller contrast class, {PE, KA, WF}.

This result would not be surprising if the committee gained additional evidence or information. If they learned, for example, that Candice changed her mind about wanting to die, then the committee would no longer seem justified in believing (WF). That is not what happens when a new option is introduced. The member who proposed active euthanasia did not give any new information to the committee. Even if we hold constant what the committee knows about the options, if they refuse to seriously consider one option and cannot give any good basis for ruling it out, then their conclusion is not justified out of a larger contrast class with that option, even if their belief is justified out of a smaller contrast class without that option.

6.2. Unqualified Judgments in Moral Epistemology

An impatient critic is likely to complain, "Enough about contrast classes, already! Is the committee *just plain justified* in believing their conclusion, (WF)?" The answer depends, of course, on what it means to call a belief just plain justified (simply, period, without qualification). We already saw in section 5.2 why "S is justified (without qualification) in believing P" cannot be analyzed in general as either "S is justified in believing P out of the extreme contrast class" or "... out of the modest contrast class" or "... out of the believer's contrast class" or "... out of the contrast class of the person who judges whether the belief is justified." The best account analyzes "S is justified (without qualification) in believing P" as "S is justified in believing P out of the *relevant* contrast class." All of the arguments for this analysis apply as well in cases with moral beliefs.

Whether a moral belief is justified (without qualification) then depends on which contrast class is presupposed to be relevant. To the extent that one sees the committee's own contrast class as the relevant contrast class, one will see them as justified (without qualification) in believing their conclusion, (WF), as long as they can rule out all other alternatives in their contrast class, even if they cannot rule out active euthanasia, since they dismiss active euthanasia as irrelevant, so (AE) is not in their contrast class. However, to the extent that one sees the larger contrast class that includes active euthanasia or (AE) as relevant, one will see the committee's belief as unjustified (without qualification) because they cannot rule out that other alternative which is in the contrast class that is supposed to be relevant. Both inclinations can be explained by analyzing "S is justified (without qualification) in believing P" as "S is justified in believing P out of the relevant contrast class." This disagreement about whether the committee's conclusion is justified (without qualification) is simply a disagreement about which contrast class is relevant.

Such disagreements are common, and often ferocious, in ethics. Hospital ethics committees really do dismiss what they see as "implausible" or "revolting" alternatives with disdain, even when they know that they lack any non-question-begging argument against those alternatives. In particular, an ethics committee in a religious hospital might refuse to consider craniotomy (which involves crushing a late fetus's skull to extract it from a pregnant woman), even when craniotomy is necessary to save the life of a pregnant woman. If the committee members admit that their refusal depends on a religious doctrine that is based on faith alone rather than on any positive ground, then they recognize that their conclusion would be at most permissively justified if they treated craniotomy as relevant. (See section 4.2.2.) Nonetheless, because they presuppose that craniotomy is not relevant, they still see their conclusion as justified (without qualification), despite having no positive ground to rule out that contrary option.

Such assumptions affect lives. An ethics committee that dismisses craniotomy as irrelevant and another ethics committee that treats craniotomy as relevant might reach different decisions. Their decisions might determine whether a pregnant woman lives or dies, even if neither committee has any more reason than the other for its own assumption about what is relevant.

My point is not that there is anything wrong with this common practice of dismissing some alternatives as irrelevant. There might be no better way to form moral beliefs. The point here is simply that these believers actually do assess their and others' beliefs as justified or not out of whichever contrast class they assume to be relevant. They presuppose (without arguing or even explicitly claiming) that some alternatives are simply irrelevant, so a lack of good grounds for ruling out those alternatives does not stand in the way of being justified (without qualification).[4]

Philosophers do the same. One well-known example comes from G. E. M. Anscombe's argument against utilitarianism or consequentialism:

> If someone says, "I agree, but all this wants a lot of explaining," then he is right, and, what is more, the situation at present is that we can't do the explaining; we lack the philosophic equipment. But if someone really thinks, *in advance*, that it is open to question whether such an action as procuring the judicial execution of the innocent should be quite excluded from consideration—I do not want to argue with him; he shows a corrupt mind. (1958, 16–17)

---

4. Compare the answer when an interviewee who had done good deeds was asked why those deeds were good: "Why is integrity important and lying bad? I don't know. It just is. It's so basic. I don't want to be bothered with challenging that" (Bellah et al. 1985, 7).

In our terms, Anscombe seems to claim to be justified (without qualification) in believing that it is always unjust or morally wrong to judicially execute an innocent person, even though she admits that she can't rule out the alternative that it is sometimes morally permissible to judicially execute an innocent person. The point is not simply that she does not actually give any good ground for rejecting this alternative. The point is that she "lack[s] the philosophic equipment" and "can't do the explaining"; yet this inability does not bother her, because she sees this alternative as irrelevant epistemically. Other philosophers make similar moves, though usually not so openly.

Views like this suggest that the important contrast class in moral reasoning might be the smaller contrast class that does not include the options that we need not and, maybe, should not consider. I am not endorsing (or opposing) these views. My point here is just that such views are coherent and popular with many thoughtful people, so any adequate framework for moral epistemology must leave room for them. To do so, we need to recognize the role of contrast classes in moral reasoning.

6.3. Relativized Moral Skepticisms

So far moral contrast classes have been discussed without reference to moral nihilism or other skeptical hypotheses. That shows that contrast classes are important to moral epistemology independent of moral skepticism. They are also useful in understanding moral skepticism.

To see how, just imagine that a member of the hospital ethics committee (probably a philosopher) argues, "Active euthanasia is not morally wrong, but neither is keeping Candice alive or killing her doctor, since nothing is morally wrong." Such moral nihilism would be dismissed with disdain and without argument by a hospital ethics committee trying to reach a practical decision. Moreover, suppose that the ethics committee members are busy doctors who have not bothered to think about any reasons for or against moral nihilism. They could not say anything to rule out moral nihilism except maybe something like, "Surely terrorism and incest are morally wrong, so *something* is morally wrong." This response clearly begs the question against moral nihilism, because it assumes the very issue at stake. So this committee seems to have no good or adequate ground for ruling out moral nihilism. Maybe other committees could rule out moral nihilism. (That issue will be addressed in part II.) But the committee in this example cannot rule out moral nihilism.

Their inability would normally not be seen as a serious defect in the committee or its performance or its grounds, because moral nihilism is not one of the alternatives that needs to be eliminated in order to meet the common or usual standards in moral epistemology, at least for ethics committees. But moral nihilism is still contrary to the committee's conclusion, (WF). Indeed, it is also contrary to (KA), (PE), and (AE); (R), (W), and (G); and (AU), (KD), (GU), and (PU). Hence, moral nihilism is included in the extreme contrast class but not in the modest contrast class for moral beliefs:

The Extreme Contrast Class for a moral belief P = all claims contrary to P, including skeptical scenarios that are systematically uneliminable.

The Modest Contrast Class for a moral belief P = all claims contrary to P that need to be eliminated in order to meet usual epistemic standards.

These are only two out of an infinite array of possible contrast classes. Moreover, the boundaries of these two classes could be specified more precisely. However, I will not bother with other classes or more precision since nothing I say here will depend on such details.

As in section 5.1, we can use these two contrast classes to distinguish two epistemic judgments:

(JM) The committee is justified out of the *modest* contrast class in believing (WF).

(JE) The committee is justified out of the *extreme* contrast class in believing (WF).

And we can shorten these judgments to:

(JM') The committee is *modestly* justified in believing (WF).

(JE') The committee is *extremely* justified in believing (WF).

If the hospital ethics committee is unable to rule out moral nihilism but is able to rule out all of (WF)'s modest alternatives, such as (KA), (PE), and (AE), then (JM) and (JM') are true, but (JE) and (JE') are false. This result follows from the principle that to be justified in believing one member out of a contrast class, a believer must be able to rule out all other members of that contrast class.

Different kinds of moral skepticism simply generalize denials:

Skepticism about *modestly* justified moral belief
= No moral belief is justified out of the modest contrast class.
= No moral belief is modestly justified.

Skepticism about *extremely* justified moral belief
= No moral belief is justified out of the extreme contrast class.
= No moral belief is extremely justified.

Both of these claims are denied by *anti-skepticism* about justified moral belief. Both claims are accepted by *strong skepticism* about justified moral belief. Still, the independence of these claims allows a promising compromise:

Moderate skepticism about justified moral belief = Skepticism about extremely justified moral belief but not about modestly justified moral belief.

Such moderate moral skepticism follows if no moral believer can rule out moral nihilism, but some moral believers can sometimes rule out all but one of the alternatives in the modest contrast class.

None of these kinds of moral skepticism are committed to any contrast class being relevant or not. Their claims are only about what can and cannot be accomplished within the specified contrast classes.

6.4. Academic Moral Skepticism

Most moral skeptics, however, do not refer to contrast classes at all. Instead, they endorse something like this:

> *Academic* skepticism about justified moral belief = Nobody is justified (without qualification) in believing any moral claim.

Since moral believers are justified (without qualification) if and only if they are justified out of the relevant contrast class, Academic skepticism about justified moral belief is equivalent to the claim that nobody is justified in believing any moral claim out of the relevant contrast class.

Academic moral skepticism has many opponents. One group includes *invariantists* about relevance, who hold that which contrast class is relevant does not vary from context to context. Different invariantists see different contrast classes as always relevant. *Extreme invariantists* see the extreme contrast class as always relevant. They can deny Academic moral skepticism only if they hold that some moral believers can rule out skeptical hypotheses, including moral nihilism. *Modest invariantists* see the modest contrast class as always relevant. They deny that skeptical hypotheses, such as moral nihilism, are ever relevant, so they can deny Academic moral skepticism even if no moral believers can ever rule out moral nihilism. This view is suggested by the quotation from Anscombe in section 6.2.

A separate group that opposes Academic moral skepticism includes *moral contextualists*, who hold that which moral contrast class is relevant varies with context. A standard version of moral contextualism holds that the modest contrast class is the relevant one in contexts like the hospital ethics committee, and the extreme contrast class is not relevant in such practical contexts but is relevant in some philosophical discussions.[5]

To appreciate this compromise, consider a philosophy class that has spent all term studying extreme positions like moral nihilism, egoism, relativism, and skepticism. The final assignment is a debate in class. Some students sincerely and thoroughly defend moral nihilism. Another student responds by claiming that withdrawing food and fluids is morally required after Candice requests it. This student appeals to common moral principles to rule out the options of keeping Candice alive, passive euthanasia, and active euthanasia (so this student goes further than the hospital ethics committee). However, this student never considers moral nihilism carefully enough to be able to rule it out. It would be natural for the students who defend moral nihilism (as well as the teacher) to claim that this student is not justified (without qualification) in believing that active euthanasia is morally wrong.

---

5. For example, Timmons 1998, 221: "Regardless of whether members of the [ethics] committee could defend their basic moral beliefs against skeptical challenges, or even whether they had justifying reasons that they might be able to rehearse, I submit that the moral conclusions reached by the committee were justified ones. In more of a detached context, in which skeptical challenges get their hold, those same beliefs would be in need of justification." In our terms, Timmons holds that skeptical challenges are irrelevant in such "engaged" contexts.

Nonetheless, according to contextualists, the hospital ethics committee can still be justified (without qualification) in reaching the same conclusion even if the committee lacks the same ability that made the student unjustified (without qualification). The point is not that the ethics committee has more information or expertise or logical acumen than the philosophy student. Whether one is justified in believing something does depend on one's other beliefs and on one's intellectual abilities. As one gathers evidence and draws inferences, one comes to be justified in more beliefs. However, that kind of variation does not explain why the hospital committee is justified when the philosophy student is not. In our example, the committee and the student have the same background beliefs and abilities, and they draw the same inferences (except that the student rules out active euthanasia while the committee does not).

The contextualist claim is, instead, that different alternatives are relevant in different contexts. Since the committee's job is to reach a practical decision in a relatively short time, they are not expected to be able to rule out extreme philosophical alternatives. In contrast, the point of the philosophy class is to consider moral nihilism and other extreme positions for a whole term, so students are expected to take those alternatives seriously and to be able to say something against them before rejecting them. That is supposed to make the student's belief unjustified (without qualification), although the committee's belief is justified (without qualification).

Moral skeptics need not deny that different alternatives *appear* relevant in such different contexts. If a member raises moral nihilism during a hospital ethics committee meeting, it does *seem* natural to dismiss that alternative as irrelevant in that context. The crucial issue, however, is not about appearances. Whether a belief *seems* justified (without qualification) depends on which contrast class *seems* relevant. However, whether a belief is *really* justified (without qualification) depends on which contrast class is *really* relevant.

The crucial issue, then, is whether moral nihilism is *really* relevant in contexts like the ethics committee. Academic moral skeptics often claim that moral nihilism is really relevant even in ethics committees. Contextualists then deny that moral nihilism is really relevant in ethics committees. Modest invariantists, as well as many practical doctors, might say that moral nihilism is not really relevant even in philosophy classes. If moral nihilism really is irrelevant, at least in practical contexts, then the ethics committee's moral beliefs can be justified (without qualification) even though the committee cannot rule out moral nihilism. This claim would be enough to refute Academic moral skepticism, even if no moral believer could ever rule out moral nihilism, as long as some moral believer is able to rule out all other alternatives in the modest contrast class. Thus, in order to determine whether Academic moral skepticism is defensible, we need to determine whether moral nihilism really is relevant or irrelevant, at least in practical contexts like that of ethics committees.

6.5. Is Moral Nihilism Relevant?

Contextualists and modest invariantists give several reasons to dismiss moral nihilism as irrelevant. Some of their arguments claim that certain features of moral nihilism itself make it irrelevant.

Many anti-skeptics argue that moral nihilism is irrelevant simply because it cannot be ruled out in practice or in principle. It is not clear why ineliminability is supposed to show that moral nihilism is irrelevant, but maybe the idea is just that its ineliminability makes moral nihilism empty or incoherent. If so, I have already criticized that idea in section 3.3.

A second line of thought might be that moral believers are justified when they have done everything they can to check out their moral beliefs because they should not be blamed for failing to do what they cannot do. However, Academic skeptics can respond that, even when believers do all that they can, they still have not done *enough* to be justified (without qualification). People do not always succeed when they do their best. The issue of whether believers are justified is not only about whether believers are to blame. It is at least partly about whether their grounds are adequate. The fact that such believers are not to blame for failing to rule out moral nihilism does not show that their grounds are adequate or that moral nihilism is irrelevant.

More technically, recall the distinction between personal and impersonal justifiedness in section 4.2.4. A believer who properly uses all available information is personally justified but still might not be impersonally or wholly justified. That is what happens in Gettier examples, and the point extends to moral beliefs: even if moral believers cannot be blamed personally for their failure to rule out moral nihilism, their grounds still might not be adequate to rule out moral nihilism given full information, and then they are not impersonally justified. Since the topic of moral epistemology includes being impersonally and not just personally justified, Academic moral skeptics can hold that the ineliminability of moral nihilism does not make that alternative irrelevant to the issues that determine whether a moral believer is justified (without qualification).

An everyday example might make this point clearer. Consider Hannah, who is trying to figure out what is inside a wrapped birthday present. She knows that it is not a bike because it is too small. She knows that it is not clothes because of how it rattles when shaken. It still might be either a puzzle or a game, for all she knows. If she believes that it is a game, her belief is not justified, even out of the modest contrast class, unless she can somehow rule out the possibility of a puzzle. Now suppose that the evil donor put the present in an impenetrable box tied with an unbreakable ribbon. In this case, Hannah can't do anything to find out what is in the box, so she is not to blame. That still does not make her justified in believing that the box contains a game as opposed to a puzzle. Nor does it make the possibility of a puzzle irrelevant. Instead, her inability keeps her belief from being justified out of any contrast class that includes a puzzle. That alternative does not cease to be relevant just because she cannot rule it out no matter what she does. Analogously, if there is nothing that any moral believer can do to rule out the hypothesis of moral nihilism, then the fact that a moral believer does everything that any moral believer could do to determine whether an act is morally wrong does not make that moral believer justified in contrast with moral nihilism. Nor does it show that moral nihilism is irrelevant.

Opponents of moral skepticism sometimes add that, if moral nihilism were true, its truth would have no effect on people's actions. That must be so in one way, since otherwise moral nihilism could be ruled out or in by observations of people's actual behavior. (Cf. section 8.1.) Still, its lack of effect on action does not make moral nihilism epistemically irrelevant. Nor does it make contrary beliefs justified (without qualification). Analogously, the fact that Hannah's acts would not be affected if there were a puzzle in the locked box does not make her justified (without qualification) in believing that there is a game in the locked box.

Maybe the point is not about truth but about belief. Belief in moral nihilism is often called "idle," which seems to mean that this belief has no effect on people's actions. This would make it pointless to believe in moral nihilism if the aim of belief were always to decide how to act. However, even if this is the only aim of substantive ethics (which I doubt), action is not the goal of meta-ethics or moral epistemology. (See section 1.1.) Besides, it is not at all clear that belief in moral nihilism would not affect action. Moral nihilists might be less inclined to engage in some kinds of morally motivated behaviors, either good or bad. (See section 1.4.) At least belief in moral nihilism could affect theoretical activities such as speech acts or mental acts of thinking about issues in moral epistemology.

A different kind of "idleness" is charged when critics claim that belief in moral nihilism does not give people any *reason* to act differently. This is obvious, in one way, since the point of moral nihilism is to deny moral reasons, not to assert or add any new reasons. Nonetheless, belief in moral nihilism might affect what people have adequate reason to do, if it undermines moral reasons to do or not to do certain acts. Of course, moral nihilists still might have other, non-moral reasons to do exactly what non-nihilists think they have moral reasons to do. However, it is hard to see why moral and non-moral reasons must always coincide in this way. And such coincidence would not make moral nihilism irrelevant epistemically.

Yet another common response is that there is no reason to believe in moral nihilism, and that makes it irrelevant to moral epistemology. Similar objections are often raised against Descartes' deceiving demon. However, section 3.2 canvassed several reasons for believing in moral nihilism. Some of those reasons are no good, and the others are not conclusive, but at least the challenge of moral nihilism cannot be dismissed as unfounded in the same way as Descartes' deceiving demon. Nobody believes in skeptical hypotheses like Descartes' deceiving demon, but actual intelligent people really do believe in moral nihilism, and they develop careful reasons, so they are not just being arbitrary or playful.[6] Commonsense morality stands accused, and the prosecution has presented its arguments. These

---

6. Descartes' deceiving demon hypothesis involves "sticking one's neck out" in the sense of hypothesizing many facts without any explanation. Why would the demon bother to deceive us at all? Why would the demon deceive us this way instead of another? How does the deception work? And so on. The competing hypothesis that I really do have hands, there are other people, and so on, leaves fewer facts unexplained. Similarly for a brain-in-a-vat hypothesis. In contrast, moral nihilism postulates no such unexplained facts, whereas opponents of moral nihilism do postulate moral facts that cannot be explained easily. Thus, defenders of moral nihilism cannot be accused of sticking their necks out farther than their opponents. Perhaps that is part of the reason why moral nihilism has more actual defenders than Descartes' deceiving demon.

arguments, though questionable, are not so weak that the defense can simply rest before presenting any arguments of its own. (Cf. section 4.3.)

Moreover, even if there were no actual opponents and no reason at all for moral nihilism, that would not show that moral nihilism is irrelevant epistemically. To see why, consider Hannah again. Even if nobody believes or has reason to believe that the box contains a puzzle, that does not make that possibility irrelevant, nor does it make Hannah justified (without qualification) in believing that the box contains a game. What matters is whether the other alternatives can be ruled *out*, not whether anyone does or could rule them *in*.

So far, then, there is no good reason to insist that moral nihilism is irrelevant to whether a moral belief is justified (without qualification). However, the preceding arguments cite features of moral nihilism itself independent of context. Contextualists, instead, usually point out aspects of particular contexts that might seem to make moral nihilism irrelevant in those contexts even if not in other contexts or in itself.

One obvious difference between the hospital ethics committee and the philosophy class, for example, is that some philosophy students think about and defend moral nihilism, whereas the hospital committee members, like most people, usually do not consciously consider the alternative of moral nihilism. But recall Hannah. She is not justified in believing that the box contains a game instead of a puzzle just because she does not consciously think of the possibility of a puzzle. In situations like hers, people seem better justified when they think of and rule out more contrary close possibilities, so someone's failure to think about an alternative seems not to be the kind of thing that could make that person's belief justified (without qualification). Even when believers would not be justified if they considered misleading evidence, their failure to consider that evidence merely prevents defeat and is not what makes their belief justified. Besides, it would beg the question here to assume that moral nihilism is misleading.

Another common answer cites the purpose of hospital ethics committees. People form and join such committees in order to reduce immoral practices in hospitals. The committees would not serve this purpose if they wasted their precious time quibbling about moral nihilism. That might seem to justify such committees in dismissing moral nihilism without worrying about whether they have any good reason against that alternative.

This argument has some force. Bad consequences would follow if ethics committees got bogged down in philosophical discussions of moral nihilism. However, these reasons are purely instrumental. Bad consequences cannot show that moral nihilism is false or that such committees have any epistemic reason for dismissing moral nihilism. Compare Hannah again, but this time, just as she is about to try to test whether the box contains a puzzle or a game, she smells smoke. Her house is on fire. That gives her strong instrumental reason not to waste time ruling out the possibility that the box contains a puzzle. However, that instrumental reason cannot make her epistemically justified in believing that the box contains a game since it cannot make her able to rule out the hypothesis of a puzzle. Analogously, even if hospital ethics committees are instrumentally justified in refusing to consider moral nihilism, that does not make them epistemically justified in any moral belief contrary to moral nihilism. Such instrumental considerations cannot show that moral nihilism is irrelevant in the epistemic way that is at issue here.[7]

In the absence of any other argument, there seems to be no good basis for dismissing moral nihilism as epistemically irrelevant either in general or in any particular context. However, this conclusion does not imply that moral nihilism *is* relevant to justified belief. There might also be no good basis for that opposite claim. An alternative is relevant only when believers need to rule it out in order to be justified (without qualification). Thus, to claim that moral nihilism is relevant in ethics committees is to claim that ethics committees must rule it out in order to be justified (without qualification). For Academic moral skeptics to assume that would beg the question against contextualists and modest invariantists.

Academic moral skeptics cannot argue that moral nihilism is relevant simply because it is contrary to positive moral beliefs. That argument assumes that all contraries are relevant. I already criticized the analysis of "S is justified (without qualification) in believing P" as "S is justified out of the extreme contrast class, which includes all contrary possibilities" (see section 5.2). Since that analysis fails, it is hard to see any good basis for insisting that all contrary possibilities are relevant.

Maybe the fact that some intelligent people sincerely believe and assert moral nihilism is supposed to make it relevant. However, if the fact that an alternative is not believed does not make it irrelevant, why would the fact that it is believed automatically make it relevant? We often argue with certain audiences that share certain of our assumptions without worrying about the known fact that other people, whom we are not addressing, might question those assumptions. When such arguments work, why can't they make us justified? We often cannot discover or understand contrary positions that other people have held, so we would not be justified (without qualification) in believing much, if anything, if we always had to be able to rule out every position that anyone ever held. For these reasons, the fact that someone holds a position does not seem to require us to rule it out. And if this requirement does not hold in general, then it cannot be used to show that moral nihilism is relevant.[8]

I know of no other argument for the claim that moral nihilism is relevant epistemically. Thus, we seem to be left with no good reason to assume either that moral nihilism is relevant or that moral nihilism is not relevant, even in a particular context. This means that we also have no good reason to agree or disagree with either modest invariantism or contextualism or to accept or deny Academic skepticism regarding justified moral beliefs.

7. See section 4.2.1. Section 4.2.4 is also helpful here, since in the case of fire Hannah can be personally justified without being impersonally justified, if the fire makes full information unavailable to her. Finally, compare philosophers and committees who dismiss alternatives as irrelevant for practical reasons with legal theorists and judges who exclude tainted evidence from trials and who exclude policy considerations from legal interpretation.

8. Compare my criticisms of Lewis's rule of attention in section 5.3.

6.6. More Problems for Relevance

These problems in deciding whether moral nihilism is or is not relevant suggest more general problems for determining relevance. Moral nihilism is just one of the many alternatives whose relevance is problematic. It is at least as difficult to show that a hospital ethics committee either should or should not treat active euthanasia or craniotomy as relevant. A Catholic hospital ethics committee, for example, could argue that their job is not to question standard Catholic moral doctrines, just as other hospital ethics committees argue that their job is not to argue against moral nihilism. But then an atheistic ethics committee could also argue that their job is not to refute Catholic doctrines that they find obscure and implausible. Such appeals to the function or purpose of the ethics committee cannot determine what is relevant in these conflicts any more than when moral nihilism is at issue.

More generally, nobody has formulated plausible rules governing when an alternative is relevant. I argued against David Lewis's rules in section 5.3, and the same points apply to moral beliefs. Such rules also seem unavailable because of difficulties in defining contexts. Imagine that the philosophy teacher leaves the class on moral nihilism and goes straight across campus to join the hospital ethics committee. (Philosophers play both such roles often these days.) Right before the committee meeting starts, another member asks the philosopher what the class discussed, and the philosopher responds, "Moral nihilism." Does this utterance make moral nihilism relevant to the committee meeting? If not, what if the chair calls the meeting to order then another member asks the philosopher, "What did you say?" The philosopher repeats, "Moral nihilism." Does this utterance make moral nihilism relevant to the ongoing committee meeting? What if the other members keep wondering what moral nihilism is, so they are thinking about moral nihilism? Or the philosopher's mind wanders during the meeting, so the philosopher is still thinking about whether moral nihilism is true? Maybe these thoughts cause the philosopher to blurt out "moral nihilism" as a reflex or as a joke in response to a serious question about what the committee should do. Does this make moral nihilism relevant? Or what if the philosopher sincerely asserts that moral nihilism is true? Maybe the philosopher has recently been convinced by the readings and discussions in the class. Can the committee members still dismiss that extreme view as irrelevant when some members hold it? And what if most people on campus are moral nihilists? What about atheists on ethics committees in Catholic hospitals? Or a Catholic hospital in a mainly Protestant or Jewish or Muslim city or state or country? How many people in what positions must believe a view in order for it to be relevant? Of course, contextualists could simply declare answers to these questions. What is hard is to find any basis for choosing one answer which favors one contrast class instead of another. What someone counts as relevant or irrelevant then seems arbitrary epistemically. This makes it attractive to seek a way of doing moral epistemology without any commitment to real relevance. As we will see, moral Pyrrhonism provides a way.

But this is not the only reason to avoid claims to relevance. As I also argued in chapter 5, a separate problem arises from difficulties in specifying any complete contrast class that could be relevant even for simple issues such as a person's name. Similar problems arise for moral beliefs. Imagine that her doctor gives Candice a certain amount of a certain anesthesia in a certain way. Does every different kind, amount, or way to administer anesthesia constitute a relevant alternative? If so, few non-specialists, or even specialists, could be justified (without qualification) in believing that the doctor did the right thing, since they could not list, much less rule out, all of the other alternatives. That seems implausible. However, if some contrary treatments are not relevant, then what makes them irrelevant? Since the doctor could choose any of the treatments, it is hard to see why any of them would be irrelevant. A dilemma, thus, arises: It is doubtful that the treatments are all relevant, although none seems irrelevant. This dilemma can be solved by, and only by, suspending belief about all claims that any contrast class is really relevant or irrelevant.

The deepest problem for contextualism is that a single claim about justified belief can cross contexts. Imagine that, during the philosophy class, the philosophy professor describes the ethics committee's decision. Then the professor asks simply, "Is the committee's belief justified (without qualification)?" A skeptical student answers, "No." The student is incorrect if the committee's context determines whether they are justified (without qualification) because their context determines which contrast class is really relevant to their conclusion, and if moral nihilism really is irrelevant in their context. However, the student is correct if the student's context determines the truth of what the student says, and if moral nihilism really is relevant in the student's context. Thus, whether the student is correct depends on which alternatives are really relevant. More generally, when one person judges whether another person's belief is justified (without qualification), we need to distinguish the judger from the believer. The judger's context can be very different from the believer's context. Then we need to ask whose context determines whether the judger is correct about the believer.[9]

In judging that a belief is justified or not, the context of the believer seems more important if the purpose of the judger is to predict whether the believer will do well as a believer. In our example, the fact that a member of the committee could not rule out moral nihilism is no basis for criticizing that believer as an ethics committee member by calling the member's belief unjustified. After all, the issue of moral nihilism rarely, if ever, comes up in ethics committee meetings, so an inability to deal with moral nihilism is no indication that the believer cannot function perfectly well on the committee.

In contrast, the context of the judger seems more important if the judger's purpose is to decide whether to endorse the belief (or the process that led to it) in

---

9. The judger and believer could be the same person. Or more than two people could be involved: if the student writes in a paper that the ethics committee is not justified and later shows this paper and the grade to a parent, then the parent might speak and believe within a new context about whether the teacher was justified in believing that the student was not justified in believing that the committee was justified in believing that its decision was morally right. Further parties in further contexts could be added. Such complications raise additional problems for real relevance.

order to determine whether the judger should use that belief (or process) in forming the judger's own beliefs. If the student calls the committee's belief justified (without qualification) in order to endorse the committee's belief (or process) and then to go on to derive further beliefs from that assumption, then the student should be held responsible for meeting the standards of the context in which the student endorses that belief. That context is the philosophy class where moral nihilism is supposed to be relevant.

Thus, we cannot specify which context matters, or which contrast class is really relevant, because that depends on the purpose of the judger. Compare the question of whether jumbo shrimp really are large (without qualification). When your purpose is to find shrimp large enough to stuff, it can be fine for you to say, "Those shrimp are large." The same assertion would, however, be ridiculous if your purpose was to win a contest in which you had to find a large crustacean. Because whether these shrimp count as large depends on the judger's purpose in classifying them as large or small, there is no way to settle disputes about whether the shrimp are really large (without qualification). Similarly, since judgments about whether a belief is justified (without qualification) depend on the purposes of the person making the judgment, there is also no way to settle disputes about whether a believer is really justified (without qualification).

Contextualists might try to solve this problem by adding an explicit reference to the judger's purpose. One attempt introduces judgments of the form "Believer B is justified in believing claim X when B is in context C and judger J has purpose P." But even this won't work, because a third party should be able to disagree with the judger about whether B is justified (without qualification), when that third party has different purposes that make a different contrast class more important. When different judgers have different purposes, there is no solid basis for claiming that one purpose is the one that determines whether a believer is justified (without qualification). Besides, this move in effect admits that what determines which contrast class is relevant is *not* a feature of the belief that is judged to be justified or not. And it allows the same belief to be called justified by one person for one purpose but then called unjustified by another person (or even the same person) for another purpose, so this is not *real* relevance. It is only an appearance from one perspective. For such reasons, adding explicit references to context cannot save real relevance.

Even if contextualists cannot solve the problems for real relevance, invariantists might seem to have an easier time. They can simply say that either the extreme contrast class or the modest contrast class is relevant in all contexts for all judgers and believers. Then cross-context judgments create no trouble. But which contrast class—modest or extreme—is always the relevant one? There is no solid basis for choice among these candidates, since, as I argued, the judger's purpose affects which contrast class is important. This difficulty in determining which contrast class is relevant does not entail that there is no fact of the matter about which contrast class is relevant. However, in the absence of any idea about how to settle on one contrast class as opposed to other candidates, it seems better to avoid any claim that any contrast class is the relevant one.

6.7. Moderate Moral Pyrrhonism

If we avoid claims to relevance in moral epistemology, then we get a kind of Pyrrhonian moral skepticism. Meta-skeptics about relevance suspend belief about all epistemic claims that presuppose that any moral contrast class really is relevant. In particular, since to call any moral belief justified (without qualification) is to say that it is justified out of the relevant contrast class (see section 5.2), meta-skeptics about relevance neither assert nor deny that any moral belief is justified (without qualification). They also neither assert nor deny Academic moral skepticism (section 6.4). This makes them Pyrrhonian moral skeptics (cf. section 5.4).

Pyrrhonists also do not side with Academic moral skepticism's traditional opponents, including contextualists and modest invariantists. Pyrrhonists see those positions as confused because, like Academic skepticism, they depend on a false presupposition, namely, that some contrast classes are really relevant. Moral Pyrrhonists avoid the whole language game in which these traditional disputes were framed. They see disputes about whether moral believers are justified (without qualification) as pointless in much the same way as disputes about whether jumbo shrimp are really large.

Pyrrhonian moral skeptics can still endorse relativized moral skepticisms (section 6.3). In particular, Pyrrhonian moral skepticism is compatible with moderate skepticism about justified moral belief, which claims that no moral believer is extremely justified (because nobody can rule out moral nihilism) but some moral believers are modestly justified (because they can rule out all other alternatives in the modest contrast class). Such relativized moral skepticisms do not imply anything about which (or whether any) contrast class is really relevant, so such relativized skepticisms can be accepted by meta-skeptics about relevance, including Pyrrhonian moral skeptics. Moderate moral skepticism is logically independent of Pyrrhonian moral skepticism, so some Pyrrhonian moral skeptics may reject moderate moral skepticism. However, the combination of Pyrrhonian moral skepticism with moderate moral skepticism provides a larger view that is coherent and attractive.

Pyrrhonian moral skeptics can also make particular relativized judgments, such as that the hospital ethics committee is justified in believing (WF) in contrast with (PE) and (KA), but not in contrast with (AE) (or moral nihilism), because they have reasons to rule out (PE) and (KA) but they have no good reason to rule out (AE) (or moral nihilism). Just as we say that certain shrimp are large *for shrimp* when we want to avoid disputes about whether they are large without qualification, Pyrrhonists can also make relativized judgments that avoid any disputes about which contrast class is relevant.

Pyrrhonian moral skeptics can even, if they want, continue to talk about whether moral beliefs are justified without explicitly specifying any contrast class.[10]

---

10. Compare Fogelin 1994, 5–10. See also my account of what Pyrrhonians mean by such assertions in Sinnott-Armstrong 2004a.

They can, for example, say simply that the hospital ethics committee is justified in reaching its conclusion, but the philosophy student is not justified in reaching the same conclusion, even if neither can rule out moral nihilism. However, what Pyrrhonists mean by these unqualified judgments must be *only* that the ethics committee is justified out of the modest contrast class and the philosophy student is not justified out of the extreme contrast class. Pyrrhonists can even admit that these contrast classes seem to be the relevant ones for those contexts. All that they need to avoid is any claim or presupposition that any contrast class is really relevant in any context.

Moral Pyrrhonism spells the end of much traditional moral epistemology, which endorsed or opposed Academic moral skepticism. However, when moderate moral skepticism is added, new light is thrown on the issues that were at stake. For example, contrast classes reveal the force and limits of skeptical hypothesis arguments. The version in section 4.3.2 claimed that nobody can rule out moral nihilism, so no moral belief can be justified (without qualification). We will see in part II whether there really is no way to rule out moral nihilism. However, even if so, that would support at most moderate moral skepticism. It would not support strong moral skepticism or skepticism about modestly justified moral belief. Moral beliefs are modestly justified if they are justified with respect to a contrast class that by definition does not include moral nihilism or any other extreme alternative that would not be taken seriously in everyday moral deliberation. Hence, there is no need to be able to rule out any extreme alternative like moral nihilism in order for a moral belief to be modestly justified. Thus, moral beliefs might be modestly justified even if skeptical hypothesis arguments are sound.

Although such moderate Pyrrhonian moral skepticism is, I hope, attractive, my argument for it cannot be complete without determining which alternatives can and cannot be ruled out. If no moral believers can rule out moral nihilism, but some moral believers can rule out all other alternatives in the modest contrast class, then moderate Pyrrhonian moral skepticism follows from my arguments against real relevance plus my analysis of unqualified judgments in moral epistemology. But whether our epistemic abilities are limited in these ways remains to be seen in part II.

THEORIES

Part I explained the essential concepts of moral epistemology and presented the basic challenge of moral skepticism. In part II, we will consider various replies to moral skepticism and ask which moral beliefs or believers can be justified on each approach. I cannot discuss every response to moral skepticism, but I will sort respondents into kinds and briefly discuss some of the most common, important, and plausible examples of each sort.

These traditional views do not employ contrast classes explicitly. Instead, they discuss whether moral beliefs or believers can be justified without qualification. To represent these views accurately, then, I will often need to suppress any mention of contrast classes. However, when I draw my own conclusions, I will introduce contrast classes explicitly.

I will argue for two theses: First, some of these theories do show how some believers sometimes can be justified in holding some moral beliefs out of some limited contrast classes, including the modest contrast class. Second, no method can show that anyone is justified in believing any moral judgment out of the extreme contrast class or out of any contrast class that includes moral nihilism. The survey of these alternatives will thereby lead to moderate moral skepticism.

I also hope to illustrate how disagreements between these theories and academic moral skepticism can often be understood as disagreements over which contrast class is relevant. When a certain theory or method shows that a moral believer is justified in believing a certain moral judgment out of a certain limited contrast class, Academic moral skeptics will insist that that this contrast class is not wide enough. They will claim that more alternatives must be ruled out for that belief to be justified without qualification, that is, out of the relevant contrast class. Defenders of the non-skeptical method will respond that this limited contrast class is the relevant one, so being justified out of that limited class is all believers need in order to be justified without qualification, that is, out of the relevant contrast class.

Throughout part II, I will remain neutral about which contrast classes, if any, are relevant and about how much is needed to be justified without qualification. My reasons for this neutrality were given in sections 5.3 and 6.5–6.6, where I argued that, even if some contrast classes *seem* relevant, there is no good reason to hold (or deny) any contrast class is *really* relevant (or irrelevant) for the substantively-neutral purposes of meta-ethics. My goal, then, is not to resolve the debate between Academic moral skepticism and its deniers but only to understand these various theories and methods and to determine how much can be achieved by each.

7

Naturalism

One common way to try to stop the regress of justified belief is by deriving moral conclusions from non-moral premises. This won't do much good if the non-moral premises themselves need to be justified but are not justified. However, it is often assumed that certain non-moral premises either do not need to be justified because they are self-evident or can be justified by observation or by some scientific method or in some other way. If so, and if such non-moral premises are enough to derive moral conclusions, then such a derivation would seem enough to justify belief in the moral conclusion.

If this method works, it provides a very strong kind of justification. Since moral nihilists usually deny only moral facts, they would presumably have to accept the non-moral premises, so a successful derivation of morality from non-moral premises could rule out moral nihilism and make moral beliefs extremely justified. This potential makes it crucial for me to determine whether or not any such derivation succeeds.

Such derivations fall into two large groups. Some philosophers claim to derive moral conclusions from premises that are normative (or evaluative) but still morally neutral. These attempts will be labeled *normativism* and will be discussed in chapter 8.

Other philosophers go further and claim to derive morality from premises that are not only non-moral but also non-normative (and non-evaluative). In traditional (but misleading) terms, they try to derive a moral "ought" from "is." This approach will be called *naturalism*, for lack of a better term. However, naturalism in moral epistemology should not be confused with naturalism about the metaphysics of moral properties or with any of the other views that go by the same name. Naturalism in moral epistemology is the topic of the current chapter.

7.1. The Original Humean Doctrine

David Hume wrote that it "seems altogether inconceivable, how this new relation [*ought* or *ought not*] can be a deduction from the others [*is* and *is not*], which are entirely different from it" ([1739–40] 1988, 469). It is not completely clear what Hume is saying here, but he is often interpreted as denying that any valid argument could have purely non-normative premises and a normative or moral conclusion. I will call this the *original Humean doctrine*.

The original Humean doctrine is accepted by a wide variety of moral theorists. It would not hold if moral language could be defined in purely non-moral or natural terms, since then such a morally neutral definition plus premises in purely natural terms would entail a moral conclusion. However, G. E. Moore presented an open-question argument against any purely naturalistic definition of moral terms.[1] Moore argued that, if any normative or moral term "M" could be defined by a purely non-normative and hence non-moral term "N," then it would not be an open question whether all N are M. For example, if "morally right" could be defined as "maximizes pleasure," then the question of whether it is morally right to maximize pleasure in a particular case would never be semantically open because a negative answer would always be either contradictory or nonsense. However, such questions are always open according to Moore. It follows that no normative or moral term can be defined by a purely non-normative term. If such a naturalistic definition were the only way to derive "ought" from "is" validly, then Moore's argument would imply the original Humean doctrine. This implication was and is drawn by many of Moore's followers.

Moore's argument is often criticized, but other arguments can be given for the original Humean doctrine. Expressivists often hold the original Humean doctrine on the ground that differences between the functions of normative and non-normative claims make it impossible to deduce one from the other. The original Humean doctrine is also often supported by a general claim that logic is conservative: "The conclusions of a valid inference are contained within the premises. You don't get out what you haven't put in" (Pigden 1991, 423). This metaphor suggests that, if you haven't put any normative content into the premises, you cannot get out any normative content from the conclusion of an argument that is valid.

7.2. Necessary Moral Truths

Despite this convergence in belief, the original Humean doctrine needs to be qualified if the term "valid" is used as logicians use it. Logicians call an argument *valid* if it is not possible for its premises to be true and its conclusion false. (Cf. Fogelin and Sinnott-Armstrong 2005, 50.) Arguments are valid in this way even if they suppress premises that are necessarily true. That makes it easy to construct a valid argument from non-normative premises to a moral conclusion. Here is an example from Judith Jarvis Thomson (1990, 15–16):

---

1. Moore 1903, 15–17. Moore focused on the term "good" so I have to generalize his argument for my purposes.

If C rings D's doorbell, he will thereby cause D pain.

_____

∴ Other things being equal, C morally ought not to ring D's doorbell.[2]

Thomson claims that this argument is valid because it is "surely a necessary truth" that "other things being equal, one morally ought not to cause others pain."[3]

Defenders of the original Humean doctrine might respond that Thomson's claim is not necessarily true. However, it would not be enough to deny the necessity in Thomson's particular example. If any moral claim is necessarily true, then some argument with completely non-normative premises and a moral conclusion will be valid in the logician's sense. Thus, the original Humean doctrine could not be defended in this way without denying that any moral claim is necessarily true. That road would be hard going.

Another response might be that the qualification "other things being equal" robs Thomson's conclusion of moral content. Her conclusion by itself does not, after all, imply that C morally ought not to ring D's doorbell. However, Thomson's original conclusion seems to have some moral force despite its qualification. It claims a moral presumption against a certain kind of act. That presumption means that such an act always needs some defeater to keep it from being the case that one morally ought not to do it. There is no such need with other kinds of acts, such as scratching my head. Thus, Thomson's conclusion locates an act inside a special morally relevant class.

Moreover, even if Thomson's qualified conclusion did not have any moral content, she could remove the qualification from her conclusion by adding another premise, "Other things are equal." This premise might have no moral content if Thomson could provide non-moral descriptions of the other things that need to be equal, or if she could list non-moral circumstances that are sufficient to ensure that nothing defeats the usual moral reason not to cause pain.[4] For example, she could add premises that (i) C rings D's doorbell intentionally and on purpose in order to cause pain to D; (ii) C suffers from no false belief, compulsion, or coercion; (iii) D did not consent and did not cause death or disability or unusual pain to anyone; and (iv) C's act of ringing the doorbell would not prevent any pain, disability, or death for anyone else. These new premises rule out excuses, underminers, and overriders. Refinements are probably needed, but the basic idea should be clear. These new premises do not seem to have any moral content, so, if they are sufficient to exclude anything that might keep it from being true that C ought not to ring D's doorbell, then Thomson's argument can be valid even if its

_____

2. I added the qualification "morally" in Thomson's conclusion, but this does not affect her point or mine.

3. Indeed, it is also valid (trivially) to argue from an irrelevant premise like "Ireland is an island" to "Other things being equal, one morally ought not to cause others pain," if this conclusion is necessarily true, as Thomson claims.

4. Thomson seems to reject this possibility, but I still want to consider its implications for moral epistemology.

conclusion claims without qualification that C morally ought not to ring D's doorbell.

The real problem is that Thomson's argument is not valid *formally*. An argument is *formally* valid if and only if it is an instance of an argument form all of whose instances are valid (cf. Fogelin and Sinnott-Armstrong 2005, 137). Since Thomson's argument becomes invalid if we substitute "pleasure" for "pain," it is not an instance of any form all of whose instances are valid, so it is not formally valid. Thomson's argument still does refute the original Humean doctrine. But it does not refute the claim that denies only formal validity to arguments with non-normative premises and normative or moral conclusions. This will be called the *qualified Humean doctrine.*[5]

Why does it matter that an argument's validity is not formal? Because formally invalid arguments depend on suppressed premises. They cannot justify their conclusions unless their suppressed premises are independently justified.

There's no problem when the suppressed premise is justified. Consider:

Lewis is my uncle.

∴ Lewis is male.

This argument is valid but not formally valid, so it depends on the suppressed premise that all uncles are male. This suppressed premise is true by definition. Its denial is semantically incoherent (assuming the words have their usual meanings). Hence, this suppressed premise can be independently justified.

Thomson's suppressed premise is not like this. Hers claims that "Other things being equal, one morally ought not to cause others pain." Even if this premise is necessarily true, and even if almost all common speakers would accept it, it still may be denied coherently. Moral nihilists, for example, deny Thomson's suppressed premise, and moral nihilism is coherent (as I argued in section 3.3), so Thomson's suppressed premise can be denied coherently and is not true by definition. Hence, it cannot be justified in the same way as "All uncles are male."

Here's another model:

This surface is red all over.

∴ This surface is not green all over.

This formally invalid argument depends on the suppressed premise that no surface is red all over and green all over at the same time. This suppressed premise is not true by definition, but many have claimed that it is necessarily true anyway. Isn't that enough for this argument to justify belief in its conclusion?

Not quite. The believer must also, at least, not believe that this suppressed premise is false. Suppose that holograms convince you that a surface could be red all over (when seen from one angle) and green all over (when seen from a different

___

5. Hume's term "deduction" suggests that he might have had formal validity in mind originally.

angle) at the same time. On this basis, you believe that the suppressed premise is false (or at least not necessarily true). Then, even if you are justified in believing its explicit premise, and even if this argument is valid, it still could not make you justified in believing its conclusion.

This argument also cannot make any believer justified if the believer fails to believe its suppressed premise. To see why, continue the story. Suppose I come to think that I might have been misled by holograms, so the suppressed premise might be true. I do not believe it or disbelieve it. I suspend belief. I do not even have a disposition to believe it. If asked whether the suppressed premise is true, after thinking about it I would honestly say that I have no opinion one way or the other. Under this thrall of agnosticism, this argument would not be enough to make me justified in believing its conclusion even if I were justified in believing its explicit premise, and even if it is in fact valid.

In addition, the belief in the suppressed premise must be justified. An unjustified belief in a premise cannot justify belief in a conclusion, or else we could be justified in believing any fool conclusion. Thus, for this argument to justify belief in its conclusion, the believer must be independently justified in believing its suppressed premise.[6]

Critics might object that, if I must be justified in believing the suppressed premise, then I need another argument with more premises, and an infinite regress looms. However, I am not assuming that the suppressed premise must be justified by another argument. It must be justified in some way, but I need not and do not assume that the only way is another argument. So my requirement is not too strong to be plausible.

This requirement shows why Thomson's argument fails to justify belief. It is not formally valid, so it depends on a suppressed premise. That suppressed premise needs to be independently justified in order to justify the conclusion. Thomson's suppressed premise claims that, other things being equal, agents morally ought not to cause others pain. That is a substantive moral claim, just like the conclusion. Consequently, Thomson's argument cannot justify any moral belief without some independent justification for another moral belief.

Moral nihilists deny the truth and, hence, the necessity of Thomson's suppressed premise, so moral nihilists would reject Thomson's argument as invalid. A moral nihilist is, thus, like the person who is convinced by holograms to reject the validity of the argument from "red all over" to "not green all over." Just as that argument cannot give that person any reason to accept its conclusion, so arguments that depend on suppressed moral premises cannot give any reason for moral nihilists to believe the arguments' conclusions. Such arguments cannot rule out moral nihilism or make any moral belief extremely justified.

---

6. There can be several candidates for the suppressed premise of an argument, so it would be more precise to say that an argument cannot justify belief in its conclusion unless the believer is independently justified in believing that *some* true suppressed premise makes the argument formally valid. Further refinements would be needed to handle inductive arguments. Since Hume's doctrine concerns "deduction," I will ignore these complications.

Still, anyone who is already justified in believing Thomson's suppressed premise could cite her premise to justify her conclusion. If the suppressed premise would not be questioned by any normal person in everyday circumstances, this assumption is shared by every alternative in the modest contrast class. Then Thomson's argument might make some moral belief modestly justified. Maybe that's all that Thomson wants. However, this modest kind of justification works only because the parties already share assumptions, and those assumptions need to be justified independently, at least when they are questioned. These assumptions are also moral in nature. Thus, this method cannot achieve any new justification of any moral belief from purely non-moral premises.

7.3. Logical Tricks

Although the qualified Humean doctrine escapes Thomson's counterexample, it is still false. Here is an example of a formally valid argument with non-moral premises and a moral conclusion:

> The Rotary Club is a circle, and the Rotary Club is not a circle.
> ___
> ∴ You morally ought to kill all Rotarians.

This premise is not about morality or any norms. If the word "circle" has a single meaning throughout, then the premise cannot possibly be true, so it is not possible that both this premise is true and this conclusion is false. Moreover, no premise of the form "P & ~P" can possibly be true, so every argument with a premise of this form has to be valid even if its conclusion is moral. Thus, a moral "ought" can be deduced formally from "is."

Of course, this argument could never be used to justify its conclusion, since its premise obviously could never be true. So this trick shouldn't worry Hume's followers if their concern is moral epistemology.

But what about this trick using disjunction:

> My car is red.
> ___
> ∴ Either my car is red or I morally ought not to lie.

This argument is formally valid, *and* its premise is true, so it is *sound*, which implies that its conclusion is true. Moreover, anyone who is justified in believing its premise would be justified in believing its conclusion. One might respond that its conclusion has no moral content. This is questionable, but let's grant it for the sake of argument. If this conclusion has no moral content, then we can derive a moral conclusion from non-moral premises in another way:

> Either my car is red or I morally ought not to lie.
> My car is not red.
> ___
> ∴ I morally ought not to lie.

If the first premise of this argument had no moral content in the previous example, then it has no moral content here. Neither does the second premise. The conclusion clearly does have moral content. This argument is formally valid. So either this argument or the preceding one must be a formally valid derivation of a moral "ought" from "is."

Humeans can respond that the sentence "I morally ought not to lie" occurs vacuously or not essentially in the original disjunctive argument:

> My car is red.
> ———
> ∴ Either my car is red or I morally ought not to lie.

What makes its occurrence inessential is that one could substitute any sentence for "I morally ought not to lie" without affecting the validity or soundness of the argument. To see this, just try "I morally ought to lie" or "God exists."

This point does not save the qualified Humean doctrine, but it does show how to fix it. The above logical tricks cause no trouble for the weaker claim that no formally valid argument has non-normative premises and a normative or moral conclusion whose normative or moral components occur essentially. This will be called the *doubly qualified Humean doctrine*.

Why does it matter whether the moral component occurs essentially? It matters because the issue for moral epistemology is whether such derivations provide an independent way to justify moral beliefs. Since "I morally ought not to lie" could be replaced by "I morally ought to lie," this form of argument could never be used to justify one of these claims in contrast with the other. Contrast classes, thus, show why this way of deriving a moral "ought" from "is" cannot suffice for any important kind of justification.

The moral sentence still might seem to occur essentially in the second disjunctive argument:

> Either my car is red or I morally ought not to lie.
> My car is not red.
> ———
> ∴ I morally ought not to lie.

In this argument the moral conclusion is essential because it could not be replaced (in both the conclusion and the first premise) by just any other sentence without affecting the soundness of the argument. Assuming the second premise is true, the disjunct "I morally ought not to lie" would have to be replaced by some truth in order to retain the truth of the disjunctive premise and hence the soundness of this argument. Thus, if "I morally ought not to lie" is true, it could not be replaced by "I morally ought to lie," since the disjunctive premise would then not be true (assuming that "ought" and "ought not" here cannot both be true). This shows that this argument cannot be used to justify belief in its conclusion without already having an independent justification for its conclusion, since one could not be justified in believing both of its premises if one did not already have a justification for believing "I morally ought not to lie." This argument is, thus, of no use whatsoever in providing any justification for any belief in its conclusion.

7.4. Appeals to Authority

This response does not apply so directly to an ingenious example by Mark Nelson (1995) using quantifiers and beliefs:

> All of Dahlia's beliefs are true.
> Dahlia believes that Bertie morally ought to marry Madeleine.
> _____

∴. Bertie morally ought to marry Madeleine.

The first premise says nothing about the content of Dahlia's beliefs, so it does not by itself imply that any moral belief is true. The second premise merely ascribes a moral belief without calling that belief true. So neither premise seems to have moral content. In contrast, the conclusion is clearly a substantive moral claim. And the argument seems formally valid. So it looks as if Nelson has derived a moral "ought" from "is."

Several objections could be raised. I will discuss three briefly and a fourth in more detail, since the fourth is most important to moral epistemology.

7.4.1. *Does the Universal Premise Have Moral Content?*

First, the universal premise "All of Dahlia's beliefs are true" might seem to have hidden moral content. If Dahlia believes propositions A, B, and C, then that universal premise might seem to imply that A, B, and C are true, which implies that A is true, even if A has moral content. That might seem to give moral content to the universal premise.

Nelson responds that the universal premise *by itself* does not imply any moral claim, because "the general interpretation is what I intend" (1995, 559). On that modern Boolean interpretation, the premise that all of Dahlia's beliefs are true does not imply that Dahlia has any moral belief or, indeed, any belief of any kind. Even a moral (or normative) nihilist, who claims that no positive moral (or normative) belief is true, could accept this premise, as long as the nihilist holds that Dahlia has no moral (or normative) beliefs. Such a nihilist could not accept the conjunction of both premises in Nelson's argument. But it would not be fair to say that a premise has moral content whenever that premise plus other non-moral premises implies a moral conclusion. That test of moral content would make the Humean doctrines empty.

The notion of moral content is very slippery, so some readers might remain unconvinced. However, this slipperiness will create at least as much trouble for any opponent's attempt to establish that this universal premise *does* have moral content. So it is at least not clear that Nelson's argument fails in this way.

7.4.2. *Is the Argument Valid Formally?*

Some defenders of the qualified Humean doctrine might question whether Nelson's argument is valid *formally*. If not, this example fails to refute the doctrine for the same reason that Thomson's example fails (section 7.2).

Is Nelson's argument formally valid? It is formally valid if and only if we can uniformly substitute other sentences for "Bertie morally ought to marry Madeleine" without affecting the validity of the argument. If the sentence "Bertie morally ought to marry Madeleine" occurs within Nelson's premise "Dahlia believes that Bertie morally ought to marry Madeleine," then the result of substituting "Bertie is bald" for "Bertie morally ought to marry Madeleine" throughout Nelson's argument yields:

All of Dahlia's beliefs are true.
Dahlia believes that Bertie is bald.
_____

∴ Bertie is bald.

This is valid, which suggests that Nelson's argument is formally valid.

Defenders of the qualified Humean doctrine might argue that, just as the word "use" does not occur within "house," so the sentence "Bertie morally ought to marry Madeleine" does not occur within the premise "Dahlia believes that Bertie morally ought to marry Madeleine." The logical form of belief ascriptions is controversial, but I am inclined to grant that "Bertie morally ought to marry Madeleine" is a component in the premise, "Dahlia believes that Bertie morally ought to marry Madeleine." If so, Nelson's argument is formally valid.

Even if not, a parallel argument at the meta-level is formally valid:

All of the sentences that Dahlia uses to express her beliefs are true.
Dahlia uses the sentence "Bertie morally ought to marry Madeleine" to express her belief.
_____

∴ "Bertie morally ought to marry Madeleine" is true.
  If "p" is true, then p.
_____

∴ Bertie morally ought to marry Madeleine.

This formulation avoids the issue of how to represent premises that ascribe beliefs. Since any sentence can be substituted for "Bertie morally ought to marry Madeleine" without affecting the argument's validity, its validity is formal. So this variant seems to refute the qualified Humean doctrine, even if Nelson's original is not formally valid.

7.4.3. *Is the Moral Component Essential?*

A third possible objection claims that the moral component of Nelson's argument does not occur essentially. As in the disjunctive examples in section 7.3, the validity of Nelson's argument would not be affected if "Bertie ought to marry Madeleine" were replaced throughout by any other sentence, including "Bertie ought not to marry Madeleine." So the argument might seem to work just as well for the opposite conclusion. But then it has no epistemological force.

However, what matters is whether the moral component can be replaced without affecting the argument's soundness, not just its validity. In this sense, the moral component of Nelson's argument is essential. Adding "not" twice yields:

All of Dahlia's beliefs are true.
Dahlia believes that Bertie morally ought not to marry Madeleine.
_____
∴ Bertie morally ought not to marry Madeleine.

This argument and its parent without "not" are both valid, but they cannot both be sound. The premises of this new argument cannot be true if the premises in the parent argument without "not" are true (assuming that here "ought" and "ought not" cannot both be true). Thus, Nelson's argument is not as flexible as the ones with disjunction in section 7.3, because Nelson's argument depends on specific premises about Dahlia's actual beliefs and reliability.

In this respect, Nelson's argument is similar to:

All that my zoology textbook says is true.
My zoology textbook says that echidnas are mammals that lay eggs.
_____
∴ Echidnas are mammals that lay eggs.

Formally, one could add two instances of "not" to get:

All that my zoology textbook says is true.
My zoology textbook says that echidnas are not mammals that lay eggs.
_____
∴ Echidnas are not mammals that lay eggs.

But that is not what my textbook actually says. The original argument might be sound and might justify me in believing its conclusion if I am justified in believing that the zoology textbook is reliable and does say that echidnas are mammals that lay eggs. None of that is changed by the possibility of adding two instances of "not."

The same possibility also does not affect the epistemological force of Nelson's argument. If arguments like these can be sound (that is, if there can be reliable authorities in ethics, as in zoology), then it might seem that such arguments can be used to justify their conclusions and thereby provide a secure basis for moral epistemology. If so, this counterexample is not trivial in the same way as arguments with disjunction.

Some Humeans might respond that they never meant to deny the formal validity of such appeals to authority or to reliable belief. Such arguments use premises of the second order (beliefs about beliefs). So Humeans can revise their doctrine to deny only that any argument with purely non-normative premises of the first order could be formally valid if its conclusion has moral content and occurs essentially. That *triply qualified Humean doctrine* is not refuted by anything in this chapter. Moreover, such a triply qualified Humean doctrine would be enough to refute some versions of naturalism in moral epistemology.

But other versions of naturalism might escape unscathed. Even though Nelson's argument works by ascending to the second order, it still derives a conclusion with moral content from premises with no normative content in a way that is formally valid. If beliefs in such non-moral premises can be justified, then arguments like Nelson's can be used to justify beliefs in moral conclusions in much the way that some naturalists claim. The retreat to the triply qualified version, thus, robs the Humean doctrine of much of its force.

7.4.4. *Are the Premises Justified?*

Since these previous responses fail, Nelson's argument shows that the doubly qualified Humean doctrine fails as a thesis in logic. A formally valid argument can cross any supposed gap between "is" and "ought" or, more precisely, between non-normative premises and moral conclusions. Maybe that is all Nelson wanted to show.

Even if so, the doubly qualified Humean doctrine still might work episte-mologically, and that might be enough to serve the primary purposes of Hume and his followers. Humeans primarily use their doctrine to limit the ways in which moral beliefs can be epistemically justified. That is what is needed to support the relevant premise in the regress argument for Academic moral skepticism (see section 4.3.1). To counter this use of Hume's doctrine, Nelson's argument must be used to justify a moral belief in its conclusion.

One could use the original argument to justify belief in its conclusion *only* if one could be justified in believing its premises. It is not enough for the premises to be true if one does not believe them or if one does not have adequate grounds to believe them. But how could anyone be justified in believing the universal premise that all of Dahlia's beliefs are true?

A simple way would be complete enumeration: identify each claim that Dahlia believes and be justified oneself in believing each of those claims. To apply this method, given the other premise, one would have to identify one of Dahlia's beliefs as the belief that Bertie morally ought to marry Madeleine. Then one would have to be justified oneself in believing that it is true that Bertie morally ought to marry Madeleine. But that is the conclusion. So one would need to be justified in believing the conclusion before one could be justified in believing the premises. The argument could not, then, provide any independent reason to believe the conclusion, if one used complete enumeration to justify belief in the universal premise. It would beg the question.[7]

This problem might be avoided by a different kind of reason to believe that all of Dahlia's beliefs are true. Imagine that you ask Dahlia many questions about mathematics, physics, biology, psychology, history, and literature, as well as par-ticular details of Bertie's and Madeleine's lives and characters. Every one of Dahlia's answers is sincere and correct. She is completely reliable over a very wide range of non-moral beliefs. Her amazing knowledge seems to justify you in ac-cepting her other beliefs, even if some of them happen to be moral beliefs.

Dahlia can then be described as an authority. Her authority is not like that of a judge whose decisions constitute the law, since morality remains independent of

---

7. Indeed, when their universal premises are justified by complete enumeration, all syllogisms beg the question. See Sinnott-Armstrong 1999c, 179–80 and 183–84.

Dahlia's beliefs. Her authority is more like that of an historian who is known to be completely reliable about many aspects of medieval life but who never mentioned cuisine before telling you that medieval kings ate peacocks. Just as the historian's authority would give you reason to trust the historian on this new matter, so Dahlia's authority is supposed to justify you in accepting her other beliefs, even if some of her beliefs happen to be moral beliefs.

Dahlia's authority might seem more questionable, because it is general. In real life, we are never justified in believing that every one of anyone's beliefs is true, so the universal premise seems too strong. But it remains possible for this belief to be justified. That is enough to refute the doubly qualified Humean doctrine insofar as it denies the possibility of a certain kind of argument. Moreover, even if no real person is infallible, we can be justified in believing that certain people are reliable in the sense that most of their beliefs are true, so, in the absence of defeating considerations, each of their beliefs is probably true. We cannot use such premises to deduce a moral "ought" from "is," but we might still use them as some or strong evidence for a moral conclusion. This is a standard pattern in gaining justification from testimony. If it works here, then it has great importance for moral epistemology.

Critics might object that an authority in one area need not be an authority in other areas. Experts on science need not know anything about art. Whenever one appeals to an authority, one must determine whether that person is an authority in the relevant area. This divergence of authority holds for morality as well. Many very intelligent and informed people hold implausible moral beliefs. They can be Nazis, terrorists, or psychopaths. Hence, one's belief that Dahlia gets everything right in all other fields might not seem to justify one in believing that she also gets things right in morality.

This objection is inconclusive. Even though *some* informed and intelligent people hold horrible beliefs about morality, reliability in other areas still might be *some* evidence of reliability in morality, if only because it reveals a tendency not to form beliefs without careful consideration. Surely it would be very impressive if Dahlia did not make a single mistake when answering a multitude of questions about a wide variety of topics. It would show at least that she is very careful before forming opinions. Wouldn't that justify you in believing that all of her beliefs are true, even if she happens to have some moral beliefs? That depends.

Many moral beliefs depend on factual presuppositions. Maybe Dahlia knows that Bertie morally ought to marry Madeleine because Dahlia knows some relevant fact that you don't know, such as that Bertie promised to marry Madeleine or that Bertie and Madeleine will suffer a great deal if they do not marry each other. If Dahlia is reliable on such factual matters, this might give one reason to trust her moral beliefs that depend on such factual matters, if one assumes that these factual matters determine what is morally right and wrong. On that assumption, the original argument could be used to justify one in believing that Bertie morally ought to marry Madeleine.

But suppose that assumption is questioned. Suppose the issue at stake is whether promises and suffering matter morally at all. Dahlia need not be reliable on such basic moral issues even if she is reliable about factual matters such as who made promises and who will suffer. The important question for moral epistemology is whether Dahlia's reliability about non-moral matters justifies us in believing that she is also reliable on basic moral issues.

As long as Dahlia sticks to common moral principles and applies them in light of her superior factual knowledge, those of us who accept these same moral principles will have no reason to doubt what she says or that her reliability and authority extend to morality. The same applies if she asserts something that we did not previously either believe or disbelieve, such as Goldbach's conjecture. But the crucial test case occurs when Dahlia asserts something that we previously believed to be false.

Suppose this happens outside morality: After showing her knowledge in all other areas, you decide to quiz Dahlia about mathematics. She says that $2 + 2 = 5$. This would give you no reason to believe that $2 + 2 = 5$. It would give you reason to believe that, no matter how reliable she is in other areas, Dahlia is confused about mathematics.

Similarly, if Dahlia says that an all-powerful and all-good God exists, but you believe that this is impossible because of evil in the world, then you would have no reason to trust Dahlia on religion, just because she is reliable on other topics. (Cf. Craig and Sinnott-Armstrong 2004, chap. 4.) Of course, this argument can be reversed. If Dahlia says that God does not exist, but you are convinced that the ontological argument proves God's existence, then again you would have no reason to trust Dahlia on religion just because she is reliable on other topics.

Why not? The ultimate explanation is that one's reason to disbelieve the conclusion gives one reason to disbelieve the conjunction of the premises. Compare the lottery paradox. In a fair lottery with a million tickets, I am justified in believing that lottery ticket #1 will lose, because the probability that it will lose is 0.999999. The same goes for tickets #2, #3, #4, and so on up to ticket #1,000,000. So I am justified in believing each of the 1,000,001 premises in this argument:

> Ticket #1 will lose.
> Ticket #2 will lose.
> Ticket #3 will lose.
> ...
> Ticket #1,000,000 will lose.
> There are only 1,000,000 tickets.
> ——
> ∴ Every ticket will lose.

This argument is valid, but I cannot be justified in believing its conclusion, since I know the lottery is fair, so this conclusion is false. Thus, even though I can be justified in believing each premise separately, I cannot be justified in believing the conjunction of them all together. It is justified belief in the conjunction of the premises, not in each premise separately, that is necessary in order for this argument to justify me in believing its conclusion. My prior reason to reject the conclusion, thus, prevents this argument from giving me any reason at all to believe its conclusion.

More technically, the point is that the reason to believe the conclusion makes each premise negatively relevant to the others in the sense that each premise is less probable given the others than without the others.[8] In such cases of negative relevance, my reasons to believe the premises separately need not give me any reason to believe the conclusion.

This explains why Dahlia's belief that $2 + 2 = 5$ does not give us any reason to believe that $2 + 2 = 5$, no matter how reliable she is in other areas. Since I have strong prior reason to believe that $2 + 2 \neq 5$, I have strong reason not to believe the conjunction of the premises that all of Dahlia's beliefs are true and that Dahlia believes that $2 + 2 = 5$, even if I do have reason to believe each of these premises separately. The same applies if Dahlia is generally reliable and believes that an all-powerful and all-good God exists (or does not exist), but I have independent reason to believe the opposite.

The point is *not* that Dahlia is not reliable enough. We are assuming that she is completely reliable in every area that was checked in advance. The point instead is that, given certain background beliefs, we cannot be justified in believing that she is reliable on the topics at issue now. Even if God does exist, and Dahlia says so, if we were previously justified in believing that God does not exist, then this belief will keep us from being justified in trusting her in this new area, despite her reliability in other areas. Maybe we should not continue to believe that God does not exist, as if Dahlia had said nothing, but her assertion still is not enough to make us justified in believing that God does exist.

This point is about what we as individual believers are personally justified in believing. (See section 4.2.4.) The proposition that God exists still might be proven or supported in some impersonal way by evidence that we don't have. On that basis, other people might be justified in believing in God and in trusting what Dahlia says about God. However, if that evidence is not available to us or is reasonably rejected by us, then the existence of that evidence cannot make us justified in believing anything in the personal way that is relevant here. Just as we are not justified in believing that Socrates had a son when objective evidence exists, but we reasonably reject it or are not aware of it; so we are not personally justified in accepting Dahlia's word if her assertions conflict with certain of our prior reasonable beliefs.

Similar situations arise in morality if Dahlia asserts moral beliefs that seem outrageous to us. Suppose Dahlia sincerely says that you morally ought to kill all Rotarians. There is no reason to believe that her claim depends on any factual truth of which you are unaware, such as that Rotarians are murderers or carry some deadly contagious disease. Then Dahlia's pronouncement would give one no reason to believe that you morally ought to kill all Rotarians, even if she is completely reliable about all non-moral matters. Insofar as her moral beliefs do not rest on her non-moral beliefs, her reliability about non-moral matters is then no evidence for reliability on moral matters in the face of strong reason to the contrary.

The same point applies to those who hold non-standard basic moral beliefs. Suppose a moral nihilist justifiably believes that all of Dahlia's non-moral beliefs

---

8. On negative relevance, see Lehrer 1974, 192–96. Lehrer 1990, 117–18, defines a parallel notion of competition in terms of reasonableness rather than probability.

are true. Then Dahlia says that Bertie morally ought to marry Madeleine. This need not give the moral nihilist a reason to believe that Bertie morally ought to marry Madeleine, if the moral nihilist thinks that this moral belief is just as clearly confused and incorrect as if Madeleine had said that $2 + 2 = 5$ or that God exists or something else that the moral nihilist previously reasonably disbelieved. Even if Dahlia cites a promise by Bertie to marry and also future despair for both without marriage, the moral nihilist need not think that those factual truths show what Bertie morally ought to do. The moral nihilist might have at least as much reason to respond that Dahlia is insincere or unreliable about morality, despite her apparent sincerity and reliability in other areas.

Whether the moral nihilist has adequate reason to doubt Dahlia's beliefs about morality depends on the moral nihilist's reasons to accept moral nihilism. Compare an ornithologist who clearly sees a live bird of a kind that was widely and reasonably thought to be extinct. When the ornithologist reports his sighting to me, my prior reason to believe the bird extinct gives me some reason to doubt the ornithologist's testimony. Still, if the ornithologist has a long enough history of accuracy and new discoveries, then my knowledge of his record can give me reason to trust his testimony, and this reason can be strong enough to override my reason to doubt his testimony based on my belief that the bird is extinct. Overall I might be justified in believing that he really did see the supposedly extinct kind of bird, so it is not extinct after all. In something like this way, Dahlia's testimony might seem to overcome a moral nihilist's reasons to doubt that any moral wrongs exist.

But there is a crucial difference. Everyone admits that the kind of bird *might* not be extinct. In contrast, most moral nihilists hold that moral beliefs not only actually are not true but necessarily are not true, maybe because moral properties are metaphysically "queer" (see sections 3.2.3–3.2.5) or cannot be essential to the best explanation of any observation or event (see section 8.1). Such a moral nihilist's reason not to trust Dahlia's moral beliefs is different in kind from my reason not to trust the ornithologist. If the moral nihilist claims necessity for his position, his position on Dahlia's testimony is more like it would be if Dahlia testified that $2 + 2 = 5$, and then it is doubtful that testimony by an authority like Dahlia could give the moral nihilist adequate reason to give up moral nihilism.

Even without any claim of necessity, moral nihilists still have reasons to distrust Dahlia that do not apply to the ornithologist. Moral nihilists admit that people believe in moral wrongs, and they explain away those common moral beliefs as illusions (see section 3.2.2).[9] There is no parallel explanation of why the ornithologist would be mistaken in my example as described. But suppose there was such an explanation: I reasonably believe there is another kind of bird in the area that looks just like the extinct one. I also reasonably believe that the ornithologist is unaware of this other kind of bird. (Maybe he has heard of them but denies that they really exist.)

9. Anti-nihilists also might try to explain belief in moral nihilism as rebellion against parental authority, or whatever. But such explanations can't rule out moral nihilism any more than nihilistic explanations rule out common beliefs. When both sides can explain away the other, but neither side can rule out the other without begging the question, then they are at a standoff, as Pyrrhonians suggest.

Now, when the ornithologist reports seeing the supposedly extinct kind of bird, this testimony would not be an adequate reason for me to believe that he saw the supposedly extinct kind as opposed to the other kind. They look the same, after all. This situation resembles that of moral nihilists listening to Dahlia. Moral nihilists think that what Dahlia claims to see—moral facts—do not really exist. They also think that they can explain why she thinks she sees moral facts. If so, they have reason to believe that she is not reliable in this area, no matter how reliable she is in other areas. Her testimony then gives them no reason to give up their moral nihilism.

Consequently, appeals to authority, as in Nelson's argument, cannot make any moral belief justified out a contrast class that includes moral nihilism. We cannot be justified in believing the premises of such appeals to authority without assuming moral beliefs that moral nihilists question. Thus, it will always beg the question against moral nihilism to assume that anyone, including an authority about all non-moral matters, is an authority about moral matters, since moral nihilists deny that there are any real authorities about moral matters (although there can be authorities about who holds which moral beliefs). The debate will always come down to whether there is some other reason to believe those background assumptions. This kind of argument cannot justify its own assumptions. Thus, extreme justification is beyond the reach of such arguments.

Besides, no actual person is as reliable as we have been assuming Dahlia to be. We all make mistakes. In realistic circumstances, then, it is even clearer that no authority can rule out moral nihilism or make any moral believer extremely justified.

This conclusion should not disturb most people, since most people do not take moral nihilism seriously anyway, at least in their everyday lives. An appeal to an authority, such as Dahlia, might make some beliefs justified out of a limited contrast class, because it might work against non-nihilists. Non-nihilists do not believe that all moral beliefs are necessarily or explicably mistaken. Hence, if a non-nihilist has a justified belief that Dahlia is infallible or very reliable on all or most non-moral matters, her non-moral reliability might provide some evidence of her reliability on moral matters. Then Dahlia's testimony on a moral matter can provide good grounds for a moral belief, as long as moral nihilism is not at issue.

Moreover, suppose as before that we have reason to believe that Dahlia is infallible about all non-moral matters. Then we identify many of Dahlia's *moral* beliefs in a wide variety of areas, and we have reason to believe that every one of them is true. This would be enough to justify us in believing in the truth of all of Dahlia's beliefs, including her *other* moral beliefs. With this background, the fact that Dahlia believes that Bertie morally ought to marry Madeleine might justify us in believing that Bertie morally ought to marry Madeleine, even if none of the moral beliefs that we checked was about Bertie or Madeleine. This inference does not cross any boundaries between areas of authority. It also need not beg any question (except against moral nihilists), if the moral beliefs that we checked were not about Bertie or Madeleine and were justified independently of Dahlia's authority and her belief about their marriage. Admittedly, if we rely on moral beliefs in establishing an authority, then our overall justification does not start from purely non-moral premises, so it cannot affect Hume's doctrine. But the point here is just that such appeals to authority can have epistemic force if, but only if, certain moral assumptions are allowed.

Overall, then, appeals to authority, as in Nelson's argument, might justify some moral beliefs out of a limited contrast class that does not include moral nihilism, but they cannot be used to rule out moral nihilism. Similar limits apply to appeals to traditions or groups as authorities. Such arguments might make some believers modestly justified, but they cannot make anyone extremely justified. This result fits nicely with my general thesis of moderate moral skepticism.

7.5. Other Naturalisms

There have been many more attempts to derive "ought" from "is." The purportedly non-normative premises might come from action theory (e.g., Gewirth [1974] 1982, 1978; and Beyleveld 1991; criticized in Regis 1984), cognitive psychology (e.g., Brandt 1979; criticized in Sturgeon 1982), developmental psychology (e.g., Kohlberg 1981), evolutionary biology (e.g., Richards 1987), sociobiology (e.g., Wilson 1975; criticized in Kitcher 1985), speech act theory (e.g., Searle 1964, 1969, 177–98; criticized in Hudson 1969),[10] views on human nature (e.g., Hurka 1993; criticized in Kitcher 1999), or generalizations about human desires (e.g., Mill [1861] 1998, chap. 4; cf. Sayre-McCord 2001). Because there are so many ways to try to derive "ought" from "is," it would be pointless and boring for me to try to cover them all. Instead, I will close by quickly suggesting why the kinds of problems that I found in the attempts that I did discuss are bound to arise for all other attempts to justify moral beliefs by inferences from purely non-normative premises.

There are only two possibilities: whenever non-normative premises are supposed to imply a moral conclusion, the argument is either formally valid or not. If it is *not* formally valid, then it assumes some suppressed premise (as in Thomson's argument in section 7.2). If that suppressed premise is strong enough to produce a formally valid argument for a moral conclusion from non-moral explicit premises, then the suppressed premise must have some moral content. So the argument depends on a moral assumption.

On the other hand, if the argument *is* formally valid, its explicit premises still need to be justified (as in Nelson's argument in section 7.4). Since the conjunction of its explicit premises entail its moral conclusion, it is hard to see how the conjunction of these premises could be justified without making some moral assumptions.

Either way, the enlarged argument (including suppressed premises and the justification for its premises) ends up depending on moral assumptions somewhere. These assumptions might be overlooked when naturalists hide them and the audience unwittingly takes them for granted. But the argument cannot justify any belief without these moral assumptions. This dependence, of course, violates

---

10. Searle is not especially interested in using his argument in moral epistemology, so he might not be bothered if his argument works semantically but cannot be used to justify moral beliefs.

the self-imposed limits of naturalism in moral epistemology. Naturalists promise an inference from purely non-moral premises, but their premises are not all purely non-moral once the needed background arguments are included.

Such arguments still might succeed in justifying their moral conclusions if their assumptions are granted and justified. But how could these moral assumptions be justified? As always, this question needs to be answered in terms of contrast classes. If its background moral assumptions are shared by all members of a limited contrast class, then a naturalistic argument might make some moral believers justified out of that limited contrast class. But that is just because those assumptions are taken for granted. If the argument's moral assumptions are denied by some member of the contrast class, such as by moral nihilism in the extreme contrast class, then the conclusion of the naturalistic argument cannot be justified out of that larger contrast class unless the argument's moral assumptions are also justified out of the larger contrast class. The naturalistic argument cannot justify its own assumptions. Hence, the naturalistic argument cannot be an independent source of extremely justified moral beliefs. So it cannot threaten moderate moral skepticism.

8

Normativism

Like naturalism, a second method in moral epistemology also tries to derive moral conclusions from purely non-moral premises. However, this new kind of argument is not naturalistic in the same way as the views discussed in chapter 7, because it openly depends on premises that are normative or evaluative. Accordingly, I will label this approach *normativism*.

Its strategy is to deploy norms that are not moral in nature. We can call a painting beautiful, a golfer awesome, a theory stupid, and a purchase a bargain without making any specifically moral judgment about the painting, the golfer, the theory, or the purchase. Similarly, normativists use premises about what is good or what ought to be done, but each premise is supposed to have no direct moral implications by itself, so normativists claim that their arguments do not rely on any substantive moral assumptions. Whether their premises really are morally neutral remains to be seen, but their goal is to pull a moral conclusion out of a non-moral hat.

This strategy could be pursued in many ways. I cannot cover all of the possibilities, so I won't try.[1] I will discuss only two of the most popular and plausible versions of normativism.

8.1. Moral Explanations

My first exemplar employs the common form of argument called "inference to the best explanation". (Cf. Lipton 1991b; and Fogelin and Sinnott-Armstrong 2005, 254–59.) A claim that one explanation is *better* than another is evaluative, so inferences to the best explanation do not start from purely non-evaluative or non-normative

---

1. One other kind of normativism bases moral beliefs on linguistic norms of proper usage. The best-known examples are Hare 1965, 1981; and Habermas 1990 (strange bedfellows!). I criticize Hare's argument in Sinnott-Armstrong 2001a. On Habermas as a response to skepticism, see Allen (forthcoming).

premises. Nonetheless, these premises still might be non-moral, since, when explanations are judged better or worse as explanations, these evaluations use epistemic standards, not moral standards. Nobody needs to claim that any explanation is morally better than any other.

Inferences to the best explanation also differ in another way from the naturalistic arguments discussed in chapter 7. Inferences to the best explanation are inductive rather than deductive, so they are not supposed to be logically valid.[2] Normativists who employ such arguments realize that it is possible for their conclusions to be false when their premises are true. Nonetheless, these arguments can still be strong by inductive standards. They might even provide overwhelming reasons to believe their conclusions.

For example, a scientist's belief that a proton is in a cloud chamber at a time seems to be justified by an inference to the best explanation of the scientist's observations of a cloud in that chamber at (or just after) that time (Harman 1977, 6–7). This justification claims that the actual presence of a proton and hence the truth of the belief in a proton is a necessary part of the best complete explanation of why the cloud forms (and why the scientist forms the belief in the cloud) at that time rather than earlier or later. Of course, this claim can be questioned in various ways, but the point here is only that the observation of the cloud gives the observer a strong reason to believe in a proton if an actual proton is needed for the best explanation of the observation.

To generalize, such inferences to the best explanation depend on the following basic principle:

> Observation O is evidence for hypothesis H1 (as opposed to H2) if the truth of H1 is a necessary part of a complete explanation of O that is better than any competing explanation (of which H2 is a necessary part).

In the above example, O is the scientist's observation of the cloud. H1 is the conclusion that there is a proton in the chamber. H2 is some competing explanation, such as that the cloud was caused by a neutron instead of a proton or the scientist was hallucinating a cloud.

This principle does not require hypothesis H1 by itself to be a complete explanation, since subsidiary principles will also be needed to complete the explanation. That is why H1 is only *part* of the complete explanation. Still, the truth of H1 must be *necessary* and not just an optional dangler. If the explanation would work just as well without H1 (or even if H1 were false), then the inference could not show that H1 is true.[3] The inference also fails when a competing hypothesis, H2, is better than or as good as H1. In this context, the better explanation is the one with more of the standard explanatory virtues, such as simplicity, modesty,

---

2. Some advocates see inference to the best explanation as a third kind of argument in addition to deduction and induction. My wider use of "inductive" is explained in Fogelin and Sinnott-Armstrong 2005, 249–53.

3. In other words, the moral fact must be a necessary enabler of the explanation. I suggest that all reasons are necessary enablers in Sinnott-Armstrong 1992.

power, depth, conservativeness, and so on (Fogelin and Sinnott-Armstrong 2005, 256–58).

To use this principle in an argument for H1, the arguer needs to claim that observation O is accurate and that H1 is necessary for the best explanation of O. If these additional premises are not justified, then the argument using them cannot justify any belief in its conclusion. Moreover, the justification for these premises must be independent of the conclusion in order to avoid begging the question. Suppose, for example, O is the "observation" that God allowed Satan to torture Job, and one theology explains this "observation" better than any other theology. Still, no inference to the best explanation of this "observation" can justify belief in that theology as opposed to atheism, which denies the supposed "observation." Even if we start with a neutral observation that Job got boils, the premise that one theology explains this "observation" better than any other theology still cannot justify that theology as opposed to atheism. If no atheistic alternative is considered, the arguer cannot be justified in believing that any theological hypothesis (H1) is really *necessary* for the best explanation of Job's boils (O).

The same general requirements apply in moral epistemology, where the crucial question becomes whether these requirements can be met by any inference to the best explanation that is supposed to justify a moral belief. A negative answer is suggested by some philosophers who argue that moral facts and truths are never necessary for any explanation.[4] Physical events, such as protons moving through cloud chambers, are supposed to be fully explainable without reference to moral facts. A person's action or guilt feelings might be explained by that person's moral beliefs, but those moral beliefs are supposed to be explained by psychology, sociology, sociobiology, and so on, without endorsing the truth or falsity of those moral beliefs and, hence, without postulating any moral facts. (See section 3.2.2.) If no moral facts are needed for any such explanation to work all the way down, then no moral belief can be justified by any inference to the best explanation.[5]

This *problem of explanatory impotence* (as Sayre-McCord 1988b dubbed it) could be solved if moral facts could be reduced to psychological facts that are needed for the best explanation of observations. That solution is proposed by Harman (1977). However, most philosophers reject such reductions of morality to psychology. If such reductions fail, then it remains hard to see how inferences to the best explanation could work in morality.

This problem might seem to lead to moral nihilism. Since moral nihilists deny the existence of moral facts, if facts are necessary for explanations, moral nihilism implies that moral explanations never work. Thus, the explanatory impotence of

---

4. The source of this argument is Harman 1977, 3–10, although Harman ends up in a different position.

5. This requirement might seem to exclude psychological and biological facts if they are reducible to facts of physics. However, since explanation is intentional, psychological and biological facts still might capture the necessary level of generality for some explanations, and then they can be supported by an inference to the best explanation. This issue of the right level of generality is also crucial for the moral case, as we will see.

moral facts might seem to provide a new argument for moral nihilism in addition to those discussed in section 3.2. However, as I argued at the end of section 3.2.2, even if moral facts are not needed to explain any moral beliefs or anything else, that explanatory impotence by itself would not give us any reason to *deny* moral facts. The most that it would do is undermine reasons to believe in moral facts. But we still might have no reason either to believe or to disbelieve moral nihilism.[6]

Thus, the real problem created by explanatory impotence lies within moral *epistemology*. In recent exchanges, Harman makes it clear that epistemology is his main concern: "My interest in moral explanations has always been an interest in the extent to which uncontroversial data might be better explained by one rather than another competing moral framework, so that the data could provide evidential support for the one framework over the other" (1998, 207–8). The issue, then, is how to decide among members of a contrast class of competing moral frameworks. Harman's conclusion is: "Whether or not [purported moral explanations] are cases in which a moral claim explains some uncontroversial facts, they are not cases that support one moral framework as compared with another" (Harman and Thomson 1996, 170). Thus, Harman's point is not to deny the possibility of moral explanations but only to deny that they have any epistemological force.

I will argue that Harman is correct to some extent but not completely. Against Harman, I will show how moral explanations can be used to adjudicate between *some* rival moral frameworks. However, this method is useful only when the contrasted frameworks share certain moral assumptions. That requirement makes this method useless against *other* frameworks, including moral nihilism, which reject those assumptions. Overall, then, inferences to the best explanation might help to make some moral beliefs modestly justified, but they cannot make any moral belief extremely justified, so they cannot take us beyond moderate moral skepticism.[7]

To see how this works, we need to survey a variety of proposed moral explanations. Nobody claims that moral facts directly explain purely physical events,[8] but moral facts are claimed to explain various aspects of human life, including acts and beliefs.[9]

6. Similarly, Thomson says, "The no-explanation argument is not an argument to the effect that there are no moral facts: it is an argument merely for the conclusion that we have no evidence that there are any" (Harman and Thomson 1996, 78).

7. The issue is not whether moral believers consciously run through an inference to the best explanation when they form moral beliefs. Few do that. Nonetheless, if someone could succeed in this kind of inference, then that ability might seem to make that person justified in believing its moral conclusion. If so, that would be enough to refute any form of moral skepticism which denies that any moral beliefs can be justified in that way.

8. Such explanations might be claimed by religions that postulate reincarnation if the moral badness of a person's life explains why that person is reincarnated as a cockroach. However, identity of a person with a cockroach is not a purely physical fact.

9. One could also distinguish attitudes from beliefs, as does Thomson (in Harman and Thomson 1996, 87–88), but that distinction would not affect my main points.

8.1.1. Purported Moral Explanations of Acts

Let's start with explanations of acts by an individual person in terms of a moral judgment about that person or that person's character. A classic example, developed by Nicholas Sturgeon, is that of Passed Midshipman Selim Woodworth, as described by Bernard DeVoto. Woodworth accepted command of the mission to rescue the Donner party who were trapped and dying in the High Sierra Mountains. Instead of leading rescue parties into the mountains, Woodworth "spent time arranging comforts for himself in camp, preening himself on the importance of his position" (Sturgeon 1984, 63). As a result, many people died who could have been saved. DeVoto concludes, "Woodworth was just no damned good" (1942, 442). Sturgeon concurs. Their idea seems to be that Woodworth would have led a rescue if he had had any goodness at all in him. More specifically, his moral vices of cowardice and vainglory are supposed to explain his actions.

To assess this explanation, we first need to clarify the explanandum, that is, the observation to be explained. If the question is why Woodworth did bad acts instead of good acts, then it seems natural to cite the moral badness of Woodworth's character. However, this question obviously assumes that Woodworth's acts were bad. Consequently, it cannot provide evidence against anyone who denies that assumption, as do moral nihilists. To get evidence that does not beg the question against moral nihilism, we need to avoid moral terms in specifying the observation. Presumably, then, what is to be explained is why Woodworth stayed in the base camp instead of going into the mountains to save the Donner party. Moral nihilists admit that fact.

This admitted fact might be easy to explain if Woodworth were (1) ignorant of the Donner party's plight, (2) coerced, or (3) trying to prevent some greater evil. But none of this was true. Woodworth had no excuse or justification for his acts. That is why DeVoto and Sturgeon explain his acts by the hypothesis that:

(4) Woodworth was no damned good.

Opponents of moral explanations respond by adding alternatives, such as:

(5) Woodworth was (at that time) more concerned about his own comfort and ambition than about the lives of those whom he had promised to rescue.

If some non-moral explanation like (5) is available, then (4) seems unnecessary to explain what Woodworth did. Moreover, the explanation with (5) seems simpler and, hence, better than the explanation with (4), because (4) is committed to moral facts that (5) is supposed to avoid.

Defenders of moral explanations might respond that the moral aspect of (4) is needed to capture the right level of generality. (Cf. Zimmerman 1984, 83–88; and Brink 1989, 193–97.) Even if the explanation with (5) works fine in the isolated case of Woodworth's failure to save the Donner party, Sturgeon and DeVoto seem to assume that Woodworth does other acts on other occasions that could also be explained by (4). These other acts could not be explained by (5), since (5) is about a particular situation. In contrast, (4) is about Woodworth in general, so it can explain a wider range of observations. In that respect, (4) seems more powerful and, thus, better as an explanation than (5).

Opponents of moral explanations can respond that, even if (5) is too narrow, it can be generalized:

(6) Woodworth is the kind of person who is regularly more concerned about his own comfort and ambition than about the lives of others.

Now (6) can explain every act that would be explained by the character trait that led Woodworth to neglect the Donner party and that led Sturgeon and DeVoto to assert (4).[10]

However, Woodworth might be bad in other ways as well. Even if Woodworth had lacked the particular character trait mentioned in (6), he might have had other vices that could have led him to abandon the Donner party. Suppose that Woodworth was vengeful and held a grudge against a particular member of the Donner party. Then he might have left them all to die just as he did in the actual case. This possibility suggests that Woodworth need not be concerned about his own comfort and ambition, so (6) need not be true for Woodworth to act just as he did. But then (6) does not seem to capture the right level of generality for an explanation of why Woodworth did what he did. To cover all of the vices that might have led Woodworth to neglect the Donner party, we seem to need something as general as (4).

These benefits of generality arise from multiple realizability. It is common and coherent to believe that a single kind of mental state can be realized in or supervene on a variety of different kinds of physical states (or on a variety of individual physical states). If so, an explanation might need to cite the mental state in order to capture the right level of generality because any realization of that same kind of mental state would cause the same result in the context. Similarly, if a single moral fact can be realized in or supervene on a variety of non-moral states, then an explanation might have to cite the moral fact in order to capture the right level of generality because any realization of that same moral fact would yield the same result.

This kind of argument is tricky, however, because overgeneralization is a constant danger. Imagine three bottles of poison on a shelf, but only two of the poisons are deadly. Sally sees the bottles, randomly picks one, drinks its contents, and dies. Why did she die? It might seem that Sally died because she drank that bottle as opposed to drinking nothing at all. However, that explanation ignores the other two bottles, so it is incomplete. With the other bottles in mind, it might seem that Sally died because she drank the particular bottle that she did as opposed to one of the other two bottles or none. However, that is not general enough to explain why she died because she would have died even if she had drunk the other deadly poison.[11] On the other hand, it would also be inaccurate to say simply that

10. Situationists might deny that any explanation by character traits is the best explanation. Compare Doris 2002. However, the problems raised by situationism apply whether character traits are described in moral terms, as in (4), or non-moral terms, as in (6). So situationism cannot resolve the issues here.

11. The fact that Sally drank this particular bottle might explain why she died in the way she died as opposed to some other way if the two deadly poisons cause death in different ways. However, I am seeking an explanation of why she died instead of living.

she died because she drank poison. That is too general to explain why she died because she would not have died if she had drunk the non-deadly poison. Instead, the best explanation of why she died is that she drank *a* deadly poison—one of the deadly poisons. The best explanation would be in terms of poison in general only if any kind of poison would do.

Analogously, an explanation with general moral terms is accurate and adequate only if any kind of immorality to which those terms apply would have the same effect. It is doubtful that this happens in any real case, because the kind of immorality always has some subsidiary effects. So it is also doubtful that the best explanation ever cites a moral feature as general as "no damned good." This problem comes out in the Donner case because not every moral defect would lead Woodworth to neglect the Donner party (just as not every poison would kill Sally). Woodworth could have tendencies to endanger others with his reckless driving, to lie to his friends or enemies, and to cheat at games, in his marriage, and on his taxes. None of these other vices would cause, or even incline, him to neglect the Donner party. But to say that he is "no damned good" seems to cover these other vices as well.[12] So (4) seems *too* general to be the best explanation.

Defenders of (4) might deny that (4) means that Woodworth has all vices and no virtues. But then they need to tell us precisely what it does mean. What exactly is necessary for someone to be "no damned good"? In the end, whether or not they hang on to (4), defenders of moral explanations need to provide some more specific account of the moral defects in Woodworth that explain his acts. Until they provide some better moral explanation, it will remain unclear whether or not moral terms really are needed to capture the right level of generality to explain Woodworth's acts in the Donner case.

In any case, the deepest and most important issue remains. Suppose that a defender of moral explanations succeeds in specifying certain character traits of Woodworth that explain his acts at just the right level of generality when those traits are described in moral terms. Nonetheless, whatever these moral defects are, given that all moral properties supervene on some (possibly very complex) non-moral properties, these moral character traits must be supervenient on some non-moral properties.[13] Hence, the same level of generality can be achieved by referring to the non-moral supervenience base for this moral property (and disjoining the multiple realizations). Let's stipulate that the relevant moral defects will be called *badness*, and the non-moral base property that underlies the supervening moral property of badness will be called *baseness*. Then we can distinguish two explanations:

---

12. If taken literally, (4) implies that Woodworth has no redeeming qualities whatsoever. That is unlikely. He probably cared for his family or friends. If so, (4) is too general to be literally true. That is another reason why it cannot be the best explanation. In any case, my argument in the text applies even if (4) is literally true.

13. Recall my distinction between moral facts (or properties) and morally relevant facts (or properties) in section 3.1. Since supervenience is weaker than entailment, the base facts or and properties under discussion count as non-moral, despite their moral relevance. Similarly, brain states count as physical rather than mental, even if mental states supervene on brain states.

(7) Woodworth is (morally) bad.

(8) Woodworth is (non-morally) base.

Since moral badness supervenes on non-moral baseness, the non-moral hypothesis, (8), explains everything that the moral hypothesis, (7), explains. Admittedly, there need not be anything that unifies baseness.[14] But there also might be nothing that unifies badness. Thus, there is no reason to prefer the moral explanation in terms of badness, (7), over the subvening non-moral explanation in terms of baseness, (8).

There is still a reason to prefer (8) over (7), according to opponents of moral explanations. The moral explanation, (7), would commit us to moral facts. Less committal explanations are simpler. Simpler explanations are better, unless the extra commitments are necessary. Moral facts are not necessary, since (8) works fine without moral facts. Hence, (8) seems better as an explanation.

Defenders of the moral explanation with (7) could respond that the moral explanation with (8) can't be better because it's not a competitor. Instead, (8) is a reason why (7) is true, assuming that, necessarily, anyone who is base is bad. On this assumption, (8) implies (7). Hence, (7) is necessary for the best explanation if (8) is necessary for the best explanation.[15] Admittedly, non-moral explanations work without any assumptions about which non-moral properties imply which moral properties. Insofar as (7) depends on such an assumption, (7) seems more committal than (8). However, if this ruled out all moral explanations, it would seem also to rule out all biological and economic explanations and evidence, insofar as biological and economic facts also supervene on physical facts just as moral facts do. Thus, this objection seems too strong to be plausible. If these other kinds of explanations are defensible, so are moral explanations, according to their defenders.[16]

Nonetheless, even if this move works, the need for such assumptions does severely limit the usefulness of inferences to the best explanation in moral episte-mology. Imagine that Gil denies that Woodworth is bad, then Nick argues that the best explanation of why Woodworth abandoned the Donner party is that Wood-worth is base and, hence, bad. This argument has real force if Gil admits that anyone who is base is bad. Given that admission, Nick need only show that Woodworth's baseness is necessary for the best explanation, and then Gil has to admit that Woodworth's badness is also necessary for the best explanation. That would be evidence that Woodworth is bad.

---

14. This objection might be suggested by Jonathan Dancy's claims about "natural shapelessness" (1993, 76). But see Sinnott-Armstrong 1999d; Jackson, Pettit, and Smith 2000; and McKeever and Ridge forthcoming.

15. In the original explanations, the corresponding assumption is that anyone who is more con-cerned about his own comfort and ambition than about the lives of others whom he promised to rescue is no damned good. Whereas (1)–(3) exclude (4)–(5) as the best explanation, (5) does not undermine but instead supports (4), on the assumption that (4) follows from (5).

16. Cf. Thomson in Harman and Thomson 1996, 80n; and Railton 1998, 178–80. It would also be interesting to consider whether other normative explanations (regarding prudence, aesthetics, and so on) are defensible, but that would require a lengthy tangent.

In contrast, suppose that Gil denies not only that Woodworth is bad but also that anyone who is base is bad. Now, even if Nick shows that Woodworth's baseness is necessary for the best explanation, this new opponent can still deny that Woodworth's badness is necessary for the best explanation. So Nick needs some independent justification of that premise. However, the only way to show that badness is necessary depends on the assumption that anyone who is base is bad. So Nick lacks the independent justification that is needed. That is why Nick's inference to the best explanation begs the question and cannot justify his moral belief in badness, or (7), as opposed to baseness, or (8).

This point applies directly to moral nihilists. Since moral nihilists deny all moral facts, including facts about badness, moral nihilists deny both that Woodworth is bad and, more generally, that anyone who is base is bad. They can, instead, cite Woodworth's baseness to explain his acts. Their explanation in terms of baseness, (8), does compete with the explanation in terms of badness, (7), according to moral nihilists, since they believe that (7) cannot be true even when (8) is true, so (8) is not a reason for (7). Consequently, anyone who tries to use such an inference to the best explanation against moral nihilism needs some independent justification for the premise that (7) is *necessary* for the best explanation. No justification is available independent of the assumption that anyone who is base is bad. But moral nihilists deny that assumption. So any such inference to the best explanation begs the question and, hence, cannot refute moral nihilism.[17]

Thus, moral explanations of individual acts succeed only in limited ways. They can be legitimate and can be used in inferences to the best explanation if certain assumptions are granted. Such inferences to the best explanation can justify moral beliefs within limited contrast classes whose members share the needed assumptions. To this extent, I disagree with Harman's claim that no moral explanation can "support one moral framework as compared with another" (Harman and Thomson 1996, 170). Nonetheless, such inferences to the best explanation cannot make moral beliefs justified out of unlimited contrast classes that include positions, such as moral nihilism, that deny the needed assumptions. This means that inference to the best explanation cannot make moral beliefs extremely justified, just as moderate moral skeptics claim.[18]

This conclusion gets reinforced when we consider purported moral explanations of actions by groups (rather than by individuals). In a standard example, we observe that the anti-slavery abolitionist movement grew in the United States during the 1830s. We wonder why. An explanation that uses moral terms is:

17. This point might not bother Sturgeon, who admits, when explaining Hitler's acts by his moral depravity, that "the only way we could be wrong about this latter case (assuming we have the non-moral facts right) would be for our whole moral theory to be hopelessly wrong" (1984, 69). That is just what moral nihilists think.

18. Another example of this pattern cites Hitler's moral depravity as the best explanation of his killing millions of innocent people. However, this explanation assumes that Hitler's acts were evil. Compare Thomson in Harman and Thomson 1996, 86n. This assumption would be accepted by almost everyone, including me, but it would be rejected by moral nihilists. So this example provides no more evidence against moral nihilism than do Woodworth's acts.

(9) The real evils in slavery became worse during the 1820s.

This explanation seems plausible, because of changes in the practice of slavery during the 1820s. A competing non-moral explanation is:

(10) The pains and losses of freedom in slavery increased during the 1820s.

Let's suppose that the problem of generality has been solved, and the remaining competitors are (9) and (10). Opponents of moral explanations will then argue that (10) is simpler because it avoids any commitment to moral facts. Defenders of moral explanations will respond that the pains and losses of freedom mentioned in (10) are reasons to believe in the real evils mentioned in (9), so (10) is not in competition with (9). However, this response assumes that pain and loss of freedom are real evils. That assumption is denied by moral nihilists, so the premise that real evils are necessary to explain the rise of abolitionism (and the fall of slavery) begs the question against moral nihilists. Thus, this inference to the best explanation cannot succeed in providing any evidence against moral nihilism. This inference still might work fine with views that share the assumption that pain and loss of freedom are evils, so it might justify a moral belief out of a limited contrast class, all of whose members share that assumption. But it cannot show that any moral belief is extremely justified, and it cannot take us beyond moderate moral skepticism.

8.1.2. Purported Moral Explanations of Beliefs

The issues are similar when an individual's moral belief is supposed to be explained by its truth. One example involves someone who does not believe that slavery is morally wrong but who converts to the belief that slavery is morally wrong as a result of reading a novel (like *Uncle Tom's Cabin*) or watching a movie (like *Roots*). (Cf. Werner 1983.) Supposedly, the conversion cannot be explained by any of this convert's former moral beliefs, so the best explanation must be that his new belief results from the real evils in slavery.

It is doubtful, however, that moral facts are necessary to explain such moral conversions. After all, religious conversions can be explained without postulating religious facts. And if a film such as *Birth of a Nation* converted someone to racist moral views, that moral conversion would not be explained by the truth of those racist views. Similarly, moral facts also do not seem necessary to explain conversion to moral views that we endorse, such as when someone comes to believe that slavery is morally wrong.

But then how *can* this desirable conversion be explained? Even if this convert did not previously believe that slavery is immoral, this convert probably did hold other moral beliefs, such as that it is immoral to cause pain and loss of freedom to intelligent humans just to benefit those who cause the pain and loss of freedom. The novel or movie can then cause this convert to recognize the extreme pain and loss of freedom caused by slavery, the intelligence of slaves, and the selfishness of the slaveholders. The change in this person's moral beliefs about slavery can then be explained by such changes in this person's non-moral beliefs about slavery.

Alternatively, the novel or movie can cause the convert to combine his beliefs in a new way. If the convert already believed all of the needed premises but never put them together in an inference, then the convert might never have formulated the belief that slavery is immoral, and then the novel or movie can stimulate him to draw that inference. There is no need for any of those moral beliefs to be true in order to understand why this person comes to hold them.

Defenders of moral explanations might respond that the convert's new belief that slavery causes extreme pain and loss of freedom are caused by the fact that slavery does cause extreme pain and loss of freedom. If that non-moral fact implies the moral fact that slavery is immoral, then that moral fact must be true for the explanation to work. This argument has force against any opponent who admits that it is immoral to cause extreme pain and loss of freedom. Without this admission, however, there is no way to show that the moral fact is necessary for the explanation. Thus, this argument begs the question against opponents who deny that assumption. In particular, moral nihilists deny that anything is immoral, so they deny that it is immoral to cause extreme pain and loss of freedom, and then they deny that the moral fact that slavery is immoral is necessary to explain the moral conversion in this example. Consequently, this argument has no force against moral nihilists, even if it can be used against some other opponents who share the necessary assumptions. As before, this kind of moral explanation can be useful but only in limited ways.

A trickier example of a moral explanation of belief does not pretend to be realistic: If there are moral facts, then it is possible for someone called Amazing Grace to be a perfectly reliable detector of all moral facts.[19] Grace believes that an act is morally wrong when and only when the act is morally wrong (and similarly for morally right, bad, good, and so on). The real moral wrongness of an act might then seem to be the best explanation of Grace's belief that an act is morally wrong (or morally right, bad, good, and so on).[20]

Judith Jarvis Thomson suggests a possible criticism of this kind of moral explanation (Harman and Thomson 1996, 84). Grace believes that the act is morally wrong because she observes the non-moral features of the act. After all, if she were not aware of those non-moral features, then she would not be justified in believing that the act was morally wrong. These non-moral features explain the moral fact that the act is morally wrong for those reasons. However, these non-moral features are *not* explained by the moral fact. This limit on what moral facts explain is supposed to distinguish moral perception from visual perception where one's belief that an apple is red is based on the fact that it appears red, and its

19. This example derives from Tolhurst 1986, 46. For an inference to the best explanation, it is not necessary for Grace to be *perfectly* reliable, but I will follow Tolhurst's description anyway. One could make the same points with an anti-expert (who always holds false moral views) or an amazing coin that reliably indicates correct answers to moral yes-no questions without having any beliefs.

20. If the supervenience base of moral wrongness has no shape (Dancy 1993, 76), we might not be able to formulate any non-moral explanation of Grace's belief. But, again, see Sinnott-Armstrong 1999d; Jackson, Pettit, and Smith 2000; and McKeever and Ridge forthcoming.

appearance *is* explained by the fact that the apple is red. However, symmetry can be reintroduced simply by saying that Grace believes that the act is morally wrong because it seems morally wrong to her. That seeming *is* supposed to be explained by the moral fact that it is wrong (Tolhurst 1998). So Thomson's criticism does not undermine this case.

A deeper (although more obvious) problem is that this example is fictional. In the actual world, a real person could cite Grace's belief as evidence for a moral fact only if that person already had adequate independent evidence that Grace is a reliable detector of moral facts. Such evidence would have to include observations that Grace's past moral beliefs were true.

This works fine in some cases. You and I might have known Grace for a long time. We might agree that she has always gotten moral matters right in the past. Then, if you and I are having a moral dispute, you can cite Grace's moral belief as some evidence against my moral view. Our shared moral assumptions about the truth of Grace's past moral beliefs can make evidence out of our observations of Grace's current moral beliefs. The best explanation of why she believes what she does might be that her beliefs are true once again.

However, this cannot work against a moral nihilist for the simple reason that a moral nihilist would deny both that Grace's positive moral beliefs were ever true and that she is now a reliable detector of moral facts. To cite Grace against moral nihilism is like postulating a reliable detector of witches or voodoo against people who deny witches and voodoo (or like hypothesizing someone with reliable religious experience against atheists). Even if Grace reliably detects moral facts, and even if moral facts are necessary for the best explanation of Grace's moral beliefs, to assume these premises without independent justification would beg the question against moral nihilism, so Grace's beliefs cannot be evidence against moral nihilists or out of any contrast class that includes moral nihilism. Consequently, Grace's beliefs and testimony, at best, can make my moral beliefs modestly justified but not extremely justified.[21]

The same limits apply within Grace's own perspective. Even if she is in fact a reliable detector of moral facts, for her to assume this without independent justification would beg the question against moral nihilism just as much as if anyone else assumes it. She needs that assumption as a premise if she is trying to use an inference to the best explanation to justify her belief. So Grace herself cannot be justified on this basis in believing any moral claim out of any contrast class that includes moral nihilism. She, like us, is at most modestly but not extremely justified in her moral beliefs.

Similar points apply to moral beliefs held by groups. Modern societies are converging on the belief that slavery is morally wrong, and almost every society at any time has agreed that torturing toddlers just for fun is morally wrong. It might seem that the best explanation of why so many people agree is that they are reacting to a real moral wrong.

---

21. This example and conclusion are, of course, very similar to Nelson's example of Dahlia and my conclusions in section 7.4.

The most common response is that such agreement or convergence can be explained at least as well by sociology, psychology, sociobiology, or some other science without any moral facts. The fact that such moral beliefs help societies thrive and survive is enough to explain why we have evolved so that so many people hold those beliefs. We already discussed these non-moral explanations of moral beliefs in the context of an argument for moral nihilism (section 3.2.2). There I argued that the availability of such explanations does not directly support moral nihilism. Nonetheless, if we can explain common moral beliefs without invoking moral facts, that does undercut any attempt to establish those moral facts on the basis of an inference to the best explanation of common moral beliefs.

Defenders of moral explanations might respond that such scientific explanations do not compete with moral explanations because the belief that such acts are morally wrong helps society by dissuading people from doing such acts. Preventing these acts helps society because such acts usually cause harm to society or to its members. That is just what makes those acts morally wrong, or so it is assumed. This assumption is quite questionable, since an individual act might be an exception to the general trend. It is hard to see why the moral wrongness of an exceptional act would follow from the fact that acts of a general kind usually cause harm to society or from the fact that it has been socially useful for societies to believe that such acts are morally wrong. (Cf. Sidgwick 1907, 489–90.) Still, if this substantive moral assumption is accepted by both parties in a dispute, then observations of moral agreement and convergence might be best explained by moral facts, and this can be cited as evidence for one of the disputing moral frameworks above another.

The story is quite different with moral nihilism. As before, moral nihilists will insist that the explanation in terms of moral facts does compete with their scientific explanation, and moral nihilists will reject the moral assumption that acts are morally wrong when they usually reduce the survival value of society. Consequently, observations of moral agreement and convergence cannot be used as evidence against moral nihilism if moral nihilists can explain that agreement without invoking moral facts.

8.1.3. *Purported Explanations of Moral Truths*

A third kind of moral explanation will complete this list of candidates. The previous patterns cite moral facts to explain non-moral facts. Thomson recently admitted that explanations in this direction never provide evidence for moral beliefs (Harman and Thomson 1996, 91). However, she went on to claim that moral evidence can be based on explanations in the other direction, that is, when non-moral facts explain moral truths, as in her example: "Alice's giving Bert a banana was her keeping her word when [she knew] it cost her a lot to do so and she could have got away with not doing so. That, it seems plausible to think, would explain the truth of 'Alice's giving Bert a banana was just'" (Harman and Thomson 1996, 93). Since what does the explaining here is non-moral fact, an inference to the best explanation would have a non-moral conclusion. Nonetheless, Thomson claims that the availability of this explanation supports the moral claim that Alice's giving Bert a banana was just. Her argument is not, then, an inference to the best explanation, as normally understood. But it is still important here, because it challenges moral skepticism.

The question, then, is whether a non-moral explanation of a moral truth can provide evidence in favor of one moral framework over another. Suppose Carol and David agree that Alice's act was just, and the dispute is about whose moral framework can best explain why it is just. Carol is a utilitarian, so David argues forcefully that Alice's act does not maximize utility, since it will cost Alice a lot to give the banana to Bert, and nobody will be hurt if Alice does not give it, since Bert doesn't need the banana anyway. If Carol admits that utilitarians cannot explain why Alice's act is just, but she still believes that Alice's act is just, then David can offer a better explanation of its justice, namely, Thomson's. This explanation of a moral fact by non-moral facts can then provide evidence in favor of David's deontological framework above Carol's utilitarian framework.

Of course, none of this works unless Carol grants that Alice's act is just, so it cannot work against a utilitarian who sticks to her theory and denies that Alice's act is just or against a moral nihilist who denies that any act is just. Against such opponents who deny the operating assumption, the argument begs the question, so it loses its force. As Harman said, "Clearly, in a context of a dispute as to whether actions like Alice's constitute justice, [the claim that the cited features of Alice's act explain why it is just] is controversial and cannot show that there is evidence in favor of one moral framework rather than another" (Harman and Thomson 1996, 170–71). Thus, moral explanations like this one can work against some opponents but not against others.

8.1.4. *Implications for Moral Skepticism*

Do these conclusions refute or support moral skepticism? As always, that depends on what moral skepticism claims.

I argued that no inference to the best explanation by itself can provide any evidence against moral nihilism, because such inferences always depend on assumptions that moral nihilists deny, so these inferences beg the question in the absence of any independent justification for those assumptions. This result implies that inferences to the best explanation cannot justify any moral belief as opposed to moral nihilism. Since moral nihilism is in the extreme contrast class for all moral beliefs, no inference to the best explanation can justify any moral belief out of the extreme contrast class. This method fails to make any moral belief extremely justified.

On the other hand, I also gave examples where moral explanations can fairly adjudicate among some moral frameworks, which grant the necessary assumptions. This part of my conclusion refutes *complete* moral skepticism, which is the claim that there cannot ever be any evidence in favor of any moral belief or theory as opposed to *any* other. Furthermore, my conclusion leaves open the possibility that sometimes all competitors in the modest contrast class can be ruled out by inferences to the best explanation. This might happen when all members of that modest contrast class share the assumptions needed for inferences to the best explanation. If so, then some moral beliefs can be modestly justified on the basis of inferences to the best explanation. This result would support my moderate moral skepticism.[22]

8.2. Contractarianism and Contractualism

Whereas inferences to the best explanation depend on epistemic norms to determine which explanation is best, other kinds of normativism appeal to other kinds of non-moral norms. The most prominent alternative appeals to norms of rationality. Norms of rationality are supposed to be non-moral in nature because to call an act (or person) *irrational* is not to call it *immoral* and, conversely, to call an act (or person) *immoral* is not to call it *irrational*.

Such non-moral norms of rationality are invoked most famously by contractarians. (Cf. Morris 1996.) The original idea behind contractarianism might have been that people in a society have moral obligations to obey certain rules because they actually agreed to some kind of social contract including those rules. Most recent versions of contactarianism, however, do not refer to any actual contract because actual contractors are often irrational, and it is hard to see how irrational choices could justify morality. That is why contemporary contractarians usually invoke norms of rationality and focus on counterfactuals about what rational people (under appropriate circumstances) would agree to.

Contractarians sometimes also invoke other norms less openly. The appropriate circumstances for choosing moral constraints often include restrictions that are supposed to ensure some kind of impartiality, which is supposed to be essential to justified moral beliefs. The claim that these circumstances are the *appropriate* ones to justify moral beliefs invokes a kind of norm. These normative premises, in addition to the norms of rationality, are what make contractarianism a kind of normativism.

Such contractarian frameworks are used for different goals, often at the same time. Some contractarians use their contract apparatus to explain the origin and shape of actual moral beliefs. Other contractarians define the meaning or truth-conditions of moral claims in terms of contracts. Other contractarians try to show that agents have practical reasons to act in accordance with moral rules. Since such explanations, linguistic theses, and reasons for action are separate from reasons for belief, these contractarian theses have no direct implications for moral epistemology.

I will focus instead on contractarianism as a position in moral epistemology. Even here, two different goals need to be distinguished. Some contractarians use their contract apparatus merely as a striking and convenient way to display interconnections among different parts of their overall view (cf. Rawls 1971, 21 and 579). The justification of moral beliefs then comes from coherence rather than from the contract as such (see section 10.4). In contrast, the contractarians who will concern us in the current chapter claim that rational agreement can stop the skeptical regress by providing an independent source of justified moral beliefs. The basic idea behind contractarianism is then that moral beliefs are justified when all

---

22. For more criticisms of this method in moral epistemology, see Copp 1990.

rational people in appropriate circumstances would agree to those moral beliefs or to some moral code that somehow implies them.

Such contractarianism is primarily about when moral belief *contents* are justified, not about when moral *believers* or even belief *states* are justified. Most people do not become justified in believing moral claims by arguing or even being able to argue that certain people would agree to their claims. Still, if contractarians are right, then people *can* be justified in believing moral contents if they are justified in believing that those moral contents are justified by some kind of agreement, and if they base their moral belief states on this contractarian argument.

Moreover, contractarianism need not apply to *all* areas of morality. Most contractarian theories are mainly about justice and not about benevolence or other virtues. Nonetheless, if any contractarian argument could make anyone justified in believing even one moral claim, this would be enough to refute universal moral skepticism. And if this argument really does depend only on non-moral norms without any substantive moral assumptions, then this approach might be enough to refute moral nihilism and even moderate moral skepticism. So we need to consider this approach carefully.

Such contractarianism comes in many different flavors. Different contractarians employ competing theories of rationality. They also specify diverse circumstances as appropriate for choosing moral constraints. And some use dissimilar norms of impartiality. The extensive menu of options creates problems for me because I can't sample them all without this book gaining too much weight. It also creates problems for contractarians because each needs to sell his or her particular flavor to us. To illustrate these problems, I will discuss three representative versions as a taste test, and leave the others for other meals. I chose these samples not because they are easy to criticize, but because they are some of the most detailed, popular, and plausible contractarian moral theories.

8.2.1. Rationality

One contractarian tradition follows Hobbes ([1651] 1962) and is represented on the contemporary scene by Gauthier. According to Gauthier, morality faces a "foundational crisis" to which the only solution is "a mode of justification that does not require the introduction of moral considerations" (1991, 15 and 19) and justifies moral beliefs "without introducing prior moral assumptions" (1986, 6). Gauthier claims that his argument solves this crisis by achieving this kind of justification, so all of his premises are supposed to be morally neutral.

Instead of premises about morality, Gauthier uses only premises about rationality. In Gauthier's view, an agent is rational to the extent that the agent's "choices and actions maximize the agent's expected utility, where utility is a measure of considered preference" (1991, 19; cf. 1986, chap. 2).[23] Since rationality

---

23. Although only considered and coherent preferences determine rationality, Gauthier does not require full information. This is important, for he assumes (1986, 174) that people are translucent but not transparent to each other.

depends only on the agent's own expected utility without regard to effects on other people, Gauthier's notion of rationality is morally neutral. If you run out of gas, get angry, and kick your car hard enough to hurt your car and your foot, then your act of kicking is irrational, but it is not immoral. It might be immoral to kick another person's car or another person. However, morality is not in play when what you kick is your own car (assuming that you did not promise not to kick your car, it is not illegal or against the rules of a game you are playing, no impressionable children are watching, and so on). Such examples suggest that Gauthier's norms of rationality are distinct from norms of morality. This independence enables his arguments to invoke norms of rationality while avoiding moral assumptions.[24]

This notion of rationality is still supposed to reach conclusions about morality. According to Gauthier, a moral practice is "justifiable" if it "is capable of gaining unanimous agreement among rational people who were choosing the terms on which they would interact with each other" (1991, 23; cf. 1986, 339). Several aspects of this apparatus are worth highlighting.

First, Gauthier's framework is hypothetical and counterfactual (1986, 9). Real people are never actually in a position to choose the rules that govern their social interactions. Gauthier's test also refers to contractors who are rational in ways that many actual people are not. As a result, Gauthier's point cannot be that we agreed to certain rules, so now we must follow them. Instead, his point is that we would agree to them if we were rational.

Second, what Gauthier calls justifiable is not a moral *belief* or *believer* but is, instead, a *practice* that constrains social interactions. Presumably, however, justifiable practices can lead to justified beliefs and believers. When a justifiable practice forbids acts of a kind, then a belief that such acts are morally forbidden can itself be justified, and believers who know that the practice is justifiable are justified in believing that such acts are morally wrong. That relation between justifiable practices and justified believers is what makes Gauthier's apparatus relevant to moral epistemology. Gauthier need not (and does not) claim that it is *necessary* for anyone to go through his argument or to believe in universal rational agreement in order to be justified in holding a moral belief. Nonetheless, if Gauthier's argument for universal rational agreement on a practice is *sufficient* to make a moral believer justified in beliefs that are based on Gauthier's argument, then this argument is supposed to be enough to refute moral skepticism.

But what, if anything, would all rational people agree on? At the most abstract level, Gauthier's answer is his principle of minimax relative concession: "In any cooperative interaction, the rational joint strategy is determined by a bargain among the cooperators in which each advances his maximal claim and then offers a concession no greater in relative magnitude than the minimax concession" (1986, 145). More concretely, Gauthier claims:

24. Some moral egoists might question whether Gauthier's theory of rationality really is morally neutral, but I want to focus on other problems.

Many of our actual moral principles and practices are in effect applications of the requirements of minimax relative concession to particular contexts. We may suppose that promise-keeping, truth-telling, fair dealing, are to be defended by showing that adherence to them permits persons to co-operate in ways that may be expected to equalize, at least roughly, the relative benefits afforded by interaction. These are among the core practices of the morality that we may commend to each individual by showing that it commands his rational agreement. (1986, 156)

Here is a simple example from Gauthier:

Suppose each of us were to assist her fellows only when either she could expect to benefit herself from giving assistance, or she took a direct interest in their well-being. Then, in many situations, persons would not give assistance to others, even though the benefit to the recipient would greatly exceed the cost to the giver, because there would be no provision for the giver to share in the benefit. Everyone would then expect to do better were each to give assistance to her fellows, regardless of her own benefit or interest, whenever the cost of assisting was low and the benefit of receiving assistance considerable. Each would thereby accept a constraint on the direct pursuit of her own concerns, not unilaterally, but given a like acceptance by others. Reflection leads us to recognize that those who belong to groups whose members adhere to such a practice of mutual assistance enjoy benefits in interaction that are denied to others. We may then represent such a practice as rationally acceptable to everyone. (1991, 23)[25]

If these constraints are moral, but his premises are non-moral, then Gauthier's argument derives morality from rationality.

Not every common moral belief can be justified in this way. In particular, Gauthier states, "A contractarian account of morals has no place for duties that are strictly redistributive in their effects, transferring but not increasing benefits, or duties that do not assume reciprocity from other persons" (1986, 16). This restriction has radical implications: "Animals, the unborn, the congenitally handicapped and defective, fall beyond the pale of a morality tied to mutuality" (1986, 268; cf. 17–18). At this point, Gauthier must make a choice. He must either admit that his system is incomplete (in that it fails to capture some justified moral duties) or claim that his system is complete (in that there are no justified moral duties other than those within his system).

Gauthier claims completeness, for example, when he writes, "If [actual moral constraints] are to be justified, we must be able to consider them as objects of hypothetical *ex ante* agreement, the rationality of which we now recognize *ex post*" (1986, 339; cf. 11, 158). This suggests that we have no direct moral duties to "animals, the unborn, the congenitally handicapped and defective..." (1986, 268). Many critics find these results objectionable. They argue that Gauthier's moral theory cannot be adequate if it leads to such counterintuitive conclusions. However, this

---

25. The phrase "rationally acceptable" seems to mean "rationally allowed." In contrast, Gauthier sometimes claims that practices "command" rational agreement, which suggests being "rationally required." Is Gauthier claiming that it is irrational for anyone not to accept such practices? It seems so.

implication does not bother Gauthier, because his goal is not to fit common moral intuitions (1986, 269; 1991, 29).[26]

Nonetheless, it is hard to see how Gauthier could show that his moral theory is complete. Why can't there be any moral constraints without reciprocity? Because not all rational people would accept them. But then why can't there be any moral constraints that not all rational people accept? Gauthier responds, "The contractarian insists that a society could not command the willing allegiance of a rational person if, without appealing to her feelings for others, it afforded her no expectation of net benefit" (1986, 11; cf. 238). The point cannot be that society is *unable* to command such allegiance. Commands can be issued. Maybe Gauthier is saying that society could not *successfully* command such allegiance, since otherwise compliance would not be stable (1991, 29), but this is mere wishful thinking, since stable societies have often been based on force, not reason. So Gauthier seems to be saying that it is not *fair* to constrain rational people without benefit to them. This assumption is a substantive moral claim of the very kind that Gauthier was supposed to avoid. So it is hard to see how Gauthier could justify his claim to completeness without violating his own methodological limits.

Gauthier could avoid these problems by renouncing his claim to completeness. Even if he cannot justify all legitimate moral constraints, his argument still might be enough to justify some. If he can show that even one moral belief is justified by mutual self-interest, then only irrational people can refuse to agree to the corresponding practice or can deny the corresponding moral belief. That seems to include moral nihilists, so Gauthier's argument might seem to refute moral nihilism. If so, his argument would be enough to make some moral believers extremely justified and, thus, to refute even moderate versions of moral skepticism. Moderate moral skeptics then need some other objection to Gauthier's argument.

Many objections could be raised against Gauthier's argument. (Cf. Vallentyne 1991; and Paul et al. 1988.) Some critics reject Gauthier's theory of rationality (Gert 1990). Gauthier raises difficulties for some competing views of rationality, but he admits, "We cannot expect to resolve this conflict in a way that all will find convincing or even plausible" (1986, 55). This lack of resolution is crucial for moral epistemology, especially with contrast classes. If we are not justified in accepting Gauthier's theory of rationality in contrast with one of its competitors, then we are not justified in using his theory of rationality to reach any moral conclusion as opposed to the alternative that would result from the competing theory of rationality. After all, philosophers can always define "rational" so that their favorite moral system would be chosen by all rational people. Utilitarians, for example, could say that people are rational only if they maximize utility for all, and then all rational people would agree on utilitarianism of some (possibly indirect) kind. That method would, however, clearly beg the question against contrary moral beliefs as long as the premises about rationality remain unjustified. Similarly, Gauthier's argument begs

---

26. Gauthier also rejects coherentism: "It is no part of my argument to show that the requirements of contractarian morality will satisfy the Rawlsian test of cohering with our considered judgments in reflective equilibrium" (1991, 29).

the question against competitors who reject his theory of rationality as long as he cannot justify his theory of rationality.

Other critics deny Gauthier's claim that all people who are rational on his theory would accept his principle of minimax relative concession or its applications to "our actual moral principles" (1986, 156). In his own example (quoted above), Gauthier claims, "Everyone would then expect to do better were each to give assistance to her fellows, regardless of her own benefit or interest, whenever the cost of assisting was low and the benefit of receiving assistance considerable" (1991, 23). What about very rich and powerful people? The cost to them of donating $100 to a charity is low. Each donation can bring considerable benefits to the needy. But the rich and powerful would not expect to do better personally if they continually made such donations "whenever" this situation arose, since this would add up to a lot. Rich and powerful people might need help themselves some day, but that risk might sometimes be low enough that their expected utility would not be increased by a constraint that required such donations, even given a like acceptance by others. Thus, even on Gauthier's own theory of rationality, not all rational people would accept this principle.

The same basic point applies to negative moral constraints, such as prohibitions on killing. Maybe all rational persons would agree to *some* rule against killing, but the agreement breaks down when we ask *which* rule they would agree to.[27] Would all rational persons agree to a moral rule against killing that would protect rational people who are so severely handicapped that they cannot reciprocate for the costs of keeping them alive? In certain circumstances, this constraint would impose more costs than benefits for non-handicapped people (even given a chance of future handicaps). That is why Gauthier says such persons "fall beyond the pale of a morality tied to mutuality" (1986, 268). However, rational but severely handicapped people clearly would not agree to any constraint that does not protect them. So neither constraint—neither Gauthier's narrow constraint that does not protect such handicapped people nor a wide constraint that does protect such handicapped people—would garner universal agreement among all rational people.[28]

The deepest problem, and the one that is most relevant to moral epistemology, arises even if Gauthier is right about rationality and even if all rational people accept his principles. To see this problem, we need to distinguish two kinds of rationality. Sometimes a person is called rational to the extent that she adjusts her beliefs to fit her evidence. If everyone who is rational in this way would accept a

---

27. Gauthier might respond that all rational persons agree to the rule, "Don't kill," even if they disagree about whom it protects. But such agreement is as empty as when two people say, "Respect all men equally," but one means all males and the other means all people. Both accept an abstract formula, but they don't accept the same normative content. Anyway, even if the abstract formula did count as a single rule, my point could be restated in terms of disagreements about the content or force of the rule.

28. Gauthier might respond that I overlooked his requirement of "equal rationality" (1986, 226–27, 270; cf. 1991, 28). However, even if this requirement did avoid the problem, it seems unjustified apart from moral assumptions of the very kind that Gauthier is trying to avoid.

moral belief, then that moral belief would be epistemically justified. However, there is no way to justify a claim that all people who are rational in this way would accept a certain moral belief without already having separate evidence for that moral belief. The agreement would not add any new evidence, since contractors agree only because of prior evidence. So, rational agreement of this kind cannot be a separate source of justified moral belief.

In any case, contractarians do not refer to such epistemic rationality. They see people as rational to the extent that these people seek or obtain good effects and avoid bad effects. But then, if all rational people accept a belief or rule, this must be because acceptance brings good effects or avoids bad effects. Such effects do not show that a moral belief is true or even likely to be true. To see this, suppose that someone will kill anyone who does not believe in Santa Claus, and everyone knows this. Then everyone who is rational in the relevant way would accept (or try to accept) the belief in Santa Claus. But this agreement does not provide any evidence that Santa Claus exists. Similarly, to show that all rational people would accept certain moral beliefs as ways to protect or improve their lives or society does not show that these beliefs are either likely to be true or justified epistemically.

Gauthier is aware of this problem and responds that his argument does not rest on contingent preferences that some people lack (1991, 23–24).[29] But such non-contingent rational agreement is still not evidence of moral truth. Even if the desire to live is contingent, suppose that a belief in Santa Claus is necessary to prevent everyone from becoming so depressed that they would lose all motivation to do anything (or would see their desires as not worth fulfilling), regardless of what they prefer to do. This would not be evidence that Santa Claus really exists. So, even if contractarian arguments do not depend on specific preferences, they still provide at most instrumental and not epistemic justification.

A second possible response is that the person who threatens to kill anyone who does *not* believe in Santa Claus could just as well threaten to kill anyone who *does* believe in Santa Claus. In contrast, it might seem that Gauthier's argument cannot be used to argue for an opposite moral belief. But this is not clear. If facts about human nature and the environment were different, so that helping people in need endangered the rest of the species, then Gauthier's style of argument might lead every rational person to agree to a prohibition on helping people in need.

The most promising response, then, is that contractarian arguments are not about effects of moral *beliefs*. Instead, they concern effects of accepting moral *constraints* or rules or standards. Such constraints have the form of imperatives (for example, "Don't kill"), so they lack any truth-value. Hence, we should not expect them to be epistemically justified. Nonetheless, we can still be epistemically justified in believing that killing is morally wrong *if* this moral claim just means that killing violates a constraint whose acceptance is justified instrumentally, and if

---

29. Why should moral theory be restricted to non-contingent desires? It is hard to see any reason for this limitation that does not depend on substantive moral assumptions.

accepting the constraint on killing has beneficial effects that do justify it instrumentally. (Cf. Morris 1996, 224; and Copp 1995, chap. 2.) The effects that justify
the constraint are, then, also what make all rational persons accept the constraint
and what make the moral claim true.

But is this what the moral claim means? I doubt it. For one thing, accepting a
rule can be beneficial in circumstances where the corresponding moral belief is
not true. Suppose that an evil demon will kill everyone who does not accept the
rule, "Don't leave cookies for Santa." Then all rational people would accept (or try
to accept) this rule, so that rule would be justified, according to Gauthier. But this
is still not evidence that it is morally wrong to leave cookies for Santa. Indeed, it
need not be morally wrong to leave cookies for Santa in these circumstances. The
demon would not kill someone who accepts the constraint "Don't leave cookies for
Santa," but who leaves cookies anyway out of a perverse desire to break the rules.
Thus, the moral belief that it is morally wrong to leave cookies for Santa cannot
be equivalent to the claim that accepting the no-cookies rule is instrumentally
justified.

This example is fanciful, but similar real cases are common. Even if it is
socially useful to believe that active euthanasia is always morally wrong (because
doctors will make too many mistakes if they think that it is ever permitted), many
people who accept this claim about social usefulness still believe that active euthanasia is *not* morally wrong in some exceptional particular cases. Similarly, some
utilitarians hold that society would be worse off if people generally accepted
utilitarianism (Sidgwick 1907, 489–90). Such moral positions might be false, but
they seem consistent at least. Yet they would be semantically inconsistent if
"morally wrong" meant "violates a constraint that is justified by effects of accepting
it" (or by agreement among everyone who is rational in a way defined by effects).
So this cannot be what the moral belief means. Consequently, moral beliefs are
neither true nor epistemically justified merely because the corresponding moral
constraints are instrumentally justified.

Contractarians might respond that such non-contractarian beliefs are not really about morality, because the only real morality is defined by rational agreement
based on effects of accepting rules. Gauthier suggests this response when he writes,
"In identifying morality with those constraints that would obtain agreement among
rational persons who were choosing their terms of interaction, I am engaged in
rational reconstruction" (1991, 25). However, when such reconstruction is too radical, it amounts to redefinition that changes the subject. You can't defend the view
that whales are not really mammals by "reconstructing" our common notions so
that an animal counts as a mammal only if it lives on land. Analogously, if all that
contractarians mean when they say that abortion is not morally wrong is that not all
rational people would accept a rule against abortion, then opponents of abortion
can admit that those acts are not wrong on contractarian definitions — they are not
contractarian-wrong. This does not imply that these acts are not morally wrong in
the sense that is claimed by opponents of abortion and denied by defenders of
abortion. Since the original issue was not about rational agreement, contractarians
cannot resolve that issue by redefining moral wrongness in terms of their own
theory. Contractarian arguments still might provide evidence for something else,

but they cannot show how *morality* can be justified epistemically.[30] Consequently, they cannot refute moral skepticism.

8.2.2. *Impartial Rationality*

To solve the problems for Gauthier's theory, some contractarians deploy impartiality in addition to rationality. They see an act as morally wrong when it violates a principle that would be accepted by everyone who is not only rational but also impartial. Claims of impartiality are often normative, but impartiality is still supposed to be morally neutral, because impartiality by itself is not sufficient either for moral action or for true or justified moral belief. Someone who is impartial is immoral if he harms or cheats indiscriminately (Gert 1998, 134–35). Impartial believers who are irrational can believe almost any fool thing about morality. So impartiality by itself seems to have no moral content. But then how can it be used to justify moral beliefs? The idea is to combine one morally neutral norm (rationality) with another morally neutral norm (impartiality) in order to justify a moral conclusion. This form of argument is then a kind of normativism.[31]

The problem, of course, is that the premises need to be justified for anyone to be justified in believing the conclusion on the basis of such an argument. Defenders of this method of justification need to be justified in believing their particular accounts of impartiality and rationality. They also need to be justified in believing that everyone who is rational and impartial (on their accounts) would agree on certain moral principles. Finally, they need to be justified in believing a bridge principle that an act is morally wrong when and only when it violates a moral principle that would be accepted by everyone who is rational and impartial (on their accounts).

Such a bridge principle contrasts with Gauthier's claim that a moral belief is justified only when the underlying principle would be accepted by all rational people even if they were partial. Since these approaches are incompatible, defenders of the impartial rational approach need to rule out Gauthier's claim in order to be justified in believing their bridge principle in contrast with Gauthier's claim. To do that, they need to justify adding impartiality to the conditions for justified moral beliefs.

One reason to introduce impartiality is to avoid problems for Gauthier's contractarianism. Rational people who are impartial among all rational people

---

30. Contractarian theories might seem to be about morality because their conclusions overlap partly with common moral beliefs. I doubt that this is the right way to tell which views are about morality. After all, religious rules often overlap in content with moral rules, but religion is still separate from morality. And moral nihilism is about morality, even though its content does not overlap with common moral beliefs. A better way to determine which views are about morality is to ask which claims are seen as consistent. Moral nihilism is not seen as consistent with moral wrongness, but denials of contractarian-wrongness are.

31. Instead of mentioning impartiality by name, some theorists in this group might talk of acceptance by all rational people who are behind a veil of ignorance (Rawls 1971) or a blindfold of justice (Gert 1998, 149). Nonetheless, the background reason for introducing such technical devices is to ensure impartiality, so they still need to justify requiring impartiality as well as their particular device for ensuring it.

would reject principles that allow killing rational people who are too severely handicapped to reciprocate adequately. Similarly, rational impartial people would seem to agree to a principle that everyone ought to assist people in great need when the cost of assisting is low. The requirement of impartiality, thus, enables impartial contractarianism to fit our intuitions better than Gauthier's version.

This fit is an advantage *if* our moral intuitions are justified. However, the fact that a theory fits certain intuitions cannot make that theory justified if the intuitions themselves are not justified. Hence, anyone who claims that some moral beliefs are justified on the basis of this method needs an independent argument that the assumed intuitions are themselves justified.

More specifically, Gauthier would deny the moral intuitions captured by impartial rationality. So would a moral egoist. Imagine a moral egoist who knows that it is in his self-interest to reject a principle requiring him to assist the needy, even when the need is great and the cost of assisting is low. This egoist could still admit that he *would* accept the principle *if he were* impartial. He might even admit that all rational impartial people would accept the principle. Despite these admissions, he can still deny that he has any adequate reason either to be impartial or to accept the principle. He can also deny that it is morally wrong to violate that principle, if he denies that morality must be impartial. Thus, he can deny the bridge principle that impartial rational agreement determines what is morally wrong.

Moral nihilists would also reject this bridge principle along with the moral intuitions that it is supposed to support. As with egoists, moral nihilists might grant that all rational impartial people would agree to certain moral principles, but they would deny that it is morally wrong to violate those principles. Thus, they would deny the bridge principle that an act is morally wrong when it violates a moral principle that all rational, impartial people would accept.

To appeal to a bridge principle to rule out positions that deny that principle would beg the question. Both moral egoists and moral nihilists deny the bridge principle that is essential to morality as impartial rationality. Thus, this approach cannot be used to rule out either moral egoism or moral nihilism. But moral egoism and nihilism are in the extreme moral contrast class, so a believer must be able to rule them out in order to be justified in holding any moral belief out of that extreme contrast class. Hence, morality as impartial rationality cannot make any moral believer justified out of that extreme contrast class.

One common response claims that the needed bridge principle is true by definition. Either morality is defined to be impartial[32] or a morally wrong action is

---

32. Gert often appeals to his definition of morality (1998, 13), but his definition incorporates his moral views, some of which are controversial. Gert defines morality as impartial, but this is denied by moral egoists and some feminists. Gert defines morality as public, but this is denied by Sidgwick, Parfit, and many other consequentialists. Gert defines morality as universal and, hence, known to all rational agents, but this is denied by Rawls and anyone who uses empirical information to determine moral rules or principles. Gert defines morality as applying only insofar as acts affect others (so that masturbation and cheating at solitaire won't be immoral), but this is denied by Kant and others who believe in obligations to oneself. Gert defines morality as applying to acts and not emotions, but that is denied by Baron (2002). Gert might be right about all of this. I agree with some of it. However, these disagreements

defined as "one that all impartial rational persons would favor not doing" (Gert 1998, 325). But how could such definitions be justified? That depends on what kind of definition they are.[33]

If such definitions were purely lexical or dictionary definitions, they could be justified merely by observing linguistic behavior. However, a dictionary definition must capture what is meant by everyone who uses the term coherently. The definitions at issue here would be denied by moral nihilists and egoists, as well as by many moral theorists who deny that impartiality is essential to morality. Such views seem coherent, as I argued in section 3.3. Even common speakers who reject such views think that they understand what such views mean. So these definitions cannot succeed as dictionary definitions.

Still, other kinds of definitions are not intended to describe common usage. Theoretical definitions, such as "Water is H_2O," are instead intended to structure or support some theory. But then such theoretical definitions cannot be justified simply by observing linguistic behavior. Just as the definition of water as H_2O needs to be established by chemical experiments, so theoretical definitions of morality or moral terms also need some kind of independent substantive justification. That justification cannot be provided by common moral beliefs or by the contractarian framework, since that would beg the question here. Thus, such theoretical definitions cannot succeed in justifying any moral belief as opposed to the extreme opponents (such as moral nihilists and egoists) who deny them.[34]

If we cannot use this form of argument to rule out moral nihilism or egoism, then, since moral nihilism and egoism are in the extreme moral contrast class, this method cannot make any moral belief justified out of the extreme contrast class. Hence, this approach also cannot cause any trouble for moderate moral skepticism.

Still, egoism and nihilism are not taken seriously in everyday life. Consequently, even if impartial rationality cannot rule out egoism and nihilism, it still might sometimes rule out every alternative that is taken seriously in everyday life. That is all that is required for a moral believer to be modestly justified. So the model of morality as impartial rationality might seem to yield modestly justified moral belief. But I doubt it.

---

are not merely verbal. Gert is not just talking past his opponents. Instead, their disagreements are substantive. Hence, they cannot be decided by definitions alone. Positions on these issues need to be justified just like other substantive moral claims. To appeal to such a controversial definition of morality as the foundation of one's moral theory is to beg the questions against all such opponents.

33. For the distinction between dictionary and theoretical definitions, see Fogelin and Sinnott-Armstrong 2005, 368–72. I assume that the definitions at issue here are not merely stipulative. If different theories merely stipulated different definitions of morality or moral terms, then they would not really disagree. But Gauthier, Rawls, Harsanyi, Gert, and Copp do disagree. They might all agree to some indeterminate formula, such as that a morally wrong act is one that all qualified persons would favor not doing. Nonetheless, they disagree about who is "qualified", so they end up disagreeing about which acts are morally wrong.

34. A related response refers to the purpose of morality. Compare Rawls 1971, 582; and Warnock 1971. However, different moral theorists ascribe different purposes to morality. Some moral theorists accept that morality has multiple purposes, but they still rank different purposes in different ways. It is hard to see how to justify such claims against competitors without relying on controversial moral assumptions.

The main reason is that there are so many ways to introduce impartiality into something like a contractarian framework. One standard way is to add restrictions on the appropriate circumstances of social choice. The best-known example is Rawls's veil of ignorance. Rawls specifies that, when choosing principles of justice, "no one knows his place in society...his fortune in the distribution of natural assets and abilities....Nor, again, does anyone know his conception of the good....More than this, I assume that the parties do not know the particular circumstances of their own society....It is taken for granted, however, that they know the general facts about human society" (1971, 137). Rawls argues that every rational person behind this veil of ignorance would choose Rawls's two principles of justice.

In contrast, Harsanyi introduces impartiality by requiring that each person would choose between social systems "under the assumption that, in either system, he would have the same probability of occupying any one of the available social positions" (Harsanyi 1982, 45). Harsanyi argues that all rational people who are impartial in this new way would choose Harsanyi's utilitarian principle over Rawls's principles.

Yet another approach to impartiality is championed by Gert. His "blindfold of justice" (1998, 149) removes all beliefs that are not rationally required, including all beliefs about which individuals will be benefited or harmed as well as all scientific beliefs (including those that Rawls allows behind his veil of ignorance). Gert argues that all rational people who are impartial in this way would endorse Gert's moral system, including his moral ideals, moral rules, and procedure for justifying exceptions to these rules.[35] The resulting system is incompatible with both Rawls's principles and Harsanyi's utilitarianism.

A final way to introduce impartiality, adopted by Copp, is to justify moral beliefs in terms of choices by society rather than by individuals.[36] Copp requires society to reach a consensus and argues that societies would reach a consensus on certain substantive moral conclusions that conflict with those of Rawls, Harsanyi, and Gert.

This variety of ways of developing morality as impartial rationality might seem to make this general framework easy to defend. If one version fails, another could be adopted without giving up the framework of morality as impartial rationality. However, this flexibility creates problems in moral epistemology. Different

---

35. Sometimes Gert argues, instead, that all rational people would choose his moral system as a universal public system. Although this formulation need not mention impartiality explicitly, Gert still owes reasons why a justified moral system must be public and universal in the particular way he requires. If publicity and universality are not tied to impartiality (or some background moral assumption, such as fairness), then why should we care that his system would be chosen under those artificial constraints?

36. Copp 1995. See my review (Sinnott-Armstrong 1996c). Copp requires that society reach a consensus. This already builds in normative assumptions. Why favor consensus over other methods of reaching a decision, such as declaration by a monarch or mere majority? Copp assumes that some methods of social choice are better than others. He might be right, but this preference cannot be justified without relying on substantive moral assumptions.

accounts of impartiality, rationality, and the appropriate circumstances imply that rational impartial persons under appropriate circumstances would agree on different moral beliefs or rules. Ingenious moral theorists can use the framework to justify many different moral beliefs. Simply adjust one's accounts of rationality, impartiality, and appropriate circumstances to fit one's favorite moral beliefs. But, if the method is this indeterminate, then it cannot justify one moral belief in contrast with another.[37] So, for this method to work in moral epistemology, we need some way to determine which view of impartiality, rationality, and the appropriate circumstances are the right ones for justifying moral beliefs.

Of course, each moral theorist who uses this approach believes that he or she has the true account of impartiality. Gert, for example, says, "Unfortunately, the blindfold of justice has not been previously put forward as a test of impartiality, so the veil of ignorance has been taken as the best test of impartiality" (1998, 149). And Rawls says, "The fault of the utilitarian doctrine is that it mistakes impersonality for impartiality" (1971, 190). Each thinks that, as soon as his opponents understand his test of impartiality, they will accept it along with the moral beliefs that it supports. Unfortunately, however, their competitors continue to disagree about the correct test of impartiality or about the kind of impartiality that is needed for justified moral beliefs. It is hard to see how such disputes could be resolved without relying on substantive moral assumptions. For example, utilitarians, such as Harsanyi, can respond to the quotation from Rawls simply by saying that, whether you call it impartiality or impersonality, a utilitarian theory captures what matters to morality. This response brings us back to the substantive moral issue of what matters morally. So the method fails to work independently of moral assumptions.

Such moral assumptions come out even more clearly when defenders of morality as impartiality try to justify a specific version of that framework by arguing that it best captures common moral intuitions. As Rawls puts it, "To justify a particular description of the initial situation one shows that it incorporates these commonly shared presumptions" (1971, 18). But then the real work is done by the moral assumptions. The general framework adds little or nothing to the justification.

If the framework of morality as impartial rationality cannot work without moral assumptions, then those assumptions need to be justified before the framework can justify any moral belief as opposed to another view that denies those moral assumptions. We have seen that theorists who defend different versions of morality as impartial rationality make different moral assumptions. Thus, the general framework by itself cannot be used to justify anyone in believing one of these moral systems as opposed to another. Each of these systems is taken seriously by some people in everyday life. A believer must be able to rule out all everyday alternatives to be modestly justified in holding any moral belief. Consequently, the general framework by itself cannot make anyone even modestly justified in holding any moral belief.

---

37. This problem of multiple contracts is similar to the problem of multiple coherent systems to be discussed in section 10.6.4.

Of course, if the moral assumptions were justified independently, then one could build them into the framework of morality as impartiality and use that framework to justify moral beliefs. But that argument cannot work without some independent source of justified moral beliefs. So that method of morality as impartial rationality by itself could not provide an independent source of justified moral belief.

This limitation might not be a problem if such theories have other goals. However, it does mean that arguments from impartial rational agreement cannot provide any independent solution to the skeptical regress problem. That is what matters here and to moral epistemology.

So far I have focused on impartiality. Other problems arise from rationality. All of the theories I have discussed agree with Gauthier that the rationality of a choice depends on the consequences of that choice or of the thing that is chosen. Harsanyi (1982, 44) defines choices to be rational when they maximize the expected utility of the chooser. For Rawls, "a rational person...follows the plan which will satisfy more of his desires rather than less, and which has the greater chance of being successfully executed" (1971, 143; although Rawls also excludes envy). Gert (1998, 39) defines rational actions in terms of increased risks of harms to the agent. And Copp (1995, 167–89) cites effects on preferences, values, and objective needs.

These theories of rationality, like Gauthier's, do not refer to epistemic rationality of beliefs. Instead, they refer to consequences. Thus, what all rational people accept depends on effects. Impartiality does not change this feature. What all rational, impartial people accept also depends on effects.

The problem is that such effects do not show that a moral belief is true or likely to be true. Imagine, as before, that an evil demon will kill everyone if anyone does not accept the rule, "Don't leave cookies for Santa" (or if anyone does not believe that it is morally wrong to leave cookies for Santa). Then all rational impartial people would accept this rule (or hold this belief) or try to do so. Hence, that rule (or belief) would be justified, if rational impartial agreement were sufficient for being justified. But this is still not evidence that it is morally wrong to leave cookies for Santa, and it might not be true that it is morally wrong to leave cookies for Santa, since whether the demon kills would hinge on acceptance (or belief) rather than on acts of leaving cookies. Similarly, to show that all rational people would accept certain moral rules or beliefs because such acceptance has beneficial consequences for all (impartially considered) does not show that these beliefs are either likely to be true or justified epistemically.[38] Hence, universal impartial rational agreement cannot make a moral belief justified epistemically as long as the kind of rationality invoked is instrumental rather than epistemic. This problem would remain even if a theory of impartiality could be justified without moral assumptions.

---

38. Defenders of this approach might respond that "morally wrong" just means something like "violates a rule or system with the best consequences, impartially considered." But I already argued against such definitions in section 8.2.1.

8.2.3. *Reasonableness*

Another variation on the contractarian tradition invokes a very different notion of rationality, which is usually called reasonableness. This approach might seem to solve some problems for the preceding versions, because its theory of reason is not fully instrumental.

The most prominent contemporary defender of this variation is Scanlon, who writes, "An act is morally wrong if its performance under the circumstances would be disallowed by any set of principles for the general regulation of behavior that no one could *reasonably* reject as a basis for unforced general agreement" (1998, 153, my emphasis; cf. 197, etc.). For example, rape is morally wrong if nobody could reasonably reject a social prohibition on rape. Scanlon (1998, 219–20) admits that there are other ways to be morally wrong. Hence the "if" without "only if." Still, as with Gauthier's, if Scanlon's theory produces any justified moral beliefs, it might seem enough to refute moral skepticism.

Although other details also matter, Scanlon's account depends crucially on the word "reasonably." Any principle could possibly be rejected by someone, so nothing would be morally wrong if Scanlon defined acts as morally wrong only when they violate principles that no one could *possibly* reject. For his theory to have any force, Scanlon needs, instead, to define moral wrongness in terms of what no one could *reasonably* reject. Thus, to show that an act is morally wrong, Scanlon needs to show that the act violates some principle such that anyone who rejects that principle is being unreasonable.

What determines whether a rejection is reasonable? Scanlon (1998, 206, 246) admits that no algorithm specifies what is reasonable, but he does list some factors that determine reasonableness. These include consequences: "When we are considering the acceptability or rejectability of a principle, we must take into account not only the consequences of particular actions, but also the consequences of general performance or nonperformance of such actions and of other implications (for both agents and others) of having agents licensed and directed to think in the way that that principle requires" (1998, 203). Scanlon's theory of reasonableness, thus, seems partly instrumental in much the same way as Gauthier's theory of rationality. One crucial difference is that Scanlon refers to consequences "for the agent *and* others." Unlike Gauthier, Scanlon does not make reasonableness depend only on self-interest, so it can be unreasonable for someone to reject a principle that is contrary to that person's interests. This difference partly explains why Scanlon refers to what is reasonable rather than what is rational and then calls his view contractualist rather than contractarian.

Gauthier and others will ask Scanlon why it is unreasonable to reject a principle on self-interested grounds without considering other people. Scanlon might answer that it is "arbitrary" to care only for oneself and not others: "We have reason to reject principles simply because they arbitrarily favor the claims of some over the identical claims of others: that is to say, because they are unfair" (1998, 212, 216). This response assumes that arbitrariness and unfairness of this kind are morally relevant. Maybe so, but this is a substantive moral assumption that Gauthier and others might deny.

Further moral assumptions come out as Scanlon specifies when a principle can be reasonably rejected. For example, he charges that utilitarianism has "highly implausible implications" because it allows atrocities for the sake of aggregated goods. In contrast, he claims, "A contractualist theory, in which all objections to a principle must be raised by individuals, blocks such justifications in an intuitively appealing way" (1998, 230). By denying that reasonable rejection can be based on aggregated goods, Scanlon ensures that utilitarians cannot "reasonably" reject anti-utilitarian principles. Similarly, Scanlon denies that it is reasonable to reject a principle on the grounds that the principle does not consider whether someone is in the worst-off group or, more generally, "such things as whether A had a very happy and successful life or, on the contrary, his main aims had been frustrated by bad luck" (1998, 227–28). This restriction makes it unreasonable to insist on something like Rawls's difference principle. Again, Scanlon claims, "Impersonal reasons [such as reasons not to destroy an ancient monument or a tree] do not, themselves, provide grounds for reasonably rejecting a principle" (1998, 220). This restriction excludes many forms of environmental ethics from his framework. Other examples could be added.

My point here is not that these contrary moral views are correct or even plausible. Maybe Scanlon is right to rule them out as unreasonable. My point is only that these features of his theory incorporate substantive moral assumptions. Scanlon admits this when he says, "The judgment that *any* consideration constitutes a relevant, possibly conclusive, reason for rejecting a principle in the context of contractualist moral thinking as I am describing it is a judgment with moral content" (:998, 217).

Because these assumptions are moral, they need justification. The point is not that his assumptions are especially problematic. Scanlon might be right to deny that "the claims of well-being are unique among moral claims in needing no further justification" (1998, 215), so utilitarian assumptions need justification, too. But that is just because both sides of the debate need justification for any assumptions about when it is reasonable to reject principles.

If Scanlon cannot justify his assumptions, then to use them in an argument against the opponents who deny them would be blatantly circular. Scanlon admits this when he says, "It would be objectionably circular to make 'reasonable rejection' turn on presumed entitlements of the very sort that the principle in question is supposed to establish" (1998, 214; cf. 194, 213, and 216). But then he responds, "It is misleading to suggest that when we are assessing the 'reasonable rejectability' of a principle we must, or even can, set aside assumptions about other rights and entitlements altogether" (1998, 214). His idea seems to be that, in a dispute between two parties, if both accept certain rights, those shared assumptions may be built into the contractualist framework, and then the framework does not beg the question against either competitor, so it can be used to settle their dispute.

Maybe so, but Scanlon's framework still *does* beg the question against anyone who denies his moral assumptions. This includes moral nihilists. Since moral nihilists deny all positive moral assumptions, Scanlon's contractualist framework cannot justify any moral beliefs as opposed to moral nihilism. So it cannot make any moral belief extremely justified. Nor can it refute moderate moral skepticism.

But that's not all. By itself, Scanlon's contractualism also cannot justify any moral beliefs as opposed to utilitarianism, Gauthier's principle of minimax concession, Rawls's difference principle, or many forms of environmental ethics, because, as I argued, his theory of reasonable rejection incorporates assumptions that these competitors would deny. Scanlon might claim to provide independent arguments for these moral assumptions, but then those other arguments do "all the work." (1998, 213). Scanlon's contractualist framework by itself cannot justify any moral beliefs as opposed to such competing positions. Since these competitors are taken seriously by real people in everyday life, they must be ruled out in order for any contrary moral belief to be modestly justified. Thus, Scanlon's contractualist framework cannot make any moral believer modestly justified. So it cannot refute extreme moral skepticism.

Nonetheless, Scanlon's framework might accomplish something. Among friends who reject minimax concession, utilitarianism, the difference principle, and environmental ethics, and who share the assumptions built into Scanlon's contractualist framework, it can be useful to ask whether an act violates principles that these friends agree could not be reasonably rejected. The contractualist framework can make them justified in accepting certain moral beliefs as opposed to the limited number of competitors that they take seriously.

Maybe that is enough to satisfy Scanlon. He denies that "the main purpose of moral theorizing is to come up with ways of deciding moral questions without appealing to intuitive judgment" (1998, 246). I agree insofar as I doubt that there is any single main purpose for all moral theorizing, especially if this includes meta-ethical theorizing. However, this response does not change the fact that his theory fails to decide moral questions without appealing to intuitive assumptions.

Scanlon could still base his justification on moral intuitions if he defends some kind of moral intuitionism. Or he could turn to moral coherentism. He suggests the latter move when he says, "A sensible contractualism, like most other plausible views, will involve a holism about moral justification" (1998, 214). Either way, Scanlon's contractualism cannot work as a separate method or theory in moral epistemology. It cannot make us justified in any moral beliefs unless we are already justified on the basis of moral intuitionism or moral coherentism. So now we need to turn to those last two moral epistemologies to see how well they fare.

9

Intuitionism

The preceding two chapters argued that naturalists and normativists who try to avoid substantive moral assumptions end up relying on them tacitly. As a result, moral believers cannot be extremely justified on the basis of deriving their moral beliefs from purely non-moral premises (whether normative or not). The only alternative starts from moral premises. But then those moral premises themselves need to be justified. How could they be justified? We seem to be caught in the skeptical regress.

The easiest way to stop the skeptical regress is simply to stop. If we can work back to some moral claim that we are justified in believing without depending on any inference from any other belief (normative or non-normative, moral or non-moral), then there is no new premise to justify, and the regress goes no further. This is how moral intuitionists try to stop the skeptical regress.

Moral intuitionism has definite attractions. Common folk often seem to appeal to moral intuitions in everyday moral disputes. Even philosophers who officially disdain moral intuitions often seem to use them when refuting opponents or supporting their own views. Indeed, it is hard to see how to construct and justify any substantive moral theory without deploying moral intuition at some point. Thus, if moral intuitionism fails, substantive moral theory and even common moral reasoning might seem impossible. That should motivate us all to consider moral intuitionism sympathetically and carefully.

9.1. What Is Moral Intuitionism?

Moral intuitionism is a group of theories with a long history.[1] Philosophers in this tradition share various views.[2] The kind of moral intuitionism that matters here is

---

1. The best-known intuitionists include Sidgwick (1907), Moore (1903), Prichard (1968), and Ross (1930). For earlier intuitionists, see selections in Schneewind 1990.

epistemological. Within moral epistemology, some traditional moral intuitionists claim that moral beliefs are self-evident, self-justified, incorrigible, indubitable, indefeasible, unprovable, psychologically or epistemically certain, causally or conceptually independent of other beliefs, and/or known by a special faculty. (Cf. Sinnott-Armstrong 2001b.) None of these claims is needed to stop the skeptical regress, so I will not define moral intuitionism in these terms.

Instead, I will define moral intuitionism by the weakest claim that is strong enough to stop the skeptical regress. Here it is:

> Some believers are justified in holding some moral beliefs independently of whether the believer is able to infer those moral beliefs from any other beliefs.

When a believer is justified in this way, I will say that the believer is justified *non-inferentially*. The defining claim of moral intuitionism is then that some believers are justified non-inferentially in holding some moral beliefs.

Although this claim is about when *believers* are justified, for simplicity I will sometimes express it by saying that some moral *beliefs* are justified non-inferentially. This expression does not mean that the content of the moral belief is justified as an abstract proposition without relation to believers. Instead, it claims that the believer is justified in being in a belief state with that content.

This claim is not about *all* justified moral beliefs. Moral intuitionists claim only that a special class of moral beliefs can be justified non-inferentially. All other justified moral beliefs are justified by inference from those foundational moral beliefs.[3]

Moral intuitionists do not agree about *which* moral beliefs are justified non-inferentially. They differ, first, on the content of those moral beliefs—on whether the foundational beliefs are about what is good (Moore 1903) or what is morally right (Prichard 1968; Ross 1930). Moral intuitionists also differ on the generality of the non-inferentially justified moral beliefs—on whether they are abstract philosophical claims (Sidgwick 1907), mid-level generalizations (Ross 1930), or judgments of particular acts or choices (Prichard 1968; Dancy 1993, 2004). These differences lead different moral intuitionists to claim different sources (experience

---

2. Most traditional moral intuitionists held *non-naturalism*, which is the metaphysical claim that moral properties are not reducible to natural or non-normative properties. Many moral intuitionists also accepted *unranked pluralism*, which is the structural claim that there is more than one basic moral principle and no general method for ranking basic moral principles in conflicts. Because such claims are often made together with moral intuitionism, the name "moral intuitionism" is often applied to non-naturalism and/or to unranked pluralism (e.g., Rawls 1971, 34–40). However, my concern here is neither with non-naturalism nor with unranked pluralism.

3. Although my official definition refers only to *some* moral beliefs, moral intuitionists need enough non-inferentially justified moral beliefs to support their construction project. Moreover, inferences from foundational moral beliefs are subject to various objections. So, even if *some* moral beliefs are justified non-inferentially, moral intuitionists still have trouble justifying all of the other moral beliefs that they want to justify. Despite such problems, I will focus on the issue of whether any moral beliefs are non-inferentially justified.

or reason) and use different models (sense perception or a priori mathematics) to explain how moral beliefs can be justified non-inferentially.[4] Moral intuitionists also sometimes add further conditions on which moral beliefs can be justified non-inferentially, such as that they must be clear and precise, apparently obvious after reflection, strong and stable, and consistent with other moral beliefs of this believer and of others.[5]

Most importantly, moral intuitionists also disagree about which features of these moral beliefs make them (and not the others) justified non-inferentially. There are four main answers. The first theory (reliabilism) claims that the non-inferentially justified moral beliefs are justified simply by the fact that the process leading to the belief is reliable.[6] The second answer (experientialism) is that they are justified because they are based on some kind of experience that is separate from belief and, hence, cannot provide premises for any inference.[7] The third position (reflectionism) is that some moral beliefs are non-inferentially justified because they are based on reflection that includes beliefs, but the moral beliefs are not inferred from those other beliefs.[8] The fourth version (contextualism) claims that some moral beliefs do not need inferential confirmation because of the social background of the beliefs.[9]

Each of these versions raises special problems of its own. Nonetheless, I will lump them together under a broad definition of moral intuitionism because my arguments will apply to the central claim that they all share, namely, that some believers are justified non-inferentially in holding some moral beliefs.

Several terms in this defining claim need to be explained. First, to say that a person *infers* a belief is just to say that the person goes through a reasoning process of which that belief is the (or a) conclusion and other beliefs are premises. In-

4. Those who use sense perception as a model are often called moral sense theorists in contrast with (rational) intuitionists. I include both varieties under my broad definition of moral intuitionism because this distinction does not affect the response to the skeptical regress.

5. For example, Sidgwick 1907, 338–42. Some of these conditions are unclear, but I will write as if such conditions do not entail that the moral belief is true, probable, or justified. If they did, the issue would become whether moral believers ever have real moral intuitions instead of whether moral believers are ever justified non-inferentially. This reformulation would complicate verbiage but would not affect my arguments.

6. The best-known general reliabilist is Goldman (1986). For an application to moral beliefs, see Shafer-Landau 2003, chap. 12. Other versions of externalism also fall under my broad definition of intuitionism.

7. Tolhurst 1990. For criticisms, see Sinnott-Armstrong 1990. Tolhurst's moral epistemology resembles the general epistemologies of Pollock (1986) and Peacocke (1986).

8. Audi 1996, 2004. It is not clear that Audi denies what I call strong moral intuitionism, since his main concern is to deny the need for actual inference. Other reflectionists still might deny strong moral intuitionism. For criticisms of general reflectionism, see Sinnott-Armstrong 1995b.

9. See Timmons 1998, 206: "One may be epistemically responsible in holding certain beliefs at some time *t*, even though one has no justifying evidence or justifying reasons for holding those beliefs at *t*." Timmons writes about epistemic responsibility, which seems close to what I called being personally justified in section 4.2.4. If Timmons does not claim that moral believers can also be impersonally and hence wholly justified non-inferentially, then he need not commit himself to all of moral intuitionism as I define it. But then he also cannot stop the skeptical regress.

ferences come in many varieties. Some are deductively valid, but others are inductive, including inferences to the best explanation, arguments from analogies, statistical generalizations, applications of such generalizations, and so on (Fogelin and Sinnott-Armstrong 2005, 249–304). Any reasoning process that starts from one or more beliefs and is supposed to provide a justification for another belief counts as an inference.

The believer is *able* to infer the belief when the person already has enough information to form other beliefs from which he would infer this belief if he had enough overall incentive plus general intelligence and no interference. This ability does not require the person to be currently self-conscious or reflective about their beliefs or their abilities. All that is needed is for the requisite information to be encoded somehow as a belief in the believer's brain.[10] This notion of ability demands very little.[11]

Negatives are crucial here. To say that a belief is *non-inferred* is to say that the believer does not actually infer it from anything. The belief is also *non-inferable* if the believer is not able to infer it from any other belief.

Some non-moral beliefs seem both non-inferred and non-inferable. For example, when I see a dark spot on my light pants, an inference might lead me to believe that I dropped some food on my pants, but my belief that there is a spot on my pants normally is not inferred from any belief. I also might seem unable to infer that belief. A similar story could be told about simple mathematical beliefs.

Some moral beliefs also seem both non-inferred and non-inferable. Many people believe that lying is (pro tanto) morally wrong even though they do not actually infer this belief from any of their other beliefs. Some of these people also seem not to believe any other premises from which they are able to infer this moral belief. Such believers might draw inferences among non-moral beliefs to determine facts about the act, such as that it is a lie, but the moral belief about that act still might not be inferred or inferable. What determines whether the moral belief is inferred or inferable in the sense that matters here is whether the believer draws or could draw an inference that has that moral belief as its conclusion.

Whether a particular person *can* infer a belief depends on the person at the time. It is not enough that a different person could infer it. Common people can hold a moral belief non-inferably even if some unknown moral philosopher could provide an abstruse inferential justification of what they believe. It is also not enough that this person could infer the belief in the future after studying moral

10. When the encoded information causally sustains the belief in the conclusion of the inference, that belief is *based on* the ability to infer. Those who wish to incorporate this basing relation into the conditions for justified belief may modify the definition of moral intuitionism accordingly. That change will not affect the skeptical regress or my main points. I omit the basing relation only for simplicity.

11. This notion of ability is so weak that some critics might deny that I am talking about real abilities. The word, however, does not matter. The issue is only whether the believer needs information that fits into an inferential structure. That need would be enough to start the regress.

philosophy. In the relevant sense, a person can infer a belief when the person at the time has enough information to form other beliefs to serve as premises in an inference that concludes with that moral belief.[12]

There is strong evidence that some people hold moral beliefs that are non-inferred (Haidt 2001). It is less clear that any real moral belief is non-infer*able*. Since there are so many kinds of inference, and abilities are so difficult to disprove, it is hard to show that the believer in a real case is unable to draw any inference of any kind to the moral belief. If no moral beliefs are non-inferable, then no moral believer holds a justified moral belief independently of an ability to infer. That consequent would spell big trouble for moral intuitionism, so some critics of moral intuitionism deny that any moral belief is non-inferable. However, in my opinion, some people do seem to hold some moral beliefs without being able to infer them from anything. I will not rely on this psychological claim, but I will grant it for the sake of argument so that we can focus on other issues.

So far this is merely a description of the moral psychology of humans. Epistemology enters the story only when the question becomes whether any beliefs of these kinds can be justified or knowledge. Psychology can tell us whether people in fact have moral intuitions, if all that means is that people have moral beliefs that arise immediately (without inference)[13] and are held confidently (without doubt) and stably (without change).[14] Psychology cannot tell us whether anyone *should* form or hold beliefs in this way or whether any or all moral intuitions have the positive normative status of being *justified*. Such normative questions carry us into the domain of epistemology.

In general epistemology, *foundationalists* assert that some believers are justified in believing some claims independently of whether they are able to infer those beliefs from any other beliefs.[15] *Moral intuitionists* are just foundationalists about moral beliefs. They claim that some moral believers are justified in believing some

12. Since inferential abilities vary with person and time, so does whether a certain belief is inferred or inferable. We cannot, then, specify a certain belief content and ask simply whether it is inferred or inferable. Instead, we need to specify a person and a time and ask whether that person at that time infers that belief or could infer it. These references to person and time will often be dropped, but they are always implicit.

13. To say that a belief arises immediately is not to say that it arises quickly. Nor is it to deny that it depends on any previous experiences, beliefs, or reflection. All it means is that no inference mediates or grounds the belief.

14. Some moral intuitionists do not require confidence or stability, but they still defend moral intuitions that are confident and stable. Also, some moral intuitionists restrict the phrase "moral intuitions" to true, probable, or justified moral beliefs. This usage forces skeptics to deny that people have moral intuitions. To avoid such confusing formulations, I will use "moral intuitions" to refer to immediate, confident, and stable moral beliefs, regardless of whether they are true, probable, or justified. This terminological choice does not affect the substance of my arguments.

15. Purely structural foundationalists might claim only that a believer is justified in a belief only if the belief is either non-inferentially justified or inferable from non-inferentially justified beliefs. Non-skeptical foundationalists then add that some beliefs are justified. I discuss the non-skeptical version because almost all foundationalists do deny skepticism, and because I am concerned with whether foundationalism (and moral intuitionism) can succeed as a response to the skeptical regress.

moral claims independently of whether they are able to infer those moral beliefs from any other beliefs.

It is natural to restate this independence claim in terms of a need.[16] If a believer is justified independently of any ability to infer the belief, then the believer does *not need* any inferential ability in order to be justified. On the other hand, if a believer would not be justified if the believer were not able to infer the belief, then the believer *needs* that ability in order to be justified. When the ability is needed, the believer is justified inferentially. Otherwise the believer is justified non-inferentially. What moral intuitionists claim, then, is that some moral believers do not need any inferential ability in order to be justified in holding some moral beliefs.[17]

Some self-styled moral intuitionists do not claim so much. They claim only that some believers do not need any *actual* inference, but they do not go so far as to claim that any believers do not need any *ability* to infer. I will call this view *weak moral intuitionism*.

It is crucial to see how weak this version is. Suppose I believe that torture is morally wrong just because it seems that way to me. I do not actually infer this moral belief from any other belief. Add that I do have the ability to justify this belief as fully as anyone could. I could infer it from the premise that torture causes pain intentionally and expresses disrespect, and any act that does that is morally wrong, so torture is morally wrong. I could also infer it from second-order beliefs about the circumstances under which my first-order moral beliefs are reliable. I even base my moral belief on my ability to infer it, since I would suspend belief or disbelieve this moral claim if I could not infer it somehow from some other beliefs. Nonetheless, although I easily could infer it, I don't bother, just because my moral belief seems so obvious to me. If this belief (or any other like it) is justified, then I do not need any actual inference in order to be justified, so weak moral intuitionism is true.

Many people are willing to accept this weak moral intuitionism. If someone could justify a moral belief by means of an inference and bases his moral belief on the ability to draw the inference, then his lack of actual performance does not seem to make his belief unjustified. There is no point in criticizing someone for not doing something when there was no need to do it, if he could easily have done it and would have done it if there had been any need. In such circumstances, the lack of actual inference is not enough to make a belief unjustified. This is all that weak moral intuitionists claim.

16. Compare Ross 1930, 29: "Without any need of proof." Since not all inferences are proofs, and Ross does not mention abilities, he might not deny the need for an inferential ability. Notice also that opponents of moral intuitionism, who claim that an inferential ability is *necessary*, do not have to claim that any inferential ability is *sufficient* to make any moral belief justified. Maybe the moral belief must also be based on the inferential ability. Other necessary conditions also might have to be met. Opponents of moral intuitionism can hold that an inferential ability is needed without specifying what else, if anything, is needed and, so, without specifying what is sufficient for justified moral belief.

17. The issue is whether the ability is needed for the belief to be *justified*, not for the belief to be *held*. Even if a believer does not need any inferential ability to hold the belief (because she would believe it even without any such ability), the believer still might need some such ability in order to be justified in holding that belief.

The stronger view that I defined as moral intuitionism (proper) is more controversial, since it implies that a moral believer can be justified even without any ability to infer. If I *cannot* infer my moral belief from anything I believe, then more people would view my moral belief as unjustified. After all, a need for justification might arise, such as if someone questioned my moral belief, and then I would not be able to fulfill that need. Hence, something useful seems missing when I lack the ability to support my belief with any inference.

Since this strong version of moral intuitionism is controversial, it would be nice for moral intuitionists to avoid it if possible. The question is, can they avoid it and still stop the skeptical regress? I think not, and here's why. Weak moral intuitionists claim only that some moral believers are justified independently of any actual inference. This claim leaves open the possibility that no moral believer is ever justified independently of an ability to infer the moral belief from some other belief. However, if all justified moral beliefs depend on an ability to draw an inference, then the skeptical regress arises for the inference that the believer must be able to draw. The reason is that the ability to draw an inference cannot make a belief justified if the beliefs in the premises of that inference are not justified themselves. That seems clear because I could be justified in believing anything if my belief could be made justified by an ability to infer my belief from unjustified beliefs. After all, any fool belief can be inferred from itself. Consequently, a mere ability to infer a belief from other beliefs is not enough to make the conclusion justified unless those other beliefs that could be used as premises are themselves justified. This requirement is enough to start the same old skeptical regress or another one very much like it. Thus, since weak intuitionism does not deny dependence on an inferential ability that leads to a skeptical regress, weak intuitionism is not strong enough to meet the skeptical challenge.

In contrast, the stronger view that I defined as moral intuitionism would be enough to stop the regress. If a belief can be justified independently of any actual inference and also independently of any ability to draw any inference, then there is no dependence on any inference with any new premise that needs to be justified. That would bring the regress to a screeching halt. So the stronger version of moral intuitionism is what (and all that) moral skeptics need to deny.

Another traditional opponent of moral intuitionism is moral coherentism. Moral coherentists claim that some moral beliefs are justified, and the only way for any moral belief to be justified is inferentially (where this includes holistic justification, as we will see in chapter 10). Most moral coherentists do not deny that some moral beliefs are justified even though they are not actually inferred. So such moral coherentists do not and need not deny weak moral intuitionism.[18]

---

18. My notion of ability corresponds to the "weak, implicit sense of availability" required by BonJour 1985, 23. Compare also Lehrer's schema: "S is justified in accepting that p at t if and only if p coheres with system X of S at t" (1990, 115). When p coheres with S's belief system in the required way, S has the information needed to be able in my weak sense to infer p from other beliefs of S, even if S does not actually bother to infer p from those other beliefs.

Similarly, naturalists and normativists claim that moral believers are justified when they *can* derive their moral beliefs from natural or (non-moral) normative premises. Most naturalists and normativists do not require moral believers actually to go through such derivations every time they form a justified moral belief. So these opponents also do not deny weak moral intuitionism.

In order to capture the contrast between moral intuitionism and its traditional opponents, and in order to locate the weakest view that is strong enough to stop the skeptical regress, I define moral intuitionism in terms of ability to infer rather than in terms of an actual inference. I will bring up weak moral intuitionism when the contrast becomes relevant; but henceforth, whenever I refer to moral intuitionism without qualification, I will mean the strong version of moral intuitionism which claims that some moral believers are justified independently of their ability to infer their moral beliefs from any other beliefs.

9.2. Which Contrast Class?

Traditional moral intuitionism does not mention contrast classes. Its defining claim is about how moral believers can be just plain justified (period, simply, without qualification). For reasons given in chapter 5, this claim presupposes that some contrast class is really relevant. A Pyrrhonian moral skeptic will not either agree or disagree with such an unqualified claim any more than with the claim that jumbo shrimp are just plain large. To assess moral intuitionism properly, therefore, I need to relativize justified moral belief to certain contrast classes.

Moral intuitionists might claim that some moral beliefs are non-inferentially justified out of the extreme contrast class, which includes moral nihilism, egoism, and other extreme positions. To be justified out of this contrast class, the believer must have some way to rule out moral nihilism. To try to do that, moral intuitionists might simply cite a moral belief that is contrary to moral nihilism and that also seems obviously true and obviously justified to most of us in most contexts. Here's one example:

(T) It is morally wrong to torture innocent children just for fun.

Almost all normal people would happily take this belief for granted. But suppose that a moral nihilist appears on the scene and denies (T). What could the moral intuitionist say against such a moral nihilist? Not much. Moral intuitionists can point out that (T) seems obvious to them even after they reflect on it carefully. However, to appeal to such a moral belief in an argument against moral nihilism clearly begs the question (in much the same way as it would beg the question to appeal to a belief about the external world in an argument against Descartes' deceiving demon hypothesis). Such moral beliefs appear obvious to almost everyone who is not a moral nihilist, but that appearance is just what would be predicted by the moral nihilist's hypothesis that all moral beliefs are evolutionary or cultural illusions (just as Descartes' hypothesis predicts our experiences). (Recall section 3.2.2.) When both of two hypotheses would predict an observation, that observation cannot be used as evidence for one as opposed to the other. This standard is accepted even outside morality: a certain fossil cannot provide evidence for or against Darwinian evolution or punctuated equilibrium theory (or creationism, for that matter) if each theory can explain why that fossil appears in the way that it does. (Recall also section 4.2.3, where the bloody boot print is not evidence against Mustard if Plum wears the same size boot.) Similarly, since moral nihilism can explain why (T) appears obvious even if (T) is false, that appearance cannot be used to rule out moral nihilism.

Some moral intuitionists might respond that moral nihilists must not really understand (T), since anyone who understands it must accept it. However, in arguing for the coherence of moral nihilism in section 3.3, I already criticized attempts to show why moral nihilists cannot understand (T). Moral nihilists can recognize the semantic entailments of (T) and use the constituent concepts in other contexts. This shows that moral nihilists understand (T) and the other moral beliefs that they deny. Thus, it begs the question against moral nihilism to assume that all people, including moral nihilists, who deny (T) cannot understand it.

In the absence of any other way to rule out moral nihilism, moral intuitionists cannot provide any justification out of any contrast class that includes moral nihilism, such as the extreme contrast class. Hence, moral intuitionists cannot show that any moral beliefs are extremely justified. Of course, moral intuitionists could (and many would) respond that they are not trying to show how anything is extremely justified. They might even claim that it is a mistake to engage in that project of extreme justification. Nonetheless, to reject a project is not to accomplish it. My point is only that moral intuitionists still do not and cannot show that anything is extremely justified.

The next question is whether moral intuitionists can show that any moral belief is modestly justified. To do that, moral intuitionists must rule out every other alternative in the modest contrast class. This class does not include moral nihilism, so moral intuitionists might accomplish this task even though they cannot rule out moral nihilism. Still, the modest contrast class does include a lot: every moral claim that would be taken seriously in any everyday context and thus needs to be ruled out in order to meet the usual epistemic standards. A moral believer must rule out all such alternatives to be modestly justified. This modest way of being justified will be the topic of the rest of this chapter. The crucial version of moral intuitionism then claims that some believers are modestly justified in holding some moral beliefs without being able to infer those moral beliefs from anything.

9.3. When Do Beliefs Need Confirmation?

In assessing this claim of moral intuitionism, the crucial question is whether certain inferential abilities are always needed for a moral believer to be justified. Moral intuitionists deny this need. Its opponents assert it. So, when do moral believers need such inferential abilities?

We cannot answer this question directly. If a moral intuitionist baldly asserts that we do *not* need inferential abilities to back up our immediate moral beliefs, then this assertion begs the question. Similarly, if a critic of moral intuitionism baldly asserts that we *do* need inferential abilities to back up our immediate moral beliefs, then this assertion also begs the question. Neither side can win so easily. We need a less direct method.

One alternative uses analogies to non-moral beliefs. This path is fraught with peril, but it might be the only way to go. What this approach does is appeal to non-moral cases to develop principles of epistemic need and then later apply those principles back to moral beliefs. Let's try it.

I will formulate my principles in terms of when confirmation is needed, but they do not claim that the believer needs to go through any process of confirming the belief. The point, instead, is only that some confirmation needs to be available at least implicitly as information stored in the believer that gives the believer an ability to infer the belief from some other beliefs. The question is when some such confirmation is needed in non-moral cases.

Suppose that I listen to my daughter in a piano competition. I judge that she played great and her rival was mediocre. Am I justified in trusting my judgment? Not if all I can say is, "Her performance sounded better to me." I am too biased for such immediate reactions alone to count as evidence. I still might be justified if I am able to specify laudable features of her performance or if I know that others agree, but some confirmation seems needed. Generalizing:

> *Principle 1*: Confirmation is needed for a believer to be justified when the believer is partial.

This principle also applies to direct perceptual judgments, such as when I believe that my daughter played F-sharp exactly two beats before the last note. This partly explains why we prefer umpires, referees, and judges not to be parents of competitors, even when we trust those parents to try to be fair. This principle should be acceptable to all epistemologists, including reliabilists, since partiality often creates unreliability.

Second, imagine that each of us adds a column of figures, and I get one sum, but you get a different sum. Maybe I would be justified in believing that I am right if you were my child and I was helping you with your homework. However, if you are just as good at arithmetic as I am, then, when we get different answers, we need to check again to find out who made a mistake before either of us can be justified in believing that his or her answer is the correct one. We owe each other that much epistemic respect. The best explanation of this natural reaction seems to be:

> *Principle 2*: Confirmation is needed for a believer to be justified in holding a belief that other people deny or doubt, when the believer has no reason to prefer one believer to the other.[19]

This principle also applies when the person on the sidewalk looks like Tom Cruise to me but not to you. If I have no reason to believe that I am better than you at this

---

19. It is not enough that there *is* a reason to prefer one believer to the other if that believer has no access to that reason and, thus, does not *have* any reason to prefer one believer to the other.

identification, then I am not justified in believing that your belief is incorrect or that mine is correct. (Cf. Sinnott-Armstrong 2002c.)

A third principle concerns emotions. When people get very angry, for example, they tend to overlook relevant facts. They often do not notice excuses or apologies by the person who made them angry. We should not generalize to all emotions, but we can still endorse something like this:

> *Principle 3*: Confirmation is needed for a believer to be justified when the believer is emotional in a way that clouds judgment.

This explains why jurors are dismissed from a case that would upset them too much. This principle applies even if their emotions do not bias them towards either side, so it is distinct from Principle 1, regarding partiality.

Next consider illusions. At least three kinds are relevant here. First, some illusions are due to context. Objects look larger when they are next to smaller objects and they look smaller when they are next to larger objects. Since our estimates of their sizes are affected by their surroundings, we are not justified in trusting our estimates until we check their sizes in other circumstances or by other methods.

A second group of illusions arises from generalizations. For example, an oval that is shaded on top looks concave but an oval that is shaded on the bottom looks convex. The explanation seems to be that our cognitive apparatus evolved in circumstances where the light usually came from above, which would produce a shadow on the top of a concave oval (such as a cave opening) and on the bottom of a convex oval (such as an egg). Since we often overextend generalizations like this, we are not justified in trusting beliefs that depend on such generalizations until we check to determine whether our circumstances are exceptional.

The third kind of illusion involves heuristics, which are quick and simple decision procedures. In a passage with a thousand words, how many seven-letter words have the form "_ _ _ _ in _"? How many seven-letter words have the form "_ _ _ _ ing"? Most people estimate more words of the latter form, although that is impossible, since every word of the form "_ _ _ _ ing" also has the form "_ _ _ _ in _." Why do people make this simple mistake? They seem to test how likely something is by trying to imagine examples and guessing high if they easily think of lots of examples. This is called the availability heuristic (Kahneman et al. 1982). Most people easily produce words that end in "ing," but they have more trouble coming up with words that end in "in _" because they do not think of putting "g" in the last place. In cases like this, the availability heuristic is misleading. Accordingly, they do not seem adequately epistemically justified in trusting beliefs based on such heuristics until they check on whether they are in circumstances where the heuristics work.

This quick survey of three common kinds of illusion suggests:

> *Principle 4*: Confirmation is needed for a believer to be justified when the circumstances are conducive to illusion.

This principle would apply as well to many other kinds of illusions.

A fifth and final principle considers the source of a belief. If you believe that George Washington never told a lie, and if this belief comes from a legend spread by Washington's supporters to gain political power, then you are not justified in believing the legend without confirmation, though it still might be true. Even if you believe only that Washington was unusually honest, this belief might be a lingering effect of this childhood story, and then its origin makes this belief need confirmation. The point can be generalized into something like:

> *Principle 5*: Confirmation is needed for a believer to be justified when the belief arises from an unreliable or disreputable source.

This principle also explains why we do not view people as justified in beliefs based only on prejudice and stereotypes propagated by competing groups, such as when men who fear competition from women spread rumors that women cannot perform certain tasks.

These five principles, though distinct, complement each other. When a belief is partial, controversial, emotional, subject to illusion, and explicable by dubious sources, then all of these principles apply. In such cases, they work together to make it even clearer that confirmation is needed for justified belief. Even if not all of these principles apply, the more that do apply, the clearer it will be that there is more need for more confirmation.

I do not claim that these principles are precise or that my list is complete.[20] What I do claim is that these principles or some close relatives seem plausible to most people and are assumed in our shared epistemic practices. I also claim that they make sense because they pick out features that are correlated with reliability and other epistemic values.

Most importantly, I claim that these principles apply in all areas of belief. My illustrations include beliefs about arithmetic, language, history, identity, value, sound, size, and shape, but the same principles apply in science, religion, metaphysics, and so on. The main question here is whether they apply to moral beliefs. Admittedly, morality *might* be a special case where these principles do not apply. However, unless someone can point to a relevant difference between these other areas and moral beliefs, it seems only fair to apply these same standards to moral beliefs when asking whether moral beliefs are justified. So that's what I will do.

9.4. Do Moral Beliefs Need Confirmation?

Some of these principles are harder to apply than others. Let's start with an easy one.

9.4.1. *Partiality*

Principle 1 says that partiality adds a need for confirmation. But what is partiality? A judge is often called partial when the judge's self-interest is affected by the outcome of the case. However, if the judge's self-interest does not influence the

---

20. One additional principle might claim that confirmation is needed when errors are costly. This principle applies to moral beliefs insofar as moral errors are costly.

judge's decision, so the judge would have made the same decision if the judge's self-interest had not been involved, then it is natural to say that the judge's *decision* is not partial even if the *judge* is partial. Analogously, *believers* can be called partial whenever their beliefs affect their self-interest either directly or indirectly (by affecting the interests of people whom they care about). *Beliefs* are then partial only when the believer's self-interest influences whether the believer holds that belief. Thus, a partial believer can hold an impartial belief (or can hold it impartially) if the believer has an interest in holding the belief, but that interest does not influence whether the believer holds that belief.

Judges are required by law to withdraw from cases when *they* are partial even if nobody claims (and it is unlikely) that their *decision* will be partial. What matters to recusal is the impartiality of the decision-maker, not of the decision (see Sinnott-Armstrong 2002d).

Similarly, partiality of a belief can't be all that triggers Principle 1. To see why, recall the examples that motivated Principle 1. Because I am biased in favor of my daughter, even after watching her play in the piano competition I need confirmation to be justified in believing that my daughter played better than her rival. Maybe my interest in her victory did not influence my assessment, but the danger of such influence is enough to create a need for confirmation. Admittedly, if I can rule out such influence, then I can be justified in believing that my daughter played better, but the only way to rule out such influence involves independent confirmation. Thus, confirmation seems needed when the believer is partial, even if the believer is not actually influenced by that partiality, so the belief is not partial. Since confirmation is also needed when the belief is partial, Principle 1 requires confirmation when either the believer or the belief is partial.

To apply this principle to moral beliefs, we need to ask whether moral beliefs affect our self-interest. The answer is that moral beliefs affect us all. The point is not that we are better or worse off if certain moral beliefs are true. The point is, instead, that we are better or worse off if we and others hold certain moral beliefs.

The clearest cases are moral beliefs held by other people. If others in our society did not believe that killing, stealing, lying, cheating, and promise-breaking are usually morally wrong, then they would be more likely to do such acts, and we would be more likely to get hurt by such acts. Life would be "solitary, poor, nasty, brutish, and short" (Hobbes [1651] 1962, chap. 13). Similarly, it can be costly if others do not believe that they are morally required to help us when we are in need.

Our own moral beliefs can also affect our interests. It can be very expensive to believe that we are morally required to help the needy. It can also cost a lot to believe that we have to tell the truth or to keep a promise. Moreover, if we did not see acts like killing, stealing, and cheating as immoral, we would be more likely to do them and then to be punished in various ways, such as by law, rebuke, ostracism, and so on.

Special interests also arise in special cases: Women and men should know that, if abortion is not seen by them and others as morally permissible, then they, their friends, or their daughters will be more likely to suffer more, if they need abortions. Moral beliefs about affirmative action affect the interests of the preferred groups and also the non-preferred groups. And so on. Finally, social groups often form around and then solidify moral beliefs. People who believe that homosexuality is immoral find it harder to get along with homosexuals and easier to get along with homophobes. Conversely, people who believe that homosexuality is not immoral find it harder to get along with homophobes and easier to get along with homosexuals. Some might try to fake moral beliefs in order to get along, but few of us are good enough actors, and those who believe that homosexuality is immoral usually also believe that they ought not to pretend otherwise in order to get along with homosexuals. Thus, our moral beliefs affect our social options along with our actions, and both affect our interests.

Despite these general trends, many particular moral beliefs might seem to have no effect on us. If I believe that it was immoral for Brutus to stab Caesar, this moral belief by itself does not seem to change my social options or to rule out any acts that I could do today. Still, given universalizability or the requirement that relevantly similar cases be judged similarly, my judgment of Brutus's stabbing seems to depend on a universal principle that does apply in similar cases where my self-interest is involved. In this indirect way, any moral belief can affect my self-interest.

Moreover, it is hard to tell when self-interest or partiality affects our moral beliefs. As Kant said:

> It sometimes happens that in the most searching self-examination we can find nothing except the moral ground of duty which could have been powerful enough to move us to this or that good action and to such great sacrifice. But from this we may not conclude with certainty that a secret impulse of self-love, falsely appearing as the idea of duty, was not actually the true determining cause of the will. For we like to flatter ourselves with a pretended nobler motive. ([1785] 1959, sec. 2)

Kant is speaking of action, but his point applies to moral belief as well. No self-examination can show that our moral beliefs are not infected by partiality. The point is not just that it is hard to prove the negative, since we always might have overlooked some influence of self-interest. The point is, instead, that we tend to be unaware of such motives when they are active. This tendency towards self-ignorance or even self-deception is widespread.

Because people's moral beliefs affect their self-interest so often in so many ways at least indirectly, and because people are so bad at telling when their own beliefs are partial, there is a presumption that moral beliefs are partial. This presumption is strong enough to create a need for confirmation of all moral beliefs. Of course, this presumption might be overridden by some reason to believe that a certain special belief is impartial. However, such a reason amounts to confirmation, since it is also a reason to believe that the belief is more likely to be accurate. This possibility of gaining confirmation does not undermine the claim of Principle 1 that some confirmation is needed.

9.4.2. *Disagreement*

Principle 2 says that disagreement creates a need for confirmation. For this principle to imply that moral beliefs need confirmation, there must be enough disagreement about morality to trigger the need. This makes it crucial to ask how much people do in fact disagree about morality.

One popular answer is a strong version of *moral relativity*, which claims that every moral principle and judgment is or would be denied by someone. This descriptive claim about actual moral beliefs must be distinguished from the normative view called *moral relativism*, which is the claim that what is morally right or wrong varies in certain ways from society to society or from person to person with no underlying universal moral principle to explain or justify the variations. Moral relativism is about what is morally right or wrong, whereas moral relativity is about moral beliefs.

Moral relativity is supported by a wide variety of disputes. Anthologies on applied ethics include thoughtful articles on both sides of abortion, euthanasia, capital punishment, terror bombing, animal rights, famine relief, pornography, homosexuality, affirmative action, and so on. Even more disagreement occurs when we look beyond affluent modern Western societies:

> Some people are cannibals, others find cannibalism abhorrent....In some [societies], a man is permitted to have several wives, in others bigamy is forbidden. More generally, the moral status of women varies greatly from one society to another in many different ways. Some societies allow slavery, some have caste systems which they take to be morally satisfactory, others reject both slavery and caste systems as grossly unjust....Infanticide is considered acceptable in some societies....(Harman in Harman and Thomson 1996, 8–9; cf. Haidt et al. 1993)[21]

The point is not just that different people hold *different* beliefs. Many people today see computer hacking as immoral. Renaissance farmers had no views about computer hacking. But differences like this do not generate a need for confirmation. The point, instead, is that different people's moral beliefs often *conflict* in such a way that they cannot both be correct. No limited set of examples could prove that people disagree about everything in morality, but the range of disagreements about morality is surely impressive.

Some of these disagreements are not fundamentally moral because they result only from disagreements over non-moral facts. If one person supports capital punishment only because she believes that it deters murder, and another person opposes capital punishment because he believes that it does not deter murder, then they might not disagree at all about whether capital punishment would be immoral if it did not deter murder. Different cultures also often hold different religious and scientific or pseudo-scientific beliefs that lead them to different moral conclusions even when the cultures share basic moral principles.

Other apparent disagreements are due to conceptual confusions. Consider one society that prohibits adultery (or bigamy) and another society that allows husbands to have sex with mistresses (or additional wives). If the concept of "marriage" in the

---

21. Similar conflicts occur within a single person at different times. Some people believe that abortion is morally wrong and later come to believe that abortion is not morally wrong, or vice versa. But opponents of moral intuitionism usually emphasize interpersonal moral disagreement, so I will too.

first society requires a commitment to sexual exclusivity, but the "husbands" in the second society never made any such commitment, then they do not count as "married" in terms of the first society, so their sexual relations can't be "adultery" in the sense that the first society condemns. Thus, it is not clear that these societies really disagree at all.

When disagreements about moral issues arise solely from non-moral disagreements and conceptual confusions that could be removed by further inquiry and reflection, informed and rational people would not disagree. Such disputes are resolvable in principle. Disagreements that are resolvable in principle cause less trouble for those moral intuitionists who claim only that believers are non-inferentially justified in moral intuitions when the believer is informed, rational, and not confused.

Still, many moral disagreements do not seem resolvable in such ways. They do not result from factual disagreements or conceptual confusions. Like many negative claims, this can't be proven, but there is substantial evidence for it.[22] Sometimes people who are discussing the same case do agree about all important non-moral facts of the case. Their beliefs might be false, unjustified, and/or incomplete, but they share all relevant non-moral beliefs. Nonetheless, they continue to hold contrary moral beliefs. Moral disagreements also arise among well-informed people. Doctors who have studied abortion in great depth often still disagree about the morality of abortion in general or in a particular case. The same goes for euthanasia, and so on.

People also disagree about imagined situations. Philosophers and teachers often stipulate relevant factors in hypothetical cases, but readers or students who accept their stipulations still disagree about what is morally right or wrong in those circumstances. Many of these cases are too simple, but some are not. Suppose that two people stipulate facts about a hypothetical society, including the effects of capital punishment on murder rates, its costs relative to life imprisonment, the chances of parole and escape, recidivism rates for convicted murders who are not executed, relative rates of death sentences for different races, sexes, classes, and so on. They agree about all of these non-moral facts because those facts are simply accepted for the sake of argument in this fictional case. Neither of them can think of any other fact that might be morally relevant. Nonetheless, they still disagree about whether capital punishment is morally permissible in these circumstances because one person sees it as inhumane whereas the other sees it as required by justice. Numerous moral disagreements like this cannot be explained away by non-moral disagreements because there are none, by hypothesis.

Admittedly, people's intuitions about stipulated cases might be affected by prior beliefs about the real world. If I believe that capital punishment deters murder in the real world, this belief might incline me to accept capital punishment even in an imaginary world where it is stipulated that capital punishment does not deter murder. This mechanism, however, hardly seems adequate to

22. For a dissent, see Brink 1989, 110–13, 142–43, and 197–209. However, Brink wants to show that moral relativity does not refute moral realism (which I grant), whereas my argument concerns moral epistemology.

explain away all or even most such moral disagreements because the grounds that people cite often include factors like inhumanity and justice, which are supposed to be independent of deterrence. Such principles often make people disagree morally while agreeing on stipulated non-moral facts.

Irresolvable moral disagreements also seem likely because of the sources of moral beliefs. Cultural training affects moral beliefs about what is inhumane, just, dishonest, disloyal, disrespectful, private, and so on. Differences between cultures (even within a single society) then cause moral disagreements. These disagreements probably cannot all be resolved by getting straight on the facts and concepts, since inclinations from early enculturation are too tenacious.

Of course, cultures also display some commonalities, but they are too thin to resolve many common disagreements about morality. If everyone agrees that we should not be inhumane, this won't resolve a dispute on capital punishment if people still disagree about whether capital punishment is inhumane. Then it is not even clear that everyone agrees substantially, since people might use different concepts of inhumanity. Similarly, even if we agree that killing is morally wrong (pro tanto), this agreement seems superficial if we still disagree about what counts as killing (passive euthanasia?), about who should not be killed (fetuses? animals?), and about which benefits could justify killing (the goals of vigilantes or terrorists?). If people and cultures agree on so little, then there is little reason to suspect that all moral disagreements will disappear once we agree on the facts. (See Snare 1980, 368–69; and Harman in Harman and Thomson, 1996, 8–9.)

It is still possible that everyone would agree about morality if they had been exposed to the same cultural influences, and that humanity will converge on such agreement someday.[23] That possibility, however, cannot show that people today are justified in their moral beliefs, since we do not find ourselves at that point yet. Today many moral disagreements persist among careful, rational, informed people who feel confident about their beliefs. Conflicts often occur even when such moral beliefs are non-inferred and non-inferable for both believers. Thus, moral intuitions do often conflict in ways that seem irresolvable.

We cannot conclude that disagreement *always* occurs, as moral relativity claims. That position seems false, because everyone does seem to agree on some claims, such as that it is morally wrong to torture babies just for fun.[24]

Since irresolvable moral disagreements occur sometimes but not always, we need to ask how often they occur.[25] No precise answer is possible. We cannot

23. It is not clear why such convergence must be on moral truth, but I'll let that pass.

24. The universality of moral beliefs about cases like this could hardly be used to justify any moral theory or any controversial moral belief, so such cases cannot get moral intuitionists all that they seem to want. Compare Descartes' "I think," which is nowhere near enough to ground science.

25. The question is about actual moral beliefs, not possible moral beliefs. There might be an infinite number of possible moral beliefs that would garner agreement from everyone who understands them as well as an infinite number of possible moral beliefs about which people would disagree. Nonetheless, there still could be a high rate of disagreement among the actual moral beliefs that people bother to form. That is what matters when we ask whether our actual moral beliefs are justified, since our actual moral beliefs are beliefs that we do bother to form.

specify a percentage of moral issues that are subject to disagreement, much less irresolvable disagreement. Luckily, exact numbers do not matter. The crucial issue here is whether the frequency, kinds, and circumstances of existing moral disagreements are enough to create a need for inferential justification.

To determine how much is enough, imagine that you are given a hundred old thermometers. You know that many of them are inaccurate but you don't know how many. It might be eighty or fifty or ten. You pick one at random and put it in a tub of water, which you have not felt. The thermometer reads ninety degrees. Nothing about this thermometer in particular gives you any reason to doubt its accuracy. You feel lucky, so you become confident that the water is ninety degrees. Are you justified? No.[26] Since you believe that a significant number of the thermometers are unreliable, you are not justified in trusting the one that you happen to randomly pick. You need to check it. One way to check it would be to feel the water or to calibrate this thermometer against another thermometer that you have more reason to trust. Such methods might provide confirmation, and then your belief might be justified, but you cannot be justified without some kind of confirmation.[27]

These thermometers are analogous to the processes by which believers form immediate moral beliefs. According to moral intuitionism, some moral believers are justified in forming immediate moral beliefs on the basis of something like (though not exactly like) a personal moral thermometer that reliably detects moral wrongness and rightness. However, the analogy to the hundred thermometers shows that, if we know that a large number of our moral thermometers are broken or unreliable in many situations, then we are not justified in trusting a particular moral thermometer without confirmation. Maybe we got lucky and our personal moral thermometer is one that works fine, but we are still not justified in trusting it, if we know that lots of moral thermometers do not work, and we have no way of confirming which ones do work. This standard applies to moral beliefs, because we do know that lots of moral thermometers do not work. That's what moral disagreements show: if two people hold contrary beliefs about a moral issue, at most fifty percent can be correct. When each of five people disagrees with the other four, at most twenty percent can be correct. The range of disagreements among

26. You might be justified permissively and personally, but remember (from section 4.2) that I am talking about whether believers are justified positively and wholly, which requires them to be justified impersonally as well as personally. Also, remember (from section 9.2) that I am talking about being justified modestly, not about whether anyone is justified without qualification. So my claim here is compatible with my Pyrrhonism.

27. According to Bayesians, if you start with the assumption that the water is eighty degrees, then the fact that this thermometer reads ninety degrees should make you move your estimate towards ninety degrees. How much your estimate should increase depends on your prior assumption about how many thermometers work. This might make it seem as if the thermometer reading can lead to justified belief. However, if your initial estimates (about temperature and the percentage of working thermometers) are unjustified, then I doubt that one reading without confirmation can ground justified belief in these circumstances. Besides, many of us do not form any of the initial estimates that are needed to start Bayesian reasoning.

immediate moral beliefs, thus, shows that many of our moral thermometers are unreliable. It doesn't matter that we do not know how many are unreliable or whether any particular believer is unreliable. The fact that moral disagreements are so widespread still reveals enough unreliability to create a need for confirmation of moral beliefs, contrary to moral intuitionism.[28]

It also does not matter whether most or all of these moral disagreements are resolvable in principle. If we are not yet justified in believing that the moral disagreement will be resolved in favor of a certain moral belief, then we cannot be justified in holding that moral belief any more than we can be justified in trusting one thermometer in the above situation without checking its accuracy. Thus, moral disagreements that are resolvable in principle still create a need for confirmation. Once resolvable disagreements are included, there are plenty of moral disagreements to create a need for confirmation of all moral beliefs.

Of course, confirmation might be available. If we know that everyone agrees with that particular moral belief, then we might have reason to trust it. But that is just because the known agreement provides confirmation, so it does not undermine the point that some confirmation is needed. That is all Principle 2 claims.

9.4.3. *Emotion*

Next consider Principle 3, which says that emotions that cloud judgment create a need for confirmation. It is hard to tell whether this principle applies to moral beliefs. Philosophers and others have argued for millennia about whether moral beliefs are based on emotion or on reason. They also argue about which emotions, if any, cloud judgment. How can we resolve these debates? Luckily, some recent empirical studies suggest an answer.

Haidt and his collaborators have been accumulating an impressive body of behavioral evidence for what they call the social intuitionist model:

> This model suggests that moral judgment is much like aesthetic judgment: we see an action or hear a story and we have an instant feeling of approval or disapproval. These feelings are best thought of as affect-laden intuitions, as they appear suddenly and effortlessly in consciousness, with an affective valence (good or bad), but without any feeling of having gone through any steps of searching, weighing evidence or inferring a conclusion.[29]

Haidt's behavioral evidence dovetails nicely with independent brain studies. Moll's group found that brain tissue associated with emotions becomes more activated when subjects think about simple sentences with moral content (e.g., "They hung

---

28. Admittedly, we do not pick a moral thermometer in the way we pick a thermometer in the analogy. However, if we had been born in different circumstances our immediate moral beliefs would have been different. If our moral thermometer actually does work, then we are simply lucky, not justified (until we confirm its reliability).

29. Greene and Haidt 2002, 517. See also Haidt 2001; and references therein. Of course, many other judgments cause emotional reactions "suddenly and effortlessly." But Haidt argues that emotions drive or constitute moral judgments rather than being effects of those judgments.

an innocent") than when they think about sentences without moral content (e.g., "Stones are made of water"; Moll et al. 2001) or disgusting non-moral sentences (e.g., "He licked the dirty toilet"; Moll et al. 2002a).[30] Similar results were found with pictures in place of sentences (Moll et al. 2002b).

Studies by Greene and his colleagues (2001) are even more fascinating because they distinguish kinds of moral beliefs. Greene's group scanned brains of subjects while they considered what was appropriate in three kinds of dilemmas: non-moral dilemmas, personal moral dilemmas, and impersonal moral dilemmas. A paradigm impersonal moral dilemma is the side-track trolley case, where a runaway trolley will kill five innocent people tied to the track unless you pull a lever to divert the trolley onto a side track where it will kill one innocent person. A standard personal moral dilemma is the fat-man trolley case, where the runaway trolley will kill five innocent people unless you push a fat man in front of the trolley so that his body will stop the trolley before it hits the five people. Most (but not all) people say that it is morally wrong to push the fat man in the second case but not to pull the lever in the first case. What matters here is that these different moral cases stimulated different parts of the brain. While considering appropriate action in impersonal dilemmas, subjects showed significant activation in brain areas associated with working memory but no significant activation in areas associated with emotion. In contrast, while considering appropriate action in personal dilemmas, subjects showed significant activation in brain areas associated with emotion and under-activation (below the resting baseline) in areas associated with working memory.[31]

It is not obvious what to make of these results. Brain scientists do not know how to interpret under-activation in general. Nonetheless, one natural speculation is this: when asked about pushing the fat man, subjects react, "That's so horrible that I can't even think about it." Emotions stop subjects from considering the many factors in these examples. If this interpretation is correct, then many pervasive and fundamental moral beliefs result from emotions that cloud judgment.[32]

Some moral intuitionists might argue that there is no need to consider anything else when the proposed action is the intentional killing of an innocent fat man. It might even be counterproductive to consider additional factors, since they might lead one away from the correct belief. Such responses, however, assume that it is morally wrong to push the fat man, so they beg the question here. When asking whether a moral belief is justified, we should not assume that the only relevant factors are those that would be relevant if the belief were true. Ridiculous moral beliefs could be defended if that method worked.

30. It would be interesting to test reactions to negations, such as "They did not hang an innocent" and "He did not lick the dirty toilet."

31. Greene et al. (2001) also reports timing studies that confirm the different roles of emotion in different moral beliefs.

32. Philosophers should notice that what Greene calls "personal dilemmas" include most proposed counterexamples to consequentialism. If those moral intuitions are unjustified, then Greene's study might help consequentialists defend their moral theory, even if other intuitions are not affected.

Still, moral intuitionism is hardly refuted by these experiments because Greene's results must be replicated and interpreted much more carefully. Some replication is reported in Greene et al. 2004, but the issue is far from settled. All I can say now is that Greene seems to provide some evidence that many moral beliefs result from emotions that cloud judgment. (For more evidence, see Nichols 2004; and Prinz forthcoming.)

Additional evidence comes from Wheatley and Haidt (2005). They gave participants the post-hypnotic suggestion that they would feel a pang of disgust whenever they saw either the word "take" or the word "often." Participants were later asked to make moral judgments about six stories designed to elicit mild to moderate disgust. When a story contained the word that elicited disgust in a participant, that participant was more likely to express stronger moral condemnation of acts in the story. Thus, moral judgments were affected by elements of the story that could not determine the accuracy or acceptability of those moral judgments. In that sense, emotions clouded their judgment. Because independently caused emotions can distort moral beliefs in such ways, moral believers need confirmation in order to be justified in holding their moral beliefs.

9.4.4. *Illusions*

To apply Principle 4 to moral beliefs, we again need empirical research but this time in cognitive science rather than brain science. I mentioned three kinds of illusions that should be considered separately.

The first kind of illusion occurs when appearances and beliefs depend on *context*. An interesting recent example comes from Unger (1996, 88–94), who found that the order in which options are presented affects beliefs about whether a given option is morally wrong. Unger also claims that people's moral beliefs about a certain option depend on whether that option is presented as part of a pair or, instead, as part of a series that includes additional options intermediate between the original pair.[33] Since order and additional options are not morally relevant factors that could affect the moral wrongness of the judged option, the fact that moral beliefs are affected by these factors shows that moral beliefs are unreliable in such cases. That is why confirmation is needed. One still might confirm one's moral belief by reconsidering the issue in several contexts over time to see whether one's moral belief remains stable, but that is just a way of seeking confirmation so it does not undermine my point that confirmation is needed.

---

33. Unfortunately, Unger does not describe the method or precise results of his informal survey, so there is room for more careful empirical work to test his claims. Some empirical evidence that order of presentation affects moral beliefs can be found in Petrinovich and O'Neill 1996; and Haidt and Baron 1996. Some philosophical support for Unger's claims about intermediate options comes from moral paradoxes, which often arise through the mechanisms that Unger describes. One example is the mere addition paradox of Parfit (1984, 419–41) in which B seems worse than A when the two are compared directly, but it seems not worse than A when Parfit interjects A+ and Divided B as options intermediate between A and B.

The second kind of illusion arises from overgeneralization. Such illusions also affect moral beliefs. Jonathan Baron (1994, 1) even argues that all "non-consequentialist principles arise from overgeneralizing rules that are consistent with consequentialism in a limited set of cases." But one need not go so far or accept consequentialism in order to admit that many people condemn defensible lying, harming, and lovemaking because they apply generalizations to exceptional cases. We probably disagree about which moral beliefs are *over*generalizations, but we should agree that many people overgeneralize in ways that create illusions of moral wrongness.[34] In any such case, the moral believer could argue that this case is not an exception to the generalization; but, as before, that is just a way of seeking confirmation, so it does not undermine my point that this kind of illusion creates a need for confirmation.

Heuristics (that is, quick and simple decision procedures) also create illusions in morality. One reason is that many moral beliefs depend on consequences and probabilities, for which we often lack adequate evidence, and then we have to guess these probabilities. Such guesses are notoriously distorted by the availability heuristic, the representative heuristic, and so on (Kahneman et al. 1982).[35] Even when moral beliefs do not depend on probability assessments, moral beliefs are affected by the so-called "I agree with people I like" heuristic (Chaiken 1980; cf. Haidt 2001, 820). When people whom we like express moral beliefs, we tend to go along and form the same belief. When people whom we dislike oppose our moral beliefs, we tend to hold on to them in spite of contrary arguments (Lord et al. 1979). This heuristic often works fine, but it fails in enough cases to create a need for confirmation.

In addition to these three kinds of illusions, moral beliefs also seem subject to framing effects, which were explored by Kahneman and Tversky (1979). In one famous experiment, they asked some subjects this question:

> Imagine that the U.S. is preparing for an outbreak of an unusual Asian disease which is expected to kill 600 people. Two alternative programs to fight the disease, A and B, have been proposed. Assume that the exact scientific estimates of the consequences of the programs are as follows: If program A is adopted, 200 people will be saved. If program B is adopted, there is a 1/3 probability that 600 people will be saved, and a 2/3 probability that no people will be saved. Which program would you choose?

The same initial story was told to a second group of subjects, but these subjects had to choose between these programs:

> If program C is adopted, 400 people will die. If program D is adopted, there is a 1/3 probability that nobody will die and a 2/3 probability that 600 will die.

It should be obvious that programs A and C are equivalent, as are programs B and D. However, 72% of the subjects who chose between A and B favored A, whereas

---

34. This lesson is also taught by arguments for particularism in Dancy 1993 and 2004.

35. Lackey (1986, 634) discusses how such heuristics might explain conflicting moral intuitions about nuclear deterrence.

only 22% of the subjects who chose between C and D favored C. More generally, subjects were risk-averse when results were described in positive terms (such as "lives saved") but risk-seeking when results were described in negative terms (such as "lives lost" or "people who die").

The question in this experiment was about choices rather than moral wrongness. Still, the subjects were not told how the policies affect them personally, so their choices seem to result from beliefs about which program is morally right or wrong. If so, the subjects had different moral beliefs about programs A and C than about programs B and D. The only difference between the pairs is how the programs are framed or described. Thus, descriptions seem to affect moral beliefs. Descriptions cannot affect what is really morally right or wrong. Hence, these results suggest that such moral beliefs are unreliable.

Moral intuitionists could respond that moral intuitions are still reliable when subjects have consistent beliefs after considering all relevant descriptions. But then moral believers would need to know that their beliefs are consistent and that they are aware of all relevant descriptions before they could be justified in holding moral beliefs. That would make them able to confirm their moral beliefs, so this response would not undermine my point that framing effects distort moral beliefs in so many cases that moral believers need confirmation for any particular moral belief.

To see how deeply this point cuts, consider Quinn's argument for the traditional doctrine of doing and allowing, which claims that stronger moral justification is needed for killing than for letting die. In support of this general doctrine, Quinn appeals to moral intuitions of specific cases:

> In Rescue I, we can save either five people in danger of drowning at one place or a single person in danger of drowning somewhere else. We cannot save all six. In Rescue II, we can save the five only by driving over and thereby killing someone who (for an unspecified reason) in trapped on the road. If we do not undertake the rescue, the trapped person can later be freed. (1993, 152)

Most people judge that saving the five is morally wrong in Rescue II but not in Rescue I. Why do they react this way? Quinn assumes that these different intuitions result from the difference between killing and letting die or, more generally, between doing and allowing harm. However, Horowitz uses a different distinction (between gains and losses) and a different theory (prospect theory) to develop an alternative explanation of Quinn's moral intuitions:

> In deciding whether to kill the person or leave the person alone, one thinks of the person's being alive as the *status quo* and chooses this as the neutral outcome. Killing the person is regarded as a negative deviation.... But in deciding to save a person who would otherwise die, the person being dead is the *status quo* and is selected as the neutral outcome. So saving the person is a positive deviation. (Horowitz 1998, 153)

The point is that we tend to reject options that cause definite negative deviations from the status quo. That explains why subjects rejected program C but did not reject program A in the Asian disease case (despite the equivalence between those programs). It also explains why we think that it is morally wrong to "kill" in Rescue

II but is not morally wrong to "not save" in Rescue I, since killing causes a definite negative deviation from the status quo. This explanation clearly hinges on what is taken to be the status quo, which in turn depends on how the options are described. Quinn's story about Rescue I describes the people as already "in danger of drowning," whereas the trapped person in Rescue II can "later be freed" if not for our "killing" him. These descriptions affect our choice of the neutral starting point. As in the Asian disease cases, our choice of the neutral starting point then affects our moral intuitions. Horowitz adds, "I do not see why anyone would think the distinction [that explains our reactions to Quinn's rescue cases] is morally significant, but perhaps there is some argument I have not thought of. If the distinction is not morally significant, then Quinn's thought experiments do not support one moral theory over against another" (1998, 155).

Admittedly, Horowitz's explanation does not imply that Quinn's moral intuitions are false or incoherent, as in the Asian disease case. It does not even establish that his moral intuitions are arbitrary. As Van Roojen says, "Nothing in the example shows anything wrong with treating losses from a neutral baseline differently from gains. Such reasoning might well be appropriate where framing proceeds in a reasonable manner."[36] Nonetheless, the framing also "might well" *not* be reasonable, so the epistemological dilemma remains: If there is *no* reason to choose one baseline over the other, then our moral intuitions seem arbitrary and unjustified. If there *is* a reason to choose one baseline over the other, then either we have access to that reason or we do not. If we have access to the reason, then we are able to draw an inference from that reason to justify our moral belief. If we do not have access to that reason, then we do not seem justified in our moral belief. Because framing effects so often lead to incoherence and error, we cannot be justified in trusting a moral intuition that relies on such framing effects unless we at least can be aware that this intuition is one where the baseline is reasonable. So Horowitz's explanation creates serious trouble for moral intuitionism whenever such framing effects could explain our moral intuitions.

The doctrine of doing and allowing is not an isolated case. It affects many prominent issues and is strongly believed by many philosophers and common people who do not seem to be able to infer it from any other beliefs. If moral intuitions are unjustified in this case, doubts should arise about a wide range of other moral intuitions as well.

9.4.5. *Origins*

Some previous principles look at origins of individual moral beliefs, but Principle 5 considers the social origins of shared moral beliefs. The two issues are related insofar as many of our moral beliefs result from training and social interaction.

---

36. Van Roojen 1999. Van Roojen might admit that Horowitz's argument undermines moral intuitionism, since he defends a method of reflective equilibrium that is coherentist rather than foundationalist.

Specifically, Principle 5 claims that problematic social origins create a need for confirmation. To apply this principle, we need to ask whether moral beliefs have problematic social origins. The social origins of moral beliefs might be problematic in two ways. First, moral beliefs might be caused by factors that are unrelated with the truth of those beliefs. Second, the origins of moral beliefs might be immoral according to those moral beliefs themselves. Although the former problem is also important, I will focus on the latter case.

Are the origins of our moral intuitions immoral by their own lights? Nietzsche ([1887] 1966) suggests as much when he argues that Christian morality results from slaves cleverly overcoming their superiors by re-evaluating values. Insofar as Christian morality condemns such subterfuge and self-promotion, Christian morality condemns its own origins, if Nietzsche is correct. Similarly, Foucault (1979) argues at length that moral beliefs express or result from social power relations. Yet these moral beliefs themselves seem to condemn the very kind of power that leads to these beliefs.[37] But I don't want to rely on Nietzsche or Foucault, at least not here, so I will consider Harman's explanation of the common moral belief that harming someone is much worse than failing to helping someone in need:

> Whereas everyone would benefit equally from a conventional practice of trying not to harm each other, some people would benefit considerably more than others from a convention to help those who needed help. The rich and powerful do not need much help and are often in the best position to give it; so, if a strong principle of mutual aid were adopted, they would gain little and lose a great deal, because they would end up doing most of the helping and would receive little in return. On the other hand, the poor and the weak might refuse to agree to a principle of non-interference or noninjury unless they also reached some agreement on mutual aid. We would therefore expect a compromise [that] would involve a strong principle of noninjury and a weaker principle of mutual aid— which is just what we now have.[38]

Remember also that rich and powerful people have usually controlled the church, the media, the government, and the schools, which in turn affect most people's moral beliefs. In this context, Harman's claim is that the self-interest of the rich and powerful in making everyone believe that harming is worse than failing to help can explain why so many people believe that harming is worse than failing to help. But most people's moral beliefs also seem to condemn such self-serving indoctrination by the rich and powerful, since morality is supposed to consider everyone's interests equally. Thus, if Harman is correct, morality condemns its own origins, as Nietzsche and Foucault claimed.

---

37. For a feminist perspective on how power relations between genders shape moral beliefs, see Walker 1996, 1998.

38. Harman 1977, 110. Compare Scheffler 1982, 113. Harman's explanation applies to all cultures, which explains the omnipresence of the moral belief that harming is worse than failing to help. However, similar stories could be told about many particular cultural traditions that also affect many of our moral beliefs.

The point is not that such moral views are internally inconsistent or self-defeating. The point is only that there are grounds for doubt when beliefs come from disreputable sources. Defenders of such moral beliefs must admit that the source of their beliefs is disreputable if Harman's explanation is accurate. Then they need additional support for their beliefs beyond the mere fact that those beliefs seem correct to them.

These speculations about the origins of moral beliefs are mere armchair psychology. Perhaps more support could be obtained from the literature on sociobiology or evolutionary psychology. Still, these explanations are likely to remain very controversial. Luckily, I don't need to prove them here. I claim only that these undermining accounts are live possibilities. They seem plausible to many people and have not been refuted.

That would not be enough if I were arguing against certain moral beliefs, such as Christian morality (from Nietzsche) or the prevalence of non-injury over mutual aid (from Harman). However, I am not drawing any conclusion about the truth or falsity of any moral beliefs from premises about their causal origins. To do so would be to commit the dreaded genetic fallacy. My argument is different. My conclusion is not about which beliefs are true. It is about which beliefs are justified. Since the point lies in moral epistemology, we can compare the epistemology of non-moral beliefs. If a belief that there are snakes on the couch is caused by ingesting hallucinogenic drugs, it might be true that there are snakes on the couch, but the drugged believer would not be justified in believing that there are snakes on the couch.[39] In this respect, drugs resemble some cultures. If a believer's culture is corrupt in certain ways that would distort moral beliefs to favor the interests of a few, and if the believer's culture causes certain moral beliefs, then this origin might show that the believer is not justified in trusting those moral beliefs, no matter how strongly held and non-inferable they are. If these disreputable origins are live possibilities, then moral believers need some independent confirmation that their beliefs are not distorted by such disreputable origins. This need for independent confirmation then undermines moral intuitionism.

Moral intuitionists might respond that, even if some moral beliefs do originate from culture, others come from biology. Of course, I do not deny that many moral beliefs are affected by nature as well as nurture. But that source is not much better. Humans were hunter-gatherers during most of the time in which our species evolved. Those early humans were at least as selfish and prejudiced as later cultures. Why should we rely today on moral beliefs that were shaped by evolutionary pressures on hunter-gatherers in very different circumstances?[40] Again, my point is not that such beliefs are false. They might be true. My point lies in moral epistemology. If our moral beliefs reflect such ancient circumstances, then moral

---

39. If the drugged believer has no way of knowing that he is under the influence of drugs, then he might be personally justified. But he is still not impersonally justified, so he is not wholly justified. See section 4.2.4.

40. As Singer (1974) says, many of our moral beliefs derive "from discarded religious systems, from warped views of sex and bodily function, or from customs necessary for the survival of the group in social and economic circumstances that now lie in the distant past."

believers need some independent confirmation that their moral beliefs are still trustworthy in the present. This creates a need for confirmation when moral beliefs arise from nature just as much as when they arise from nurture. And this need for independent confirmation still undermines moral intuitionism.

9.4.6. *Togetherness*

Don't forget that Principles 1–5 complement each other. If I am right, moral beliefs are partial, controversial, emotional, subject to illusion, and explicable by dubious sources, so all of the principles apply. However, even if I am wrong about some of this, so not all but only several of these principles apply, they still work together to make it clear that confirmation is needed for justified moral belief. That is enough to undermine moral intuitionism.

9.5. Objections

None of my arguments is conclusive, so opponents can object at several points. I cannot respond to every objection or to any objection thoroughly. But I will quickly run through the most formidable and common objections.

9.5.1. *Special Moral Beliefs and Believers*

Many opponents object that, even if Principles 1–5 apply to *some* moral beliefs, they do not apply to *all* moral beliefs. As I admitted, some moral beliefs are not controversial. For example, almost everyone (except moral nihilists) agrees that it is morally wrong to push a fat man in front of a trolley when this won't save any lives just because you are angry with him for beating you in a game. Such cases also do not seem due to context, heuristics, overgeneralization, or framing effects. Still, such moral believers are partial and emotional. So Principles 1 and 3 do seem to create a need for confirmation even in such clear cases.

Furthermore, if enough moral beliefs need confirmation in order to be justified, then other moral beliefs cannot be immune from this need. To see why, compare a country with lots of barn facades that look just like real barns when viewed from the road (cf. Goldman 1976, 772). If someone looks only from the road, then he is not justified in believing that what he sees is a real barn (at least if he should know about the barn facades). To become justified, a barn believer needs to get confirmation by looking more closely from some new angle off the road. This need exists even for a believer with good vision who happens to be looking at a real barn, as long as there are enough barn facades in the area. These barn facades are analogous to situations that produce distorted moral beliefs. Because such distortions are so common, morality is like a land of barn facades. We cannot tell which moral appearances are deceptive unless we look closer and get some kind of confirmation. By analogy, then, we are not justified in believing that certain acts really are morally wrong, for example, when these moral beliefs are based only on immediate reactions without any confirmation. Just as barn believers with good vision in front of real barns still need confirmation in a land of barn facades, so moral believers still need confirmation even when distorting factors are absent from their actual circumstances. These moral believers are lucky not to be faced with a deceptive appearance at present, but they are not justified in assuming such luck without checking. Because there are so many deceptive appearances in the area of morality, all moral believers need to confirm that the appearance on which they rely is not one of the many moral appearances that are misleading. This need applies to every moral appearance, so no immediate moral belief is justified without confirmation.

This argument can be presented as a dilemma: if a moral believer is an educated modern adult, then she should know that many moral beliefs are problematic in the ways indicated in section 9.4. She either knows or does not know that her moral belief is an exception to this trend. If she does *not* know that her belief is exceptional, then she should apply the general rate to her particular belief and accept at least a significant probability that her belief is one of the problematic ones. And if she accepts such a significant probability, then she cannot be justified in holding her moral belief without confirmation. Alternatively, if she *does* know that her moral belief is exceptionally reliable in her circumstances, then she has enough information to draw an inference like this:

My moral belief is exceptionally reliable.
Exceptionally reliable beliefs are probably true.

––––––

∴ My belief is (probably) true.

If this moral believer does not have the information in these premises, then it is hard to see why we should call her or her belief justified. If she does have the information in these premises, then she has the ability to draw this inference to justify her belief. Either way, she is not justified without being able to infer her moral belief from other beliefs. So, moral intuitionism fails.

The same dilemma arises for a related response: Some moral intuitionists might insist that they themselves are special. Other people's moral beliefs are partial, emotional, and subject to illusions and distortion by culture. Nonetheless, these moral intuitionists might claim that they personally remain impartial and unemotional when they think about moral issues. They might claim that they can see through the illusions that mislead other people. They might claim to think for themselves independently of distorting culture and outdated evolutionary pressures.

All of this is possible. Some people might be better than others at forming moral beliefs. Still, moral intuitionists who claim such powers (at least after reading section 9.4) should know that partiality, emotion, illusion, and cultural distortion are widespread in humans generally. They should also know that those whose moral beliefs are distorted in these ways are usually not aware of their own mistakes. Self-deception abounds. On this basis, moral intuitionists should assume that they themselves are also subject to these problems, unless they have some special reason to think that they are immune. But if they do have such a special reason to trust their own strongly held non-inferable moral beliefs, then that special reason is itself confirmation for those moral beliefs. The possibility of gaining such confirmation is completely compatible with my conclusion that confirmation is needed.

9.5.2. *Must Confirmation Be Inferential?*

Moral intuitionists might object that, even if some *confirmation* is needed, that does not show that any *inferential ability* is needed. If we can confirm color beliefs simply by looking again in different light, perhaps we can confirm moral beliefs simply by reflecting on the moral issue again in a different mood without involving any substantive moral principle from which we could infer our moral belief.

I grant that confirmation does not require any actual inference. To avoid the skeptical regress, however, moral intuitionists must deny more than the need for an actual inference. They must deny the need for any *ability* to infer the moral belief, as I argued in section 9.1. I also grant that confirmation does not require moral beliefs to be inferred from moral principles. That is not the only kind of inference that can satisfy the need. Nonetheless, it is still hard to see how you could confirm a moral belief in any way without gaining enough information to make you *able* to draw *some* kind of inference to the moral belief.

This point can be supported by a survey of kinds of confirmation. Moral beliefs might be confirmed by deriving them from substantive moral principles. That form of confirmation is clearly inferential. Another way to confirm moral beliefs is to draw analogies to similar cases. Then the believer has the information needed for an inductive argument from analogy or an inference to the best explanation. Yet another way to confirm moral beliefs is to check with other people. Then the believer is able to draw another kind of inductive inference: an appeal to authority or to popular opinion. A moral belief also might be confirmed just by rethinking the issue in different moods. That confirmation is hardly adequate unless the believer thinks that her or his moral beliefs are reliable when they are constant across moods. This belief can then serve as a premise in a second-order inference to the conclusion that this moral belief is (probably) true. Every type of confirmation, thus, seems to make the believer able to draw *some* kind of inference. The believer need not explicitly formulate the inference, but the confirmation provides enough information to make the believer *able* to support the belief with an inference, at least in the weak sense of ability defined in section 9.1. Thus, if confirmation is needed, inferential ability is needed.

More abstractly, if any believer has confirmation of any kind for any belief, then that confirmation must put the believer in circumstances that make that belief more reliable or likely to be true. Otherwise, the confirmation would not be epistemic in the way that matters here (section 4.2.1). If the believer is *not* aware of the confirmation, then the believer does not have that confirmation in a way that could make the moral belief justified in the face of the problems raised in section 9.4 (just as awareness is needed for justified beliefs in the cases of thermometers in 9.4.2 or barn facades in 9.5.1). And if the believer *is* aware of the confirmation, then the believer has enough information to be able to argue like this:

I hold this moral belief in circumstances like these.
If I hold a moral belief in circumstances like these, then it is usually true.

———

∴ This moral belief is (probably) true.

This second-order inference might seem odd because it refers to the belief itself. Nonetheless, any kind of inference can lead to a skeptical regress, because it has premises that need to be justified, so moral intuitionists have to deny dependence on any kind of inference or ability to infer. Justified moral belief does depend on an ability to draw the above kind of inference, since, if the moral believer does not at least implicitly believe its premises (or something like them), then it is hard to see why the moral believer is justified in holding the moral belief. Thus, at least this minimal inferential ability is needed for justified belief.

9.5.3. *Being Justified Without Knowing It*

At this point, critics sometimes accuse me of confusing whether a belief *is* justified with whether the believer *knows* or can *show* that it is justified. I plead innocent. I might be guilty of such a level confusion if I claimed that justified believers must *actually* draw inferences like those in section 9.5.2. But all I claim is that justified moral believers must be *able* to infer their moral beliefs in some way from something. That ability requires only that certain information be stored in the believer. I do not require that the believer be reflective or conscious of this information or this ability. Hence, I do not assume that justified believers must know or be justified in believing (or even be able to know or be justified in believing) that they are justified.

I also do not assume that reliability is *never* enough for justified belief. Instead, I argue that reliability by itself is not enough for justified belief *in cases where* Principles 1–5 in section 9.3 apply. I do claim that these principles extend indirectly throughout morality, so reliability by itself is never sufficient for justified *moral* belief. But I do not just assume that conclusion. I argued for it in section 9.4. Hence, I do not beg the question against reliabilism or other forms of externalism.

It still might seem too strict to require an inferential ability because then young children cannot have justified moral beliefs since they cannot formulate the needed inferences.[41] Now, I love children. I grant that they can have justified beliefs in other areas, such as beliefs about food or parents. Nonetheless, it is not as clear that very young children (say, one to three years old) can be justified in

———

41. Tolhurst (1998, 301) raises this objection against me: "To hold that a mental state, seeming or belief, entitles one to hold a particular belief only if one has reason to believe that the state was reliably produced is to impose a demand that will render it impossible for children and non-human animals to have justified beliefs." I do not, however, require believers to have actually, explicitly, consciously formulated reasons to believe that their seemings or beliefs are reliable. All I require is that believers be *able* in my weak sense to give some reason to believe in the reliability of their seemings or beliefs. Moreover, this is required only when no other kind of inference is available, so the status of the belief as justified depends completely on the seeming or belief in question.

holding *moral* beliefs. Some studies do suggest that children as young as three years old distinguish moral beliefs from conventional beliefs (Nichols 2005, chap. 8, sec. 2.2). However, very young children often base their normative beliefs on fear of punishment (Kohlberg 1981). If someone believes that stealing is wrong just because he believes that he is likely to get punished if he steals, then it is not even clear that the belief is a moral belief. It might be purely prudential. Moreover, some children's moral beliefs might be based on deference to authorities, such as parents or teachers. Authorities can make believers justified, but only if they are justified in trusting those authorities. Maybe young children are justified in trusting their parents, for example, but then they are able to infer like this:

> My parents are trustworthy.
> My parents tell me that I shouldn't pull my sister's hair.
> ───────
> ∴ I shouldn't pull my sister's hair.

Children can also draw similar inferences from consensus as soon as they find out whether other people agree with their moral beliefs. If a young child is not able to draw any inference like this, then this child does not seem justified (even if her parents are trustworthy, even if others do agree, and even if her belief is true). Those who think otherwise are too soft on their kids.

A related objection claims that, if a moral believer cannot know that moral beliefs are subject to controversy, partiality, illusion, and so on, then that moral believer does not need to guard against these problems by getting confirmation. Children and some adults (such as isolated medieval peasants) might have no way of discovering such problems for moral beliefs. They certainly lack access to the psychological research that I cited in section 9.4. So maybe these ignorant moral believers do not need confirmation for their moral beliefs.

I do not deny that such believers are justified personally. Children and medieval peasants are not responsible for their epistemic failures if they do the best they can with the information they have. My claim is only that such ignorant moral believers are not justified *wholly*, because they are not justified *impersonally*, as defined in section 4.2.4. These ignorant moral believers are analogous to believers in Gettier examples. Observers with full and accurate information would not assess their grounds as adequate because these observers would be aware of facts like those I cited in section 9.4. That is why such ignorant moral believers are neither impersonally nor wholly justified.

Moreover, even if children and medieval peasants were justified in their moral beliefs, that would not save moral intuitionists or my readers from the need for confirmation. Moral intuitionists and my readers are neither children nor medieval peasants. They are modern educated adults. Modern educated adults can know that moral beliefs are problematic in the ways that I outlined (at least if they read section 9.4). So my readers and other modern adults need confirmation for moral beliefs regardless of what they think about other people. Moral intuitionists might seem to avoid this point if they claim only that *some* moral believers are justified. However, moral intuitionists always include themselves among those who are justified. Similarly, I assume that my readers want to know whether they themselves are justified moral believers. If it turns out that the only moral believers who are justified without confirmation are children, medieval peasants, and others who are ignorant of the factors canvassed in section 9.4, then it is not so great to be justified.

9.5.4. *Defeasibility*

Some moral intuitionists accuse me of forgetting that a moral believer can be defeasibly justified without being adequately justified. Again, I plead innocent.

To say that a moral believer is defeasibly justified is to say that the believer would be justified in the absence of any defeater. Defeaters come in two kinds (defined in section 4.2.3). An *overriding* defeater of a belief provides a reason to believe that the belief is false. For example, if one newspaper predicts rain tomorrow, but a more reliable newspaper predicts clear skies, then the latter prediction overrides the former even if I still have some reason to believe the former. In contrast, an *undermining* defeater takes the force out of a reason without providing any reason to believe the opposite. If I find out that the newspaper that predicts rain based its prediction only on a crystal ball, then this new information keeps the prediction from making me justified in believing that it will rain, but the new information does not make me justified in believing that it will not rain since a crystal ball is as likely to yield a true prediction (in propitious circumstances). When my only justification is undermined completely in this way, I have no reason left for believing that it will rain or that it will not rain.

The factors in Principles 1–5 cannot be overriding defeaters since they do not provide any reason to believe that the moral belief is false. Even when moral beliefs are partial, controversial, emotional, subject to illusion, and due to disreputable sources, that does not show that those beliefs are false. Thus, the factors in Principles 1–5 seem to be undermining defeaters. That suggests that we have no reason to trust our immediate moral beliefs before confirmation. Admittedly, some defeaters might not completely undermine a justification. They might leave some weaker reason that makes believers partially justified. However, the manifold underminers in Principles 1–5 add up, so that it is hard to see why there is any reason left to hold immediate moral beliefs without confirmation. At least there is not enough of a reason left to make such beliefs adequately justified.

Moreover, I am not just talking about *possible* underminers. I argued in section 9.4 that the underminers in Principles 1–5 actually exist for many moral beliefs. Actual moral believers are partial and emotional. They actually do disagree often. Cultures actually are disreputable in ways that affect moral beliefs. There is even empirical evidence for actual widespread illusions in morality. These actual defeaters might be absent from some moral beliefs. Still, as I argued in section 9.5.1, actual defeaters are common enough to create a need for confirmation of moral beliefs where no actual defeater has yet been found in a particular case. Even if there are no barn facades in front of you, you still need to look more closely when there are lots of actual barn facades in the area. (See also section 9.4.2 on broken thermometers.)

Moral intuitionists can still say that some immediate moral beliefs are *prima facie* justified if that means only that they *would* be adequately justified *if* they were not undermined by the factors in Principles 1–5. This counterfactual claim is compatible with their actually not being justified at all, but only appearing to be justified. Such moral believers might have no real reason for belief but only the misleading appearance of a reason (as with the newspaper's weather prediction based on a crystal ball). In contrast, to call a belief *pro tanto* justified is to indicate some actual positive epistemic force that is not cancelled or undermined even if it is overridden. If the factors in Principles 1–5 are underminers, as I argued, then immediate moral beliefs are not even pro tanto justified. At most, they misleadingly appear to be justified when they are not really justified at all.

Besides, even if moral intuitions were pro tanto justified independently of any inferential ability, this status would not make them adequately justified. As I said in section 4.2.3, skeptics win if no moral belief is adequately justified. Hence, moral intuitionists cannot rest easy with the claim that moral intuitions are merely pro tanto justified.

9.5.5. Do My Principles Lead to Disaster?

Another possible objection is that my argument assumes or leads to general skepticism, since only skeptics would accept my five principles. If so, and if general skepticism is disastrous, then that is a reason to reject my principles 1–5. Actually, however, many non-skeptics accept my principles. I argued in section 9.3 that my principles are accepted by common sense in a wide variety of non-moral examples. One reason why non-skeptics accept my principles is that they do not apply to every belief. If my belief that a pen is in front of me is not subject to disagreement or illusions and has no disreputable sources, and if I am neither partial nor emotional about pens, then I might be justified in holding that non-moral belief without being able to support it with any inference. Thus, my argument against moral intuitionism does not assume or lead to general skepticism.

My argument still might seem to assume or lead to *moral* skepticism. If so, and if moral skepticism is unacceptable, then something must be wrong with my argument. However, my argument in this chapter *by itself* does not lead to moral skepticism. My thesis is not that moral intuitions are not justified, but only that they are not justified non-inferentially because they need confirmation. Such confirmation still might be possible somehow. Even if moral intuitionism is rejected, there are other non-skeptical methods in moral epistemology, including coherentism, normativism, and naturalism. Moral skepticism rises only after all of these other approaches fall. So my principles by themselves do not yield moral skepticism.[42]

---

42. Indeed, my principles and my claim that moral intuitions need confirmation might seem incompatible with meta-skepticism about relevance, which denies that any particular contrast class is really relevant in the sense that believers need to rule out all other alternatives in that class in order to be justified without qualification. However, there might be no need to rule out any particular contrast class, even if there is a need to give evidence of a certain kind. The issue of what needs to be ruled out is separate from the issue of what is needed to rule something out.

My argument would still be questionable if it implied that we should never trust any moral intuitions. That would make it impossible to do moral theory or even to make everyday moral decisions. But nothing like this follows from my view. My argument is completely compatible with everyday moral reasoning. In their everyday lives, people do have to make some assumptions that they do not actually infer from anything else. Otherwise, they could never get anywhere. This practice is acceptable, since it is often hard to see why two people must actually give or even look for reasons behind their assumptions when they agree. Nonetheless, this is not enough to show that they are justified in holding such assumptions without any *ability* to infer them from any other beliefs. Although they do not need to formulate actual inferences, they still might need to be *able* to infer their moral beliefs in order to be justified. For example, suppose a scientist tests the water of a lake and finds that its pH is 3. On this basis she infers that there are no live fish in that lake. In normal circumstances, that inference is enough to justify her in believing that there are no live fish in that lake. But that justification is superficial. She assumes without any inference that fish cannot live in a lake with a pH of 3. This superficial justification is adequate only because she has enough expertise to be able to infer her assumptions from other beliefs if she needed to. Science works as it does because such deep justifications are available, even if scientists do not always cite them explicitly. Moral beliefs might be similar. One can give superficial justifications that depend on non-inferred assumptions because one is able to go deeper if a need arises. The fact that there is usually no present practical need to go deeper does not show that one's justification does not depend on one's ability to go deeper. If it does so depend, then our actual practices of superficial justification cannot do anything to support moral intuitionism as I defined it.

A related objection is that my principles lead to absurdity. Some moral beliefs seem so obvious that we cannot doubt them. It is morally wrong to rape violently just to relieve sexual tension or to express dominance. Isn't that obvious? Yes. But that does not show that it is justified non-inferentially. Most people believe moral principles about harm or respect from which they could infer the moral wrongness of such rape. That wrongness still seems obvious to them. Thus, obviousness does not show that a belief is not based on inference, much less that it is justified non-inferentially.

This objection might be supplemented by the claim that such obvious moral beliefs cannot be doubted. As a matter of psychological fact, most people could not bring themselves to give up their belief that it is morally wrong to rape. If a believer really cannot doubt or give up a moral belief, then there is no point in telling the believer that the belief is unjustified, if this implies that the believer ought to doubt or give up the belief. "Ought" implies "can" for epistemological norms just as much as for moral norms.[43] Or so the argument goes. However, the lack of any point in saying something does not make it false. If you are addicted to gambling,

---

43. For criticisms of this general principle, see Sinnott-Armstrong 1984. I will not repeat those criticisms here because, even if this general principle held, it would not support moral intuitionism in the way that this objection claims.

there might be no point in my telling you that gambling is stupid, since you are going to continue gambling anyway. Still, it might be true that gambling is stupid. Similarly, it might be true that someone ought to doubt a moral belief when there is no point in saying that he ought to doubt it, maybe because he just won't listen to what we say. Moreover, there might be a point in saying that someone's belief is not justified even if the believer cannot doubt that belief. If you are deluded into believing that you are Napoleon, there might be some point in me telling someone else that your belief is unjustified, even if you cannot give up that delusion. Finally, it is not clear that there is any moral belief that you cannot give up. If moral nihilism is coherent, as I argued in section 3.3, then it might take long argument or training to make you wonder whether it is true, but you can start to wonder, and then you doubt your initial moral beliefs. Most people would not be willing to undertake such a process of conversion to moral nihilism, but it might be possible after a long time. If so, this objection cannot be used to save moral intuitionism.

Most important, this argument has no tendency to establish the truth of a belief, since even unavoidable delusions might not be true. For example, I cannot stop thinking that there is more matter than space inside a rock. I know that rocks are 99% empty space (between their subatomic particles) according to modern science. Still, when I am not making a conscious effort to correct my beliefs, I believe that a rock contains more matter than space. This would not show that my belief about rocks is epistemically justified, however incurable it might be. Similarly, some people cannot help but believe in God. Others might be able to stop believing in God, but this would destroy their lives. There might be no point in telling these people not to believe in God or to blame them for believing in God. But none of this shows that belief in God is justified epistemically or that there is any evidence that God exists. Unavoidability confers no evidence or epistemic justification.

9.6. Qualifications and Conclusions

There is still a trivial way in which some immediate moral beliefs might be modestly justified. Recall my standard example:

(T) It is morally wrong to torture innocent children just for fun.

Let's grant that (T) would not be seriously questioned in any everyday context. The modest contrast class was defined to include all and only those views that need to be ruled out to meet the usual epistemic standards. This includes all and only alternatives that would be taken seriously in some everyday context. Thus, if we assume that some member of the modest contrast class is true, (T) must be true. In section 5.5.3, I proposed that S is modestly justified in believing p if and only if S is extremely justified in believing p, given that skeptical hypotheses are false. Given the falsity of all views that would not be taken seriously in any everyday context, (T) must be true. This technical point seems to make belief in (T) modestly justified, even if this belief in (T) is not inferred from anything.

This result is merely an artifact of what modestly justified belief is. To call a belief modestly justified is, in effect, to say that it is justified given our everyday assumptions. It should not be surprising that our everyday moral assumptions are justified given themselves (just as astrological beliefs are justified given astrological assumptions). That triviality does not begin to show that such beliefs are true or even likely to be true. It also does not show that there is any evidence for these beliefs, since no belief can be evidence for itself. All it shows is that these beliefs are assumed to be true in everyday contexts.

Moreover, this point will apply only to very weak moral beliefs. If any normal person would ever have any serious doubts about a moral belief, then that belief will not be modestly justified in this technical way. One can avoid all everyday doubts only by qualifying the moral belief so that its application will be in dispute (such as "It is morally wrong to harm *without an adequate reason*") or by limiting it so much that it applies to very few, if any, real acts (such as "It is morally wrong to torture babies *just for fun*"). Consequently, no serious dispute will be resolved by claiming that a moral belief is modestly justified in this technical way.

The same point applies within more limited contrast classes. I am trivially justified in believing Kantian moral claims out of any contrast class all of whose members imply Kantian moral claims. I am also trivially justified in believing the denial of Kantian moral claims out of any contrast class all of whose members imply the denial of Kantian moral claims. The same goes for utilitarian moral claims. This trick neither supports nor undermines either Kantian or utilitarian ethics. Similarly, the fact that everyday moral assumptions are justified out of a contrast class all of whose members imply them does not pose any problem for the denial of those assumptions.

This leaves moral intuitionism with no way to show how any moral belief could be justified even modestly except in a trivial technical way.[44] As always, I am talking about being justified epistemically, positively, wholly, and adequately. Moral intuitions might be justified *instrumentally* (as opposed to epistemically) if denying those intuitions would disrupt everyday life in harmful ways. Moral intuitions also might be justified *permissively* (as opposed to positively) when the believer has no reason to deny them. Moral intuitions might even be justified *personally* (as opposed to wholly) if the believer personally has no access to any information that suggests any inadequacy in the believer's grounds. The question of whether moral intuitions can be justified *defeasibly* (as opposed to adequately) was discussed in section 9.5.4. But what matters here is that moral intuitionism cannot show how any moral believer or belief can be justified in any way that is sufficient to stop the skeptical regress. So we need to look to other responses to that regress.

---

44. I am, as always, talking about substantive moral beliefs (section 1.1). If "murder" means "wrongful killing," then a belief that murder is wrong is not substantive. Hence, the fact that such beliefs can be justified by a dictionary definition does not show that any substantive moral belief is justified.

10

Coherentism

The main challenge in moral epistemology was laid down by the skeptical regress argument in section 4.3.1. In part II so far, I have discussed three groups of attempts to meet this challenge: naturalism, normativism, and intuitionism. I argued that each of these approaches meets the challenge only partly; each shows how some moral beliefs can be justified in some limited ways, but no theory so far can show how any moral beliefs could be justified out of the extreme contrast class that includes moral nihilism. The only remaining response is coherentism. I will defend a version of coherentism and bring out its advantages over rival views. Nonetheless, my version will still be limited in ways that support moderate moral skepticism.

Before developing my version, I need to explain the basic ideas behind coherentism in general. Coherentists in general epistemology respond to the skeptical challenge by claiming that some beliefs are justified by relations among beliefs. According to coherentism, a belief is justified when it has the right relation to a system of beliefs that have the right relation to each other. The right relation is called coherence. Thus, the defining claim of coherentism is that a person S is justified in believing a proposition p when p coheres with a coherent system of beliefs held by S.[1]

Most coherentists also claim that *all* justified beliefs are justified by coherence. If so, relations among beliefs are not only sufficient but also necessary for justified belief. This claim is controversial, because some simple beliefs, such as my belief that I am in pain, do not seem to need relations to other beliefs in order to be justified. Luckily, I do not need to settle this general issue here. The belief that I am in pain has no analogue among moral beliefs, since moral beliefs are

---

1. For example, Lehrer 1990, 115. Since coherentists allow degrees of justified belief, as we will see, it would be more accurate to define coherentism in terms of a belief being justified *to the extent* that it coheres with a more coherent set. My initial formulation in the text overlooks this complication in order to match traditional versions of coherentism.

universalizable, so they imply beliefs about other people. Furthermore, I argued in section 9.4 that moral beliefs need inferential confirmation. If so, they cannot be justified apart from their relations to other beliefs. Thus, a moral coherentist can claim that all moral beliefs are justified by coherence, so coherence is necessary for justified moral belief, regardless of whether coherence is necessary for justified beliefs outside morality.

Still, moral coherentists don't have to claim that much in order to stop the skeptical regress for moral beliefs. All they need to claim is that some moral beliefs are justified by relations among beliefs.[2] If coherence with a coherent system is sufficient for justified moral belief, that solves the regress problem even if coherence is not necessary because there are other ways to justify moral beliefs and avoid the regress. Consequently, I will take the crucial claim of moral coherentism to be that coherence with a certain coherent system of belief is sufficient to make some believers justified in holding some moral beliefs.

10.1. What Is Coherence?

A major problem for coherentism, as I mentioned in section 4.3.1, is circularity. If a particular belief (A) is justified by its coherence with other beliefs (B-Z), and each of those other beliefs (including Z) is also justified by coherence with the other beliefs (A-Y), then one belief (A) is justified partly by its relation to another belief (Z) that is justified partly by its relation to the original belief (A). Thus, each belief is justified partly by a relation to itself. That seems circular.

Coherentists respond that this circularity is a special kind or size that is not vicious. It would be vicious to argue that a crystal ball's predictions will be reliable because it predicts that its predictions will be reliable. However, most coherentists do not have in mind linear arguments of that kind. They claim, instead, that what justifies beliefs is holistic.[3] For a detective to be justified in believing that Mrs. White committed a certain murder, the detective needs to be able to fit together a large number of facts, including facts about not only White's motives and opportunity but also other suspects, witnesses and their reliability, fingerprints or blood drops (or the lack of these), the observations and science behind such evidence, and so on.

Of course, most detectives do not and need not cite such background beliefs explicitly. In normal discussions, a detective may simply say, "Her own friends testified against her! What more do you need?" Such local justification does not cite coherence explicitly. Nonetheless, coherentists claim that such local justification depends on the *availability* of more systematic justification (Brink 1989,

---

2. Most coherentists claim that many moral beliefs (not just some) are justified by coherence, but that stronger claim is not needed to stop the skeptical regress.

3. The difference between linear and holistic justification is not always clear, but the basic idea seems to be that what makes a belief justified is not merely its relation to a small set of premises but rather its relation to a whole body of beliefs. See section 10.1.3. The way holism avoids vicious circularity will be clarified in section 10.6.3.

123–24). Detectives would not be justified if they could not support their local justification with further background beliefs. If they do have the right kind of coherent system, then the cohering beliefs are justified.[4] The same holds for historians, scientists, and so on. Moral coherentists claim that it also holds for moral beliefs.

That's the basic idea, but we still need to determine exactly what counts as coherence on such a view. In other words, we need to specify the kinds of relations that are supposed to make beliefs justified, according to coherentism. The best account is that of Sayre-McCord (1985): a system of beliefs is coherent to the extent that its beliefs are jointly consistent, connected, and comprehensive. To understand coherence, we need to look at these three c's.

10.1.1. *Consistency*

The minimal condition that must be met for any system of belief to be coherent is consistency. Two beliefs are inconsistent when it is impossible that both beliefs are true. For example, if I believe that my pet is a cat, and I also believe that my pet is not a cat, then my beliefs are logically inconsistent. Similarly, if I believe both that Cleo is a cat and also that Cleo is not a mammal, then my beliefs are semantically inconsistent.

What's so bad about inconsistency? At least one member of each inconsistent pair must be false, so inconsistency should be disappointing to believers who want to avoid error.[5] Moreover, what makes justification epistemic is a connection to truth or at least probability (section 4.2.1). No coherence relation with an inconsistent set of premises can increase the probability that a conclusion is true, since the opposite conclusion also follows validly.[6] Thus, an inconsistent belief system cannot make a belief epistemically justified.[7]

This does not mean that a believer whose belief system is inconsistent cannot have any epistemically justified beliefs. That restriction would be too stringent, for almost everyone holds some inconsistent beliefs, at least in some philosophical paradoxes (see Sorensen 2001, chap. 8). Luckily, not every inconsistency undermines every justified belief.[8] People with inconsistent beliefs can still be justified in some beliefs if they know that both those beliefs and the beliefs on which they

---

4. If the background beliefs turn out to be faulty, then the detective still might be personally justified but is not impersonally justified in the sense of section 4.2.4 because a fully informed observer would not trust the detective's grounds.

5. Someone can believe every truth by believing both P and ~P for every P, but the cost is an equal number of errors. The fact that one of each contradictory pair is true cannot help epistemologically if we can't tell which one it is.

6. Except in paraconsistent logics, which do not affect my point in epistemology.

7. Except in the unusual case of a belief that the system is inconsistent.

8. If a contradiction implies everything (pace paraconsistent logics), then anyone with any inconsistent beliefs is committed to everything. Hence, they believe everything, if such commitments are beliefs, as some philosophers suggest. However, coherentism is about beliefs as mental states or performances, not commitments. In this sense, even if I do hold some inconsistent beliefs, I do not believe that $2 + 3 = 4$, so I do not believe everything. That is why an isolated inconsistency does not prevent all of my beliefs from being justified.

are based will be retained in the best resolution of the inconsistencies, maybe because these beliefs would survive any plausible resolution. Such beliefs are justified not because of the inconsistent belief system but only because of a consistent subset.[9] That is how inconsistent believers can have justified beliefs, according to coherentists.

In addition to logical and semantic consistency, some coherentists require what is called epistemic consistency.[10] Belief P is epistemically inconsistent with belief Q if and only P is an epistemic reason not to believe Q, or vice versa. For example, suppose I believe that Claire has naturally red hair and my only evidence is that I am looking at her hair right now. However, I also believe that I am colorblind, so I cannot distinguish red hair from other colors of hair just by looking. My colorblindness is a reason not to believe that something is red when my only evidence is my visual experience. Again, suppose I believe that lots of people in the area dye their hair so that it looks indistinguishable from naturally red hair. This is a reason for me not to believe that Claire's hair is naturally red solely on the basis of my vision, even if I am not colorblind. Such beliefs are, then, epistemically inconsistent. They are neither logically nor semantically inconsistent, since they might all be true. Claire's hair might be red despite my colorblindness and other people's dye jobs. Hence, epistemic inconsistency might not seem to be real inconsistency. The word doesn't matter. If you want, you may instead talk about that beliefs *conflicting* or *competing* epistemically.

What does matter is whether a belief set with such epistemic conflicts can make a belief justified. The answer seems to be negative for much the same reason as with logical and semantic inconsistency. When belief P is an epistemic reason not to believe Q, Q is less probable given P than given not-P. Thus, epistemically inconsistent belief sets are less likely to be true than epistemically consistent beliefs sets. For that reason, epistemic inconsistency must be disappointing to believers who seek to gain truth and avoid error. As before, not every epistemic inconsistency in my belief set is essential to every belief that I hold, so I can be justified in holding some beliefs even if my total belief set is epistemically inconsistent. Nonetheless, it is an epistemically consistent subset rather than the total epistemically inconsistent belief set that makes me justified. Thus, coherentists can (and usually do) say that epistemic as well as logical and semantic consistency are necessary for a belief set to have the kind of coherence that makes beliefs justified.

In addition to logical, semantic, and epistemic consistency, some moral coherentists require a special kind of practical consistency. (Cf. Sinnott-Armstrong 1988, chap. 6.) Suppose Pat mistakenly makes two incompatible promises. Pat believes that she has a defeasible moral reason to keep the first promise. She also

---

9. I do not claim that a consistent subset is sufficient for justified belief. If one consistent subset supports P and another consistent subset supports ~P, then (other things being equal) neither subset can make the believer adequately justified in believing either as opposed to the other.

10. Compare Sayre-McCord 1985; and Lehrer 1990, 117–18, on competition, which is reduced to probability in Lehrer 1974.

believes that she has a defeasible moral reason to keep the second promise. Since Pat cannot keep both promises, her beliefs might seem inconsistent in a practical way. However, her beliefs are not logically or semantically inconsistent. Nor are they epistemically inconsistent (at least not in any obvious way). So I see no reason why a belief system must be consistent in this practical way in order to epistemically justify moral or other beliefs.

Pat's belief set would be semantically inconsistent if Pat believed that she had an overriding moral reason to keep the first promise and also an overriding moral reason to keep the second promise. A reason cannot override a reason that overrides it. This kind of inconsistency does seem to keep a system of moral beliefs from justifying anything. But this is plain old semantic inconsistency, not any special new kind of practical inconsistency. Thus, it seems enough to say that coherence requires logical, semantic, and epistemic consistency, without requiring any special practical consistency, even for moral belief systems.

10.1.2. *Connectedness*

Consistency is not enough for coherence. If my only beliefs are that the moon is roughly round, grass is usually green, and the square root of 9 is 3, then my beliefs are all true and consistent, but they are not coherent because they are not connected. On a larger scale, if I know a lot about physical forces and about which chemicals bond with which, but I do not know how physical forces make chemical bonds work, then my beliefs about chemistry might be coherent, and my beliefs about physics might also be coherent, but my beliefs overall are not as coherent as they would be if I connected my knowledge of chemistry to my knowledge of physics.

At least three kinds of connections matter to coherence. The first is logical or semantic entailment. If I believe that all cats have some hair, and I also believe that all dogs have some hair, then my beliefs become more coherent if I add beliefs that all mammals have some hair and that cats and dogs are mammals. These new beliefs entail the previous beliefs, so the whole system becomes better connected when the new beliefs are added. Admittedly, some entailments are trivial. Whenever I believe P and also believe Q, I could add a belief in the material conditional $P \supset Q$ that will yield an entailment from P to Q. This trick works regardless of what P and Q are. But this kind of entailment adds little to coherence. It is hard to specify what kinds of entailments are more significant, but almost all coherentists agree that at least some kinds of entailments increase coherence.

Other connections also increase coherence. First, even if P does not entail Q, P is connected with Q if P increases the probability of Q (because the conditional probability of Q given P is higher than the conditional probability of Q given not P). Similarly, P is connected with Q if P is evidence for Q. Again, P is connected with Q if P explains Q. For example, my belief that my wife is at her office is connected to my belief that she left for her office an hour ago (since this increases the probability that she is at her office), with my belief that her secretary just told me that she is with a client (since this is evidence that she is at her office), and with my belief that she wants to keep her job (since this explains why she is at her office).[11]

All of these connections are inferential. I can infer that my wife is at her office from a premise that she left for her office an hour ago, from a premise that her secretary told me that she is with a client, or from a premise that she wants to keep her job (plus other premises). I can also infer my conclusion from premises that entail it, such as that my wife always goes to work on Monday morning, except when she is sick or on vacation, and it is now Monday morning, but she is not sick or on vacation. For a belief to cohere with a system is for that belief to have one or more of these connections with other beliefs in that system. Hence, if *P* coheres with *S*'s system, then *S* can infer *P* from other beliefs of *S*.

The fact that such connections make inferences available explains why such connections matter to justified moral belief. If my beliefs are connected, then I have all it takes (other than general intelligence) to be able to infer one belief from other beliefs. In short, I am *able* to infer that belief. This ability is necessary for justified moral belief, as I argued in section 9.4. Of course, the other beliefs also need to be justified, so they must also be connected to still other beliefs. Then, if the whole set of beliefs forms a connected system, each belief can be justified because the believer has the ability to support each belief with an inference from other beliefs. This is how coherentists solve the regress problem and why they claim that something important is missing when beliefs are not connected.

10.1.3. *Comprehensiveness*

Consistency and connectedness are not enough for the kind of coherence that can make beliefs justified. Imagine that my only beliefs are (a) Sam is a loving parent, (b) Sam never hits his daughter, (c) Judy is a loving parent, (d) Judy never hits her son, and (e) no loving parents ever hit their sons or daughters.[12] (a)-(d) are some evidence for (e). Also, (e) plus (a) and (c) entail (b) and (d). Thus, each belief in my system is connected to some other belief. My system of belief is also consistent. But that is not enough to make these beliefs justified by themselves.

Why not? One reason is that I need more than just two bits of evidence for (e). A deeper reason is that, whenever I could infer a (non-analytic) conclusion from premises, I can consistently avoid the conclusion by rejecting a premise. This option becomes salient when we encounter evidence against the conclusion. If I believe (e) and (a), and I recognize that they imply (b), but I see Sam hit his daughter, then I have to make a decision. I could give up (e) and admit that loving

---

11. Arguments from analogy are also common in moral reasoning. If they are separate from inferences to the best explanation, then coherentists should add analogy to the connections that increase coherence. However, I think that all good arguments from analogy are basically inferences to the best explanation. See Fogelin and Sinnott-Armstrong 2005, 266–67.

12. Any real person who held *only* these beliefs would be insane. Luckily, my argument does not depend on the claim that any real person has such a small belief set. My point is that such a small set would not be adequate to justify anything, even if some crazy person did hold these beliefs alone.

parents sometimes hit their children, perhaps as punishments to help the children learn. Or I could give up (a) and accept that Sam does not love his daughter. Or I could hold on to (b) and believe that I did not really see Sam hit his daughter (maybe it was someone else or an accident or a hallucination). Our choice among these options cannot be based on (a)-(e) by themselves. We need to bring in other beliefs about the reliability of our vision under the circumstances, about parents' motives and child-raising practices, about Sam as an individual, and so on. A larger set of beliefs is needed to rule out contrary consistent and connected positions and, thereby, to make a believer justified in holding a particular belief.

This familiar point leads to corporatism, which is the claim that beliefs get tested and justified in large groups rather than alone.[13] Limited corporatists claim that these groups of beliefs are limited, so some beliefs play no part in justifying certain other beliefs. Holistic corporatists claim that every belief plays some part in justifying every other belief. The holistic version might seem unrealistic (see section 10.6.1), but it presents an ideal that gives direction to thinking. The more beliefs one has on various subjects, the more varied premises one has available, thus the more alternatives one will be able to rule out. The ideal is to be able to rule out as many positions as possible. That is why coherentists hold that a more comprehensive system is more coherent in a way that makes beliefs better justified.

It is not so clear how to apply this notion of comprehensiveness to moral beliefs. Some moral theorists assume that a moral belief system is more comprehensive and better when it tells us what we morally ought to do in more situations. But there are exceptions. We do not want a moral system to tell us whether to part our hair on the left or the right. We don't even want to be told what to do in unresolvable moral conflicts (Sinnott-Armstrong 1988, sec. 2.3). Suppose that I accidentally make conflicting promises. My belief system does not include any belief that either promise is more binding or important. Adding such a belief would make my moral belief system more useful for decision-making. However, my belief system might suffer in other ways. For one thing, it might not be true that either promise is overriding. Moreover, a belief that prefers one of the conflicting promises might not be connected to any of my other beliefs. Without connectedness and consistency, mere comprehensiveness is no good. Of course, this is no problem for coherentists, since they require all three (consistency, connectedness, and comprehensiveness) for the kind of coherence that makes beliefs justified.

10.2. First-Order Coherence

This general account of coherence can be applied to moral beliefs at several levels. The simplest application occurs when people try to connect disparate moral beliefs about particular cases by inferring them from general moral principles. This goal is called narrow reflective equilibrium (Daniels 1979).

---

13. This term comes from White (1981, 20), who presents Duhem as a fellow limited corporatist and Quine as a holistic corporatist.

To see how this works, let's quickly run through a few standard examples:

The Watching Case: A baby crawls into a pool of water. A bystander can save the baby's life easily at little cost. Otherwise the baby will drown.

The Watching Judgment: It is morally wrong for the bystander to let the baby drown.

The Triage Case: A doctor has only five doses of a medicine. The only way to save one patient's life is to give that patient all five doses. The only way to save five other patients is to give one dose to each.

The Triage Judgment: It is not morally wrong to let the single patient die (and give the doses to the five patients).[14]

Letting die benefits nobody much in the Watching case, but it saves five lives in the Triage case. Thus, if S believes the Watching and Triage judgments, it is natural (although hasty) for S to generalize to the principle that letting die is morally wrong unless it prevents more loss of life. Similar examples involving other harms and benefits lead some to the more general utilitarian principle that an act is morally wrong when and only when it leads to more harm than benefit overall.

Such principles notoriously run into trouble in other cases:

The Transplant Case: A doctor can save the lives of five sick people by and only by cutting up one healthy person and distributing that person's organs to the five (heart to one, liver to another, and so on).

The Transplant Judgment: It is morally wrong to cut up the healthy person.

If S adopts the Transplant judgment, it seem natural (even if hasty) for S to give up the utilitarian principle in favor of a deontological principle, such as that it is morally wrong to kill one person just to save the lives of five other people. Similar examples lead some to the more general Doctrine of Doing and Allowing, which claims that it takes more to justify doing harm than merely allowing harm (Quinn 1989a). This doctrine is supposed to explain why it is not morally wrong to *allow* the harm in the Triage case, but it is morally wrong to *do* harm in the Transplant case, even though the acts in both cases save five lives.

Although many people accept some doctrine like this, it seems problematic in other cases:

The Trolley Case: A runaway trolley will kill five people on the main track unless a bystander pulls a lever that will redirect it onto a side track where it will kill one person.[15]

The Trolley Judgment: It is not morally wrong to pull the lever.

14. For doubts about the triage judgment, see Taurek 1977.
15. This famous example comes from Foot 1967. For discussion and variations (including the Loop Case), see Thomson 1976 and 1985.

Redirecting the trolley seems to cause a death and to count as killing.[16] Thus, if S comes to believe the Trolley judgment, then S cannot consistently hold the principle that it is always morally wrong to kill one to save five. Without this, however, S has no principle that implies the Transplant judgment. To construct a new principle, it seems natural to focus on the agent's means, since the doctor in the Transplant case uses the healthy patient's body as a means to save the lives of the five, but the redirector in the Trolley case does not use the body or death of the one as a means to save the five. Accordingly, S might turn to the principle that it is morally wrong to use a person's death or body as a means only to save the lives of five people. Similar examples lead some to the more general Doctrine of Double Effect, which claims that it takes more to justify causing harm intentionally (as an end or as a means) than merely causing harm as a foreseen but unintended side effect (Quinn 1989b).

Unfortunately, this new doctrine runs into trouble when the Trolley case is modified:

> *The Loop Case*: A runaway trolley will kill five people on the main track unless a bystander pulls a lever to redirect it onto a side track where it will kill one person. The side track loops back to the main track so that the trolley will still kill the five if it does not stop, but the body of the person on the side track will slow the Trolley down enough to stop it before it reaches the other five.

> *The Loop Judgment*: It is not morally wrong to pull the lever in the Loop Case.

This redirector (assuming that he knows the facts of the case) uses the body of the person on the side track as a means to save the five, so pulling the lever should be morally wrong, according to the Doctrine of Double Effect. Thus, if S believes the Loop judgment, S cannot consistently keep the Doctrine of Double Effect.[17]

Of course, S could deny the Loop judgment. Or S could reformulate the Doctrine of Double Effect so that it allows the Loop judgment. Many moves are possible. The point here is not to defend or criticize these moves but simply to illustrate how narrow coherence works.[18]

If S believes the Watching, Triage, Transplant, Trolley, and Loop judgments, then S's moral beliefs are both consistent and comprehensive enough to cover all of these cases. However, these beliefs are not yet connected, since none of them implies any of the others. At this level, S cannot connect these judgments except by introducing general principles that imply the particular judgments (with the help

16. This might be denied, but, if you redirected a trolley away from your five family members onto my wife, I would think you killed my wife, even if justifiably.

17. Other problems for this doctrine are discussed by MacIntyre 2001 and Sinnott-Armstrong 1996d.

18. After S decides on judgments and principles about killing persons, S needs to think about non-human animals and fetuses. Then S needs judgments and principles about cheating, lying, and promise-breaking when nobody is killed. And so on. I obviously cannot illustrate the whole process here, so I will restrict myself to the simple example in the text.

of added premises).[19] These general principles explain and thereby help S understand the particular judgments.[20] General principles are also needed to increase the comprehensiveness of S's moral beliefs by applying to many cases beyond the original ones. For these reasons, S's moral beliefs cannot be coherent without some general principles to connect and extend S's particular moral judgments.

It is often hard, however, to find general principles to do the job. Indeed, there is no consensus on how to handle the trolley problem or other cases.[21] A principle can always be constructed by conjoining the particular judgments, but such a principle would not explain or extend the particular judgments. When S adds more significant general principles, their power creates a danger of conflict. S might have to give up one of the original beliefs (such as the Loop Judgment) in order to consistently hold on to a principle (such as the Doctrine of Double Effect) that explains the other original beliefs. But S also could consistently give up the general principle and hold on to the original belief. So S has a choice about how to construct a coherent system of moral beliefs.

When general moral principles conflict with particular moral judgments, some moral theorists seem to assume that we should *always* adjust the general principles (Dancy 1993, 2004). But that's too simple, since our particular judgments might be questionable in ways that the principles reveal. Nor is it any better to assume that we should *always* adjust our particular judgments to fit general principles. This would leave us with no adequate test of which moral principles to hold. So, it seems that sometimes we need to give up particular judgments, and sometimes we need to give up general principles.

A similar choice arises when general principles conflict. For example, the principle of utilitarianism sometimes conflicts with agent-centered restrictions on lying, breaking promises, and killing innocent people. In such conflicts, we need to decide which principle to give up.

Such choices might seem easy when one and only one of the conflicting moral beliefs leads to many other conflicts and inconsistencies. However, each of these new conflicts just creates more choices for S about how to construct a coherent moral system. The question is how S can choose among the various ways to resolve epistemic conflicts throughout the system.

One standard method assigns an initial credence level for each particular belief or general principle and then prefers the consistent system with the highest total credence. When a general principle conflicts with a particular judgment, if S's initial credence in the general principle is high enough, and if other things are

---

19. If the principles in question relate moral properties to non-normative properties, they enable naturalistic arguments as discussed in section 7.2.

20. Explanatory connections play a special role in moral beliefs on some accounts. If an act morally ought not to be done only when there is a moral reason not to do it, then a moral believer might need to know what that moral reason is in order to understand what makes it true that this act morally ought not to be done. First-order coherence ensures principles that reveal *why* acts morally wrong, not just *that* they are wrong. Second-order principles are less revealing in this way, as we will see in section 10.3.

21. My favorite other cases include Boorse and Sorensen 1988 on ducking harm, and Parfit 1984, chapters 17–19, on the repugnant conclusion and mere addition.

equal, then S maximizes credence by abandoning or adjusting the particular judgment to remove the conflict with the general principle. But if S's initial credence in the particular judgment is high enough, then S maximizes credence by abandoning or adjusting the general principle to bring it in line with the particular judgment.

The problem is that this standard answer just reshuffles prejudices. If one person finds the general principle more attractive, then that person will give up the particular judgment. If another person finds the particular judgment more attractive, then that person will give up the general principle. It is hard to see any basis for the choice beyond prior beliefs. But these initial beliefs might not be reliable or justified, and they can be brought into narrow coherence even if they are unreliable and unjustified. So it is not enough to maximize credence.[22]

We want credibility, not just credence. For that, we must look beyond our initial beliefs in the conflicting principles and judgments themselves. Then we are not seeking only narrow first-order coherence.

10.3. Second-Order Coherence

To solve the problems for narrow coherence, we need some way to distinguish beliefs that are credible from those that are not. One natural move invokes second-order beliefs about which first-order beliefs are reliable or likely to be true.[23] Consider vision. Past experience teaches us that we are not reliable at identifying persons by sight when the light is bad, the distance is far, we do not know the person well enough, and so on. We often make mistakes and get corrected in such circumstances. In the absence of these conditions, however, our visual identifications seem reliable because they are rarely mistaken. When I say "Hi, Ken" to someone standing nearby who looks like a close friend, I have rarely been corrected. That's why I believe that I can reliably identify close friends by vision over short distances in good light. Given these second-order beliefs, suppose that I also believe that I am in such circumstances looking at my close friend, Ken. Then I can infer that it probably is Ken whom I see. The connection and, hence, coherence with my second-order beliefs about circumstances of reliability, thus, justify me in believing that it is Ken.

This approach in general epistemology can be extended to moral beliefs (Brink 1989, 125–43). Moral beliefs can also be justified by connections to second-order meta-ethical beliefs about the circumstances in which moral beliefs are reliable or unreliable. Most of us have learned by experience that we are more likely to change our moral beliefs later when we form moral beliefs quickly without adequate non-moral information, when we do not feel confident about our moral

22. This point is pressed by critics of coherentism, including Brandt (1979, 16–23), who asks, "Is one coherent set of fictions supposed to be better than another?"

23. In non-moral epistemology, this move is developed by BonJour 1985, who builds on the work of Wilfrid Sellars and Brand Blanshard.

beliefs, when we form our moral beliefs under the grip of strong emotions, when we have a personal stake in a certain moral belief, when other people disagree with us, and so on (section 9.4). Of course, the fact that we change our moral beliefs does not prove that the earlier moral beliefs were false. Still, while holding our current moral beliefs, if we now look back on former contrary moral beliefs, then we believe that those earlier beliefs were incorrect, which suggests to us that the circumstances of those earlier moral beliefs are less conducive to reliability than are our current circumstances.

Most of us have observed similar phenomena in other people. Teachers of ethics often encounter students with strong moral opinions who change their moral beliefs when they learn more facts about the topic or when they calm down emotionally or when the issue is described so as to exclude partiality. Friends and family follow the same patterns. Of course, we might agree with their earlier views, when they were ignorant, emotional, and partial. Still, since such circumstances so often change moral beliefs, and the earlier and later views cannot both be correct, moral beliefs seem more reliable when they remain stable even in the face of further information, emotional changes, or partiality.

This list of conditions is crude and incomplete. Added information is sometimes misleading. Some emotions support correct moral beliefs in some circumstances.[24] Confidence and stability in moral beliefs can result from close-mindedness. A more precise theory of the conditions of reliability for moral beliefs would need to add qualifications about the relevant kinds of information, emotion, and partiality. It would also take into account illusions of various kinds and social origins of moral beliefs (section 9.4). Luckily, I do not need to develop detailed second-order beliefs for my purposes here.

My point is only that moral believers can adopt and refine some such second-order beliefs about the circumstances in which their first-order moral beliefs are reliable. Moreover, these second-order beliefs can be justified by observations about the conditions under which people change their moral beliefs and see their former beliefs as mistaken. The general pattern of justification looks like this: S holds first-order moral beliefs A–M and remembers giving up earlier moral beliefs N–Z. S also holds non-moral beliefs A*–Z* about the circumstances under which A–Z are or were held. Together A–Z and A*–Z* enable S to generalize to second-order beliefs about the circumstances under which moral beliefs are reliable or unreliable.

These second-order beliefs can get further support from observations about when other people's moral beliefs are reliable or unreliable, according to S. It is not necessary for every moral believer to be reliable or unreliable under the same

24. Some critics might deny that emotions distort moral belief, since immorality *should* upset us. In my view, however, we should not ask simply *whether* emotions distort but, rather, *which* emotions distort in *which* circumstances. In particular, we need to distinguish the emotions that result from moral belief from those that exist prior to moral belief. When prior anger (or disgust), for example, makes someone's moral beliefs harsher, those moral beliefs will change when the anger (or disgust) fades. Such prior emotions, thus, introduce unreliability.

circumstances. However, in the absence of contrary indications, it is reasonable for S to assume that S's own moral beliefs are subject to the same influences as other people's moral beliefs. This third-person perspective is important, because most people are too confident and too reluctant to admit unreliability in their own moral beliefs.

Once these second-order beliefs are developed and justified, they can be used to justify first-order moral beliefs. A second-order belief about reliability under certain circumstances plus a corresponding description of the circumstances of a certain first-order moral belief implies that the first-order moral belief is reliable or likely to be true. This inference connects the second-order belief to the first-order belief, so the whole system gains coherence. The second-order beliefs give S's moral beliefs credibility, and not just credence, so S can answer the critic of narrow coherence who asks why any of the moral beliefs that cohere at the first-order level are credible.

It is admittedly not enough for S to have only a few second-order beliefs. If S forms second-order beliefs about several distorting factors but overlooks another distorting factor that makes S's moral belief unreliable in S's current circumstances, then S's system might not be comprehensive enough to justify S's moral belief. But that just shows why coherence requires comprehensiveness in addition to connectedness. A fair degree of comprehensiveness can be achieved. If S identifies enough distorting factors to explain all of the mistaken beliefs that S has identified in a wide survey of moral beliefs by S and others, then S has some reason to believe that S's second-order beliefs take account of all of the distorting factors that are likely to infect S's current moral belief. That would seem to justify S to an adequate degree.

Other problems arise in identifying S's circumstances. Even if we have a complete list of distorting factors, it is often hard to detect these factors in particular moral beliefs. It is usually easy to tell whether my vision is operating in good light, at short distances, and so on, but it is hard to tell whether a moral believer is adequately informed or impartial. Did this moral believer miss some relevant fact? Is self-interest involved in some roundabout way? Moral beliefs are almost never formed with complete information. They almost always affect the believer's welfare somehow (section 9.4.1). Still, there are ways to check. We can ask other people with more information and different interests. We can never be sure, but, if we are careful, we can have some reason to believe that our moral beliefs are not distorted by ignorance, partiality, or other factors in our second-order beliefs.

All of this together is supposed to justify some moral believers. If a moral believer finds that, in the absence of a certain range of factors, moral beliefs rarely need to be revised, are widely accepted by other people, and support and explain one another, then all of this together is *some* reason to believe in the reliability of moral beliefs formed under such circumstances. Moral believers cannot ever be sure that they did not overlook some crucial fact or that their self-interest is not operating below the surface, but some moral believers can still have some reason to believe that some moral beliefs are not distorted in such ways. Moreover, that reason is not defeated by any other beliefs, if the believer's system is comprehensive and coherent. So that reason seems adequate for the belief that some believers' moral beliefs are not distorted. In such a situation, moral believers can be justified in believing that a particular moral belief is true. The belief still *might* be false but that does not remove the reason to believe that it is true, since justification can be fallible.

Such second-order coherence can work without moral principles. Just as I can be justified in believing that the person I see is my friend Ken, even if I have no principle from which I can infer that it is Ken; so I can be justified to some extent in believing that an act is morally wrong if it seems morally wrong in circumstances that I am justified in believing to be conducive to reliability, even if I have no principle from which I can infer that it is wrong. Such justified beliefs still depend on inference, even if it is a second-order inference without substantive principles.[25]

If we ever achieve such second-order coherence in this way, it is quite an accomplishment. It is even more of an accomplishment if such second-order coherence converges with first-order coherence. This convergence is neither obvious nor inevitable. Some believers could find that their particular moral judgments cohere with certain general moral principles, but then their second-order beliefs imply that either the particular judgments or the general principles are unreliable. Or when such moral believers use their second-order beliefs to limit their first-order moral beliefs, they might find that these limited first-order moral beliefs do not cohere with each other at the first-order level.

When first-order coherence and second-order coherence do converge, moral believers are able to answer various challenges. At the first-order level, general moral principles explain why particular acts are morally wrong and, hence, why particular moral judgments are true. Second-order meta-ethical beliefs then provide reasons to believe that the first-order beliefs are not just coherent fictions but are, instead, true or at least probable. We can also use second-order beliefs to decide which first-order belief to reject when two first-order beliefs conflict.

10.4. Wider Coherence

We can go even further. Second-order coherence brings in other people's moral beliefs as evidence for second-order beliefs about reliability. Other people's moral beliefs can also lead more directly to new justified moral beliefs when other people tell us what they believe and we have reason to believe that they are reliable. We discussed this kind of testimony in section 7.4. The point here is just that coherentists can incorporate a role for testimony once they have second-order beliefs about when other people are reliable.[26]

---

25. It seems natural to describe such cases as know-how: just as I know how to pick Ken out of a crowd, so I know how to tell right from wrong, even if no principle implies that the act is wrong. My view, thus, captures a truth behind particularism (Dancy 1993, 2004) as well as the view that moral knowledge is (or can be) a kind of know-how (section 2.1).

26. Walker shows the importance of interpersonal coherence in 1996 and 1998.

Appearances can be relevant in a similar way. When a stick in water looks bent, I still might not believe that it is bent, so its appearance is distinct from belief. Nonetheless, if a stick looks straight, and if I have reason to believe that appearances are reliable in the circumstances, then this appearance gives me some reason to believe that the stick is straight (approximately). Analogously, if an act seems morally wrong, and if I have reason to believe that such moral seemings or appearances are reliable in the circumstances, then its appearance of moral wrongness gives me some reason to believe that the act is morally wrong. Such moral appearances are distinct from beliefs, since an act might seem wrong without my believing that it is wrong if I believe that appearances are misleading in the circumstances. Consequently, such appearances cannot fit into inferences directly as premises. Nonetheless, beliefs about appearances can provide premises for inferences. If I *believe* that the act *appears* immoral and I also believe that moral appearances are reliable in the circumstances, then I am able to infer that the act is probably immoral. In this way, moral appearances can be connected to moral beliefs so as to increase coherence.[27]

Moral emotions and feelings follow. To feel guilty is to feel bad in a certain way as a result of an appearance that some act you did was immoral (Roberts 1988). Our guilt feelings can then give us reason to believe that some acts are morally wrong insofar as they involve appearances that the act is morally wrong, but only if we have reason to believe that appearances are reliable in the circumstances. Our moral beliefs are better justified when they cohere with our emotions and feelings in this way (Tolhurst 1990; Nussbaum 1990, 40–42).

Many moral theorists (especially contractarians and contractualists) also derive moral principles from beliefs about rationality and impartiality. Arguments of this kind cannot provide independent justification for moral beliefs, as I argued in section 8.2. Nonetheless, the fact that the principles can be derived in this way shows that they cohere with certain accounts of impartiality and rationality. When such a story can be told about a wide range of moral beliefs, this reveals coherence in the set of moral beliefs. That makes the moral beliefs more justified at least if the accounts of rationality and impartiality have independent plausibility.

Meta-ethical beliefs also belong in the mix. If some moral beliefs better explain beliefs in deontic logic, then these connections provide reason to prefer those moral beliefs (Sinnott-Armstrong 1992). The same holds if some moral beliefs fit better with independently plausible definitions of moral terms or of morality. (See section 8.2.2, note 32.)

Even metaphysical views play a role. Rawls (1958, secs. 5–6) argues that his contractarian theory of justice incorporates a more plausible account of persons than does utilitarianism, which overlooks the separateness of persons. Parfit (1984, esp. chap. 15) counters by criticizing the view of personal identity that underlies non-utilitarian moral theories. Scheffler (1982, 67, 112–13, and 128) argues that the

---

27. Moral coherentism thereby incorporates the insights of Tolhurst 1998. This incorporation does not turn coherentism into foundationalism because moral seemings do not justify moral beliefs apart from inferences from second-order beliefs about when seemings are reliable.

need to take account of "personal independence" provides a rationale for agent-centered prerogatives that is lacking from but needed for agent-centered restrictions. Despite their differences on substantive morality, these philosophers all agree that moral beliefs need to be brought into coherence with non-moral beliefs about persons.

Rawls (1971) and his followers (such as Daniels 1979) also require justified moral beliefs to cohere with social science and with ideals of society. Admittedly, findings of social science and ideals of society are often controversial. Nonetheless, a moral belief that depends on an implausible view of how society actually works is itself implausible.

Even the historical origins of moral beliefs can provide reasons to reject inconsistent moral beliefs with dubious origins. Other historical facts, such as about how slavery fell, can also become important if one moral theory provides a better explanation of those facts than a competing theory, given shared assumptions (as discussed in section 8.1).

Other non-moral facts become relevant, not only because they are needed to apply general moral principles to specific cases, but also because moral principles can imply non-moral facts. For example, the principle that it is never morally wrong to maximize utility plus the principle that it is always morally wrong to punish an innocent person together imply that it never maximizes utility to punish any innocent person (Sturgeon 1984, 51). Whether someone believes the non-moral conclusion then determines whether that believer can consistently hold both of the moral principles.

In the end, there is no limit to the kinds of beliefs that might be used to test moral beliefs. By bringing all of these beliefs into the coherent system that makes moral beliefs justified, coherentists can incorporate the virtues of alternative moral epistemologies without their vices. This makes coherentism more plausible than any competing view that restricts itself to a more limited diet. None of the competitors alone is enough for what they can achieve together under the mantle of coherentism.

10.5. Which Contrast Class?

Let's assume that someone's moral belief system is completely coherent in all of these ways. The next question asks what this coherence achieves by way of justified belief. If this question asks what is justified without qualification, then it cannot be answered, for reasons I gave in sections 5.3 and 6.5–6.6. Pyrrhonists like me abjure all such unqualified epistemic judgments. So we need to distinguish contrast classes.

First, can coherence make any moral belief justified out of the extreme contrast class? Moral nihilism is in the extreme contrast class, so a believer cannot be justified out of that class unless the believer can rule out moral nihilism. A believer cannot rule out an alternative if the believer's grounds beg the question against that alternative. However, even a completely coherent moral belief system would beg the question against moral nihilism. First-order coherence obviously

uses moral beliefs that moral nihilists deny and explain away. Second-order coherence still depends on the same first-order moral beliefs to justify second-order
beliefs about conditions of reliability. Indeed, whenever coherentists include
moral beliefs in the overall system that makes a belief justified, that system as a
whole must beg the question against moral nihilism. Since moral nihilists do not
grant any moral beliefs, the coherence method cannot get started against moral
nihilism.[28]

It might seem that a coherentist could rule out moral nihilism if moral nihilism is less coherent overall than its denial. To see why that can't work, consider
a moral belief system that is as coherent as possible. Subtract all of its positive moral
beliefs. Compare the resulting nihilistic system with the original moral system by
the standards of coherence (section 10.1). Taking away all of the moral beliefs
cannot introduce any logical or semantic inconsistency or any epistemic conflict.
The nihilistic system will also be just as connected as the original moral belief
system. The logical, probabilistic, evidential, and explanatory relations among non-
moral beliefs in the original system will still hold in the nihilistic system, since
none of these connections depends on moral beliefs. As I argued in section 8.1,
there will always be non-moral explanations for non-moral facts within a completely coherent system. Finally, the nihilistic system includes all of the same non-
moral beliefs as the moral system, so the nihilistic system is just as comprehensive
apart from its lack of moral beliefs. That lack doesn't make moral nihilism less
comprehensive any more than lacking astrological beliefs makes non-astrological
systems less comprehensive than astrological systems. If there are moral facts, the
nihilistic system is missing something. But if there are no moral facts, the nihilistic
system misses nothing, and the moral system is deluded. Without an independent
reason to believe in positive moral facts, then, it begs the question to claim that the
nihilistic system is less comprehensive than the original moral system. Since the
nihilistic system is just as consistent, connected, and comprehensive, it is just as
coherent. So coherence cannot be used to rule out moral nihilism.

This should not be surprising. Coherence among empirical beliefs cannot rule
out general skeptical hypotheses about deceiving demons and brains in vats.[29]
Moral nihilism plays the parallel role in moral epistemology, so we should not
expect that coherence can rule out moral nihilism. In both areas, the most coherent possible belief system cannot be adequate to make any belief justified out of
the extreme contrast class.

Coherence still might make some moral believers justified out of the modest
contrast class. Imagine a moral believer with a completely coherent moral system
that implies that it is morally wrong for a doctor to lie to a certain patient about
that patient's diagnosis just so that the doctor can leave earlier on his vacation. The
moral believer has confirmed every non-moral fact that might seem relevant and

---

28. The illegitimacy of using non-shared moral beliefs in coherence arguments is admitted by Rawls
1951, 183; Daniels 1979, 259, and 1980, 85–89; and Brink 1989, 132. These coherentists do not, however, see
the relevance of this "independence constraint" to moral nihilism.

29. Despite valiant efforts at meta-justification by BonJour (1985, sec. 8.3) and Haack (1993, 213–22).

has compared every alternative moral belief that any normal person would take seriously in an everyday situation. The moral believer has achieved first-order coherence, so he can infer this particular belief from a general moral principle that plausibly explains why this act is wrong. The believer has also achieved second-order coherence, so he believes and has reason to believe that the circumstances under which he holds this particular belief are conducive to reliability. The believer has even achieved interpersonal coherence by asking many people with various backgrounds about the case, and they all agree with him (or any disagreement is easy to explain away as distorted by partiality, emotion, or illusion). This belief even fits with the believer's emotions and follows from principles that would be accepted by everyone who is rational and impartial in this believer's view. Add more levels of coherence if you want. The point is that this much coherence seems enough to make a moral believer justified out of the modest contrast class.

Thus, coherence can make some moral believers modestly justified, but coherence cannot make any moral believers extremely justified. This conclusion supports my moderate moral skepticism.

10.6. Objections

Critics raise many objections to coherentism. I cannot respond to them all adequately but I will quickly run through the main ones. I will focus on objections not to my claims about the limits of coherence but instead to my claims about what coherence can accomplish. My general thesis will be that these objections succeed in showing why coherence cannot make any moral beliefs justified out of the extreme contrast class, but they fail to show that no moral believer is ever justified out of more limited contrast classes.

10.6.1. *Back to Reality*

One common objection is that coherentism makes it too hard to be justified. When we inspect actual people's belief systems, they are never even close to completely coherent. First, everyone (or almost everyone) holds inconsistent beliefs, as paradoxes show. Second, they lack any beliefs to connect many different areas (such as history and physics, or economics and aesthetics). Third, their belief sets are far from comprehensive, since nobody knows more than a small part of all there is to know. We do gain a tremendous and varied body of information as we go through life, including information about when certain sources of belief are reliable. But there's always an awful lot left to learn. Thus, if justified belief required a completely coherent belief system, nobody would actually be justified in believing anything, even out of the modest contrast class.

This problem might seem to be ameliorated by my admission that actual inference is not required for justified belief. A believer need not work through any coherent system (or even be justified in believing that any system is coherent) in order to be justified in believing a particular belief within that system. All the believer needs is an ability to infer in the weak sense of having the requisite information encoded somehow in the believer's brain. But even that is lacking. No real brains encode enough information for a completely comprehensive and connected system.

Further, real people lack the ability to achieve coherence. Maybe some people could gain consistency by giving up lots of conflicting beliefs, but then they would lose connectedness and comprehensiveness. Since we cannot make our beliefs coherent, it might seem unfair for coherentists to say that we ought to make our beliefs coherent or for coherentists to condemn our beliefs as unjustified because we lack completely coherent belief systems.

Coherentists could respond by denying that "ought" implies "can" (Sinnott-Armstrong 1984). They could also deny that we ought to make our beliefs completely coherent. Coherentism is, after all, a theory about the conditions under which beliefs are justified, not a practical method that gives people advice about what they ought to do or believe.

Critics still might object that no actual believers are justified according to coherentism. This objection assumes that some believers are justified, so some skeptics might counter by arguing that epistemologists should not depend on that assumption. An account of what is needed to prove Goldbach's conjecture should not assume that anyone can prove that conjecture. Similarly, an account of what is needed for justified moral belief should not assume that people can have justified moral beliefs. Coherentism might give an accurate account of what is needed to be justified in believing something, even if it implies that nobody is or can be justified in believing anything. (Cf. section 1.4 on the problem of the criterion.)

Luckily, a more conciliatory response is available. The difficulty of achieving complete coherence would reveal serious problems for coherentism *if* coherentists claimed that believers are not justified *at all* when they fail to achieve a *completely* coherent belief system. However, coherentists need not and should not make that claim. Instead, they should distinguish degrees of coherence and of justified belief.[30]

One belief set is more coherent than another when the former is more consistent, connected, and comprehensive, that is, when it includes fewer inconsistencies, more inferential connections, and more beliefs in a wider variety of areas. On this basis, actual people's belief sets can be ordered by their coherence.[31] Degrees of coherence can then reflect degrees of justified belief. At the bottom of

---

30. Degrees of justified belief are excluded by many other moral epistemologies. A belief either is or is not validly derivable from non-normative or non-moral premises. On any particular point, either all rational impartial people agree or they do not all agree. Hence, such versions of naturalism and normativism do not allow moral beliefs to be justified to varying degrees. Moral explanationists might talk about how many observations a moral belief explains. Some moral intuitionists may refer to different levels of reflection or moral experience, so they can allow moral beliefs to be justified to different degrees. But even these moral epistemologists usually don't emphasize degrees. This might explain why this objection to coherentism seems so strong to such theorists.

31. This ordering will be weak in the sense that sometimes neither of two sets will be ranked above the other. Also, one set might be more coherent than another in ways that affect a certain belief and its status as justified, even though the other set is more coherent with respect to a different belief. But these complications do not affect my main points here.

this scale, some belief sets have so little coherence that beliefs in those sets are not justified at all. Somewhat higher up on the scale, some belief sets have a little coherence, maybe even enough to make believers pro tanto justified, but not enough to make believers adequately justified. Further up the scale, some believers' systems are as coherent as any actual person's system and as coherent as these or any believers could make them. All of these degrees can exist even if no actual belief system is at the very top of the scale.

Coherentists have to admit that no actual believer is maximally justified in believing anything, because nobody actually has a maximally coherent belief system, and a believer is maximally justified in believing only what coheres with a maximally coherent belief system of that believer. But this claim yields no objection. The fact that the believer's system is not maximally consistent, connected, and comprehensive means that further information might make the believer stop believing, or might make him unjustified in believing, what he now believes. So it would be epistemically best to be maximally justified.[32] That does not imply (or even suggest) that nothing whatsoever is accomplished when believers fall short of being maximally justified. Believers can be justified to some degree without being maximally justified.

The next question is whether the best actual moral system is coherent enough to make any moral belief justified *adequately*. The term "adequate" is tricky. The answer depends on which contrast class is at stake.

Believers cannot be justified out of the extreme contrast class unless they can rule out moral nihilism. Grounds for ruling out any alternative are not adequate if they beg the question. But all available grounds beg the question against moral nihilism, as I argued in section 10.5. Thus, moral believers cannot be adequately justified out of the extreme contrast class. To this extent, the objection succeeds.

Now suppose that moral nihilism is out of the question, so we are considering only whether coherence can make any moral belief adequately justified out of the modest contrast class. I think that it can. For some moral beliefs, all of the alternatives that would be taken seriously by normal people in everyday contexts conflict with moral beliefs formed under circumstances that usually lead to moral beliefs that are reliable according to other shared moral beliefs, and there is no support for those alternatives except beliefs that were formed in circumstances that usually distort moral beliefs, again according to shared moral beliefs. Sometimes the reliable moral beliefs also fall under general moral principles and fit well with non-moral beliefs. When all of this comes together in the right way, coherence can make moral beliefs adequately justified out of the modest contrast class. And it does seem to come together in the right way for some actual believers about some obvious moral issues, although they are still not maximally justified out of the modest contrast class (or even adequately justified out of the extreme contrast

32. It might be prudentially better to remain unjustified and deluded. It might also be an epistemic improvement for some actual people to admit that some of their beliefs are inconsistent. My point is only that the epistemic ideal is maximally justified belief.

class). This method can work even in some cases where moral beliefs were controversial before being tested by coherence.

Of course, there will be many other cases where everyday conflicting moral
beliefs cannot be dismissed as distorted, and where the believer does not have
adequate reason to believe in the reliability of his or her own moral beliefs. Then
the moral believer is not adequately justified even out of the modest contrast class.
This might happen either because everyday alternatives are overlooked or because
moral believers rely on grounds that are inadequate from a fully informed perspective. Many or even most of our actual moral beliefs fall into this class, because of the problems surveyed in section 9.4. Moral believers are often much
more confident than they have any epistemic right to be. But the fact that the
coherence method fails in most or even almost all cases does not show that coherence cannot make any moral beliefs modestly justified.

It is important not to overestimate this claim. The modest contrast class just
takes for granted that moral nihilism and other extreme views are false. To be
justified modestly in believing that lying is wrong is merely to be extremely justified in believing that lying is wrong given our everyday moral assumptions.
Nothing has been done to show that those assumptions themselves are true. Those
assumptions need not beg the question against other positions inside the moderate
contrast class. If every position in the contrast class includes those assumptions, but
those assumptions are enough to rule out some of the positions in the contrast
class, then those that are ruled out are incoherent.

Extreme skeptics might object that the best actual belief system still might not
be good enough. However, nothing would be gained by raising the standards in
this way. Indeed, we would lose any distinction between those who do well and
those who fall short epistemically. Compare a tough multiple-choice test. The best
performance is 50% correct, the class average is 30%, and the worst is 10%. The
teacher could fail all of the students on the grounds that they all got less than 60%.
The disadvantage would be a lack of discrimination. The best student and the
worst student would get the same grade even though the best student got five times
as many answers correct. Assuming otherwise normal circumstances, it seems
better to grade on a curve, so that the best student gets an adequate grade (maybe
even an A), and only the worst students fail.

Analogously, the test of coherence is tough. Few, if any, actual people get
close to even 60% comprehensiveness. Nonetheless, some people do much better
than others. If we say that nobody is ever adequately justified even out of a limited
contrast class, then we obliterate distinctions between the believers who are best
and worst off epistemically because they have the most and least coherent belief
systems. To regain those distinctions, we need to grade on a curve and hold that
some moral belief systems are coherent enough to make some moral believers
adequately justified out of some limited contrast classes.[33]

33. The analogy to grading on a curve was suggested by remarks of Nomi Arpaly in a very different
context. It is also useful to grade on a curve when assessing how much people help the needy. See Sinnott-
Armstrong 2002b, 151.

This point does not apply to extremely justified belief because all grounds beg the question against moral nihilism. The proper analogy is then to a test where students are asked to prove a theorem from axioms 1–4 alone without assuming axiom 5, and they all prove the theorem easily but only by assuming axiom 5 from the start. Even if some students give more convoluted arguments from axiom 5, they all fail equally as answers to the one question that was asked. Similarly, no moral believer has grounds that could begin to count as adequate for ruling out moral nihilism. That is why no moral believer can have extremely justified moral beliefs, even if some do have modestly justified moral beliefs.

10.6.2. *Problems of Truth*

Another group of problems concerns truth. It is easy to see why consistency increases the chance of truth, but coherentists also claim that we are better justified when our beliefs cohere with systems that are more comprehensive and connected. To make our belief systems more comprehensive and connected, we need to add more beliefs. We add beliefs about general principles to make our system more connected. We add beliefs about new topics to make our beliefs more comprehensive. The problem is that these new beliefs introduce new chances of error. Thus, a system is more likely to be false when it is more connected and comprehensive. Coherence reduces the probability of truth. But what makes a belief justified epistemically is supposed to increase the probability of truth. So how can coherence make a belief justified in an epistemic way? (Cf. Sayre-McCord 1985; Loeb 1996.)

This charge is misleading. It is less likely that all of a coherent system is true. Still, it is more likely that a coherent system contain more truths. It is also more likely that a higher percentage of a coherent system is true, compared with an equally comprehensive system that is not coherent (consistent and connected). And a certain belief can still be very likely given the coherent system. Besides, although coherence is not evidence of truth, coherentists need not claim that it is (Sayre-McCord 1996). What does get cited as evidence is a particular belief. When asked for evidence that theft is immoral, one might give first-order evidence by saying that theft is harmful and it is immoral to do what is harmful, or one might give second-order evidence by saying that reliable sources (authorities, emotions, and so on) show that theft is immoral. What one does not do is lay out one's entire coherent system of belief. That system is necessary for the evidence to be forceful, according to coherentists, but that does not mean that the system as a whole is the evidence. Consequently, what is the evidence can increase the probability that the belief is true, even though the system as a whole is less likely to be true than a smaller system.

What matters is that evidence for a belief can increase the conditional probability of that belief, given other beliefs; and the probability becomes more accurate as more evidence and counterevidence are added to the condition. What's the probability that Joe owns a Ford truck? Not very high if we don't know much about Joe. Then we find out that Joe is patriotic, so he always buys American products when he can; and he is a farmer, so he has many uses for a truck. Further information might point the other way: maybe he owns stock in General Motors, and not in Ford. But then more information can raise the probability again: maybe a friend reported seeing Joe driving a Ford truck. Or maybe Joe himself told us that he owns a Ford truck. Joe still might have been lying. Indeed, the more beliefs we form about Joe, the more chance that at least one of them is false. Nonetheless, our estimate of the unconditional probability that Joe owns a Ford truck will be more accurate if we consider its conditional probability given all of the information we have. If the probability given all of our information together is high enough, then we are (modestly) justified in believing that Joe owns a Ford truck.

That explains why coherence makes beliefs justified modestly but still epistemically. Our system of belief includes all of the information we have. If our belief system is consistent, then we can determine whether a belief is likely to be true, given our total information. If our belief system is comprehensive, then no further information would reduce the probability that our belief is true. That is why we seem justified in believing what is likely to be true given our coherent belief system. This way of being justified is epistemic because it requires high probability of truth.[34]

Critics still might object that high conditional probability given a belief system is not high probability of truth. Coherence requires only relations among beliefs inside a system. For the system to be coherent, its beliefs must be consistent, connected, and varied. But, except in special cases, whether beliefs are true depends on their relations to something other than just more beliefs. Beliefs are supposed to be true only when they correspond to facts that exist independently of whether those facts are actually believed, at least on one common view. This correspondence view of truth makes it hard to see how internal coherence could be evidence of truth (or even of probable truth).[35]

Some coherentists might respond that one has done as much as one can and as much as can be expected if one checks a moral belief against as many other beliefs as possible. Then one cannot be faulted, and one is permissively personally justified. This response does not solve the real problem. Permissive personal justification does not show that one's moral belief is true or likely to be true. Even if coherence is the best tool for forming moral beliefs, it still might have no relation to truth since even the best tools might fail most of the time.

An adequate response must begin by invoking second-order beliefs about reliability. If the process that produces a belief is reliable in the total circumstances, then the belief is likely to be true. The total circumstances would be considered in a comprehensive system. Thus, if a believer holds a coherent system that implies

34. If strict probabilities seem inapplicable to moral beliefs, I can replace "probable" with "reasonable," as in Lehrer 1990, 127–28. Then I could ask whether a moral belief is reasonable, given our total information. This way of being justified is still epistemic insofar as reasonableness is tied to truth.

35. This problem would not arise for moral constructivists or non-realists who hold that true moral beliefs are no more than justified moral beliefs. When such a view is combined with coherentism about justified belief, coherence is sufficient for truth, by definition. However, I already gave arguments against such views in sections 2.2 and 3.3.3.

that a belief results from a reliable process, then that believer has reason to believe that the belief is probably true.

It is still possible that the whole coherent system is way off base. Maybe none of its first-order moral beliefs are true, so neither are any its second-order beliefs that moral beliefs are reliable in certain circumstances. However, this hypothesis of massive delusion is an extreme position that is not and need not be taken seriously in everyday life. Thus, this alternative is excluded from the modest contrast class, which includes only positions that would be taken seriously by normal people in everyday life and need to be ruled out to meet the usual epistemic standards. Hence, even if second-order coherence cannot be used to rule out the possibility of massive delusion, second-order coherence still might make some moral beliefs epistemically justified out of the modest contrast class. Since a comprehensive system includes so much and connections within the system ensure that believers cannot give up one part without also giving up many others, when a belief coheres with a coherent system, the only way to question whether the belief is true is to reject massive parts of the coherent system. Such alternatives will be so extreme that, although we cannot rule them out, we do not need to be able to rule them out in order to achieve modestly justified belief.

Some critics still might ask why we need general moral principles if we already have a comprehensive set of moral beliefs about all particular cases. The answer depends on assumptions. If we assume that the physical world is interconnected causally and that causal connections depend on general laws, then a comprehensive set of true beliefs about the physical world must also be connected by general laws. Similarly, if we assume that acts are not just plain immoral but are immoral for reasons and that moral reasons depend on general moral principles, then a comprehensive set of true moral beliefs must also be connected by general principles. This assumption about the moral world is built into the widely accepted principle of universalizability. Once such assumptions are granted, it seems natural to include general principles in the epistemic ideal of coherence.

Of course, moral nihilists and others might deny that any moral principles are true.[36] Still, insofar as universalizability is built into common moral assumptions, the denial of all moral principles is an extreme position that would not be taken seriously in everyday life. Hence, it would not fall within the modest contrast class, so moral believers need not be able to rule it out in order to be justified out of the modest contrast class. Thus, the problems regarding general moral principles do not show that coherence cannot make any moral beliefs modestly justified.

My overall response to the problem of truth can be summarized in an analogy to a crossword puzzle.[37] When our answers fit the clues as well as the number of spaces throughout the entire puzzle, we seem justified in believing that our answers are correct. Our answers still might be incorrect in some systematic way, so

---

36. This might be denied by particularists, such as Dancy 1993 and 2004. However, there are strong reasons to doubt the truth and even coherence of the kind of particularism that excludes all general moral principles. See Sinnott-Armstrong 1999d; Hooker and Little 2000; and McKeever and Ridge forthcoming.

37. Modified from Haack 1993, 81–89, who used a similar analogy for a different purpose.

that they fit together. We also might have been using the wrong clues for these puzzle spaces. Such chances of global error cannot be ruled out by what we have available to us, if we have only the spaces and the clues. However, we can still be justified in believing our answers given that we are not misled in any such global way. Analogously, if our moral beliefs are comprehensive enough and fit together with each other and with all of our non-moral beliefs, then we cannot rule out massive delusion, so we cannot be justified extremely, but we can still be justified epistemically out of the modest class, that is, given that we are not way off base globally. This result, of course, leads directly to moderate moral skepticism.

10.6.3. *Circularity*

The next objection is that coherentism cannot solve the regress problem without lapsing into circularity. As before, suppose that S holds first-order moral beliefs A–M, gave up moral beliefs N–Z, holds non-moral beliefs A*–Z* about the circumstances under which A–Z are or were held, and generalizes to second-order beliefs, 1–9, about when moral beliefs are reliable. According to my coherentism, what justifies a certain first-order belief, A, is second-order beliefs, 1–9, plus A*. What justifies those second-order beliefs is first-order beliefs, B–Z, and their circumstances, B*–Z*. But then what justifies each of those other first-order moral beliefs, such as B, is the same second-order beliefs, 1–9, plus B*. And what justifies those second-order beliefs is the remaining first-order moral beliefs, A and C–Z. Thus, A is part of the justification of itself.

That part might not seem essential. However, if you are not allowed to use any more than C–Z to justify the second-order beliefs that justify the first-order belief B, then you are not allowed to use any more than D–Z to justify the second-order beliefs that justify the first-order belief C, and you are not allowed to use any more than E–Z to justify the second-order beliefs that justify the first-order belief D, and so on. This series leaves nothing when you work all the way down to justifying the last first-order belief that is supposed to be justified. So coherentists cannot escape the circularity. They do better to admit that circularity and explain why it is not vicious.

When is circularity vicious? If I argue that God exists because the Bible says so, and the Bible is correct because God wrote it, then my argument is circular. This circularity is vicious because, if this is my only reason to believe in God, I have no reason to rule out the contrary view that God did not write the Bible. I have no adequate response to critics who deny that assumption.

To determine whether the circles in moral coherentism are vicious in this way, we need to ask: can moral coherentists answer their critics? That depends. If moral coherentists claim to be justified out of the extreme contrast class, then they need to be able to rule out moral nihilism. But we already saw (section 10.5) that the most coherent set of moral beliefs begs the question against moral nihilism, so it cannot provide any adequate reason to rule out moral nihilism. Against this opponent, the circularity of coherentism is vicious in just the same way as the biblical argument for the existence of God.

The picture is very different when moral coherentists claim only to be justified out of the modest contrast class. That contrast class includes only views that would be taken seriously by normal believers in everyday life, so they must be ruled out to meet the usual epistemic standards. Moral nihilism is excluded. Normal believers assume that certain acts are morally wrong. This shared assumption provides a starting point to justify second-order beliefs and apply them back down to justify first-order moral beliefs. Thus, when S's moral belief system is coherent at both levels, S can answer critics. Imagine that S's moral beliefs cohere among themselves (first-order coherence) and also with meta-ethical beliefs about reliability (second-order coherence). First-order coherence helps S understand why S's moral beliefs are true. Second-order coherence gives S reason to believe that S's moral beliefs are true. A critic who questions a first-order belief can be answered by either a moral principle or a second-order belief about reliability or both. A critic who questions a first-order principle can be answered by particular first-order beliefs that provide evidence for the general principle or by a second-order belief about reliability or both. And a critic who questions a second-order belief about reliability can be answered by appealing to shared first-order beliefs made under the circumstances that are conducive to reliability according to the second-order principle. The only critic who cannot be answered is a critic who questions all of these beliefs together, that is, who rejects particular moral judgments, general moral principles, and also second-order beliefs about when moral beliefs are reliable. But the only critic who rejects all of those beliefs is a moral nihilist or, at least, an extreme position that is not included in the modest contrast class. Thus, every position within the modest contrast class can be handled by the coherence method. This shows why the circularity of coherentism is not vicious when only the modest contrast class is at stake.

10.6.4. *Something from Nothing*

A related objection argues that you cannot get something from nothing. If an argument starts from premises that are not justified, then the argument cannot justify its conclusion. But then, if individual beliefs are not justified apart from coherence, how can they become justified when they fit into a coherent system?

The answer is that starting points don't have to be positively justified as long as they are at least permissively justified (Sayre-McCord 1996). To see how this works, imagine that you remember that there was no lake in a certain valley last year. While driving today, you look into the valley from a distance, and you seem to see a lake. Your visual image is distinct enough that it is not epistemically irresponsible or wrong for you to believe that there is a lake, so you are permissively justified in believing that there is a lake, as opposed to a mirage. Nonetheless, you are not yet positively justified in believing this, because your evidence from the visual experience is balanced by your beliefs that there was no lake there last year and that lakes usually do not form so quickly. Then you drive farther on. From a different angle you still see a lake, but again your visual image is just distinct enough that by itself it would make you permissively justified but not positively justified in believing that there is a lake, as opposed to a mirage. Repeat ten times as you drive along. Now you can apply your background beliefs that lakes look the same from different angles, but mirages do not. Given that assumption, your collection of visual experiences from different angles make you positively justified in believing that there is a lake as opposed to a mirage. The point is that each visual perception alone would make you only permissively justified, but all of them together make you positively justified in believing that there is a lake in the valley. In this way, lots of permissively justified beliefs can together create positive justification.

Contrast a different kind of addition. Suppose that a believer seems to see her hand, seems to see her arm, seems to see her leg, and so on. Since there is no reason to deny these appearances, the believer is permissively justified in believing that each body part exists in the external world. Do these permissively justified beliefs add up to positive justification for believing that there is an external world? It seems not. Why not? The difference is that the hypothesis of a mirage would explain each visual experience individually but could not explain the conjunction of all the visual experiences together, since a normal mirage does not look the same from different angles. In contrast, the hypothesis that there is no external world but only appearances of an external world would explain the conjunction of all of the appearances of body parts. That is why the appearances cannot be used to rule out the hypothesis that explains them all together.

Now compare moral beliefs. Suppose that an act seems morally wrong from the perspective of the agent. It also seems morally wrong from the perspective of each of the affected parties. It also seems morally wrong from the perspectives of uninvolved bystanders with various backgrounds. Each of these beliefs by itself might be permissively but not positively justified. All together, can they become positively justified? That depends on the contrast class.

Suppose the contrast class includes moral nihilism. That hypothesis is supposed to include an explanation of the conjunction of all of the moral appearances together, just like the hypothesis that there is no external world but only appearances of external objects. Consequently, permissively justified moral beliefs cannot add up to positive justification out of a contrast class that includes moral nihilism.

Nonetheless, if the contrast class does not include moral nihilism or any other extreme hypothesis, then how could a contrary hypothesis explain the permissively justified beliefs? One suggestion might be that one person's moral beliefs are distorted by some special self-interest. But if that self-interest is not shared by other people, then it could not explain why other people also have the same permissively justified moral belief.[38] And if that kind of self-interest is shared by all of the other

38. Early on many people *might* have been permissively justified in believing that it was fair to deny votes to women, because this belief was shared by almost everyone, including women, except a few whose moral beliefs were dismissed as self-interested and uninformed. However, as women became better educated, and as more men embraced female suffrage, it became harder to use self-interest or ignorance to explain away the widespread permissively justified moral beliefs that it is unfair to deny votes to women. This might be part of the reason why successful political movements usually emphasize diversity.

people, then it leads to a much more radical hypothesis that is not part of the modest contrast class. Similarly, a variety of descriptions can limit framing effects, a variety of moods can limit effects of emotions, and a variety of cultures can reduce the effects of cultural distortions. Thus, permissively justified moral beliefs become harder to explain away if they are stable across descriptions, moods, and cultures. When the consensus is broad enough, the only undermining explanation would be too extreme to be included in the modest contrast class. Then it could not preclude modestly justified moral belief.

Overall, then, permissively justified moral beliefs can add up to make moral beliefs positively justified when moral nihilism is *not* included in the contrast class but not when moral nihilism *is* included in the contrast class. This new perspective again points in the direction of moderate moral skepticism.

10.6.5. Underdetermination

Another common objection to coherence theories is that incompatible belief systems can be equally coherent. This possibility must be granted as an abstract point about belief systems without reference to believers. A moral belief system based on the Doctrine of Double Effect (section 10.2) might be just as coherent as a contrary moral belief system that denies that doctrine.

What is not so clear is why this is an objection to coherentism. The point might concern truth. Incompatible beliefs cannot both be true. They are both justified if coherence makes beliefs justified. But that shows at most that some justified beliefs are false. That's not news. Nor is it a problem. Coherentists admit from the start that justification is fallible.

Justified contrary beliefs are easy to understand once believers enter the discussion. Suppose Jay's moral beliefs form a coherent system including the Doctrine of Double Effect. Kay's equally coherent moral belief system denies that doctrine. Then, according to coherentism, Jay is justified in believing the Doctrine of Double Effect, and Kay is justified in believing its denial. How does this happen? Simple: they use different experience and beliefs. Jay uses his. Kay uses hers. When they use different evidence, different believers can be justified in contrary beliefs. Jay might be justified in believing that Elle is in New York because Jay seems to see Elle there (or Elle tells Jay that she is in New York), while Kay is justified in believing that Elle is not in New York because Kay seems to see Elle in Boston (or Elle tells Kay that Elle is in Boston). Since Jay and Kay base their beliefs on different visual experiences (or testimony) that might be equally reliable, Jay and Kay can be equally justified in holding contrary beliefs. Analogously, if Jay and Kay base their contrary moral beliefs about the Doctrine of Double Effect on different moral emotions and background beliefs that are equally reliable, then Jay and Kay can also be equally justified in holding contrary moral beliefs.

If their systems of belief are comprehensive, Jay and Kay must include beliefs that the other person has (and is justified in) a contrary belief. Then each needs some explanation of why the other is misguided. But such explanations might be available to both Jay and Kay (even if the other person has reason to discount the explanation and hold on to the contrary belief). In the end, it is not surprising or problematic that different people can be equally justified in holding contrary moral beliefs.

It would be a problem if a single person were justified in holding contrary beliefs. But that can't happen. If Em is justified in believing the Doctrine of Double Effect as opposed to some contrary moral principle, then Em cannot also be justified in believing that contrary principle as opposed to the Doctrine of Double Effect. The reason is simple: to be justified in believing D as opposed to C, a believer must be able to rule out C and not able to rule out D (section 5.1). But then this believer cannot be able to rule out D and not C. So this believer cannot also be justified in believing C as opposed to D. This exclusion holds for all moral epistemologies, including coherentism.

It should not be surprising that moral believers cannot be justified in believing either of two contrary moral beliefs when they could just as coherently believe either one or the other. If both moral beliefs cohere with everything that this particular believer believes (including beliefs about reliability, about emotions, and about other people's beliefs), then this believer has no basis for choosing between the contrary beliefs. That is why the believer is not justified in believing either of them.

The deepest charge is that this situation arises all the time.[39] Whenever a moral believer accepts a coherent belief system, that believer always could instead find some incompatible system that is equally coherent. Indeed, if a moral believer wants to reject any particular conclusion, the believer can always deny that conclusion and modify other principles to form another system that is just as consistent, connected, and comprehensive as the original system. Abstractly, if a moral believer holds the generalization:

(G) All acts of kind K are morally wrong.

and accepts the fact that:

(F) Act A is of kind K.

then the moral believer can infer:

(W) A is morally wrong.

However, if the moral believer wants to reject the conclusion, (W), then the moral believer can find some additional property P of A and replace (G) with:

(G-) All acts of kind K, except those with property P, are morally wrong.

Now the moral believer can consistently reject (W).

---

39. This problem is analogous in some respects to Goodman's new riddle of induction (1979, 72–83). In terms of contrast classes, Goodman's problem can be partly resolved by saying that past experience justifies us in believing that emeralds are green as opposed to blue but does not justify us in believing that emeralds are green as opposed to grue.

For example, suppose a doctor believes:

(L) All acts of a doctor lying to a patient about that patient's diagnosis to prevent the patient from becoming depressed are morally wrong.

The doctor then diagnoses a patient with a terminal illness, so he infers that:

(M) My lying to this patient would be morally wrong.

But this case is complicated. The patient is just about to leave for a week of family vacation. The week away will not interfere with any treatment for the patient, and the patient is unlikely to suffer from any symptoms during that week. Moreover, the doctor knows the family well and believes that the vacation will help to strengthen the patient's family, so the family and the patient will be better able to deal with the patient's coming illness and demise. The doctor also believes that, if she reveals the diagnosis to the patient, this patient will become depressed and the depression will hurt the vacation and the family. So the doctor wants to reject (M). Easy! Just replace (L) with:

(L-) All acts of a doctor lying to a patient about that patient's diagnosis to prevent the patient from becoming depressed, except when lying would help everyone involved, are morally wrong.

A doctor who adopts (L-) must allow lying in all other cases where this exception applies. If that is acceptable, then the doctor can form a belief system without (L) that is just as consistent, connected, and comprehensive as the doctor's earlier belief system with (L).

There is a complication: the doctor needs to explain the exception in order for the new system to have as many connections as in the old system. Sometimes that won't be easy. If the new principle says that it is morally wrong for doctors to lie except on Tuesday, then it will be hard to explain what is morally special about Tuesday. Still, normal people do not cite unimportant features when they make an exception. They usually (maybe even always) have some reasons to allow the exceptions that they allow. Their reasons will depend on features of the case that can explain the desired exception clauses. So it might seem as if people can always modify principles and avoid conclusions that they dislike.

In *practice*, this problem usually gets solved by believers being unwilling or unable to modify their beliefs in the required ways. Many doctors who want to lie to a particular patient will find themselves incapable of accepting the changes that they need to make in their moral beliefs to maintain consistency. They cannot make the revised beliefs seem plausible to themselves; nor can they bring their emotions and practices in line with the revised moral beliefs.

In *principle*, however, they *could* make those changes. That possibility raises the question of whether they are justified in believing the principle that they hold. However, such questions about being justified without qualification are misguided, for reasons given in sections 5.3 and 6.5–6.6. Whether a moral believer in this situation is justified depends on the contrast class at issue.

If a particular moral believer could in principle hold a coherent system with (L) or a contrary equally coherent system with (L-), then that moral believer is not justified in believing (L) as opposed to (L-). Nonetheless, that particular moral believer might be justified in believing (L) as opposed to many other alternatives, including every alternative that this particular believer is capable of believing. Indeed, if the only exception clauses that would allow the believer to avoid (L) are too ad hoc to be explicable in any way that would be acceptable to any normal believer, then this person's background beliefs and moral experiences might make this person able to rule out every other alternative that would be considered seriously by any normal person in an everyday situation, as well as every alternative that must be ruled out to meet any usual epistemic standards. If so, then coherence can make moral believers modestly justified in some cases.

10.7. Conclusions

All of this leads to moderate moral skepticism. Even maximal coherence cannot rule out moral nihilism or other extreme alternatives because the moral assumptions in the coherent system beg the question against such extreme opponents, and moral nihilism can be as coherent as its denial. Since moral nihilism is in the extreme contrast class, moral believers are never justified in holding any moral beliefs out of that extreme contrast class. Extremely justified moral belief is unattainable. That's the skeptical side of my conclusion.[40]

Nonetheless, moral nihilism is not in the modest contrast class, because no normal person takes moral nihilism seriously in any everyday situation, so moral believers do not need to rule out moral nihilism in order to meet the usual epistemic standards. A high enough degree of coherence can in principle make some moral believers able to rule out every alternative in the modest contrast class. Such moral believers can in principle be justified in holding moral beliefs out of the modest contrast class. Modestly justified moral belief is attainable. That's the moderate side of my skepticism.

Is any actual person's system of moral beliefs coherent enough to make any actual moral believer modestly justified? This question would require detailed analysis of some actual person's actual moral beliefs. It would also require a complete list of the alternatives in the modest contrast class. I have not engaged in that enterprise. Consequently, I cannot show that any actual person is modestly justified in any moral belief.

It does seem clear, nonetheless, that some actual moral believers are justified out of more limited contrast classes. Although most people are overconfident when forming moral beliefs, we can be careful, and some of us are very careful. This happens with obvious beliefs, such as that it is morally wrong to torture children just for fun. It can even happen in some previously controversial cases: sometimes the moral beliefs of a hospital ethics committee are coherent enough to rule out all of the options or alternative moral beliefs that they consider. And sometimes they

---

40. Some critics see this side of my conclusion as obvious, but part II has discussed several philosophers who deny it.

consider quite a few alternatives (when they have enough time). They might even develop their position to a point where they will have a response to any alternative that any actual person would seriously suggest. Such actual moral believers are then justified in holding moral beliefs out of large but limited contrast classes.

Impatient critics will still ask: are any moral believers justified (without qualification)? As I argued in chapter 5, this question means: are any moral believers justified out of the relevant contrast class? We can't answer that question without knowing which contrast class is the relevant one. But I argued in sections 5.3 and 6.5–6.6 that we should suspend belief about which contrast class is the relevant one. For that reason, I refuse to say whether anyone in principle or practice is justified without qualification in holding any moral belief. That is the Pyrrhonian side of my position.

Is my overall position, then, really skepticism? Some critics (and friends) tell me that I am not really a moral skeptic, either because I do not claim that no moral believers are justified without qualification or because I allow that (and show how) some moral believers are justified out of limited contrast classes. I honestly do not care whether or not my position gets labeled "skepticism." I call it by that name to reveal its connections to the Pyrrhonian tradition. But the name does not matter to any issue of substance.

What does matter is what we can accomplish and what we cannot accomplish when we try to justify our moral beliefs. It also matters which debates in epistemology make sense and which do not. I hope that this book has made a contribution towards clarifying those issues, whether or not my conclusions get classified as skeptical.

References

Achinstein, Peter. 2001. *The Book of Evidence*. New York: Oxford University Press.

Allen, Amy. Forthcoming. "Discourse Ethics versus Moral Skepticism: The Foucault/ Habermas Debate Reconsidered."

Annis, David B. 1978. "A Contextualist Theory of Epistemic Justification." *American Philosophical Quarterly* 15:213–19.

Anscombe, G. E. M. 1958. "Modern Moral Philosophy." *Philosophy* 33:1–19.

Audi, Robert. 1993. *The Structure of Justification*. New York: Cambridge University Press.

———. 1996. "Intuitionism, Pluralism, and the Foundations of Ethics." In *Moral Knowledge? New Readings in Moral Epistemology*, ed. Walter Sinnott-Armstrong and Mark Timmons: 101–36. New York: Oxford University Press.

———. 1998. *Epistemology*. London: Routledge.

———. 2002. "An Internalist Theory of Normative Grounds." *Philosophical Topics* 30:19–46.

———. 2004. *The Good in the Right: A Theory of Intuition and Intrinsic Value*. Princeton: Princeton University Press.

Austin, J. L. 1961. "A Plea for Excuses." In *Philosophical Papers*. New York: Oxford University Press.

Ayer, A. J. 1946. *Language, Truth, and Logic*. 2nd edition. London: Gollantz. 1st edition published 1935.

Baron, Jonathan. 1994. "Nonconsequentialist Decisions." *Behavioral and Brain Sciences* 17:1–42 (including comments and response).

Baron, Marcia. 2002. "Character, Immorality, and Punishment." In *Rationality, Rules, and Ideals*, ed. Walter Sinnott-Armstrong and Robert Audi:243–58. Lanham, MD: Rowman and Littlefield.

Bellah, R. N., Madson, R., Sullivan, W. M., Swindler, A., and Tipton, S. M. 1985. *Habits of the Heart*. New York: Harper and Row.

Beyleveld, Deryck. 1991. *The Dialectical Necessity of Morality*. Chicago: University of Chicago Press.

Bird, Alexander. 2001. "Scepticism and Contrast Classes." *Analysis* 61:97–107.

Blackburn, Simon. 1973. "Moral Realism." Reprinted in *Essays in Quasi-Realism*. New York: Oxford University Press, 1993.

———. 1984. *Spreading the Word*. New York: Oxford University Press.

———. 1985. "Supervenience Revisited." Reprinted in *Essays in Quasi-Realism*. New York: Oxford University Press, 1993.

———. 1988. "Attitudes and Contents." Reprinted in *Essays in Quasi-Realism*. New York: Oxford University Press, 1993.

———. 1993. *Essays in Quasi-Realism*. New York: Oxford University Press.

———. 1996. "Securing the Nots: Moral Epistemology for the Quasi-Realist." In *Moral Knowledge? New Readings in Moral Epistemology*, ed. Walter Sinnott-Armstrong and Mark Timmons: 82–100. New York: Oxford University Press.

———. 1998. *Ruling Passions*. Oxford: Clarendon Press.

BonJour, Laurence. 1985. *The Structure of Empirical Knowledge*. Cambridge: Harvard University Press.

———. 2002. *Epistemology*. Lanham, MD: Rowman and Littlefield.

Boorse, Christopher, and Sorensen, Roy. 1988. "Ducking Harm." *Journal of Philosophy* 85:115–34.

Boyd, Richard. 1988. "How to Be a Moral Realist." In *Essays on Moral Realism*, ed. Geoffrey Sayre-McCord. Ithaca: Cornell University Press.

Brandt, Richard. 1954. *Hopi Ethics*. Chicago: University of Chicago Press.

———. 1979. *A Theory of the Good and the Right*. Oxford: Clarendon Press.

Brennan, Geoffrey, and Pettit, Philip. 2004. *The Economy of Esteem*. New York: Oxford University Press.

Brink, David. 1989. *Moral Realism and the Foundations of Ethics*. New York: Cambridge University Press.

Burgess, J. A. 1998. "Error Theories and Values." *Australasian Journal of Philosophy* 76(4):534–52.

Burgess, J. P. 1979. "Against Ethics." Unpublished manuscript, Department of Philosophy, Princeton University.

Chaiken, S. 1980. "Heuristic versus Systematic Information Processing and the Use of Source versus Message Cues in Persuasion." *Journal of Personality and Social Psychology* 39:752–66.

Chisholm, Roderick M. 1982. "The Problem of the Criterion." In *The Foundations of Knowing*. Minneapolis: University of Minnesota Press.

———. 1989. *Theory of Knowledge*. 3rd edition. Englewood Cliffs, NJ: Prentice-Hall.

Clifford, W. K. 1879. "The Ethics of Belief." In *Lectures and Essays*. London: Macmillan.

Copp, David. 1990. "Explanation and Justification in Ethics." *Ethics* 100:237–58.

———. 1991. "Moral Skepticism," *Philosophical Studies* 62:203–33.

———. 1995. *Morality, Normativity, and Society*. New York: Oxford University Press.

Copp, David, and Zimmerman, David, eds. 1984. *Morality, Reason, and Truth*. Totowa, NJ: Rowman and Allanheld.

Craig, William Lane, and Sinnott-Armstrong, Walter. 2004. *God? A Debate between a Christian and an Atheist*. New York: Oxford University Press.

Dancy, Jonathan. 1993. *Moral Reasons*. Oxford: Blackwell.

———. 2004. *Ethics without Principles*. New York: Oxford University Press.

Daniels, Norman. 1979. "Wide Reflective Equilibrium and Theory Acceptance in Ethics." *Journal of Philosophy* 76:256–82.

———. 1980. "Reflective Equilibrium and Archimedian Points." *Canadian Journal of Philosophy* 10:83–103.

Davidson, Donald. 1967. "The Logical Form of Action Sentences." In *The Logic of Decision and Action*, ed. N. Rescher. Pittsburgh: University of Pittsburgh Press.

Dawkins, Richard. 1976. *The Selfish Gene*. Oxford: Oxford University Press.

DePaul, Michael, and Ramsey, W., eds. 1998. *Rethinking Intuition: The Psychology of Intuition and Its Role in Philosophical Inquiry*. Lanham, MD: Rowman and Littlefield.

DeRose, Keith. 1999. "Contextualism: An Explanation and Defense." In *The Blackwell Guide to Epistemology*, ed. John Greco and Ernest Sosa. Oxford: Blackwell.

DeRose, Keith, and Warfield, Ted, eds. 1999. *Skepticism: A Contemporary Reader*. New York: Oxford University Press.

Descartes, René. 1641. *Meditations*.

DeVoto, Bernard. 1942. *The Year of Decision: 1846*. Boston: Houghton Mifflin.

Doris, John. 2002. *Lack of Character*. New York: Cambridge.

Dorr, Cian. 2002. "Non-Cognitivism and Wishful Thinking." *Nous* 33:558–72.

Dreier, James. 1996. "Expressivist Embeddings and Minimalist Truth." *Philosophical Studies* 83:29–51.

Dretske, Fred. 1970. "Epistemic Operators." *Journal of Philosophy* 67:1007–23.

Dworkin, Ronald. 1996. "Objectivity and Truth: You'd Better Believe It." *Philosophy and Public Affairs* 25:87–139.

Fogelin, Robert. 1967. *Evidence and Meaning*. New York: Routledge.

———. 1994. *Pyrrhonian Reflections on Knowledge and Justification*. New York: Oxford University Press.

Fogelin, Robert, and Sinnott-Armstrong, Walter. 2005. *Understanding Arguments*. 7th edition. Belmont, CA.: Thomson/Wadsworth.

Foot, Philippa. 1967. "The Problem of Abortion and the Doctrine of the Double Effect." *Oxford Review* 5. Reprinted in *Virtues and Vices*. Berkeley: University of California Press, 1978.

———. 1978. *Virtues and Vices*. Berkeley: University of California Press.

Foucault, Michel. 1979. *Discipline and Punish*. Trans. Alan Sheridan. New York: Random House.

Frankfurt, Harry. 1971. "Freedom of the Will and the Concept of a Person." *Journal of Philosophy* 68:5–20.

Garner, Richard. 1994. *Beyond Morality*. Philadelphia: Temple University Press.

Gauthier, David. 1986. *Morals by Agreement*. Oxford: Clarendon Press.

———. 1991. "Why Contractarianism?" In *Contractarianism and Rational Choice*, ed. Peter Vallentyne: 15–30. New York: Cambridge University Press.

Geach, P. T. 1960. "Ascriptivism." *Philosophical Review* 69:221–25.

———. 1965. "Assertion." *Philosophical Review* 74:449–65.

Gert, Bernard. 1990. "Rationality, Human Nature, and Lists." *Ethics* 100:279–300.

———. 1998. *Morality*. New York: Oxford University Press.

Gettier, Edmund. 1963. "Is Justified True Belief Knowledge?" *Analysis* 23:121–23.

Gewirth, Alan. 1974. "The 'Is-Ought' Problem Resolved." Reprinted in *Human Rights*. Chicago: University of Chicago Press, 1982.

———. 1978. *Reason and Morality*. Chicago: University of Chicago Press.

Gibbard, Allan. 1990. *Wise Choices, Apt Feelings*. Cambridge: Harvard University Press.

———. 2003. *Thinking How to Live*. Cambridge: Harvard University Press.

Goldman, Alvin. 1976. "Discrimination and Perceptual Knowledge." *Journal of Philosophy* 73:771–91.

———. 1986. *Epistemology and Cognition*. Cambridge: Harvard University Press.

Goodman, Nelson. 1979. *Fact, Fiction, and Forecast*. 3rd edition. Indianapolis: Hackett Publishing Company.

Gowans, Christopher, ed. 2000. *Moral Disagreements*. London: Routledge.

Greene, Joshua. Forthcoming. *The Terrible, Horrible Truth about Morality*.

Greene, Joshua, and Haidt, Jonathan. 2002. "How (and Where) Does Moral Judgment Work?" *Trends in Cognitive Science* 6:517–23.

Greene, Joshua, Nystrom, L. E., Engell, A. D., and Darley, J. M. 2004. "The Neural Bases of Cognitive Conflict and Control in Moral Judgment." *Neuron* 44:389–400.

Greene, Joshua, Sommerville, R., Nystrom, L. E., Darley, J. M., and Cohen, J. D. 2001, September. "An fMRI Investigation of Emotional Engagement in Moral Judgment." *Science* 293:2105–8.

Haack, Susan. 1993. *Evidence and Inquiry*. Oxford: Blackwell.

Habermas, Jürgen. 1990. *Moral Consciousness and Communicative Action*. Trans. C. Lenhart and S. Weber. Cambridge: MIT Press.

Haidt, Jonathan. 2001. "The Emotional Dog and Its Rational Tail: A Social Intuitionist Approach to Moral Judgment." *Psychological Review* 108:814–34.

Haidt, Jonathan, and Baron, Jonathan. 1996. "Social Roles and the Moral Judgment of Acts and Omissions." *European Journal of Social Psychology* 26:201–18.

Haidt, Jonathan, et al. 1993. "Affect, Culture, and Morality, or Is It Wrong to Eat Your Dog?" *Journal of Personality and Social Psychology* 65:613–28.

Hare, R. M. 1952. *The Language of Morals*. Oxford: Clarendon Press.

———. 1965. *Freedom and Reason*. Oxford: Clarendon Press.

———. 1981. *Moral Thinking*. Oxford: Clarendon Press.

Harman, Gilbert. 1977. *Morality*. New York: Oxford University Press.

———. 1998. "Responses to Critics." *Philosophy and Phenomenological Research* LVIII: 207–13.

Harman, Gilbert, and Thomson, Judith Jarvis. 1996. *Moral Relativism and Moral Objectivity*. Oxford: Blackwell.

Harsanyi, John. 1982. "Morality and the Theory of Rational Behavior." Reprinted in *Utilitarianism and Beyond*, ed. A. Sen and B. Williams. Cambridge: Cambridge University Press.

Hawthorne, John. 2004. *Knowledge and Lotteries*. Oxford: Clarendon Press.

Hinckfuss, Ian. 1987. "The Moral Society: Its Structures and Effects." Preprint Series in Environmental Philosophy, Department of Philosophy, 16, Australian National University.

Hintikka, Jaakko. 1969. "Deontic Logic and its Philosophical Morals." In *Models for Modalities*. Dordrecht, Netherlands: Reidel.

Hobbes, Thomas. 1651. *Leviathan*. New York: Macmillan, 1962.

Hooker, Brad, ed. 1996. *Truth in Ethics*. Oxford: Blackwell.

Hooker, Brad, and Little, Margaret, eds. 2000. *Moral Particularism*. Oxford: Clarendon Press.

Horowitz, Tamara. 1998. "Philosophical Intuitions and Psychological Theory." In *Rethinking Intuition: The Psychology of Intuition and Its Role in Philosophical Inquiry*, ed. Michael DePaul and W. Ramsey. Lanham, MD: Rowman and Littlefield. An earlier version appeared in *Ethics* 108 (1998): 367–85.

Hudson, W. D., ed. 1969. *The Is-Ought Question*. New York: St. Martin's.

Hume, David. 1739–40. *A Treatise of Human Nature*, ed. L. A. Selby-Bigge. Oxford: Clarendon Press, 1888.

———. 1748. *Enquiries Concerning Human Understanding and Concerning the Principles of Morals*, ed. L. A. Selby-Bigge. Oxford: Clarendon Press, 1888.

Hurka, Thomas. 1993. *Perfectionism*. New York: Oxford University Press.

Jackson, Frank. 1998. *From Metaphysics to Ethics*. Oxford: Clarendon Press.

Jackson, Frank, and Pettit, Philip. 1998. "A Problem for Expressivism." *Analysis* 58:329–51.

Jackson, Frank, and Pettit, Philip, and Smith, Michael. 2000. "Ethical Particularism and Patterns." In *Moral Particularism*, ed. Brad Hooker and Margaret Little:79–99. Oxford: Clarendon Press.

James, William. 1896, June. "The Will to Believe." *New World*:327–47.

Joyce, Richard. 2001. *The Myth of Morality*. New York: Cambridge University Press.

Kahneman, D., Slovic, P., and Tversky, A., eds. 1982. *Judgment under Uncertainty: Heuristics and Biases*. Cambridge: Cambridge University Press.

Kahneman, D., and Tversky, A. 1979. "Prospect Theory: An Analysis of Decision under Risk." *Econometrica* 47:263–91.

Kant, Immanuel. 1785. *Foundations of the Metaphysics of Morals*. Trans. Lewis White Beck. Indianapolis: Bobbs-Merrill, 1959.

Kaplan, David. 1989. "Demonstratives." In *Themes from Kaplan*, ed. Joseph Almog, John Perry, and Howard Wettstein:481–563. New York: Oxford University Press.

Karjalainen, Antti, and Morton, Adam. 2003. "Contrastive Knowledge." *Philosophical Explorations* VI(2):74–89.

Kitcher, Philip. 1985. *Vaulting Ambition*. Cambridge: MIT Press.

———. 1999. "Essence and Perfection." *Ethics* 100:59–83.

Kohlberg, Lawrence. 1981. "From *Is* to *Ought*: How to Commit the Naturalistic Fallacy and Get Away with It in the Study of Moral Development." In *Essays on Moral Development*, Vol. I, *The Philosophy of Moral Development*:101–89. San Francisco: Harper and Row.

Kvanvig, Jonathan. 2003. *The Value of Knowledge and the Pursuit of Understanding*. Cambridge: Cambridge University Press.

Lackey, Douglas. 1986. "Taking Risk Seriously." *Journal of Philosophy* 83:633–40.

Lehrer, Keith. 1974. *Knowledge*. Oxford: Clarendon Press.

———. 1990. *Theory of Knowledge*. Boulder: Westview.

Levi, Isaac. 1980. *The Enterprise of Knowledge*. Cambridge: MIT Press.

Levinson, Stephen. 1983. *Pragmatics*. New York: Cambridge University Press.

Lewis, David. 1996. "Elusive Knowledge." *Australasian Journal of Philosophy* 74:549–67.

Lipton, Peter. 1991a. "Contrastive Explanation." In *Explanation and Its Limits*, ed. D. Knowles. Cambridge: Cambridge University Press.

———. 1991b. *Inference to the Best Explanation*. New York: Routledge.

Lockhart, Ted. 2000. *Moral Uncertainty and Its Consequences*. New York: Oxford University Press.

Loeb, Don. 1996. "Generality and Moral Justification." *Philosophy and Phenomenological Research* 56:79–96.

———. 1998. "Moral Realism and the Argument from Disagreement." *Philosophical Studies* 90:281–303.

Lord, C. G., Ross, L., and Lepper, M. R. 1979. "Biased Assimilation and Attitude Polarization: The Effects of Prior Theories on Subsequently Considered Evidence." *Journal of Personality and Social Psychology* 37:2098–99.

MacIntyre, Allison. 2001. "Doing Away with Double Effect," *Ethics* 111:219–55.

Mackie, J. L. 1946. "A Refutation of Morals." *Australasian Journal of Philosophy* 24:77–90.

———. 1977. *Ethics: Inventing Right and Wrong*. Harmondsworth, Middlesex, UK: Penguin.

———. 1978. "The Law of the Jungle: Moral Alternatives and Principles of Evolution." *Philosophy* 53:455–64.

———. 1980. *Hume's Moral Theory*. London: Routledge.

McKeever, Sean, and Ridge, Michael. Forthcoming. *Principled Ethics: Generalism as a Regulative Ideal*. New York: Oxford University Press.

Mill, John Stuart. 1861. *Utilitarianism*, ed. Roger Crisp. New York: Oxford University Press, 1998.

Miller, Geoffrey. 2000. *The Mating Mind*. New York: Doubleday.

Moll, Jorge, et al. 2001. "Frontopolar and Anterior Temporal Cortex Activation in a Moral Judgment Task: Preliminary Functional MRI Results in Normal Subjects." *Arq. Neuropsiquiatr* 59:657–64.

Moll, Jorge, et al. 2002a. "Functional Networks in Emotional Moral and Nonmoral Social Judgments." *Neuroimage* 16:696–703.

Moll, Jorge, et al. 2002b. "The Neural Correlates of Moral Sensitivity: A Functional Magnetic Resonance Imaging Investigation of Basic and Moral Emotions." *Journal of Neuroscience* 22:2730–36.

Moore, G. E. 1903. *Principia Ethica*. Cambridge: Cambridge University Press.

Morris, Christopher. 1996. "A Contractarian Account of Moral Justification." In *Moral Knowledge? New Readings in Moral Epistemology*, ed. Walter Sinnott-Armstrong and Mark Timmons: 215–42. New York: Oxford University Press.

Nelson, Mark. 1995. "Is it Always Fallacious to Derive Values from Facts?" *Argumentation* 9:553–62.

———. 2003. "Sinnott-Armstrong's Moral Scepticism." *Ratio* 16:63–82.

Nichols, Shaun. 2005. *Sentimental Rules: On the Natural Foundations of Moral Judgment*. New York: Oxford University Press.

Nietzsche, Friedrich. 1887. *On the Genealogy of Morals*. In *Basic Writings of Nietzsche*, trans. W. Kaufmann. New York: Random House, 1966.

———. 1888. *Twilight of the Idols*. In *The Portable Nietzsche*, trans. Walter Kaufmann. New York: Viking Press, 1954.

Nozick, Robert. 1981. *Philosophical Explanations*. Cambridge: Harvard University Press.

Nussbaum, Martha. 1990. *Love's Knowledge*. New York: Oxford University Press.

Parfit, Derek. 1984. *Reasons and Persons*. Oxford: Clarendon Press.

Paul, Ellen Frankel, Miller, Fred. D., and Paul, Jeffrey, eds. 1988. *The New Social Contract*. Oxford: Basil Blackwell.

———, eds. 1994. *Cultural Pluralism and Moral Knowledge*. New York: Cambridge University Press.

———, eds. 2001. *Moral Knowledge*. New York: Cambridge University Press.

Peacocke, Christopher. 1986. *Thoughts*. New York: Blackwell.

Peirce, Charles Saunders. 1934. *Collected Papers*, Vol. 5. Cambridge: Harvard University Press.

People v. Young, 11 N. Y. S. 2d 274 (1962).

Petrinovich, Lewis, and O'Neill, Patricia. 1996. "Influence of Wording and Framing Effects on Moral Intuitions." *Ethology and Sociobiology* 17:145–71.

Pettit, Philip. 1997. "The Consequentialist Perspective." In *Three Methods of Ethics*, M. Baron, P. Pettit, and M. Slote: 92–174. Oxford: Blackwell.

Pigden, Charles. 1991. "Naturalism." In *A Companion to Ethics*, ed. Peter Singer. Oxford: Blackwell.

Plato. 1997a. *Meno*, in *Complete Works*, ed. John Cooper. Indianapolis: Hackett.

———. 1997b. *Theaetetus*, in *Complete Works*, ed. John Cooper. Indianapolis: Hackett.

Pollock, John. 1986. *Contemporary Theories of Knowledge*. Totowa: Rowman and Littlefield.

Prichard, H. A. 1968. *Moral Obligation*. Oxford: Oxford University Press.

Prinz, Jesse. Forthcoming. *The Emotional Construction of Morals*. Oxford: Oxford University Press.

Prior, A. 1964. "Conjunction and Contonktion Revisited." *Analysis* 24:191–95.

Putnam, Hilary. 1981. *Reason, Truth, and History*. New York: Cambridge University Press.

Quinn, Warren. 1989a. "Actions, Intentions, and Consequences: The Doctrine of Doing and Allowing," *Philosophical Review* 98:287–312. Reprinted in *Morality and Action*. New York: Cambridge University Press, 1993: 149–74.

———. 1989b. "Actions, Intentions, and Consequences: The Doctrine of Double Effect." *Philosophy and Public Affairs* 18:334–51. Reprinted in *Morality and Action*. New York: Cambridge University Press, 1993: 175–93.

———. 1993. *Morality and Action*. New York: Cambridge University Press.

Rachels, James. 1971. "Egoism and Moral Skepticism." In *A New Introduction to Philosophy*, ed. Steven M. Cahn. New York: Harper and Row.

Radford, Colin. 1966. "Knowledge—By Examples." *Analysis* 27:1–11.

Railton, Peter. 1998. "Moral Explanation and Moral Objectivity." *Philosophy and Phenomenological Research* 58:175–82.

Rawls, John. 1951. "Outline of a Decision Procedure for Ethics." *Philosophical Review* 60:177–97.

———. 1958. "Justice as Fairness." *Philosophical Review* 47:164–94.

———. 1971. *A Theory of Justice*. Cambridge: Harvard University Press.

Regis, Edward, ed. 1984. *Gewirth's Ethical Rationalism*. Chicago: University of Chicago Press.

Richards, Robert J. 1987. "A Defense of Evolutionary Ethics." Appendix to *Darwin and the Emergence of Evolutionary Theories of Mind and Behavior*. Chicago: University of Chicago Press.

Roberts, R. C. 1988. "What an Emotion Is: A Sketch." *Philosophical Review* 97:183–209.

Robinson, R. 1948. "The Emotive Theory of Ethics." *Proceedings of the Aristotelian Society, Supplementary Volume*.

Ross, W. D. 1930. *The Right and the Good*. Oxford: Oxford University Press.

Ruse, Michael. 1998. *Taking Darwin Seriously*. Amherst, NY: Prometheus.

Ruse, Michael, and Wilson, Edward O. 1986. "Moral Philosophy as Applied Science." *Philosophy* 61:173–92.

Russell, Bertrand. 1905. "On Denoting." *Mind* 14:479–93.

———. 1948. *Human Knowledge: Its Scope and Limits*. New York: Allen and Unwin.

Ryle, Gilbert. 1958. "On Forgetting the Difference between Right and Wrong." In *Essays in Moral Philosophy*, ed. A. I. Melden. Seattle: University of Washington Press.

Sanford, David. 1984. "Infinite Regress Arguments." In *Principles of Philosophical Reasoning*, ed. James H. Fetzer. Totowa, NJ: Rowman and Allanheld.

Sartwell, Crispin. 1991. "Knowledge Is True Belief." *American Philosophical Quarterly* 28: 157–65

———. 1992. "Why Knowledge Is Merely True Belief." *Journal of Philosophy* 89:167–80.

Sayre-McCord, Geoffrey. 1985. "Coherence and Models for Moral Theorizing." *Pacific Philosophical Quarterly* 66:170–90.

———, ed. 1988a. *Essays on Moral Realism*. Ithaca: Cornell University Press.

———. 1988b. "Moral Theory and Explanatory Impotence." *Midwest Studies in Philosophy* 12:433–57.

———. 1996. "Coherentist Epistemology and Moral Theory." In *Moral Knowledge? New Readings in Moral Epistemology*, ed. Walter Sinnott-Armstrong and Mark Timmons: 137–89. New York: Oxford University Press.

———. 2001. "Mill's 'Proof' of the Principle of Utility: A More Than Half-Hearted Defense." In *Moral Knowledge*, ed. Ellen Frankel Paul, Fred D. Miller, and Jeffrey Paul: 330–60. New York: Cambridge University Press.

Scanlon, T. M. 1998. *What We Owe to Each Other*. Cambridge: Harvard University Press.

Schaffer, Jonathan. 2004. "From Contextualism to Contrastivism." *Philosophical Studies* 119:73–103.

Scheffler, Samuel. 1982. *The Rejection of Consequentialism*. Oxford: Clarendon Press.

Schneewind, Jerome, ed. 1990. *Moral Philosophy from Montaigne to Kant*, Vols. I and II. New York: Cambridge University Press.

Searle, John. 1962. "Meaning and Speech Acts." *Philosophical Review* 71:423–32.

———. 1964. "How to Derive 'Ought' from 'Is.'" *Philosophical Review* 73:43–58.

———. 1969. *Speech Acts*. Cambridge: Cambridge University Press.

Sextus Empiricus. 1996. *Outlines of Pyrrhonism*. In *The Skeptic Way*, trans. Benson Mates. New York: Oxford University Press.

Shafer-Landau, Russ. 2003. *Moral Realism: A Defense*. New York: Oxford University Press.

Shope, Robert. 1983. *The Analysis of Knowing*. Princeton: Princeton University Press.

Sidgwick, Henry. 1907. *Methods of Ethics*. 7th edition. New York: Macmillan.

Singer, Peter, 1974. "Sidgwick and Reflective Equilibrium." *Monist* 58:490–517.

Sinnott-Armstrong, Walter. 1984. "'Ought' Conversationally Implies 'Can.'" *Philosophical Review* 93:249–61.

———. 1987. Review of *Spreading the Word*, by Simon Blackburn. *Philosophy and Phenomenological Research* 48:163–66.

———. 1988. *Moral Dilemmas*. Oxford: Blackwell.

———. 1990. "Moral Experience and Justification." *Southern Journal of Philosophy* 29, Supplement:89–96.

———. 1992. "An Argument for Consequentialism." In "Ethics," special issue, *Philosophical Perspectives* 6:399–421.

———. 1993. "Some Problems for Gibbard's Norm-Expressivism." *Philosophical Studies* 69:297–313.

———. 1995a. "Nihilism and Skepticism about Moral Obligations." *Utilitas* 7:217–36.

———. 1995b. Review of *The Structure of Justification*, by Robert Audi. *Philosophical Quarterly* 45:394–97.

———. 1996a. "Moral Skepticism and Justification." In *Moral Knowledge? New Readings in Moral Epistemology*, ed. Walter Sinnott-Armstrong and Mark Timmons. New York: Oxford University Press.

———. 1996b. "Moral Dilemmas and Rights." In *Moral Dilemmas and Moral Theory*, ed. H. E. Mason: 48–65. New York: Oxford University Press.

———. 1996c. Review of *Morality, Normativity, and Society*, by David Copp. *Philosophical Review*, 105:552–54.

———. 1996d. Review of *Morality and Action*, by Warren Quinn. *International Journal of Philosophical Studies* 4:193–96.

———. 1999a. "An Argument for Descriptivism." *Southern Journal of Philosophy* 37(2): 281–91.

———. 1999b. "'MPP, RIP' RIP." *Philosophical Papers* 28:125–31.

———. 1999c. "Begging the Question." *Australasian Journal of Philosophy* 77:174–91.

———. 1999d. "Some Varieties of Particularism." *Metaphilosophy* 30:1–12.

———. 1999e. "Explanation and Justification in Moral Epistemology." In *The Proceedings of the Twentieth World Congress of Philosophy*, Vol. 1, Ethics, ed. Klaus Brinkman. Bowling Green: Philosophy Documentation Center.

———. 2000a. "Expressivism and Embedding." *Philosophy and Phenomenological Research* LXI(3):677–93.

———. 2000b. "From 'Is' to 'Ought' in Moral Epistemology." *Argumentation* 14:159–174.

———. 2001a. "R. M. Hare." In *A Companion to Analytic Philosophy*, ed. A. P. Martinich and David Sosa: 326–33. Oxford: Blackwell.

——. 2001b. "Moral Intuitionism." In *Encyclopedia of Ethics*. 2nd edition, ed. Lawrence Becker and Charlotte Becker: 879–82. New York: Routledge.

——. 2002a. "What's in a Contrast Class?" *Analysis* 62:75–85.

——. 2002b. "Gert Contra Consequentialism." In *Rationality, Rules, and Ideals*, ed. Walter Sinnott-Armstrong and Robert Audi: 145–63. Lanham, MD: Rowman and Littlefield.

——. 2002c. "Moral Relativity and Intuitionism." In "Realism and Relativism," special issue, *Philosophical Issues* 12:305–28.

——. 2002d . "Recusal and *Bush v. Gore.*" *Law and Philosophy* 21:221–48.

——. 2004a. "Classy Pyrrhonism." In *Pyrrhonian Skepticism*, ed. Walter Sinnott-Armstrong. New York: Oxford University Press.

——, ed. 2004b. *Pyrrhonian Skepticism*. New York: Oxford University Press.

——. Forthcoming. "A Contrastivist Manifesto." *Social Epistemology*.

Sinnott-Armstrong, Walter, and Audi, Robert, eds. 2002. *Rationality, Rules, and Ideals*. Lanham, MD: Rowman and Littlefield.

Sinnott-Armstrong, Walter, Moor, James, and Fogelin, Robert. 1986. "A Defense of Modus Ponens." *Journal of Philosophy* 83:296–300.

Sinnott-Armstrong, Walter, and Timmons, Mark, eds. 1996. *Moral Knowledge? New Readings in Moral Epistemology*. New York: Oxford University Press.

Smith, Michael. 1994. *The Moral Problem*. Oxford: Blackwell.

——. 2001. "Some Not-Much-Discussed Problems for Non-Cognitivism in Ethics." *Ratio* 14:93–115.

Snare, Francis. 1980. "The Diversity of Morals." *Mind* 89:353–69.

Sober, Elliott, and Wilson, David Sloan. 1998. *Unto Others: The Evolution and Psychology of Unselfish Behavior*. Cambridge: Harvard University Press.

Sorensen, Roy. 2001. *Vagueness and Contradiction*. Oxford: Clarendon Press.

Sosa, Ernest. 2004. "Two False Dichotomies: Foundationalism/Coherentism and Internalism/Externalism." In *Pyrrhonian Skepticism*, ed. Walter Sinnott-Armstrong. New York: Oxford University Press.

Stevenson, Charles. 1944. *Ethics and Language*. New Haven: Yale University Press.

Stine, Gail. 1976. "Skepticism, Relevant Alternatives, and Deductive Closure." *Philosophical Studies* 29:249–61.

Stoljar, Daniel. 1993. "Emotivism and Truth Conditions." *Philosophical Studies* 70:81–101.

Strawson, Peter. 1950. "On Referring." *Mind* 59:320–44.

Sturgeon, Nicholas. 1982. "Brandt's Moral Empiricism." *Philosophical Review* 91:389–422.

——. 1984. "Moral Explanations." In *Morality, Reason, and Truth*, ed. David Copp and David Zimmerman: 49–78. Totowa, NJ: Rowman and Allanheld.

——. 1994. "Moral Disagreement and Moral Relativism." In *Cultural Pluralism and Moral Knowledge*, ed. Ellen Frankel Paul, Fred. D. Miller, and Jeffrey Paul. New York: Cambridge University Press.

Tarski, Alfred. 1944. "The Semantic Conception of Truth." *Philosophy and Phenomenological Research* 4:341–75.

Taurek, John. 1977. "Should the Numbers Count?" *Philosophy and Public Affairs* 6:293–316.

Thomson, Judith Jarvis. 1976. "Killing, Letting Die, and the Trolley Problem." *The Monist* 59:204–17. Reprinted in *Rights, Restitution, and Risk*, ed. W. Parent. Cambridge: Harvard University Press, 1986.

——. 1985. "The Trolley Problem." *Yale Law Journal* 94:1395–1415. Reprinted in *Rights, Restitution, and Risk*, ed. W. Parent. Cambridge: Harvard University Press, 1986.

——. 1986. *Rights, Restitution, and Risk*, ed. W. Parent. Cambridge: Harvard University Press.

——. 1990. *The Realm of Rights*. Cambridge: Harvard University Press.

Timmons, Mark. 1996. "Outline of a Contextualist Moral Epistemology." In *Moral Knowledge? New Readings in Moral Epistemology*, ed. Walter Sinnott-Armstrong and Mark Timmons. New York: Oxford University Press.

———. 1998. *Morality without Foundations: A Defense of Ethical Contextualism*. New York: Oxford University Press.

Tolhurst, William. 1986. "Supervenience, Externalism, and Moral Knowledge." *Southern Journal of Philosophy* 24, Supplement:43–55.

———. 1987. "The Argument from Moral Disagreement." *Ethics* 97:610–21.

———. 1990. "On the Epistemic Value of Moral Experience." *Southern Journal of Philosophy* 29, Supplement:67–87.

———. 1998. "Seemings." *American Philosophical Quarterly* 35:293–302.

Unger, Peter. 1996. *Living High and Letting Die*. New York: Oxford University Press.

Vallentyne, Peter, ed. 1991. *Contractarianism and Rational Choice*. New York: Cambridge University Press.

Van Fraassen, Bas C. 1980. *The Scientific Image*. Oxford: Clarendon Press.

Van Roojen, Mark. 1996. "Expressivism and Irrationality." *Philosophical Review* 105:311–35.

———. 1999. "Reflective Moral Equilibrium and Psychological Theory." *Ethics* 109:846–57.

Vogel, Jonathan. 1990. "Are There Counterexamples to the Closure Principle?" In *Doubting: Contemporary Perspectives on Skepticism*, ed. M. Roth and G. Ross. Dordrecht: Kluwer.

Walker, Margaret Urban. 1996. "Feminist Skepticism, Authority, and Transparency." In *Moral Knowledge? New Readings in Moral Epistemology*, ed. Walter Sinnott-Armstrong and Mark Timmons. New York: Oxford University Press.

———. 1998. *Moral Understandings*. New York: Routledge.

Warnock, Geoffrey. 1971. *The Object of Morality*. London: Methuen.

Watson, Gary. 1975. "Free Agency." *Journal of Philosophy* 72:205–20.

Wellman, Carl. 1971. *Challenge and Response: Justification in Ethics*. Carbondale: Southern Illinois University Press.

Werner, Richard. 1983. "Moral Realism." *Ethics* 93:653–79.

Wheatley, T., and Haidt, J. 2005. "Hypnotic Disgust Makes Moral Judgments More Severe." *Psychological Science*.

White, Morton. 1981. *What Is and What Ought to Be Done*. New York: Oxford University Press.

Williams, Bernard. 1981. "Internal and External Reasons." Reprinted in *Moral Luck*:101–13. Cambridge: Cambridge University Press.

Williamson, Timothy. 2000. *Knowledge and Its Limits*. Oxford: Oxford University Press.

Wilson, E. O. 1975. *Sociobiology: The New Synthesis*. Oxford: Oxford University Press.

Zangwill, Nick. 1994. "Moral Mind-Independence." *Australasian Journal of Philosophy* 72:205–18.

———. 2000. "Against Analytic Moral Functionalism." *Ratio* 13.

Zimmerman, David. 1984. "Moral Realism and Explanatory Necessity," In *Morality, Reason, and Truth*, ed. David Copp and David Zimmerman:79–103. Totowa, NJ: Rowman and Allanheld.

Index